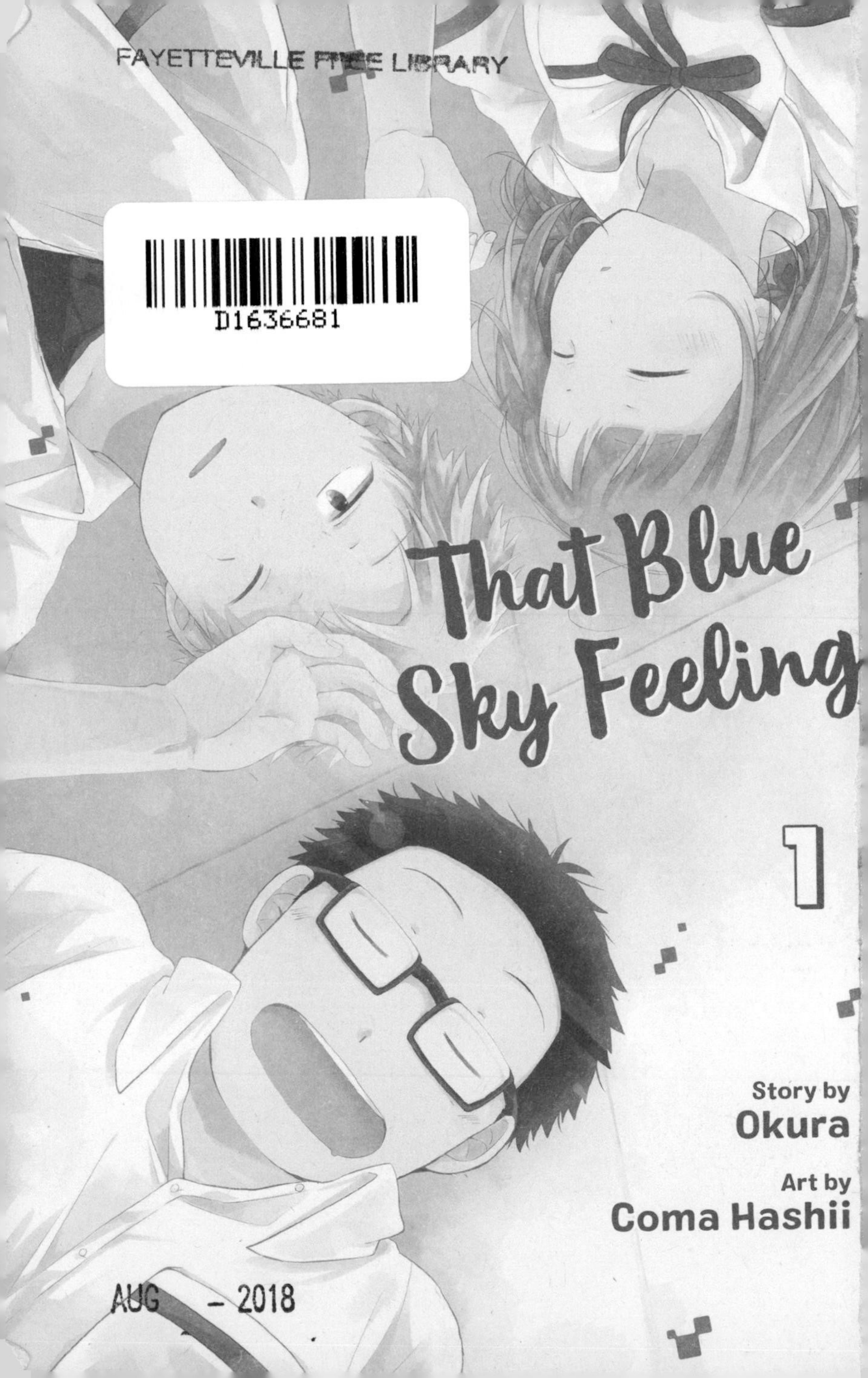
That Blue Sky Feeling
1
Story by
Okura
Art by
Coma Hashii

CONTENTS

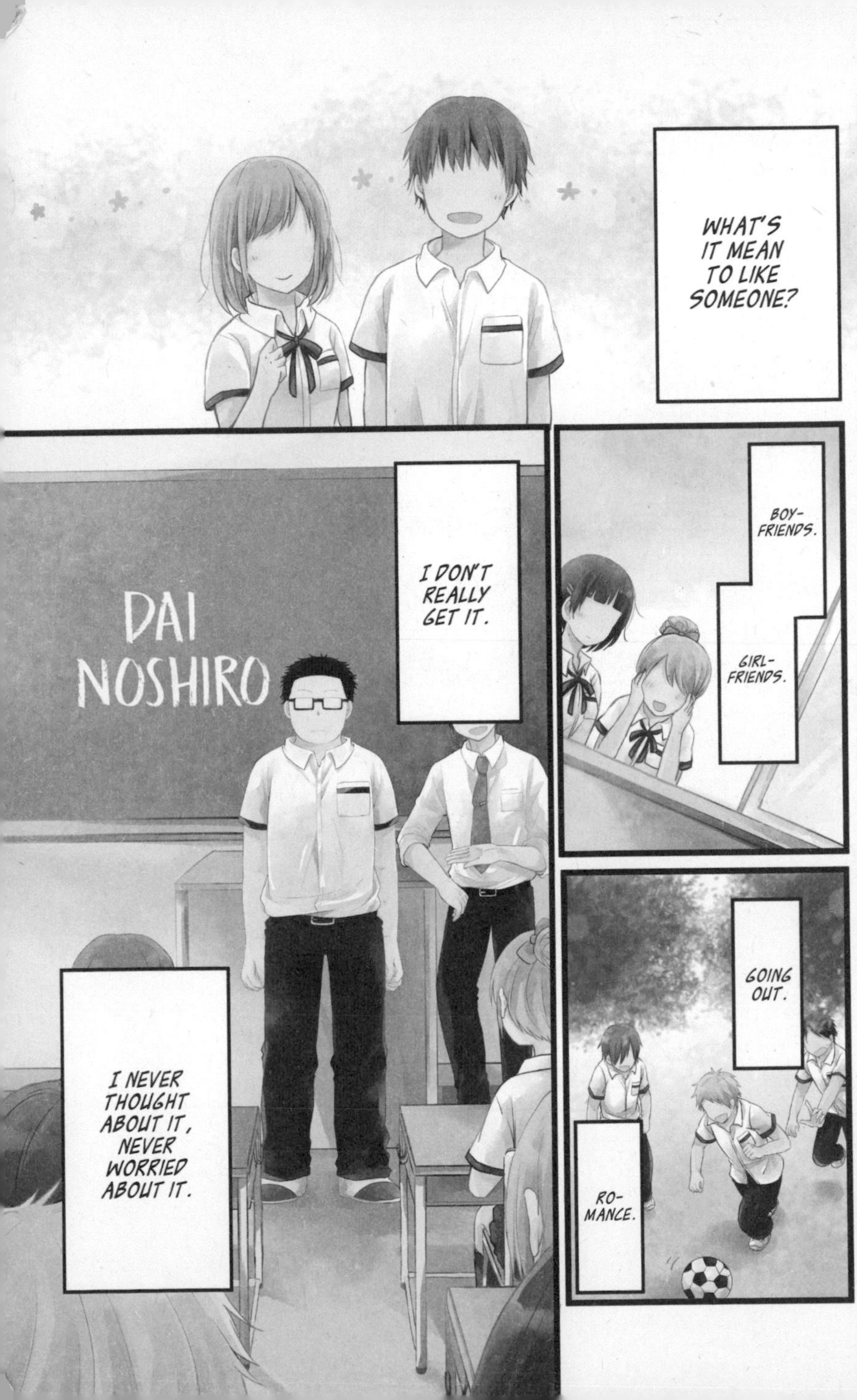
WHAT'S IT MEAN TO LIKE SOMEONE?
BOY-FRIENDS.
GIRL-FRIENDS.
GOING OUT.
RO-MANCE.
I DON'T REALLY GET IT.
DAI NOSHIRO
I NEVER THOUGHT ABOUT IT, NEVER WORRIED ABOUT IT.

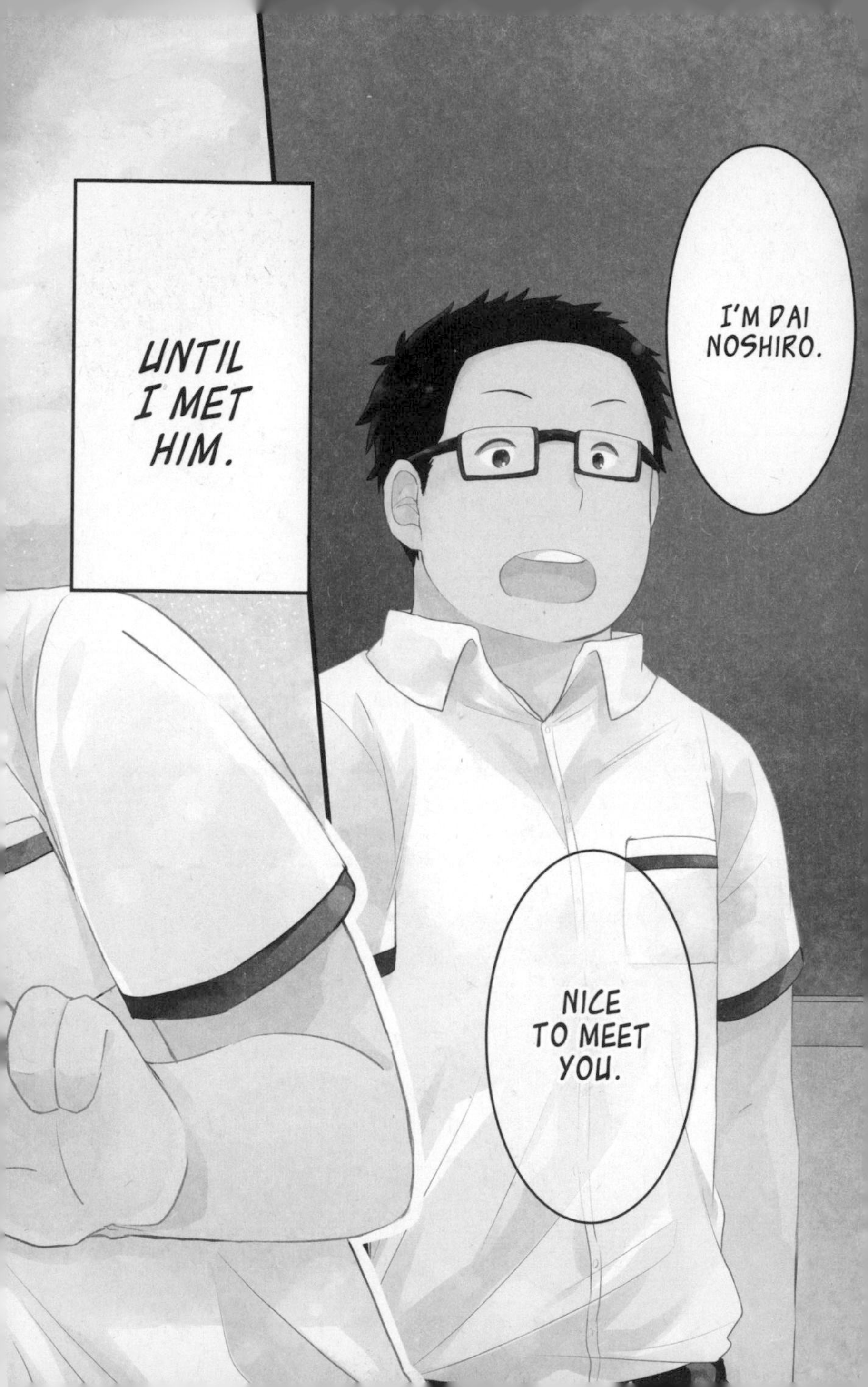
I'M DAI NOSHIRO.
UNTIL I MET HIM.
NICE TO MEET YOU.

Chapter 1: I heard that guy's a homo.

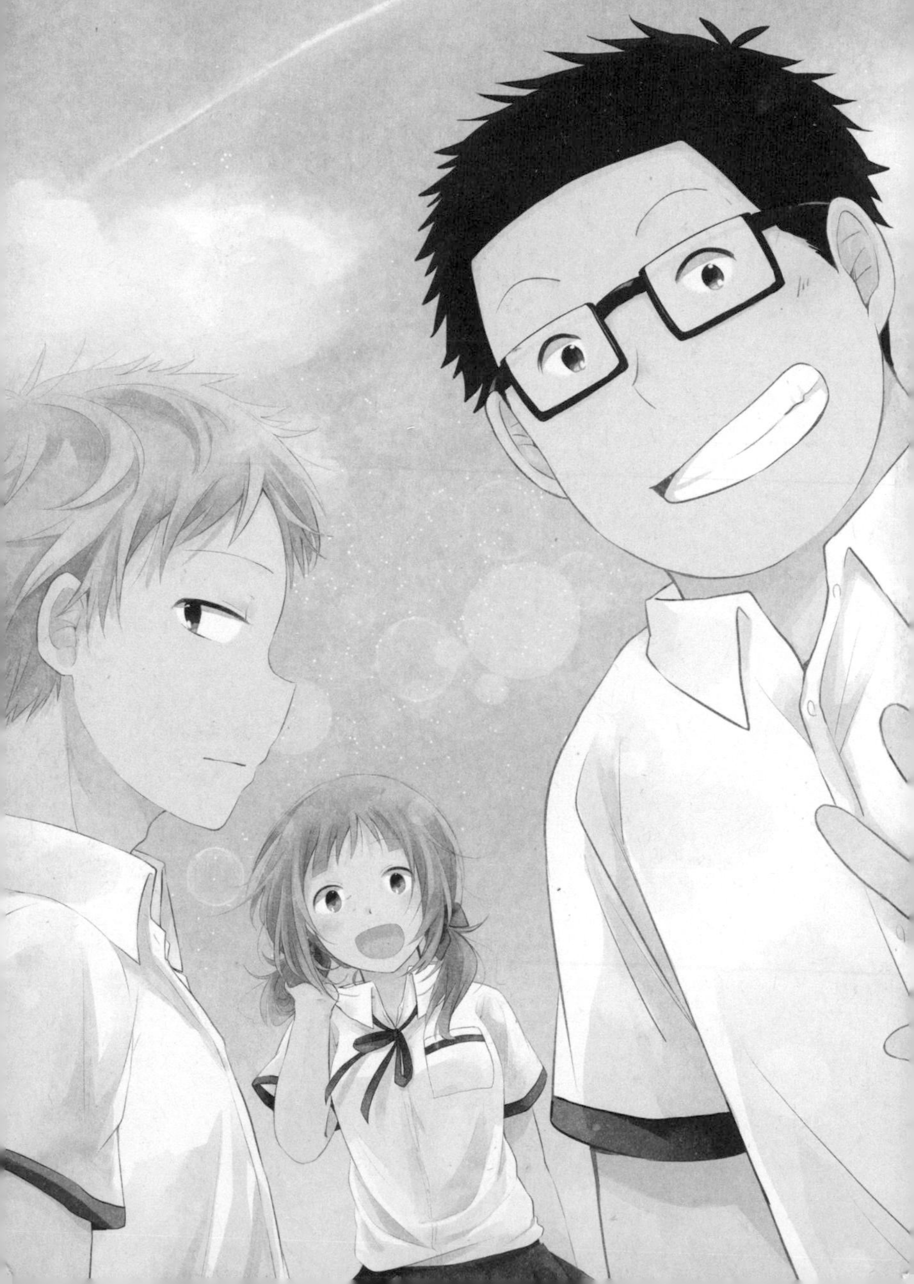

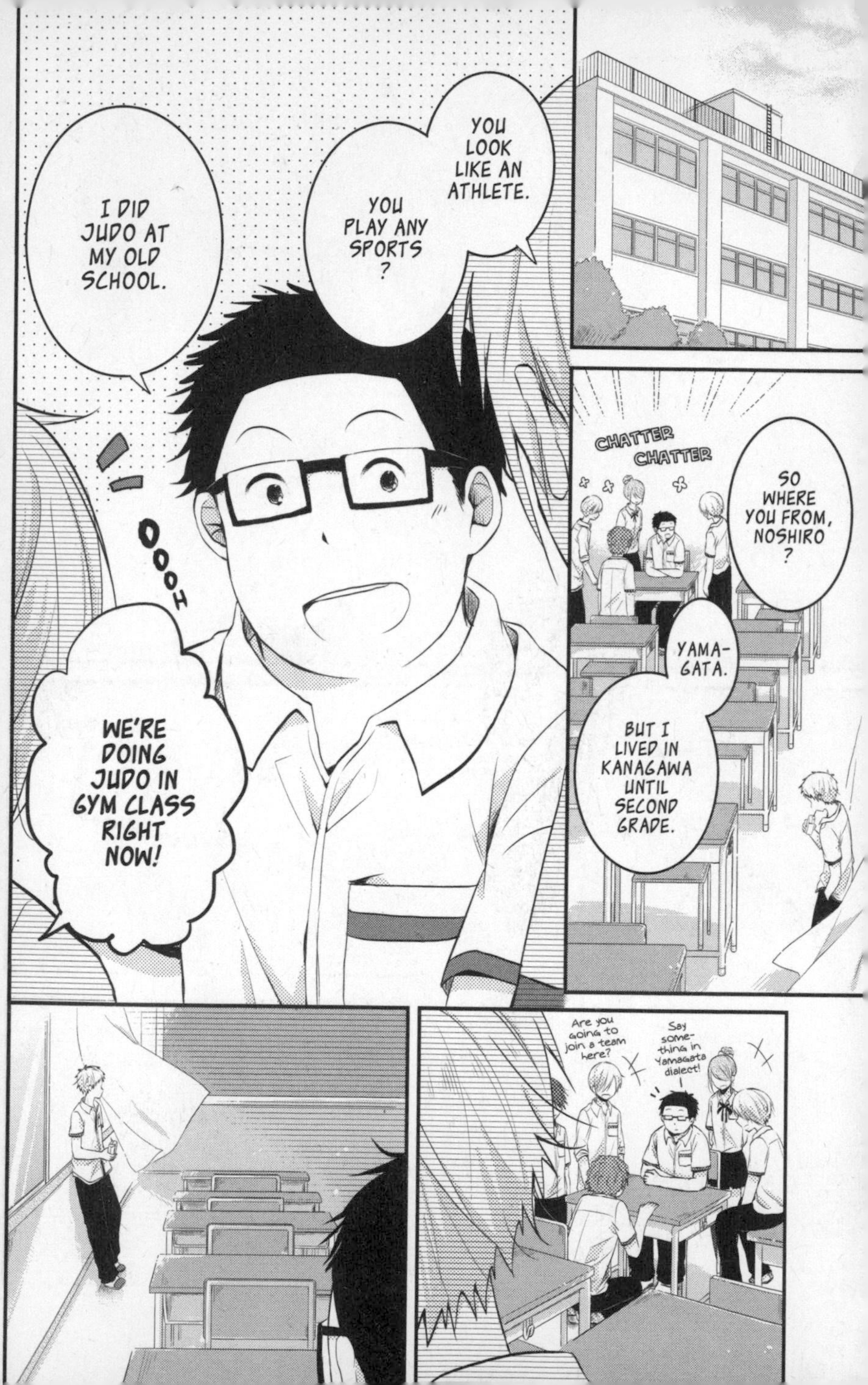
CHATTER CHATTER
SO WHERE YOU FROM, NOSHIRO?
YAMA-GATA.
BUT I LIVED IN KANAGAWA UNTIL SECOND GRADE.
YOU LOOK LIKE AN ATHLETE.
YOU PLAY ANY SPORTS?
I DID JUDO AT MY OLD SCHOOL.
OOOH
WE'RE DOING JUDO IN GYM CLASS RIGHT NOW!
Say something in Yamagata dialect!
Are you going to join a team here?

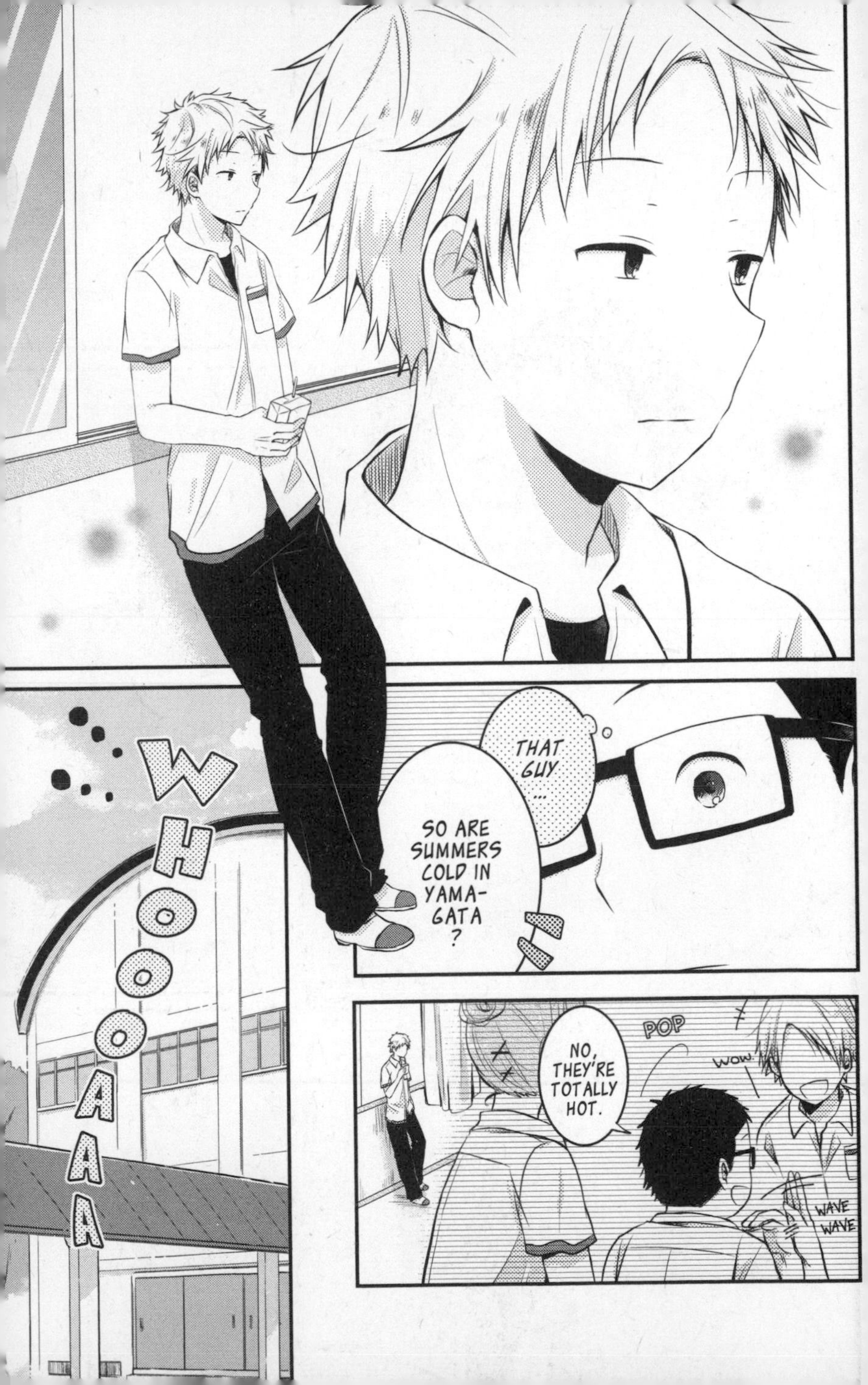
THAT GUY ...
SO ARE SUMMERS COLD IN YAMAGATA?
POP
WOW.
NO, THEY'RE TOTALLY HOT.
WAVE WAVE
WHOOOOAAAA

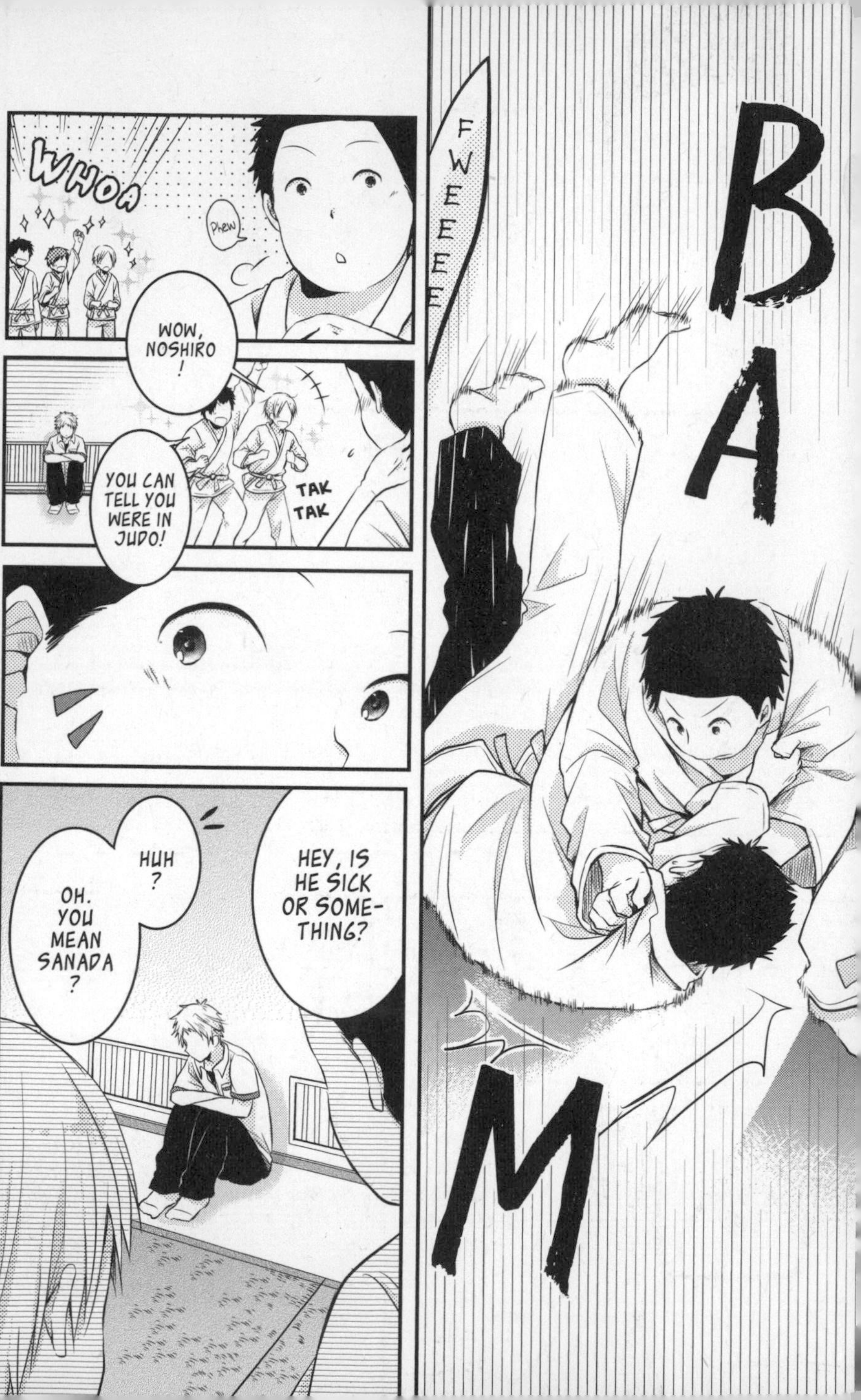
FWEEEE
BAM
Phew
WHOA
WOW, NOSHIRO!
TAK TAK
YOU CAN TELL YOU WERE IN JUDO!
HEY, IS HE SICK OR SOMETHING?
HUH?
OH. YOU MEAN SANADA?

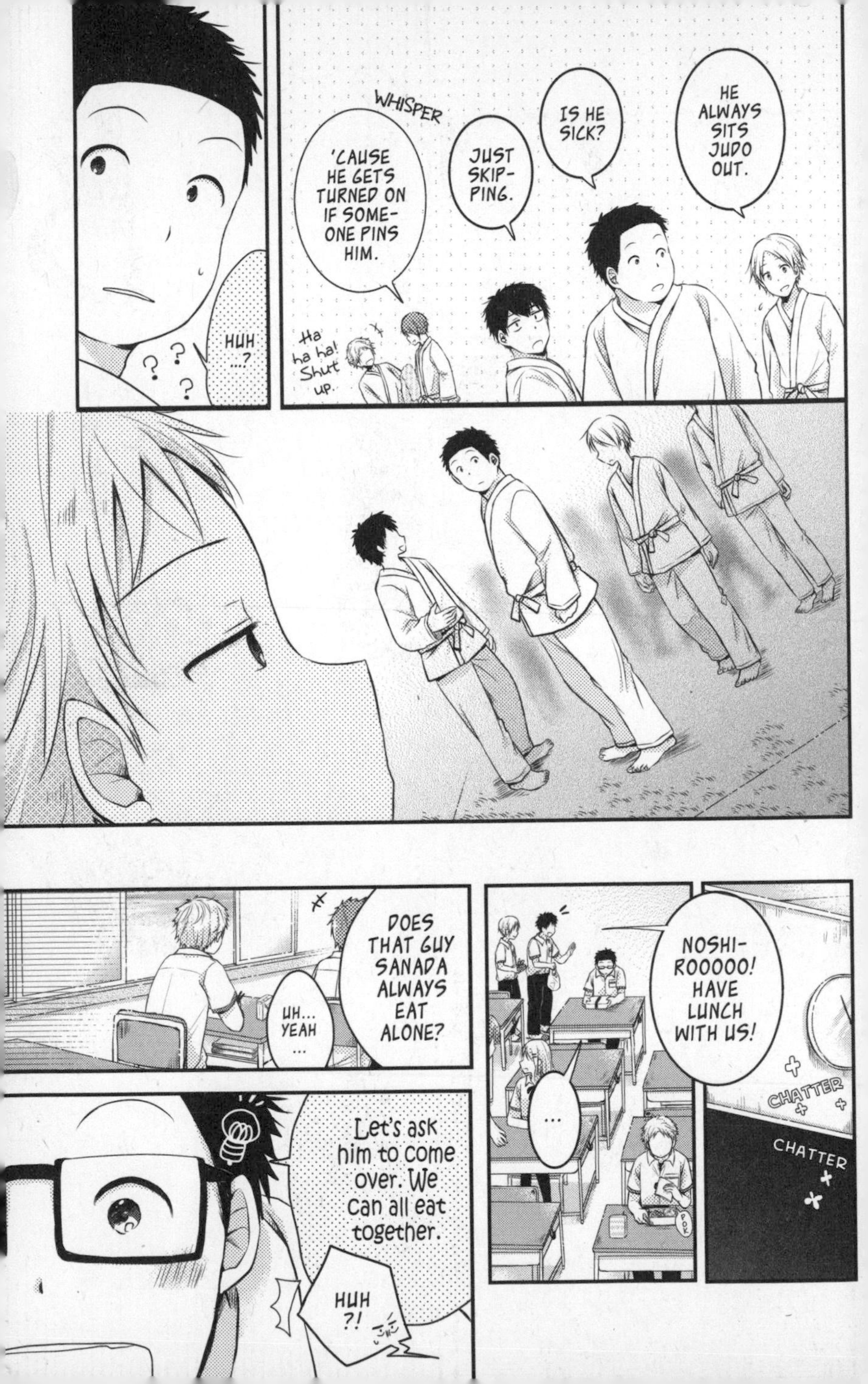
HE ALWAYS SITS JUDO OUT.
IS HE SICK?
JUST SKIP-PING.
WHISPER
'CAUSE HE GETS TURNED ON IF SOME-ONE PINS HIM.
Ha ha ha! Shut up.
HUH ...?
NOSHI-ROOOOO! HAVE LUNCH WITH US!
CHATTER
CHATTER
...
POK
DOES THAT GUY SANADA ALWAYS EAT ALONE?
UH... YEAH ...
Let's ask him to come over. We can all eat together.
HUH ?!

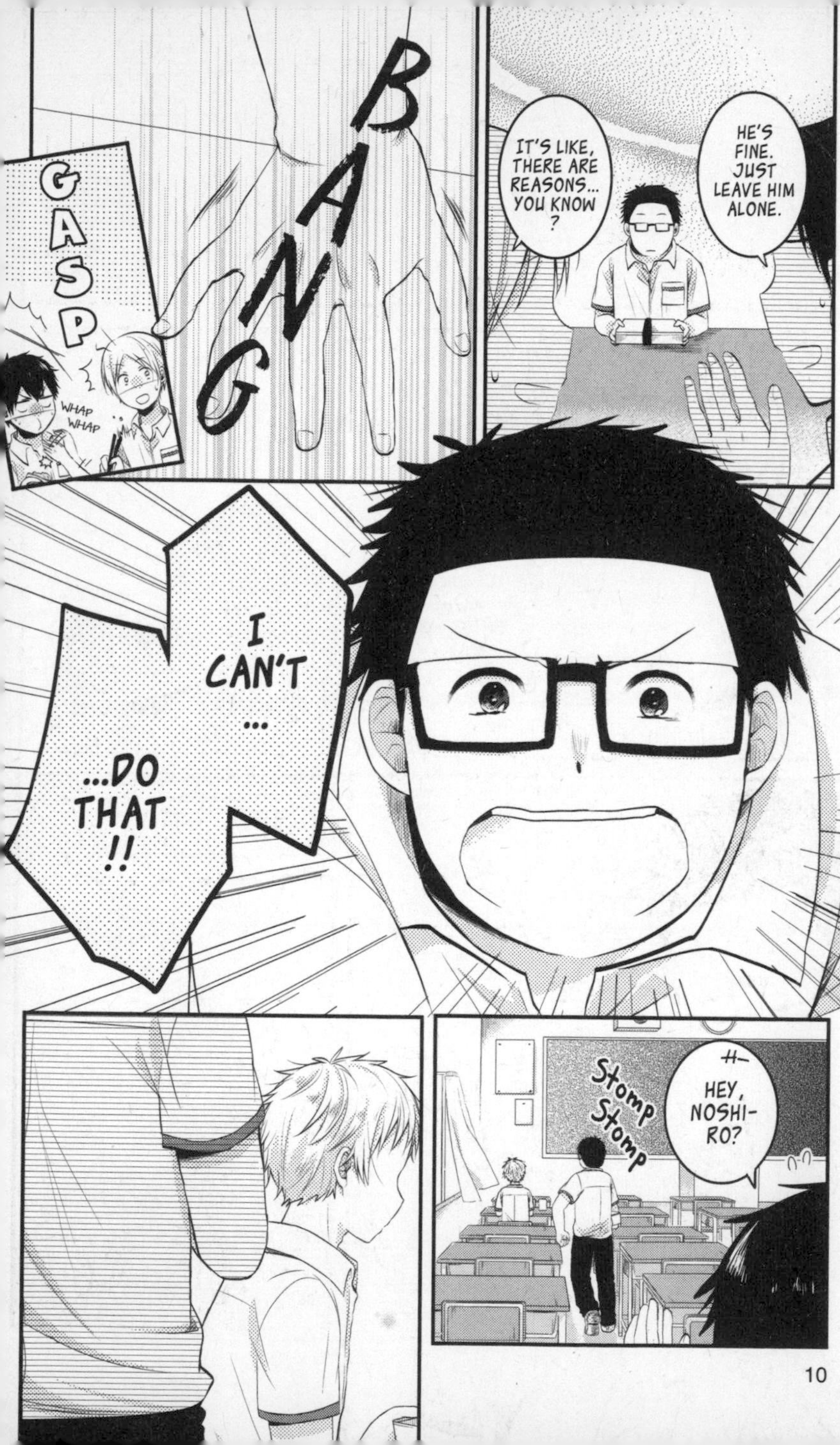
HE'S FINE. JUST LEAVE HIM ALONE.
IT'S LIKE, THERE ARE REASONS... YOU KNOW?
BANG
GASP
WHAP WHAP
I CAN'T... ...DO THAT!!
H-HEY, NOSHIRO?
Stomp Stomp

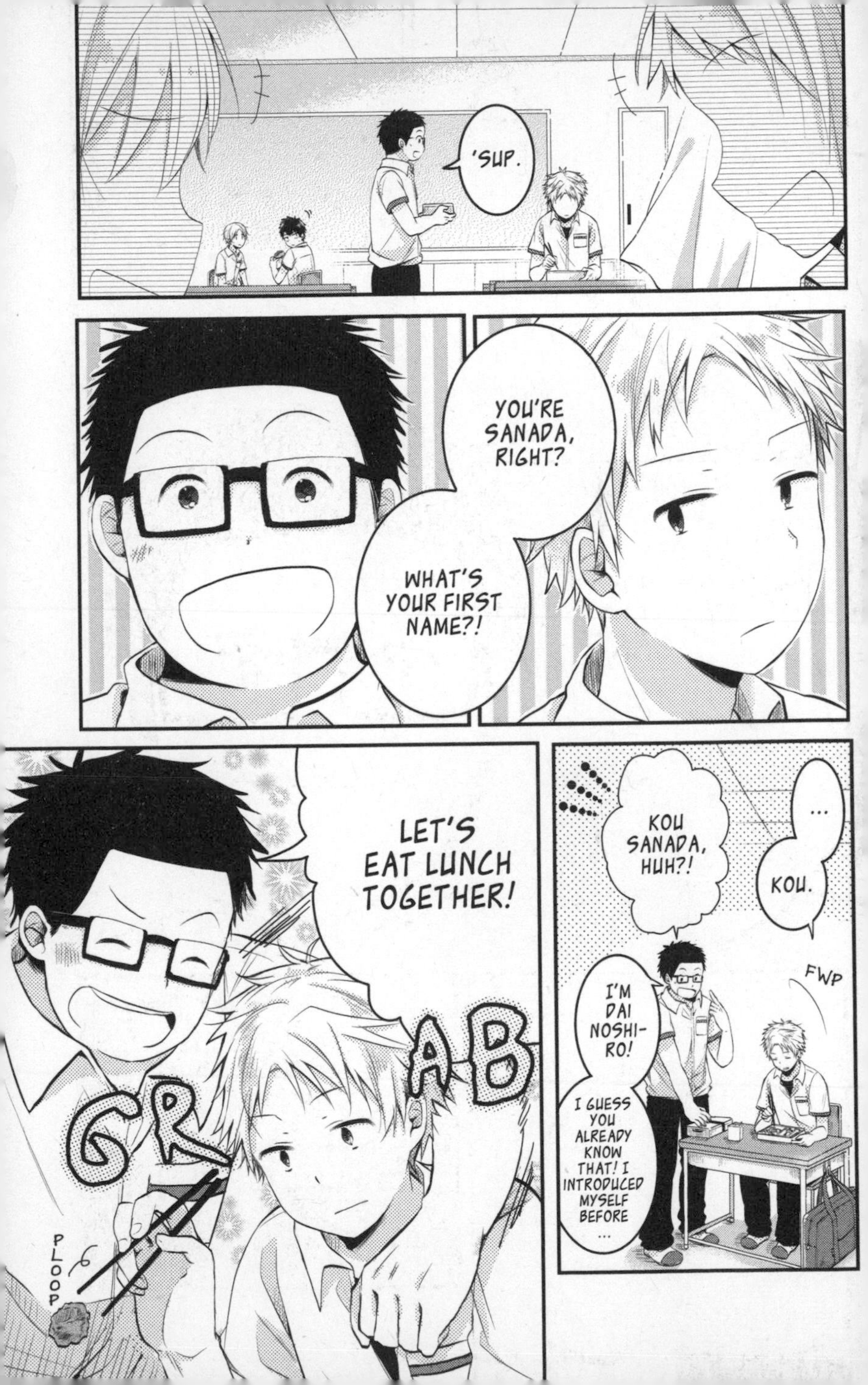
'SUP.
YOU'RE SANADA, RIGHT?
WHAT'S YOUR FIRST NAME?!
... KOU.
KOU SANADA, HUH?!
FWP
I'M DAI NOSHIRO!
I GUESS YOU ALREADY KNOW THAT! I INTRODUCED MYSELF BEFORE ...
LET'S EAT LUNCH TOGETHER!
GRAB
PLOOP

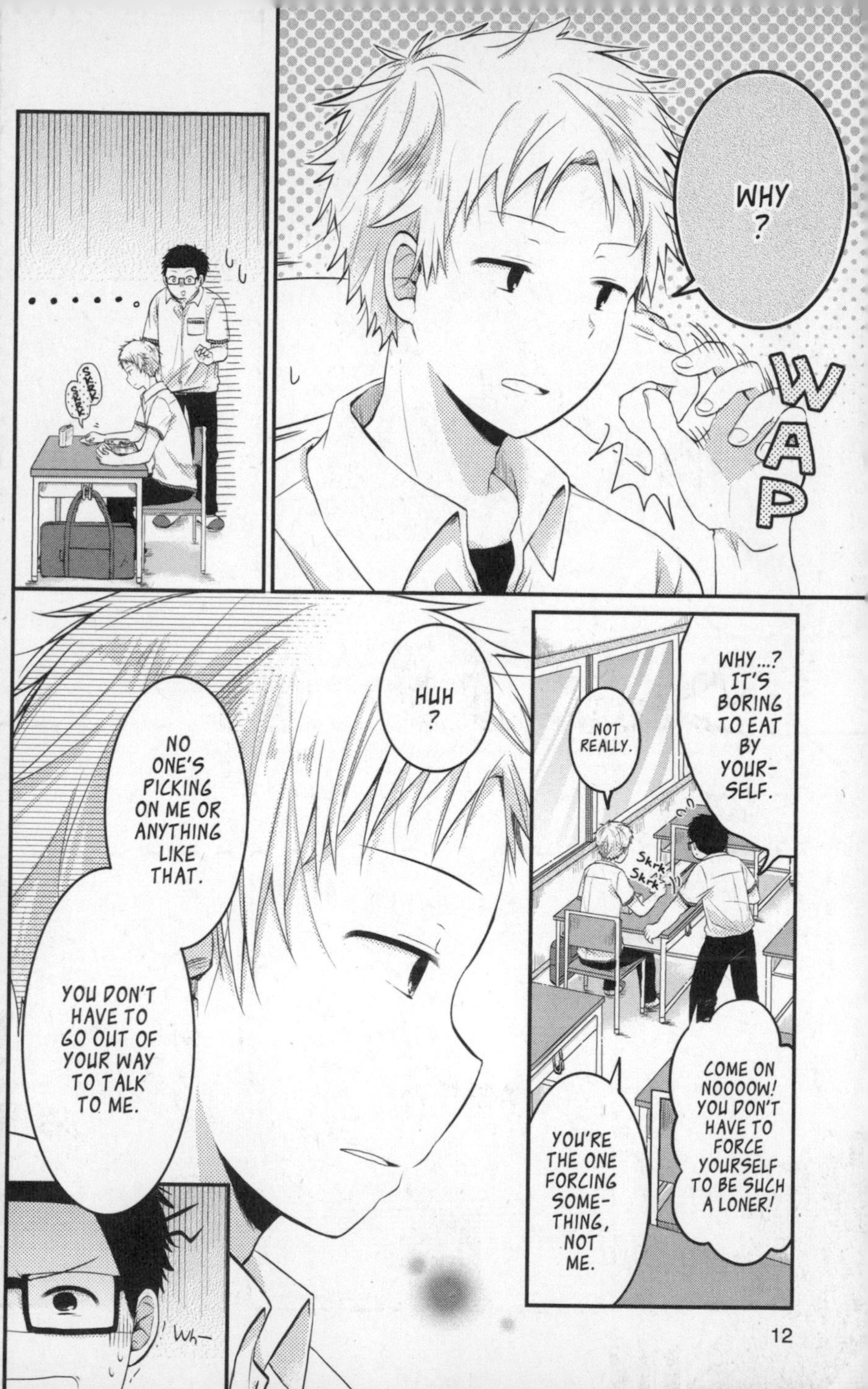
WHY?
WAP
......
SKRK SKRK
WHY...? IT'S BORING TO EAT BY YOURSELF.
NOT REALLY.
Skrk Skrk
COME ON NOOOOW! YOU DON'T HAVE TO FORCE YOURSELF TO BE SUCH A LONER!
YOU'RE THE ONE FORCING SOMETHING, NOT ME.
HUH?
NO ONE'S PICKING ON ME OR ANYTHING LIKE THAT.
YOU DON'T HAVE TO GO OUT OF YOUR WAY TO TALK TO ME.
Wh-

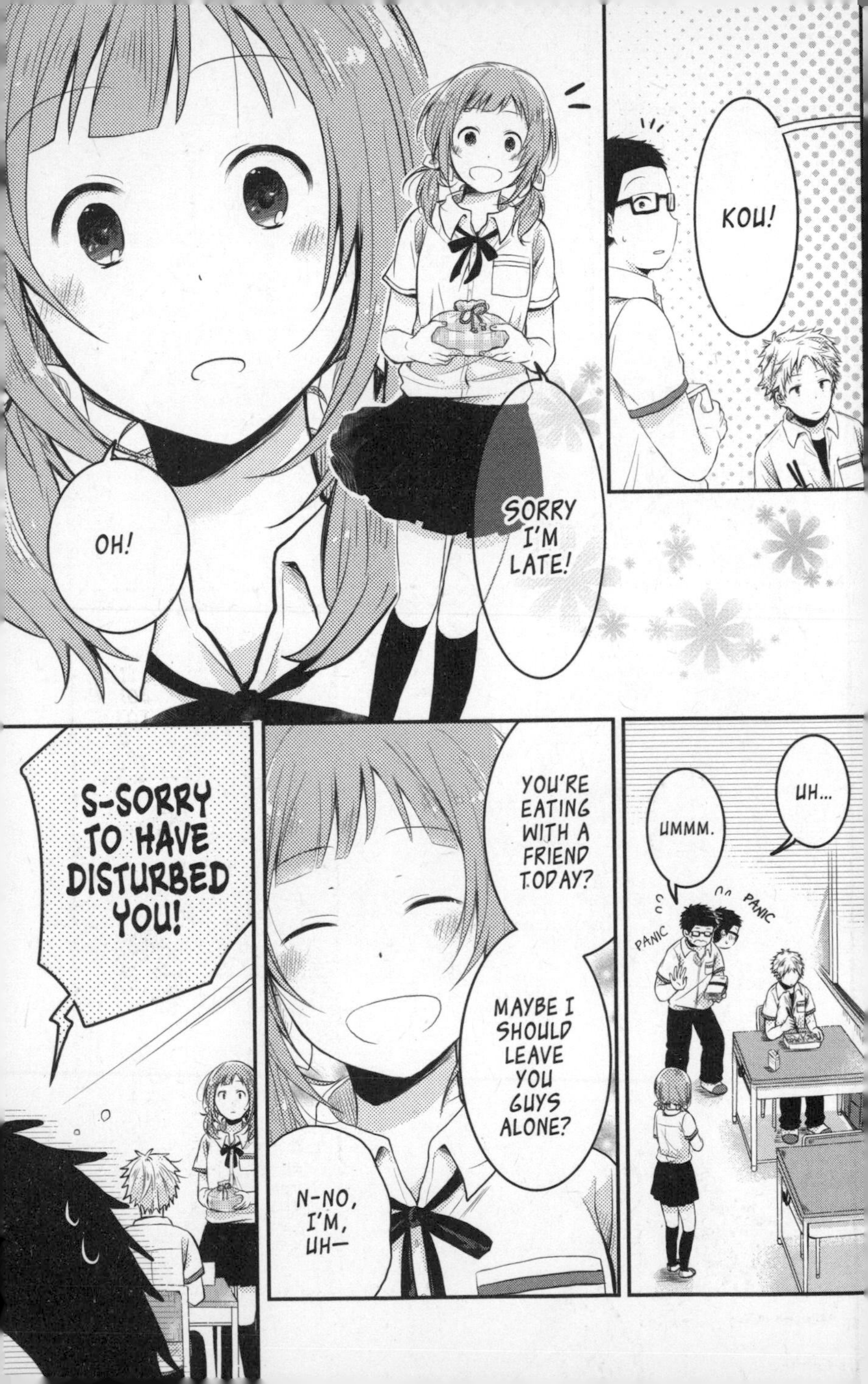
KOU!
SORRY I'M LATE!
OH!
UH...
UMMM.
PANIC
PANIC
YOU'RE EATING WITH A FRIEND TODAY?
MAYBE I SHOULD LEAVE YOU GUYS ALONE?
N-NO, I'M, UH—
S-SORRY TO HAVE DISTURBED YOU!

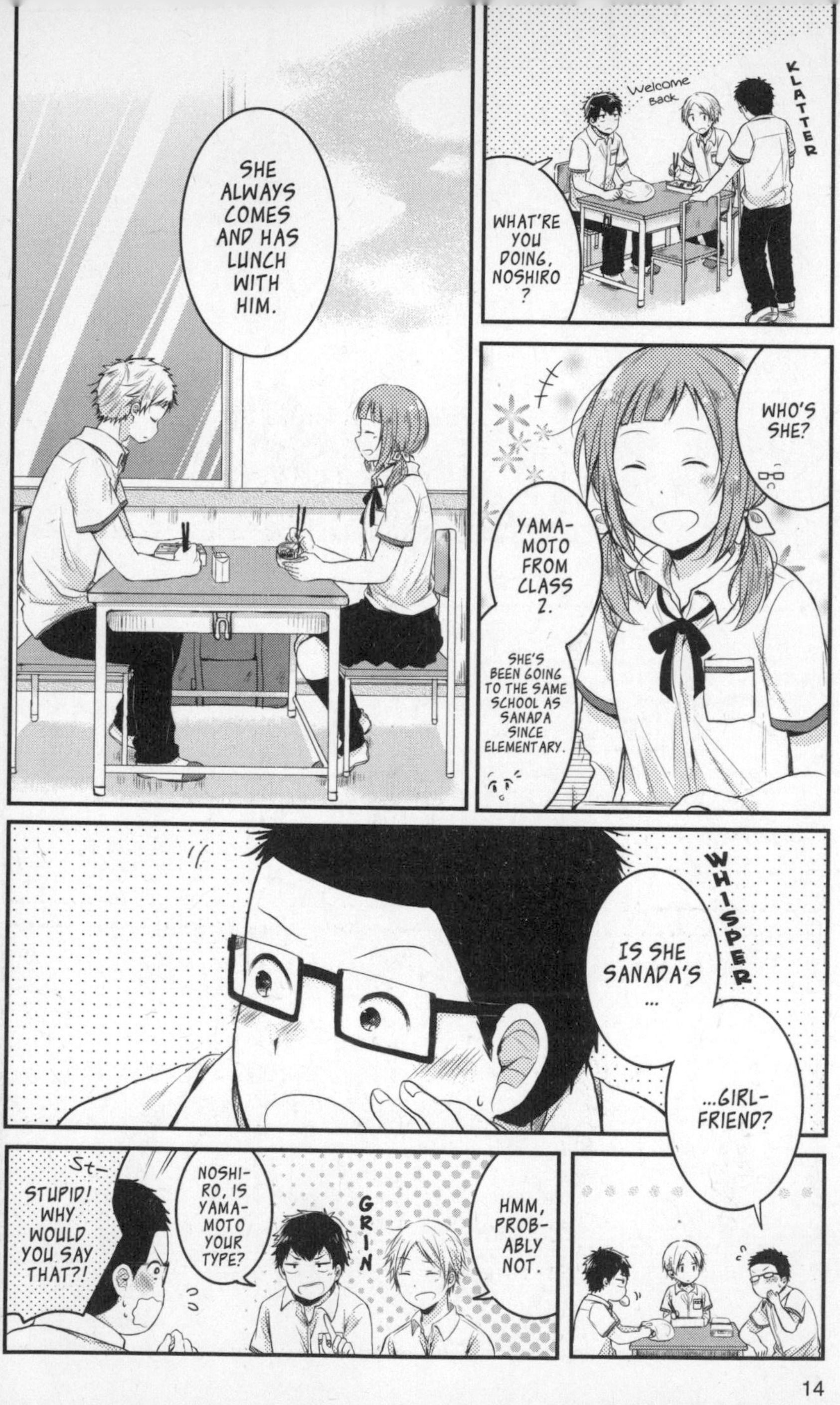
KLATTER
Welcome back
WHAT'RE YOU DOING, NOSHIRO?
WHO'S SHE?
YAMAMOTO FROM CLASS 2.
SHE'S BEEN GOING TO THE SAME SCHOOL AS SANADA SINCE ELEMENTARY.
SHE ALWAYS COMES AND HAS LUNCH WITH HIM.
WHISPER
IS SHE SANADA'S ...
...GIRLFRIEND?
HMM, PROBABLY NOT.
GRIN
NOSHIRO, IS YAMAMOTO YOUR TYPE?
St-
STUPID! WHY WOULD YOU SAY THAT?!

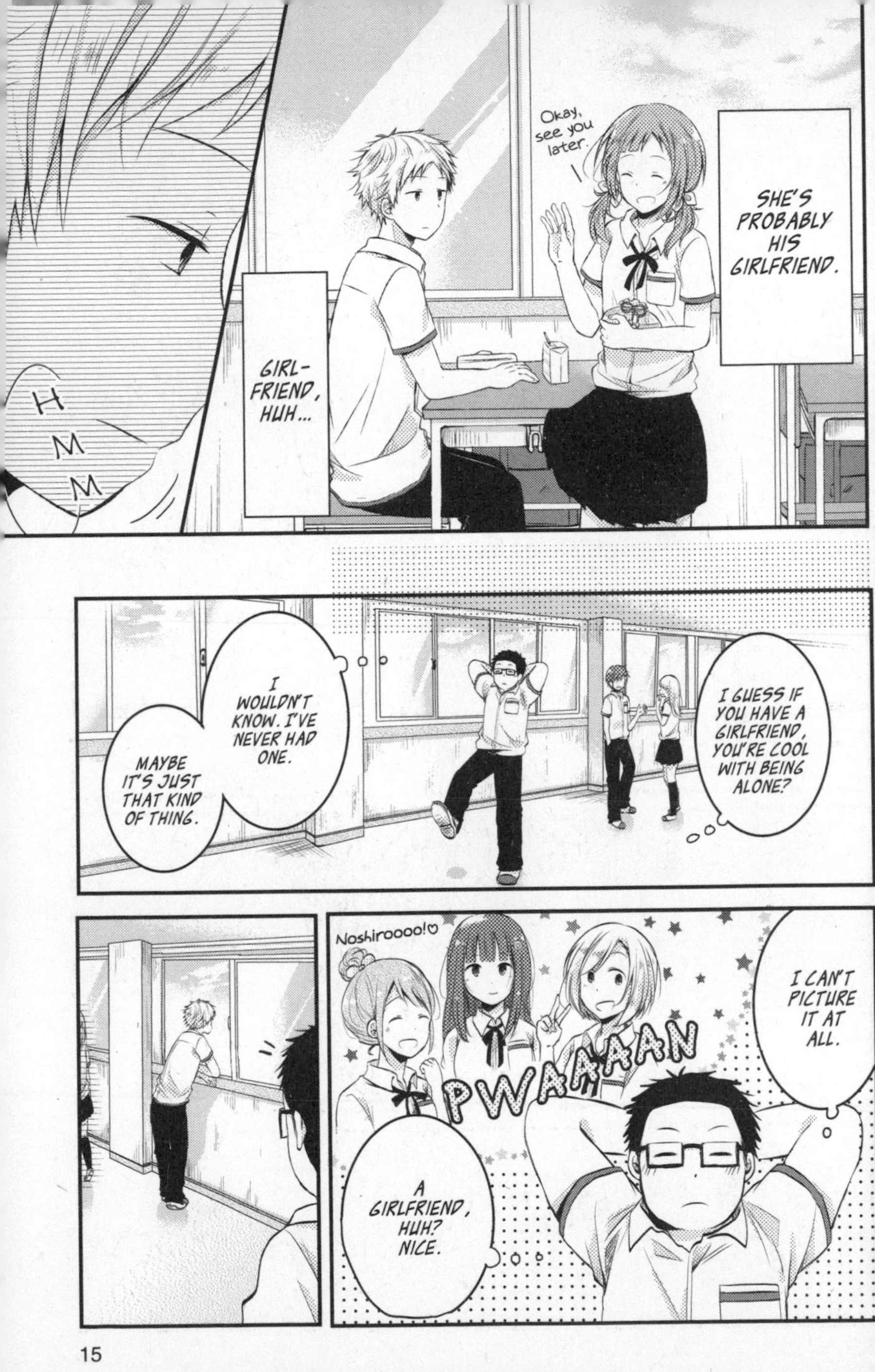

SHE'S PROBABLY HIS GIRLFRIEND.
Okay, see you later.
GIRL-FRIEND, HUH...
HMM
I GUESS IF YOU HAVE A GIRLFRIEND, YOU'RE COOL WITH BEING ALONE?
I WOULDN'T KNOW. I'VE NEVER HAD ONE.
MAYBE IT'S JUST THAT KIND OF THING.
I CAN'T PICTURE IT AT ALL.
Noshiroooo!♡
PWAAAAAN
A GIRLFRIEND, HUH? NICE.

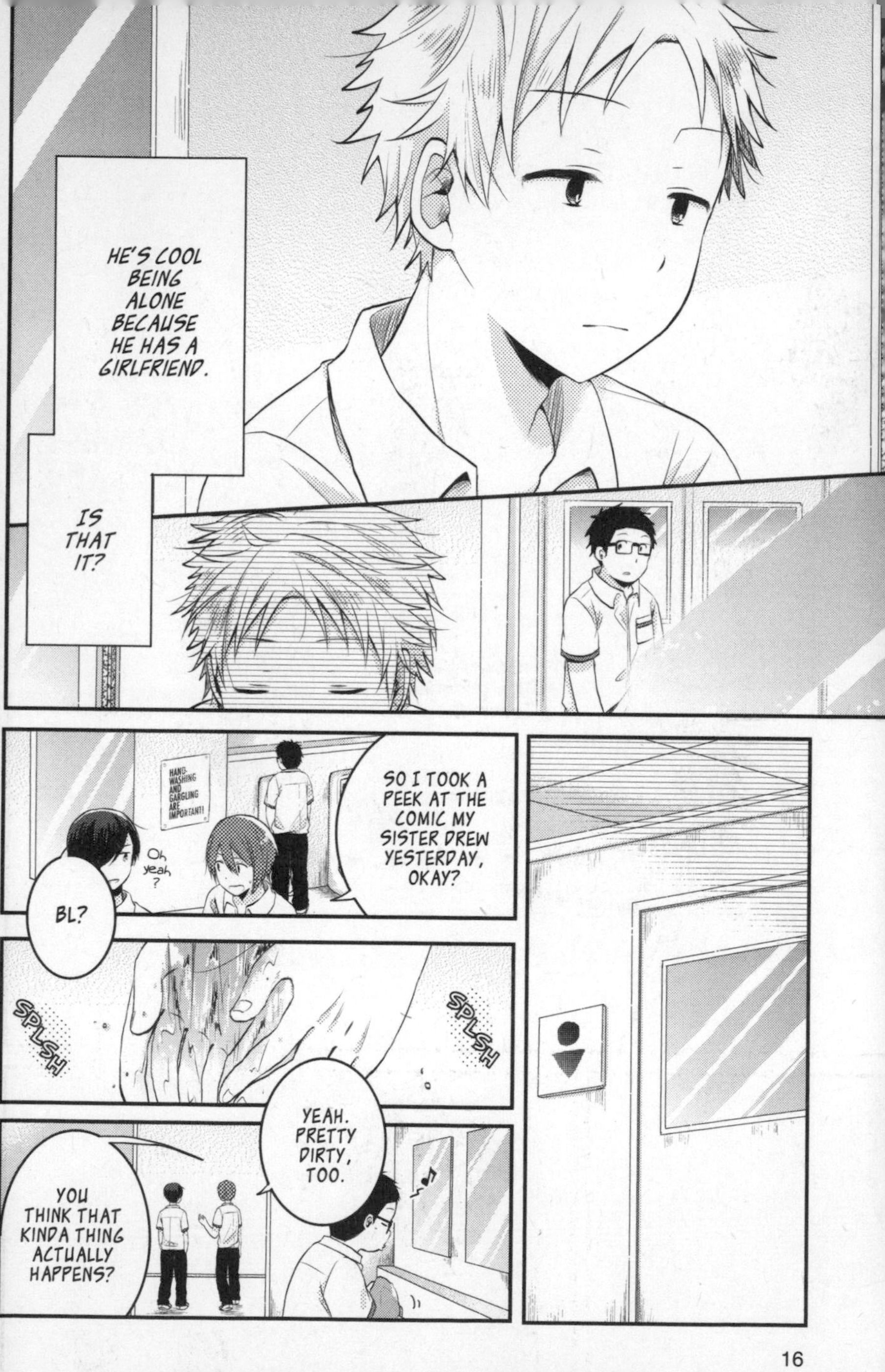
HE'S COOL BEING ALONE BECAUSE HE HAS A GIRLFRIEND.
IS THAT IT?
SO I TOOK A PEEK AT THE COMIC MY SISTER DREW YESTERDAY, OKAY?
HAND-WASHING AND GARGLING ARE IMPORTANT!
Oh yeah?
BL?
SPLSH
SPLSH
YEAH. PRETTY DIRTY, TOO.
YOU THINK THAT KINDA THING ACTUALLY HAPPENS?

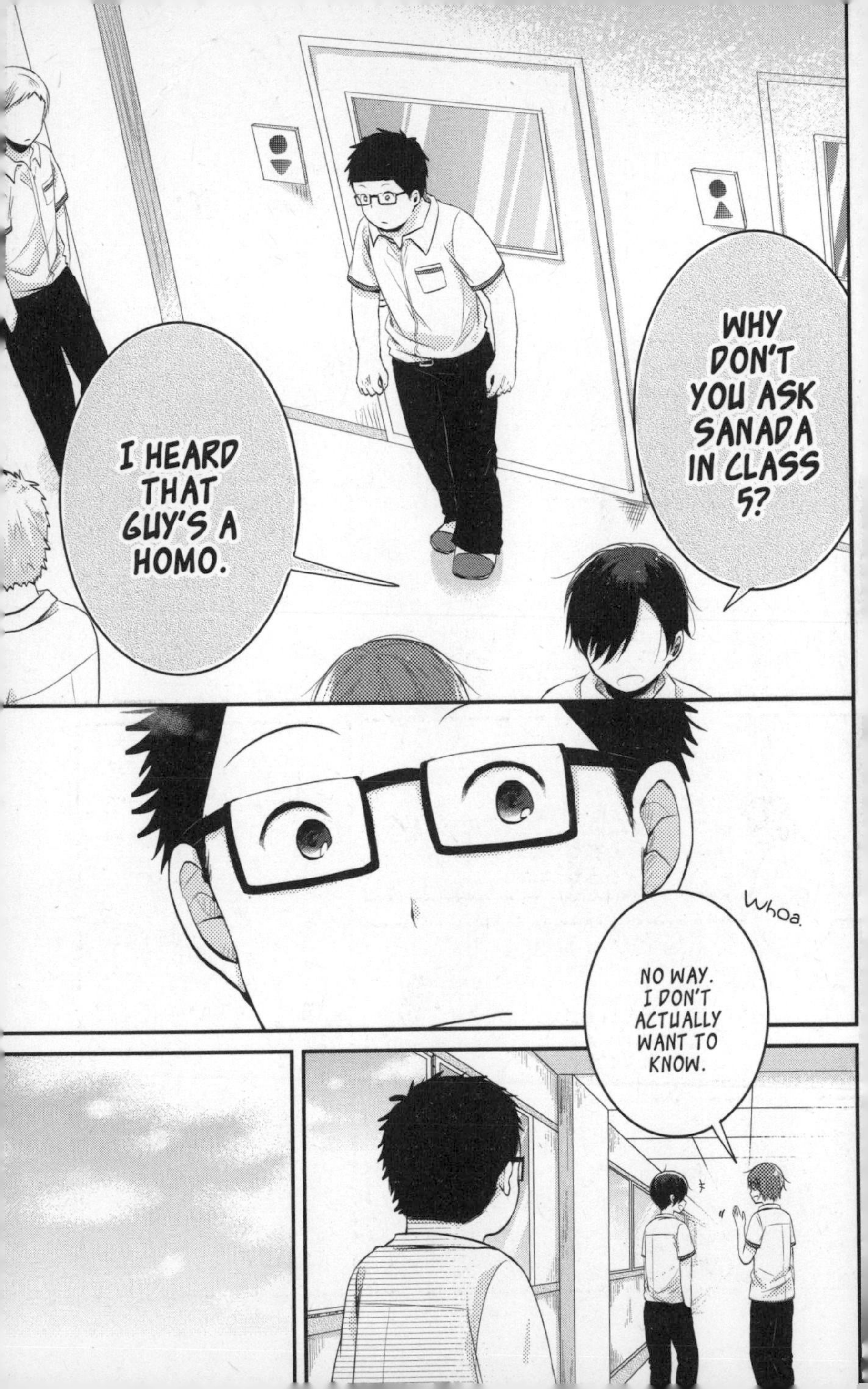
WHY DON'T YOU ASK SANADA IN CLASS 5?
I HEARD THAT GUY'S A HOMO.
Whoa.
NO WAY. I DON'T ACTUALLY WANT TO KNOW.

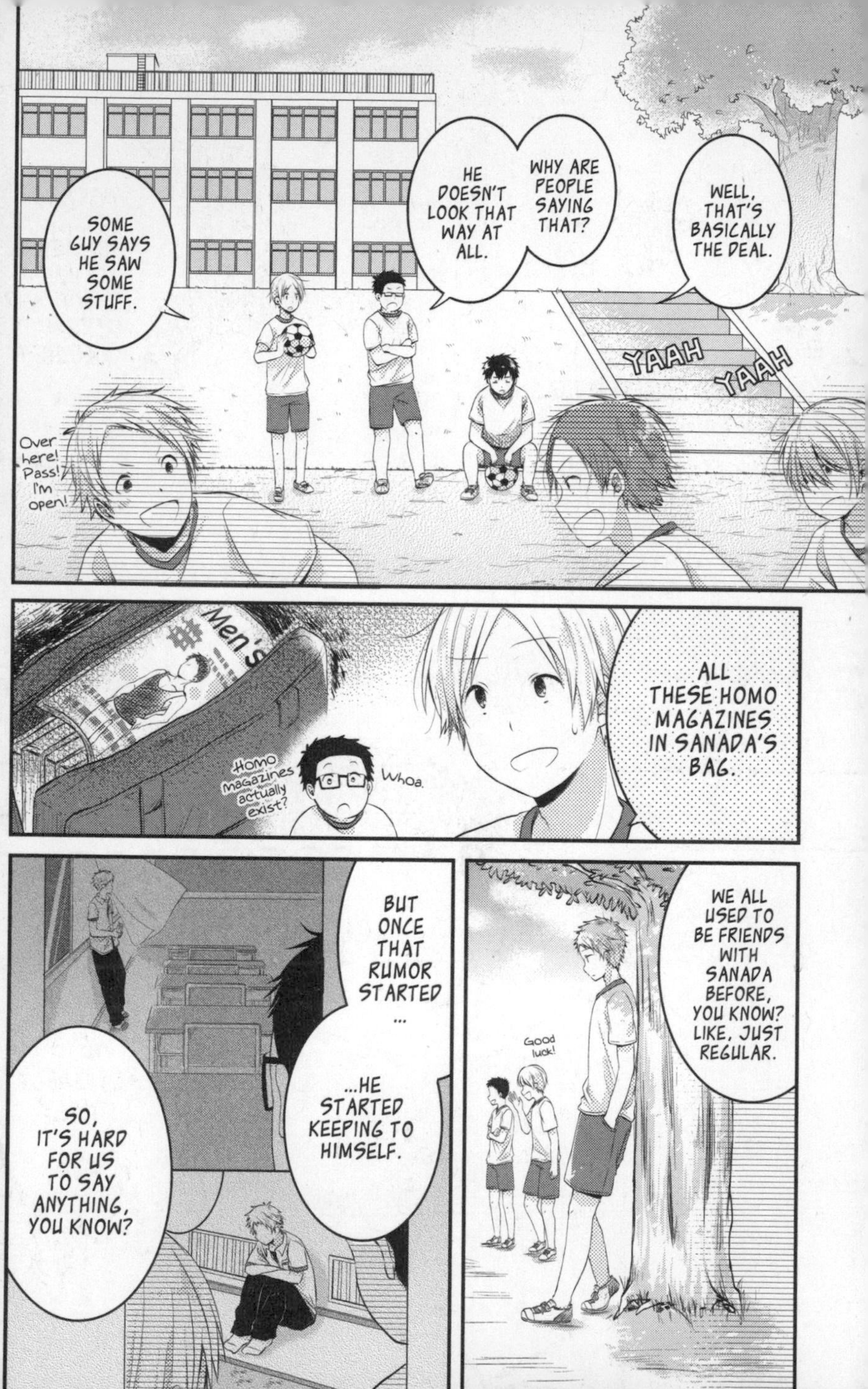
WELL, THAT'S BASICALLY THE DEAL.
YAAH
YAAH
WHY ARE PEOPLE SAYING THAT?
HE DOESN'T LOOK THAT WAY AT ALL.
SOME GUY SAYS HE SAW SOME STUFF.
Over here! Pass! I'm open!
ALL THESE HOMO MAGAZINES IN SANADA'S BAG.
Whoa.
Homo magazines actually exist?
Men's
WE ALL USED TO BE FRIENDS WITH SANADA BEFORE, YOU KNOW? LIKE, JUST REGULAR.
Good luck!
BUT ONCE THAT RUMOR STARTED...
...HE STARTED KEEPING TO HIMSELF.
SO, IT'S HARD FOR US TO SAY ANYTHING, YOU KNOW?

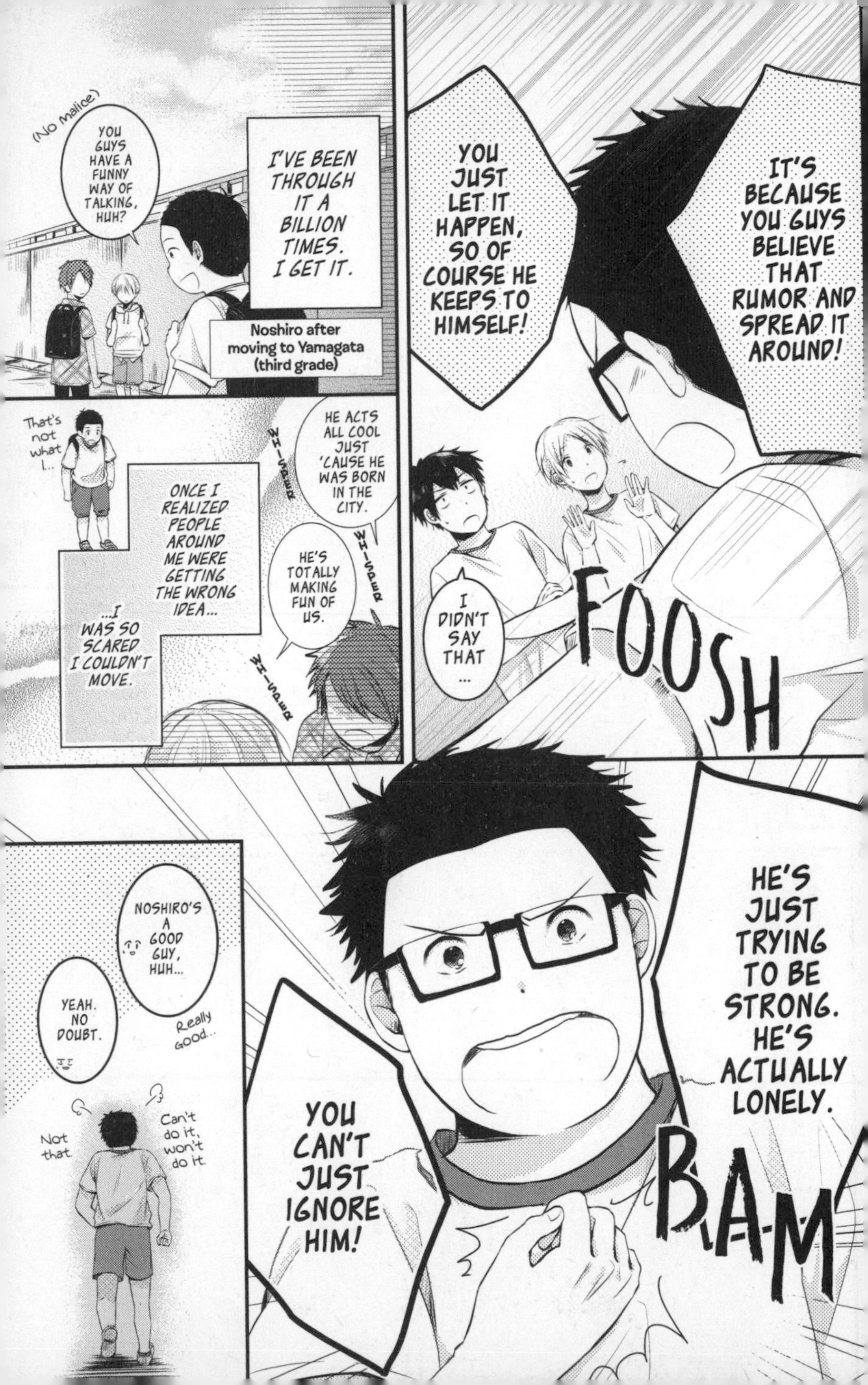

IT'S BECAUSE YOU GUYS BELIEVE THAT RUMOR AND SPREAD IT AROUND!
YOU JUST LET IT HAPPEN, SO OF COURSE HE KEEPS TO HIMSELF!
I DIDN'T SAY THAT ...
FOOSH
I'VE BEEN THROUGH IT A BILLION TIMES. I GET IT.
YOU GUYS HAVE A FUNNY WAY OF TALKING, HUH?
(No malice)
Noshiro after moving to Yamagata (third grade)
HE ACTS ALL COOL JUST 'CAUSE HE WAS BORN IN THE CITY.
WHISPER
ONCE I REALIZED PEOPLE AROUND ME WERE GETTING THE WRONG IDEA...
That's not what I...
WHISPER
HE'S TOTALLY MAKING FUN OF US.
...I WAS SO SCARED I COULDN'T MOVE.
WHISPER
HE'S JUST TRYING TO BE STRONG. HE'S ACTUALLY LONELY.
YOU CAN'T JUST IGNORE HIM!
BAM
NOSHIRO'S A GOOD GUY, HUH...
YEAH. NO DOUBT.
Really good...
Can't do it, won't do it.
Not that.

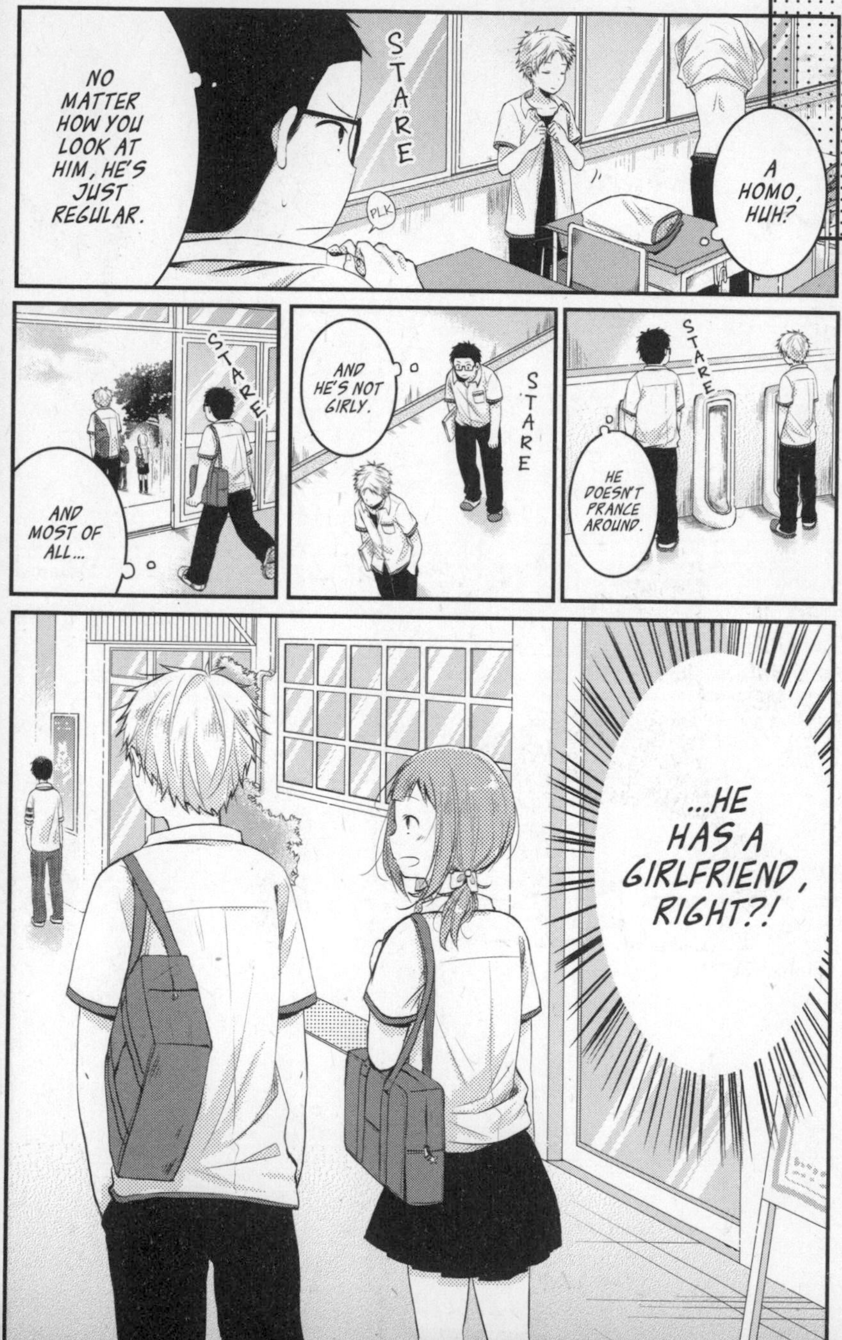
A HOMO, HUH?
STARE
PLK
NO MATTER HOW YOU LOOK AT HIM, HE'S JUST REGULAR.
STARE
HE DOESN'T PRANCE AROUND.
STARE
AND HE'S NOT GIRLY.
STARE
AND MOST OF ALL...
...HE HAS A GIRLFRIEND, RIGHT?!

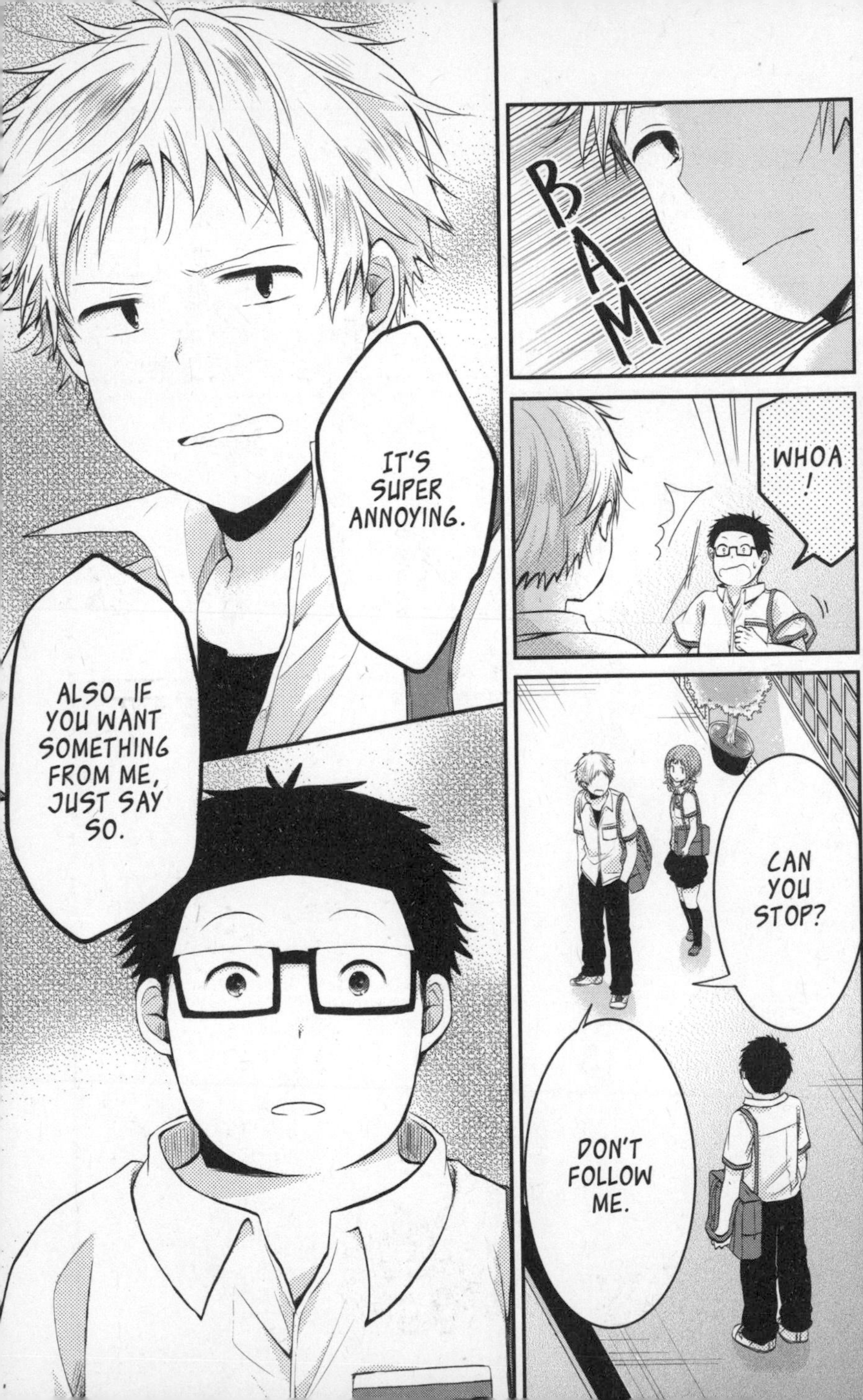
BAM
WHOA!
CAN YOU STOP?
DON'T FOLLOW ME.
IT'S SUPER ANNOYING.
ALSO, IF YOU WANT SOMETHING FROM ME, JUST SAY SO.

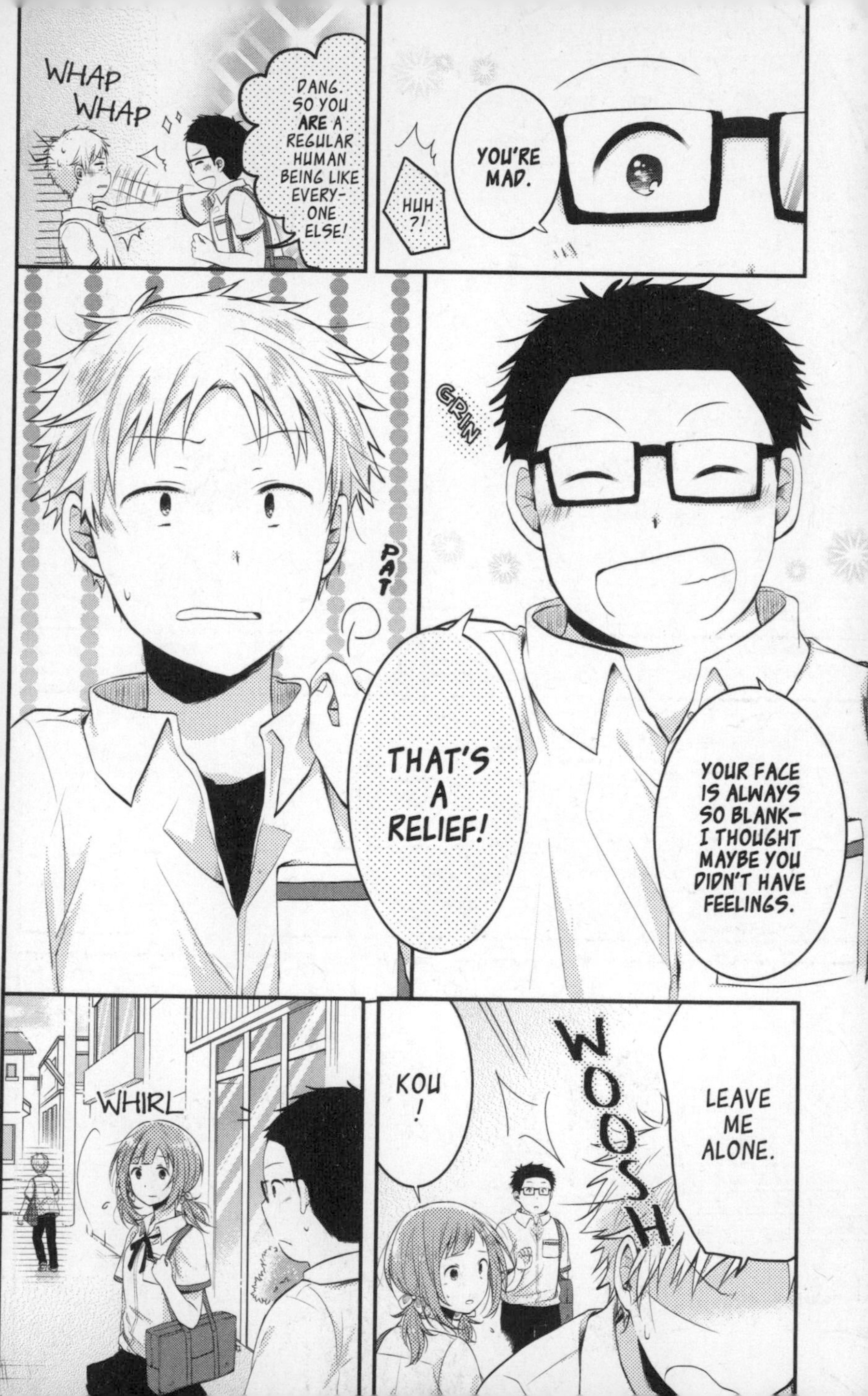
YOU'RE MAD.
HUH?!
DANG. SO YOU ARE A REGULAR HUMAN BEING LIKE EVERY-ONE ELSE!
WHAP WHAP
GRIN
YOUR FACE IS ALWAYS SO BLANK- I THOUGHT MAYBE YOU DIDN'T HAVE FEELINGS.
PAT
THAT'S A RELIEF!
LEAVE ME ALONE.
WOOSH
KOU!
WHIRL

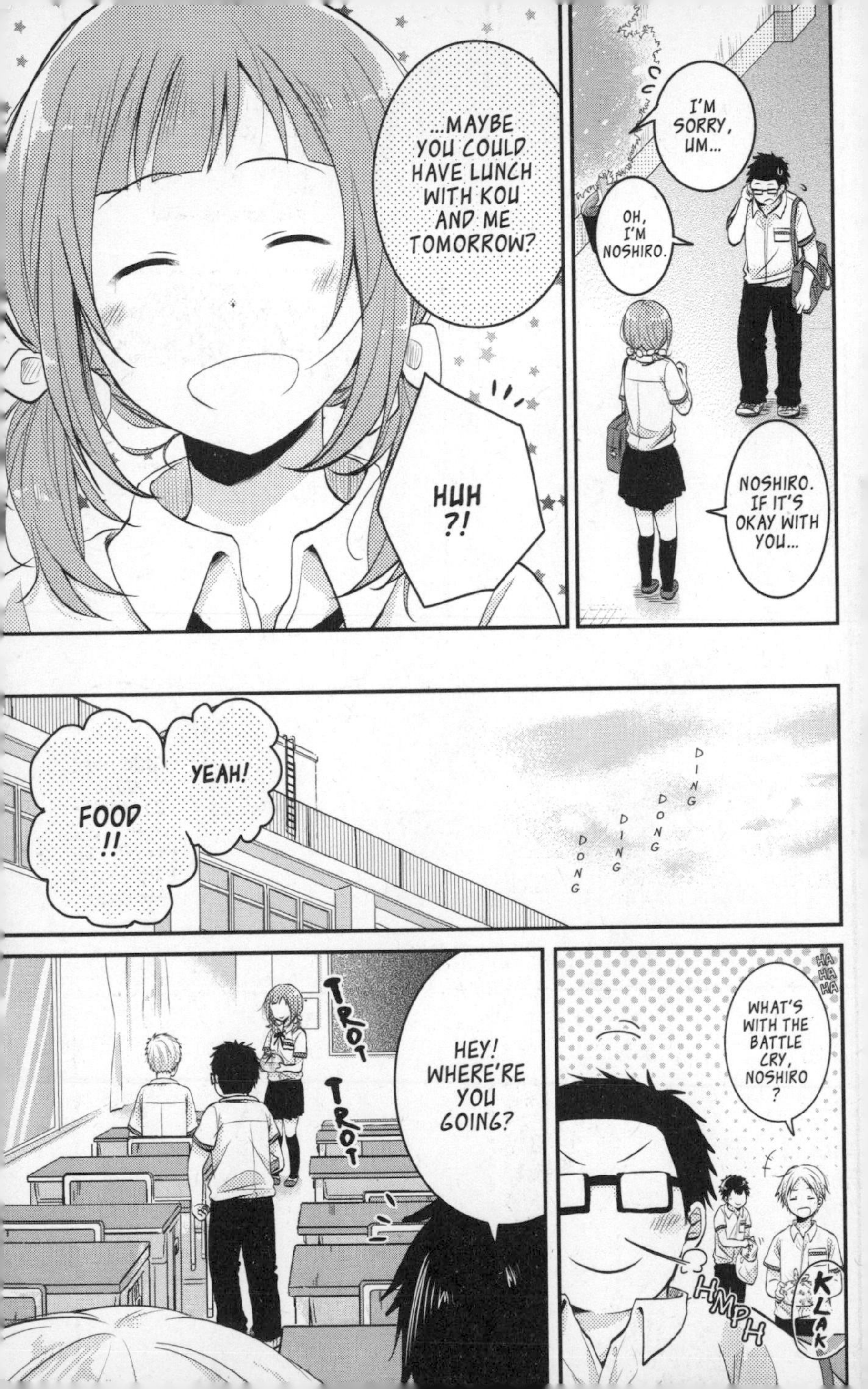
I'M SORRY, UM...
OH, I'M NOSHIRO.
NOSHIRO. IF IT'S OKAY WITH YOU...
...MAYBE YOU COULD HAVE LUNCH WITH KOU AND ME TOMORROW?
HUH?!
DING DONG DING DONG
YEAH!
FOOD!!
HA HA HA
WHAT'S WITH THE BATTLE CRY, NOSHIRO?
KLAK
HMPH
HEY! WHERE'RE YOU GOING?
TROT TROT

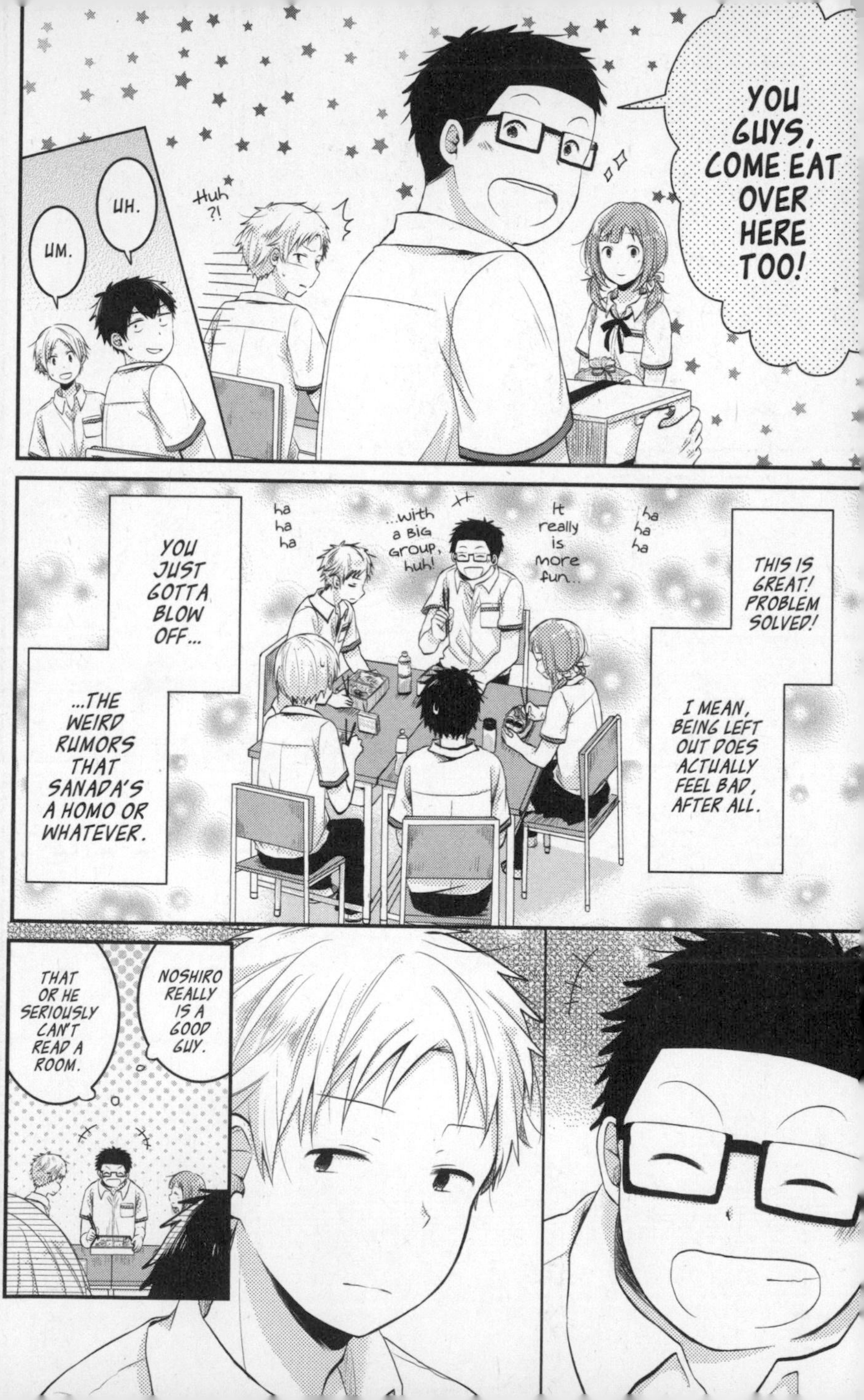
YOU GUYS, COME EAT OVER HERE TOO!
Huh ?!
UH.
UM.
THIS IS GREAT! PROBLEM SOLVED!
I MEAN, BEING LEFT OUT DOES ACTUALLY FEEL BAD, AFTER ALL.
ha ha ha
It really is more fun...
...with a Big Group, huh!
ha ha ha
YOU JUST GOTTA BLOW OFF...
...THE WEIRD RUMORS THAT SANADA'S A HOMO OR WHATEVER.
NOSHIRO REALLY IS A GOOD GUY.
THAT OR HE SERIOUSLY CAN'T READ A ROOM.

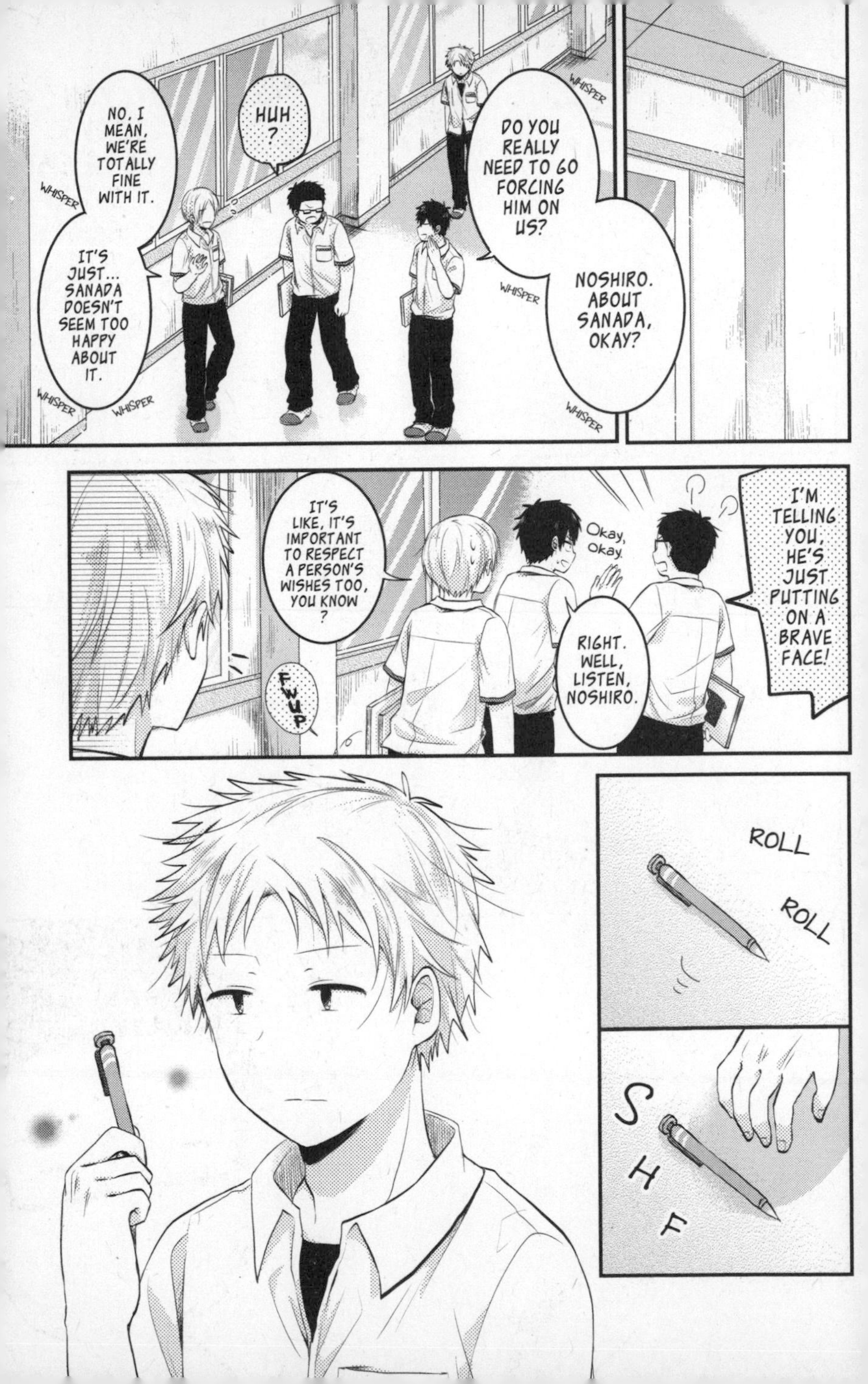
WHISPER
DO YOU REALLY NEED TO GO FORCING HIM ON US?
NOSHIRO. ABOUT SANADA, OKAY?
WHISPER
WHISPER
HUH?
NO, I MEAN, WE'RE TOTALLY FINE WITH IT.
IT'S JUST... SANADA DOESN'T SEEM TOO HAPPY ABOUT IT.
WHISPER
WHISPER
WHISPER
I'M TELLING YOU, HE'S JUST PUTTING ON A BRAVE FACE!
Okay, okay.
RIGHT. WELL, LISTEN, NOSHIRO.
IT'S LIKE, IT'S IMPORTANT TO RESPECT A PERSON'S WISHES TOO, YOU KNOW?
FWUP
ROLL
ROLL
SHF

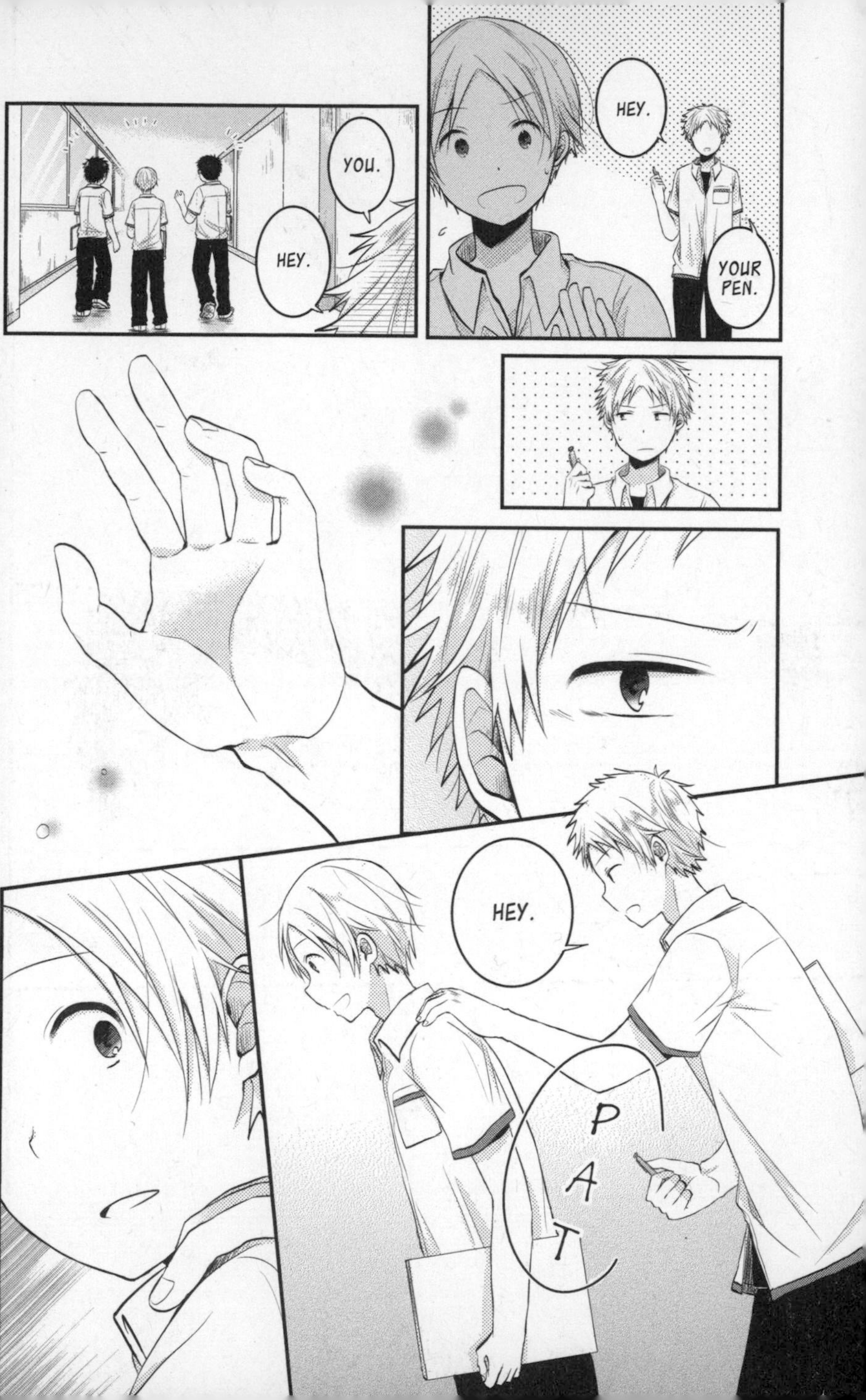

HEY.
YOUR PEN.
YOU.
HEY.
HEY.
PAT

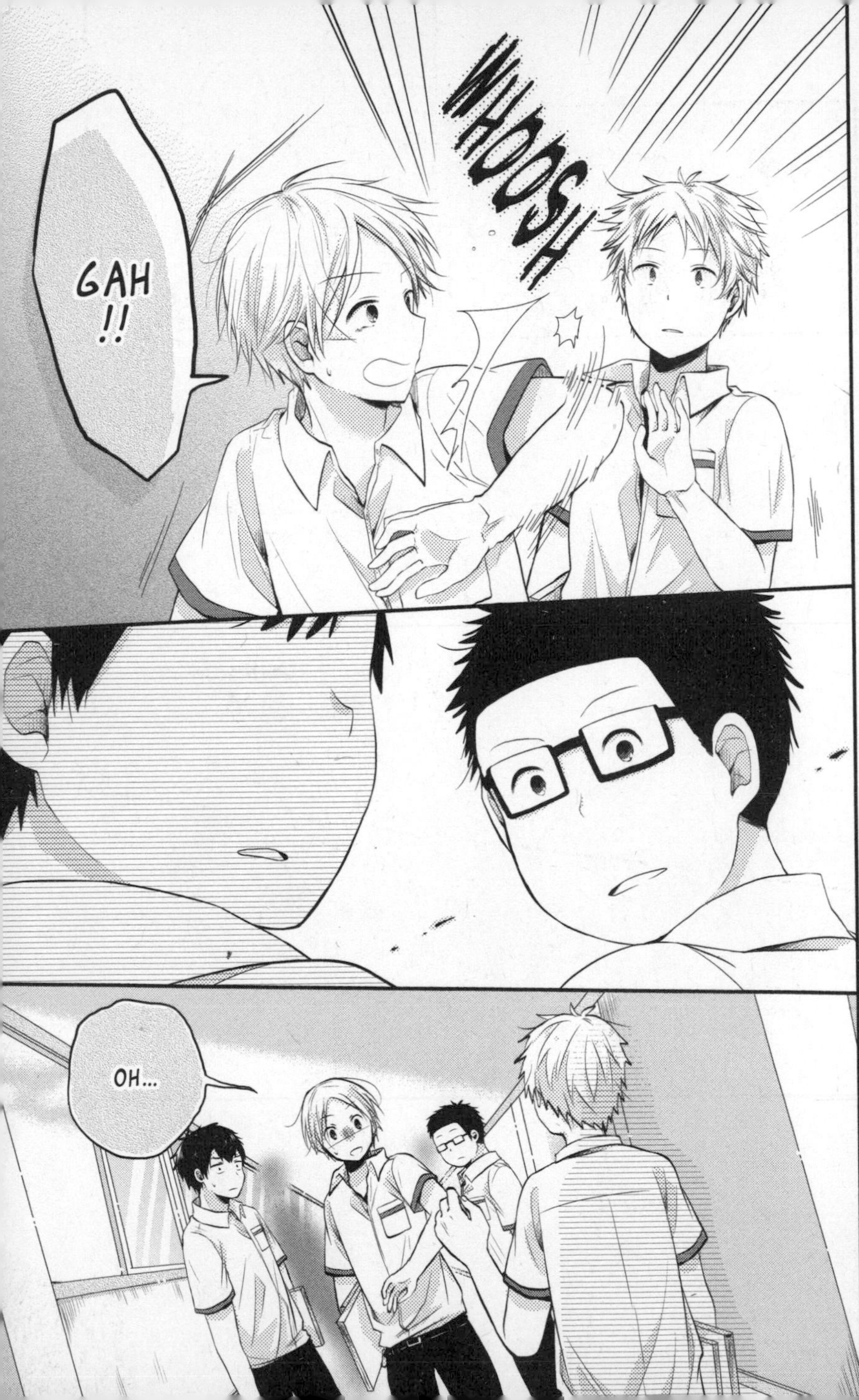
WHOOSH
GAH!!
OH...

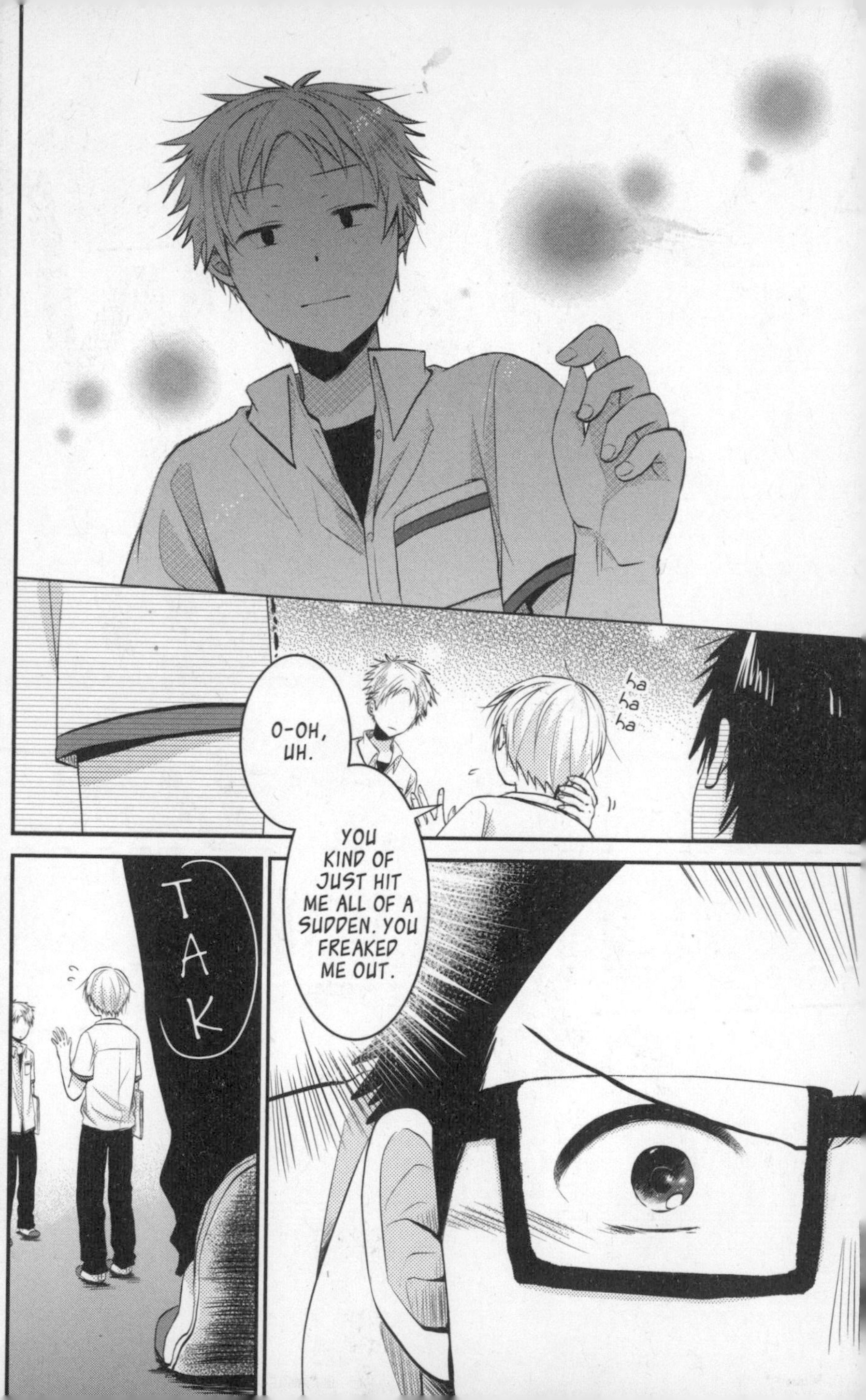
ha ha ha
O-OH, UH.
YOU KIND OF JUST HIT ME ALL OF A SUDDEN. YOU FREAKED ME OUT.
TAK

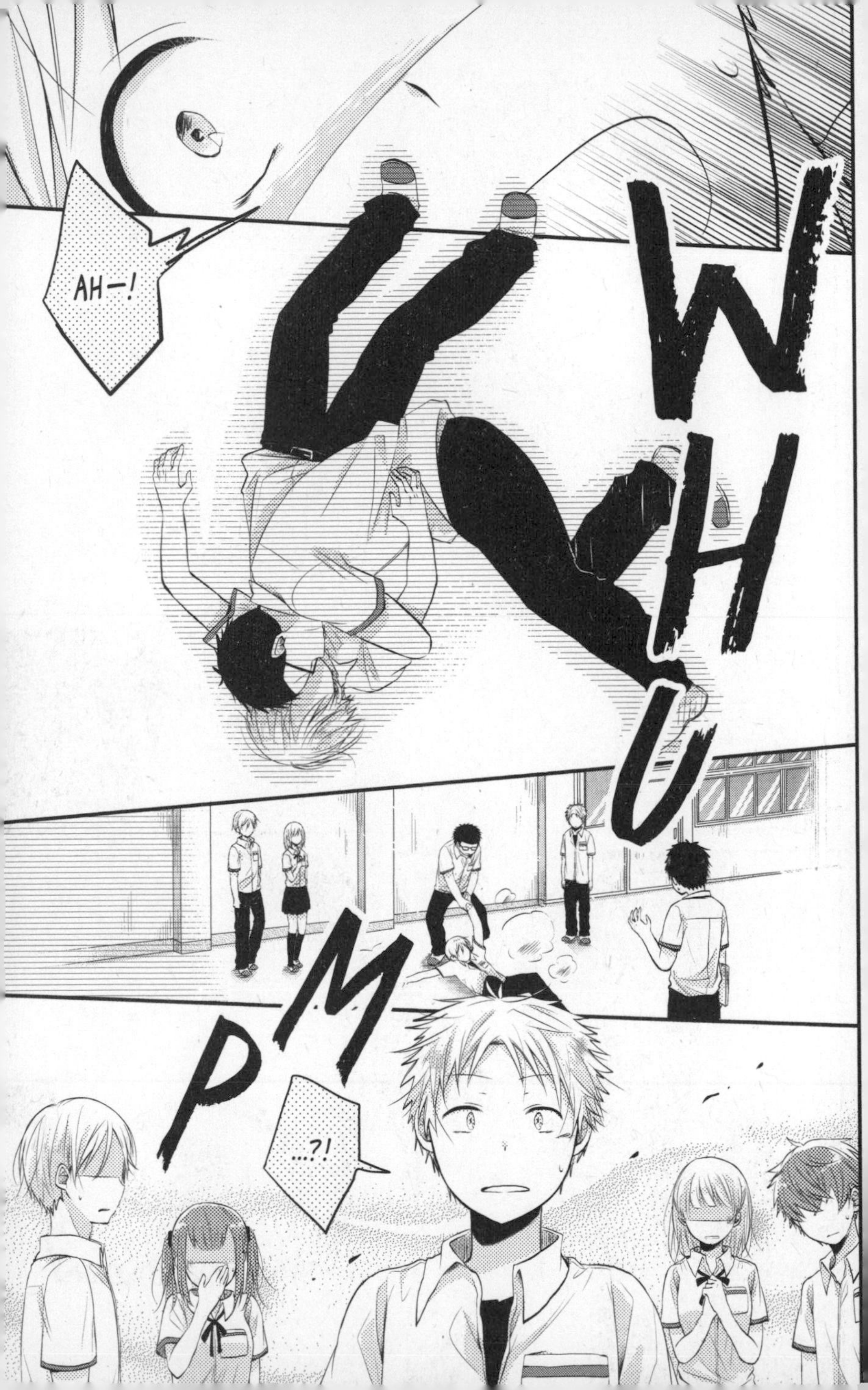
WHUMP
AH—!
...?!

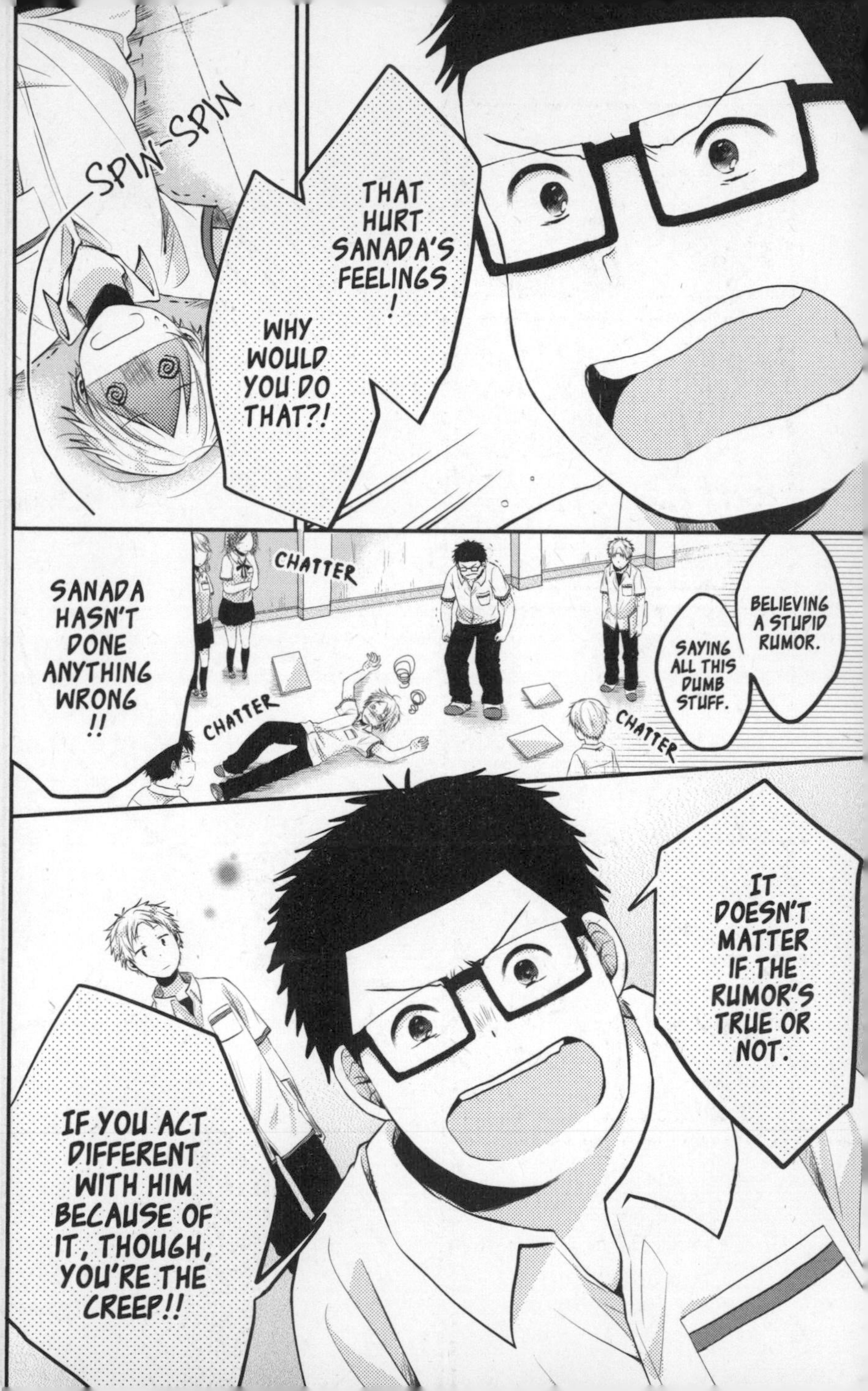
THAT HURT SANADA'S FEELINGS!
WHY WOULD YOU DO THAT?!
SPIN-SPIN
BELIEVING A STUPID RUMOR.
SAYING ALL THIS DUMB STUFF.
CHATTER
CHATTER
SANADA HASN'T DONE ANYTHING WRONG!!
CHATTER
IT DOESN'T MATTER IF THE RUMOR'S TRUE OR NOT.
IF YOU ACT DIFFERENT WITH HIM BECAUSE OF IT, THOUGH, YOU'RE THE CREEP!!

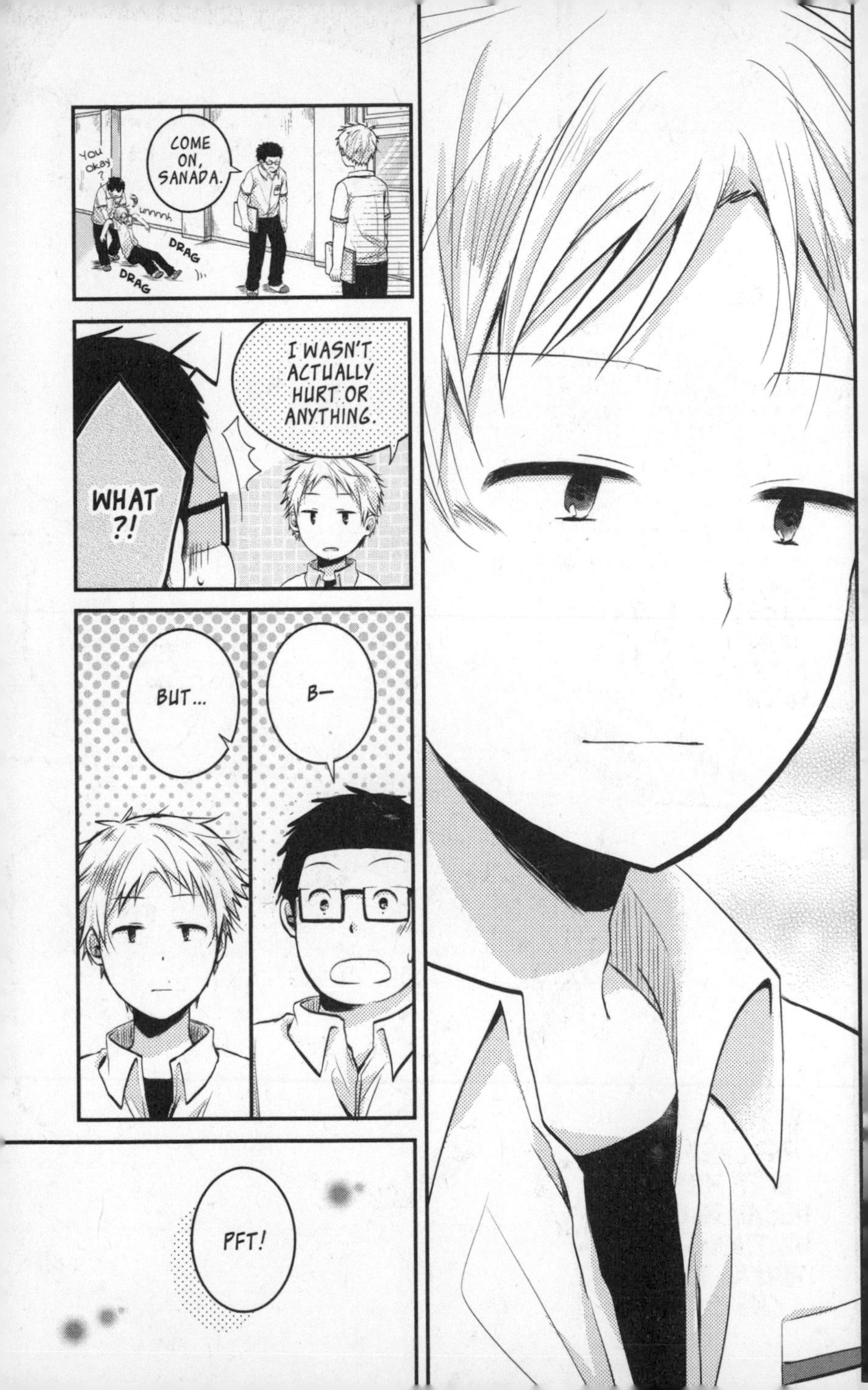
COME ON, SANADA.
You okay?
unnnh
DRAG
DRAG
I WASN'T ACTUALLY HURT OR ANYTHING.
WHAT?!
B—
BUT...
PFT!

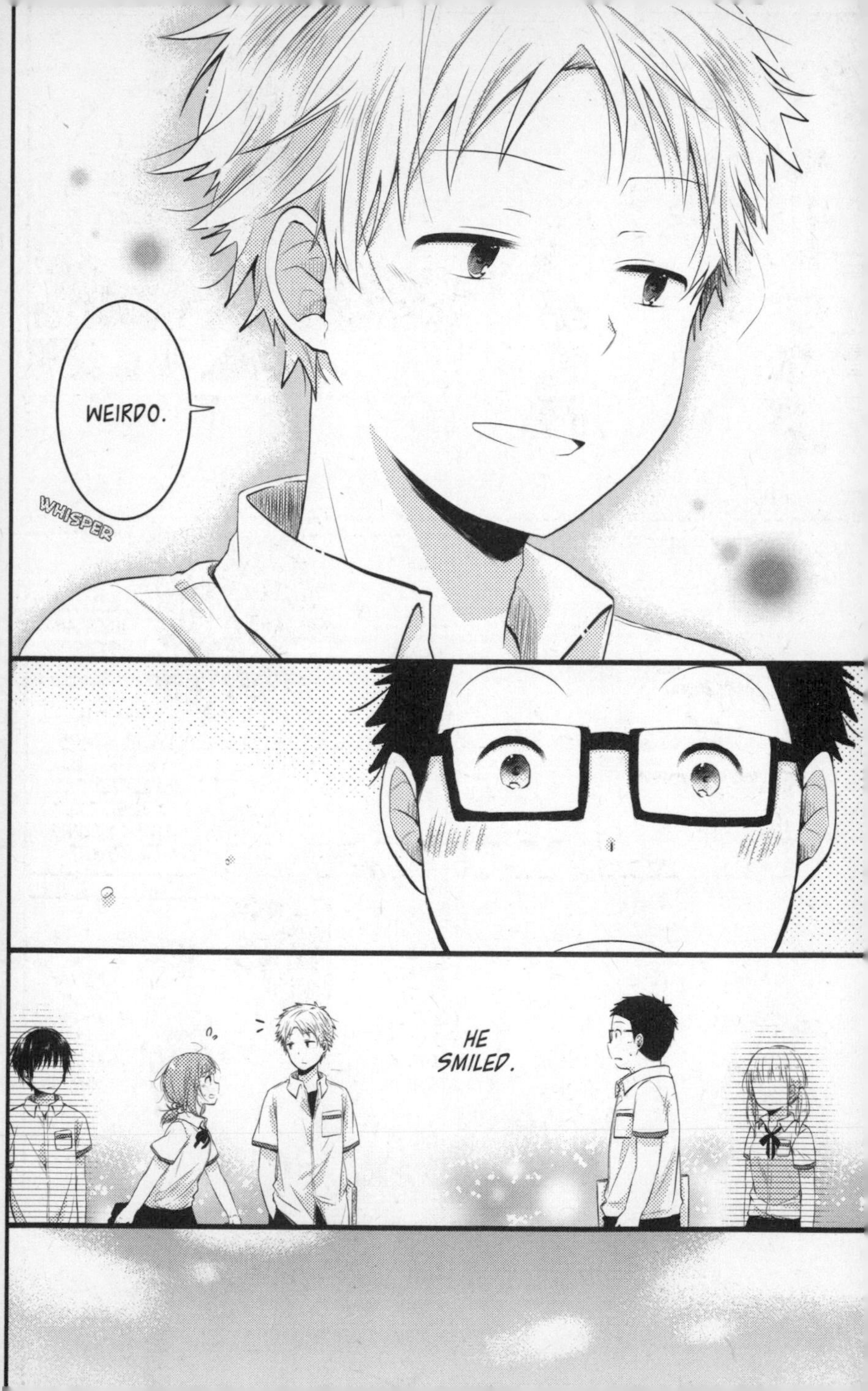
WEIRDO.
WHISPER
HE SMILED.

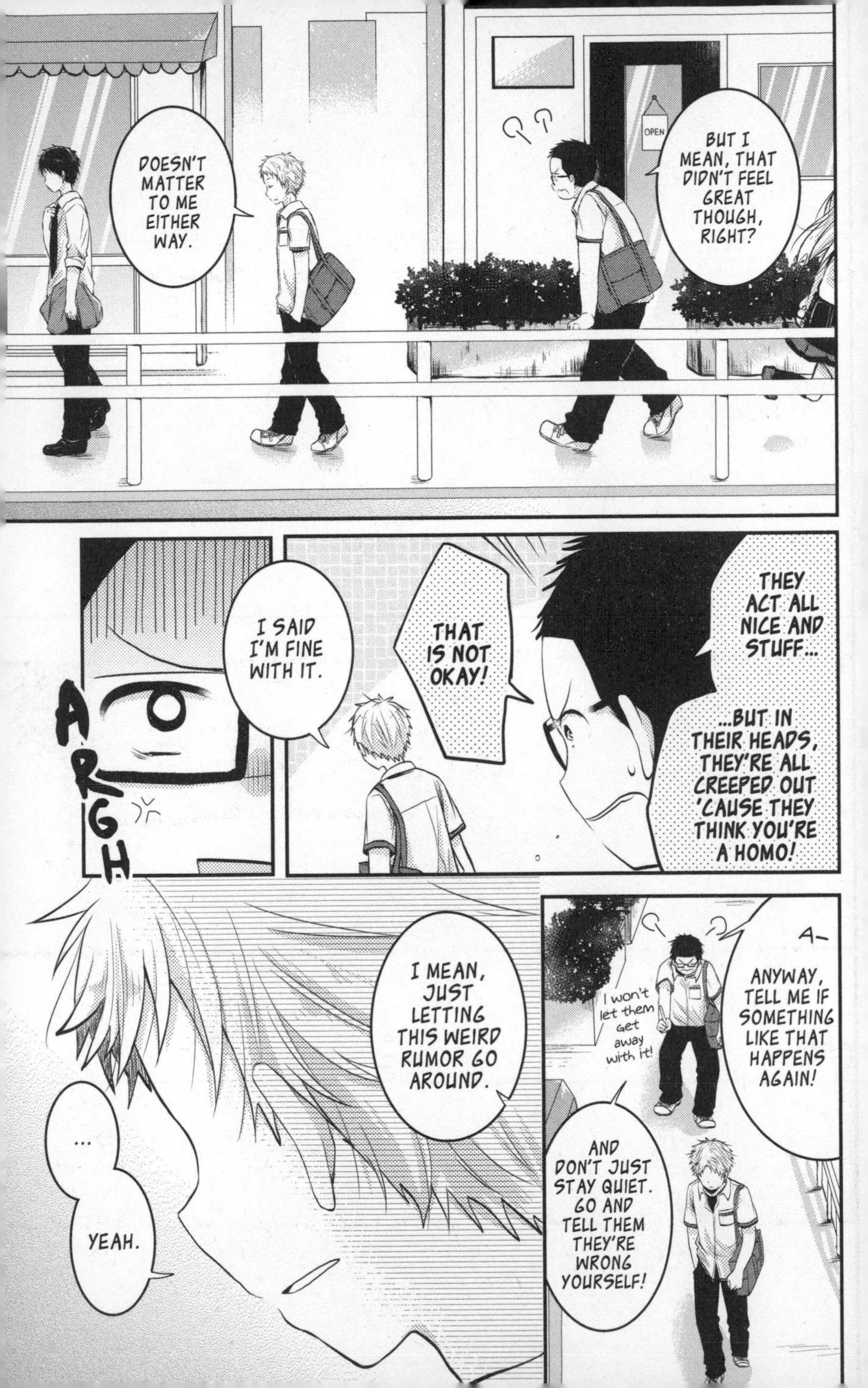
OPEN
BUT I MEAN, THAT DIDN'T FEEL GREAT THOUGH, RIGHT?
DOESN'T MATTER TO ME EITHER WAY.
THEY ACT ALL NICE AND STUFF...
...BUT IN THEIR HEADS, THEY'RE ALL CREEPED OUT 'CAUSE THEY THINK YOU'RE A HOMO!
THAT IS NOT OKAY!
I SAID I'M FINE WITH IT.
ARGH
A—
ANYWAY, TELL ME IF SOMETHING LIKE THAT HAPPENS AGAIN!
I won't let them get away with it!
AND DON'T JUST STAY QUIET. GO AND TELL THEM THEY'RE WRONG YOURSELF!
I MEAN, JUST LETTING THIS WEIRD RUMOR GO AROUND.
...
YEAH.

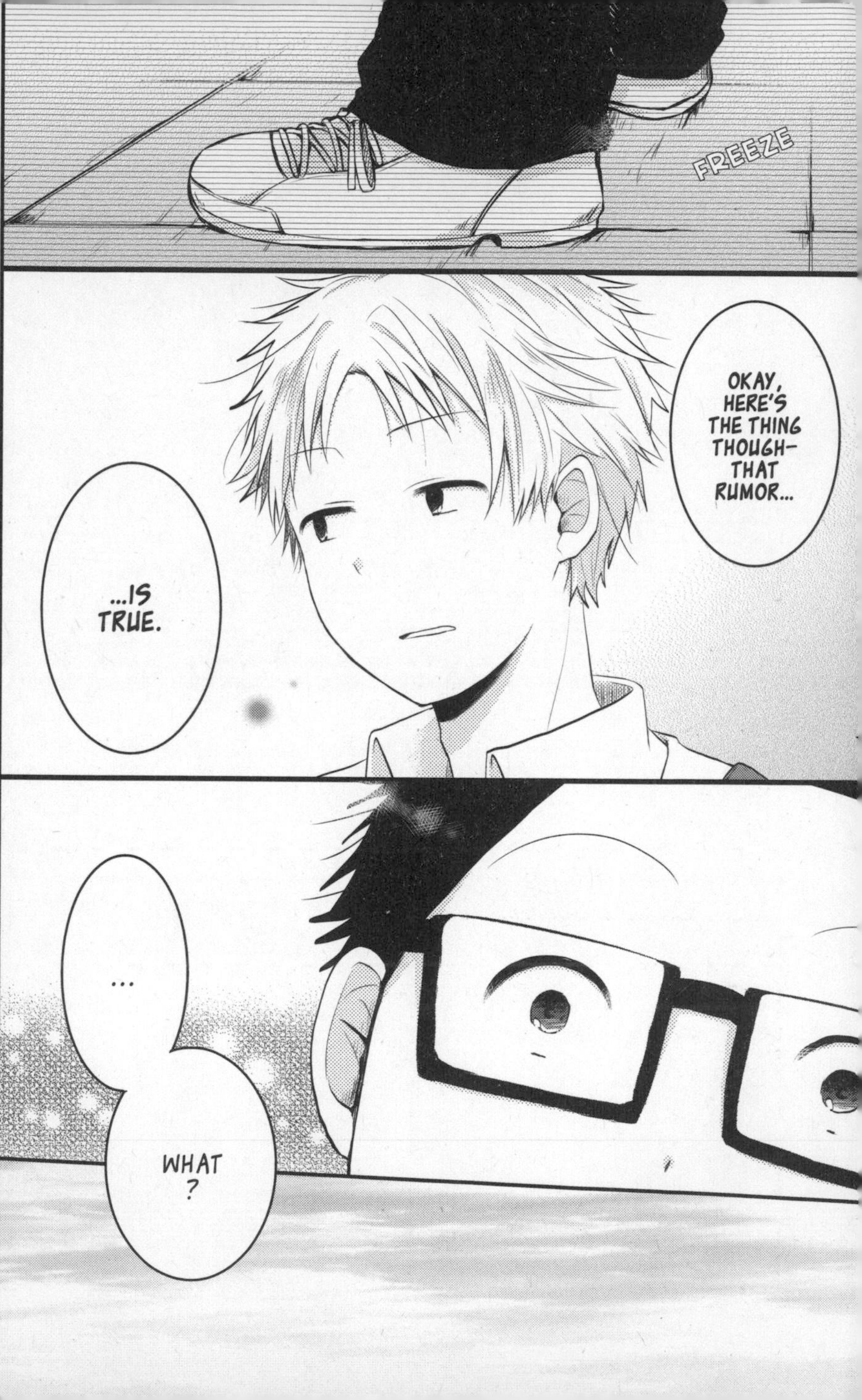
FREEZE
OKAY, HERE'S THE THING THOUGH-THAT RUMOR...
...IS TRUE.
...
WHAT?

That Blue
Sky Feeling

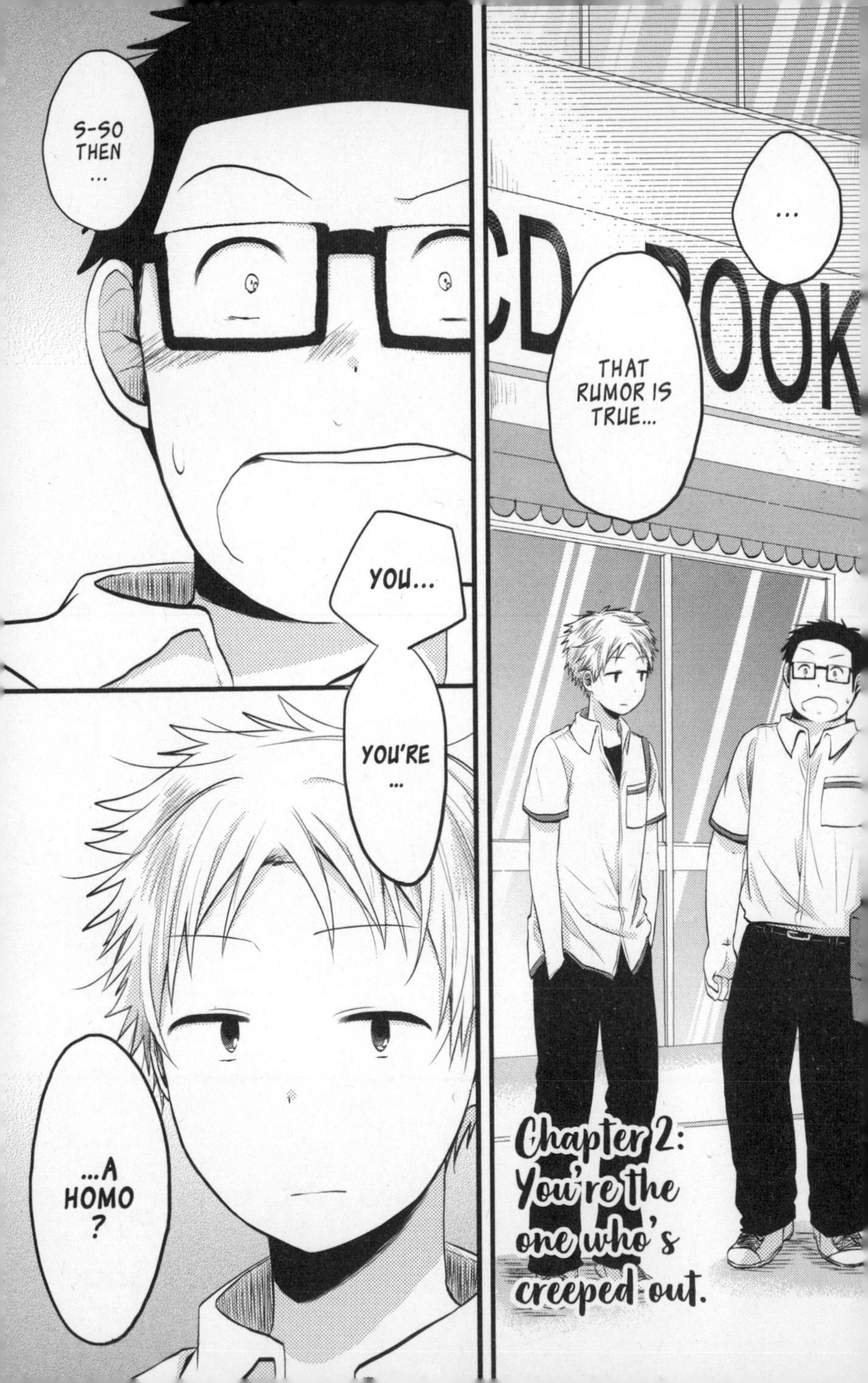
...
THAT RUMOR IS TRUE...
Chapter 2: You're the one who's creeped out.
S-SO THEN ...
YOU...
YOU'RE ...
...A HOMO ?

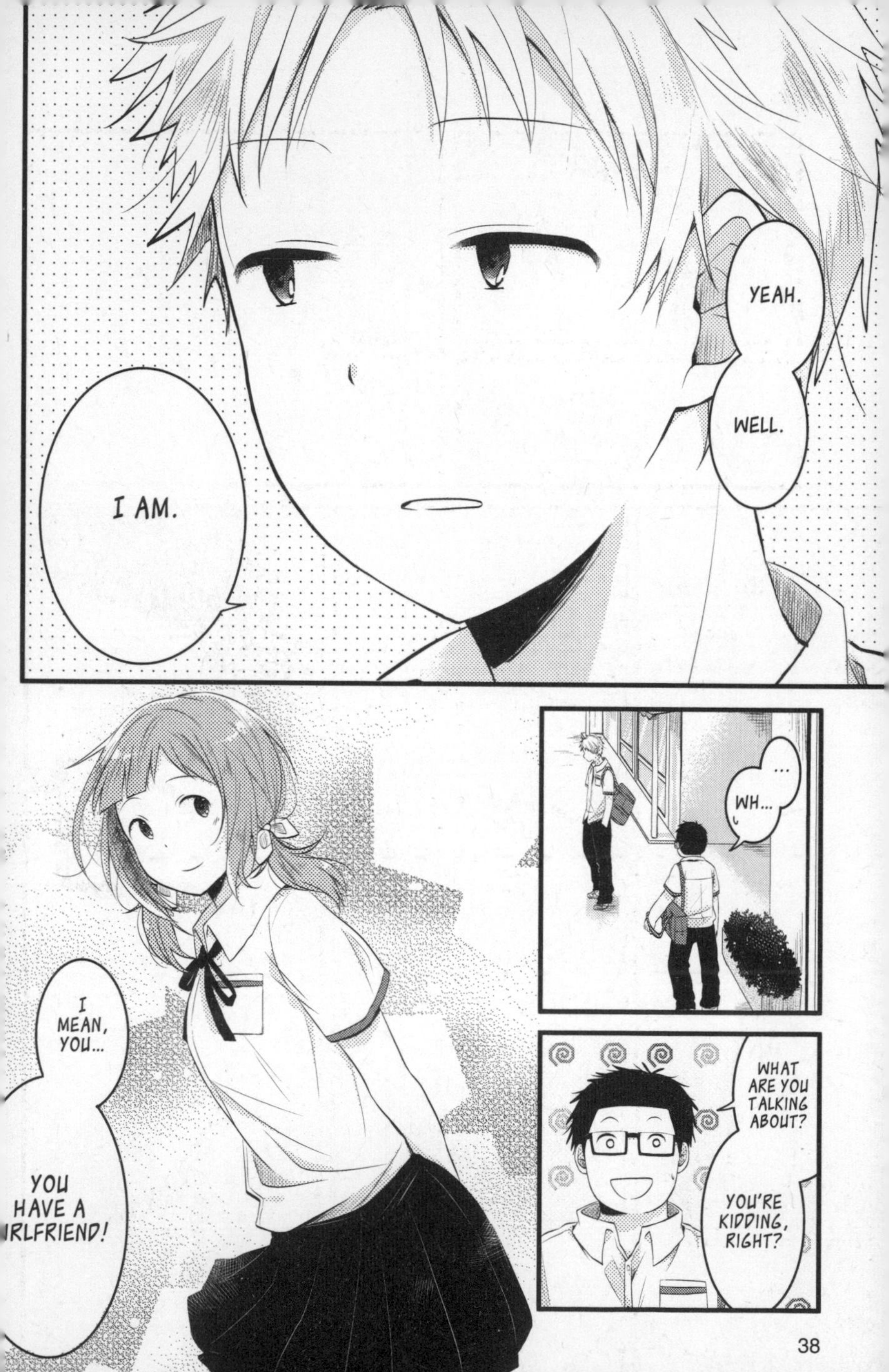
YEAH.
WELL.
I AM.
... WH...
WHAT ARE YOU TALKING ABOUT?
YOU'RE KIDDING, RIGHT?
I MEAN, YOU...
YOU HAVE A IRLFRIEND!

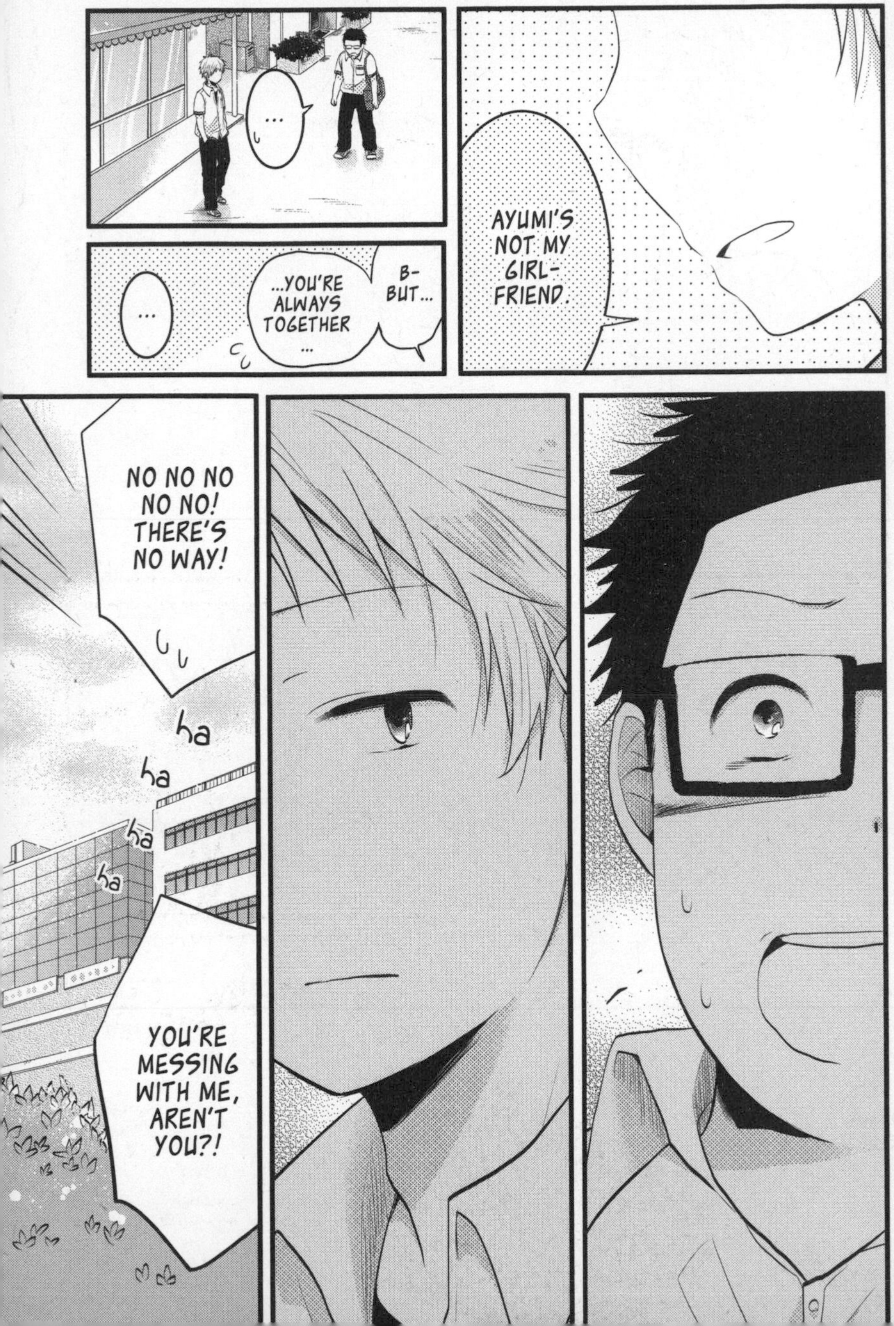
...
AYUMI'S NOT MY GIRL-FRIEND.
B-BUT...
...YOU'RE ALWAYS TOGETHER ...
...
NO NO NO NO NO! THERE'S NO WAY!
ha ha ha ha
YOU'RE MESSING WITH ME, AREN'T YOU?!

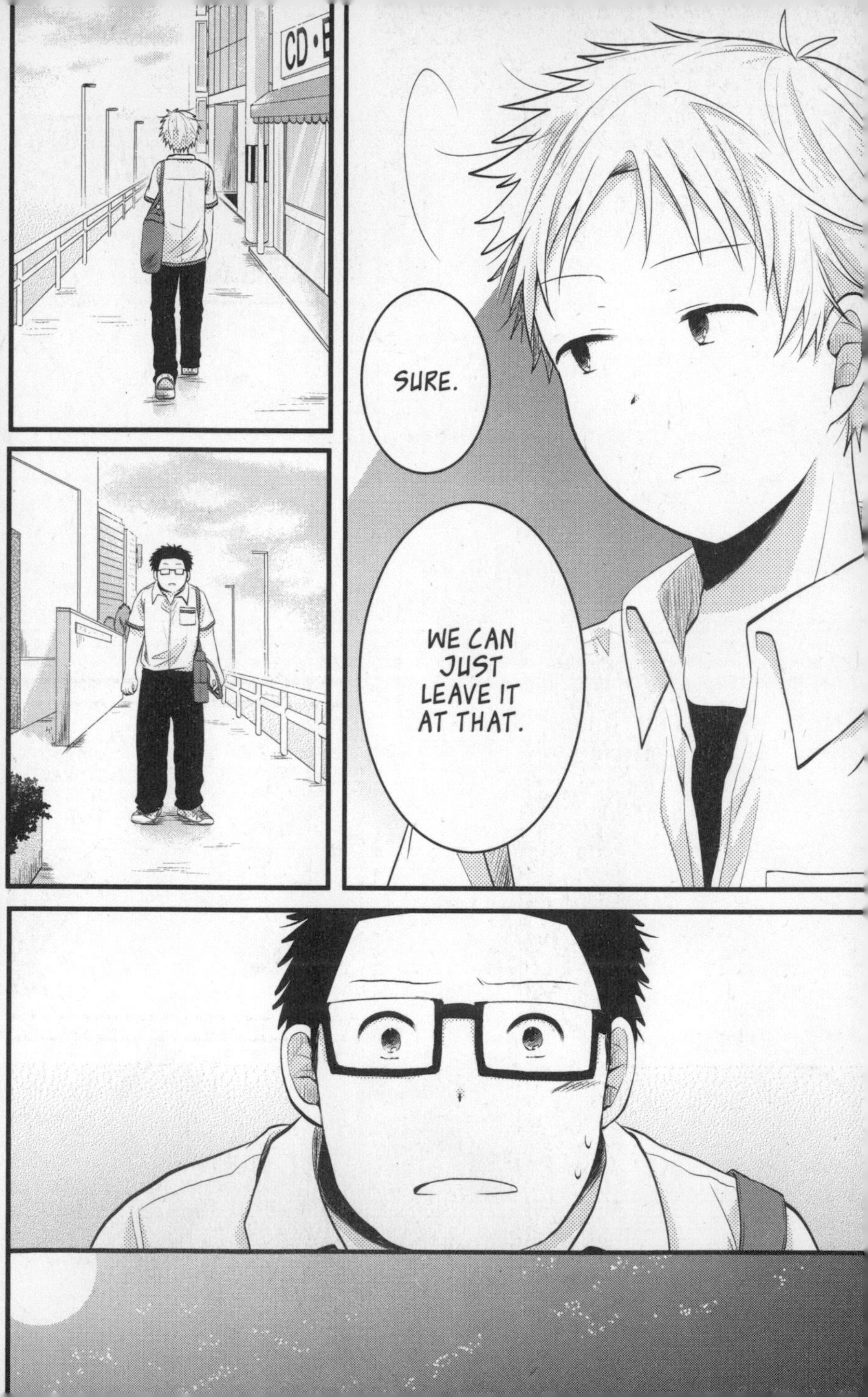
SURE.
WE CAN JUST LEAVE IT AT THAT.

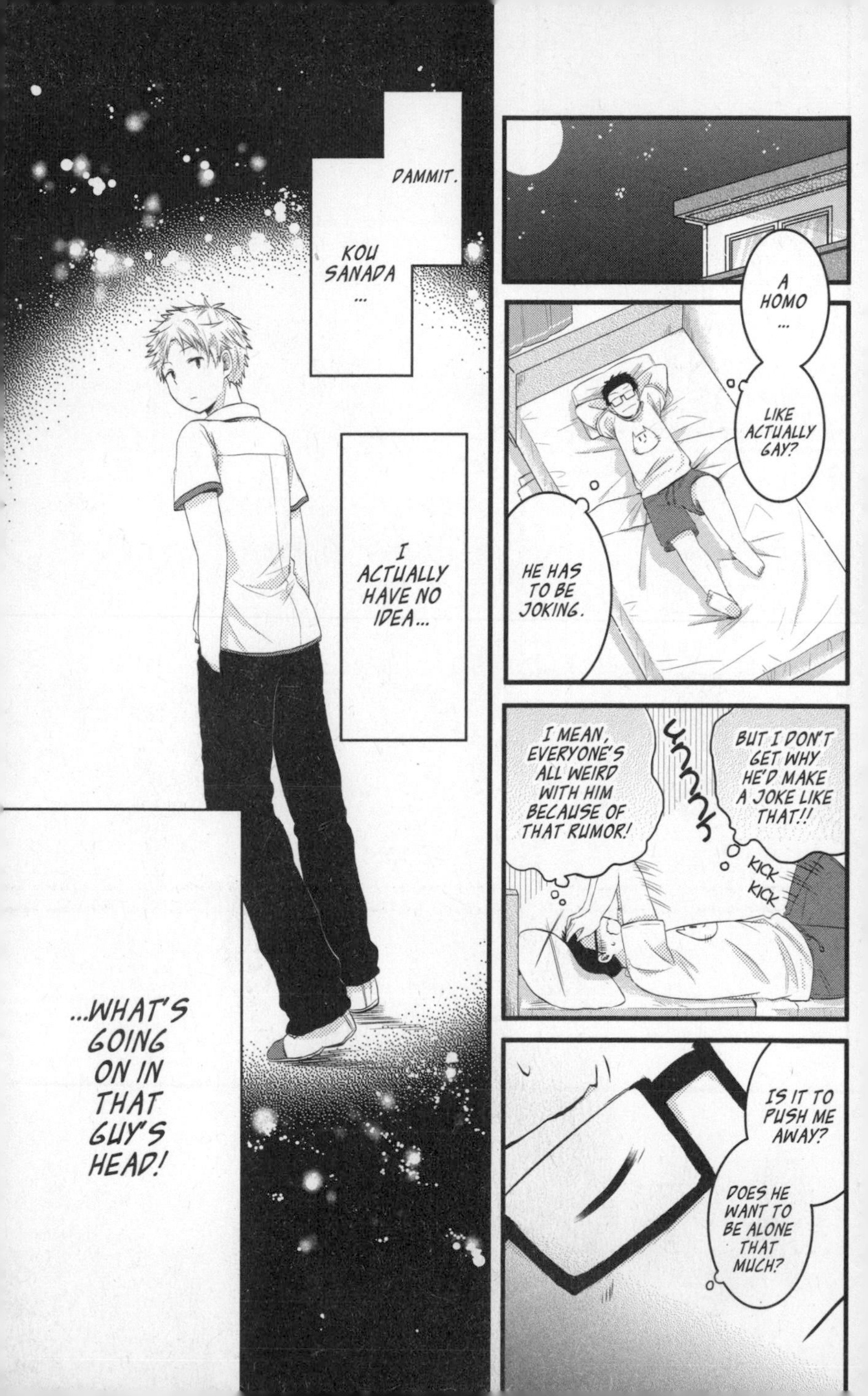
A HOMO...
LIKE ACTUALLY GAY?
HE HAS TO BE JOKING.
BUT I DON'T GET WHY HE'D MAKE A JOKE LIKE THAT!!
UNNNH
I MEAN, EVERYONE'S ALL WEIRD WITH HIM BECAUSE OF THAT RUMOR!
KICK KICK
IS IT TO PUSH ME AWAY?
DOES HE WANT TO BE ALONE THAT MUCH?
DAMMIT.
KOU SANADA...
I ACTUALLY HAVE NO IDEA...
...WHAT'S GOING ON IN THAT GUY'S HEAD!

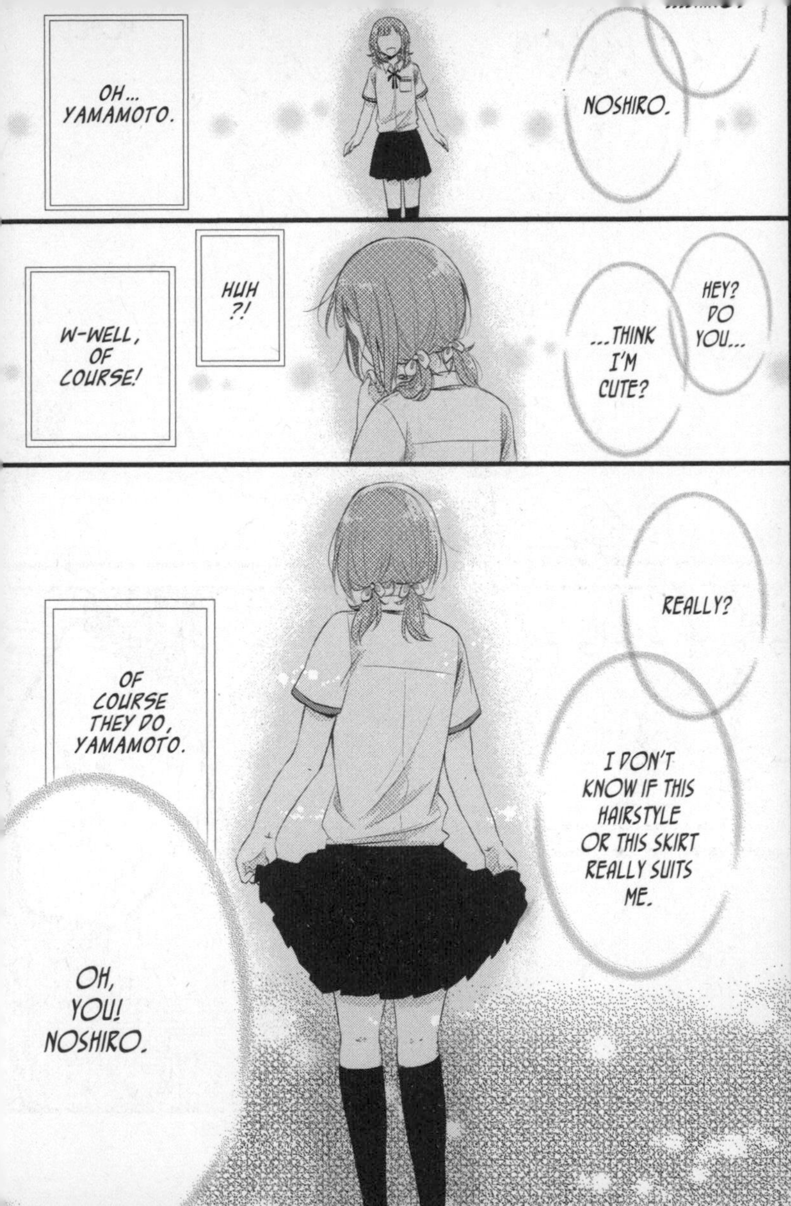
NOSHIRO.
OH... YAMAMOTO.
HEY? DO YOU...
...THINK I'M CUTE?
HUH ?!
W-WELL, OF COURSE!
REALLY?
I DON'T KNOW IF THIS HAIRSTYLE OR THIS SKIRT REALLY SUITS ME.
OF COURSE THEY DO, YAMAMOTO.
OH, YOU! NOSHIRO.

WHIRL

I'M NOT YAMA-MOTO.

I'M SANADA!

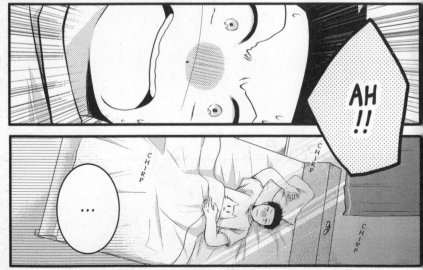

AH!!

CHIRP

CHIRP

CHIRP

CHIRP

...

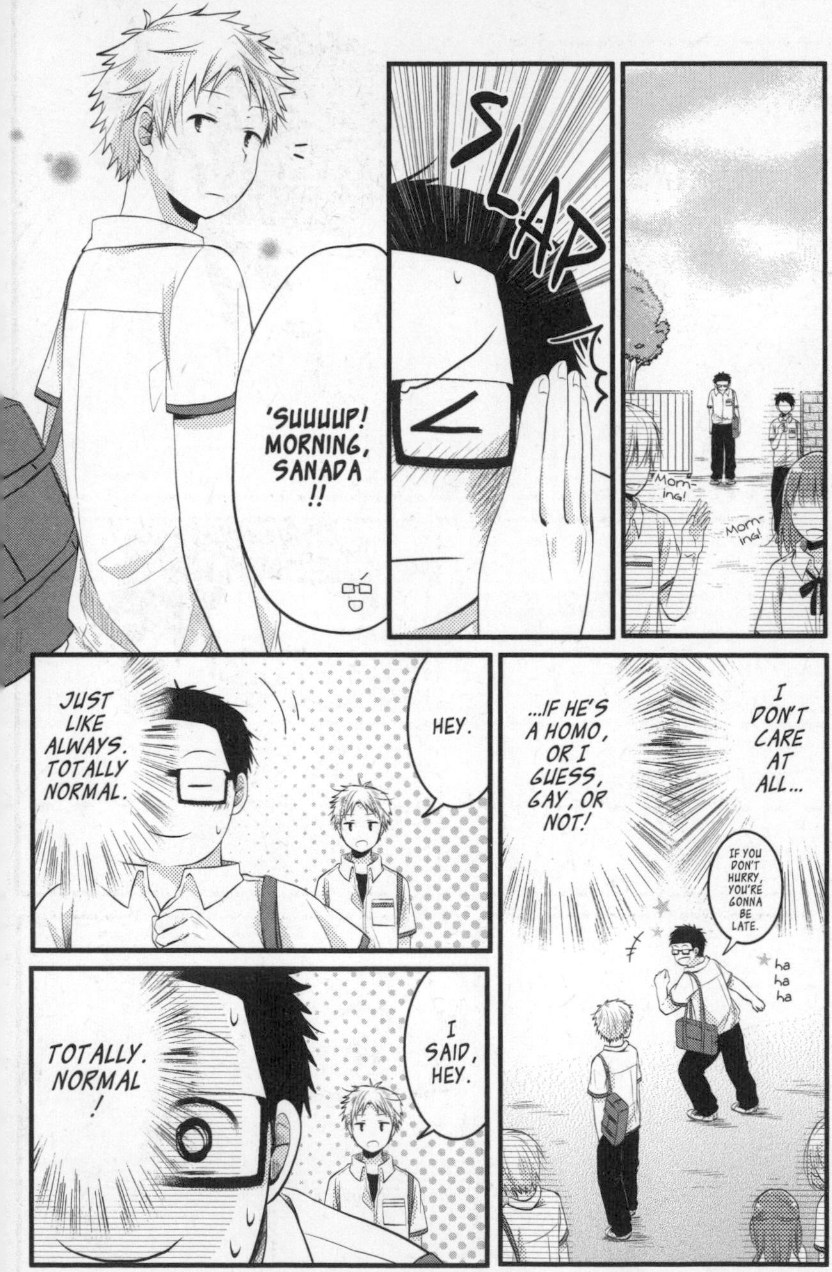
Morn-ing!
Morn-ing!
SLAP
'SUUUUP! MORNING, SANADA!!
I DON'T CARE AT ALL...
...IF HE'S A HOMO, OR I GUESS, GAY, OR NOT!
IF YOU DON'T HURRY, YOU'RE GONNA BE LATE.
ha ha ha
HEY.
JUST LIKE ALWAYS. TOTALLY NORMAL.
I SAID, HEY.
TOTALLY. NORMAL!

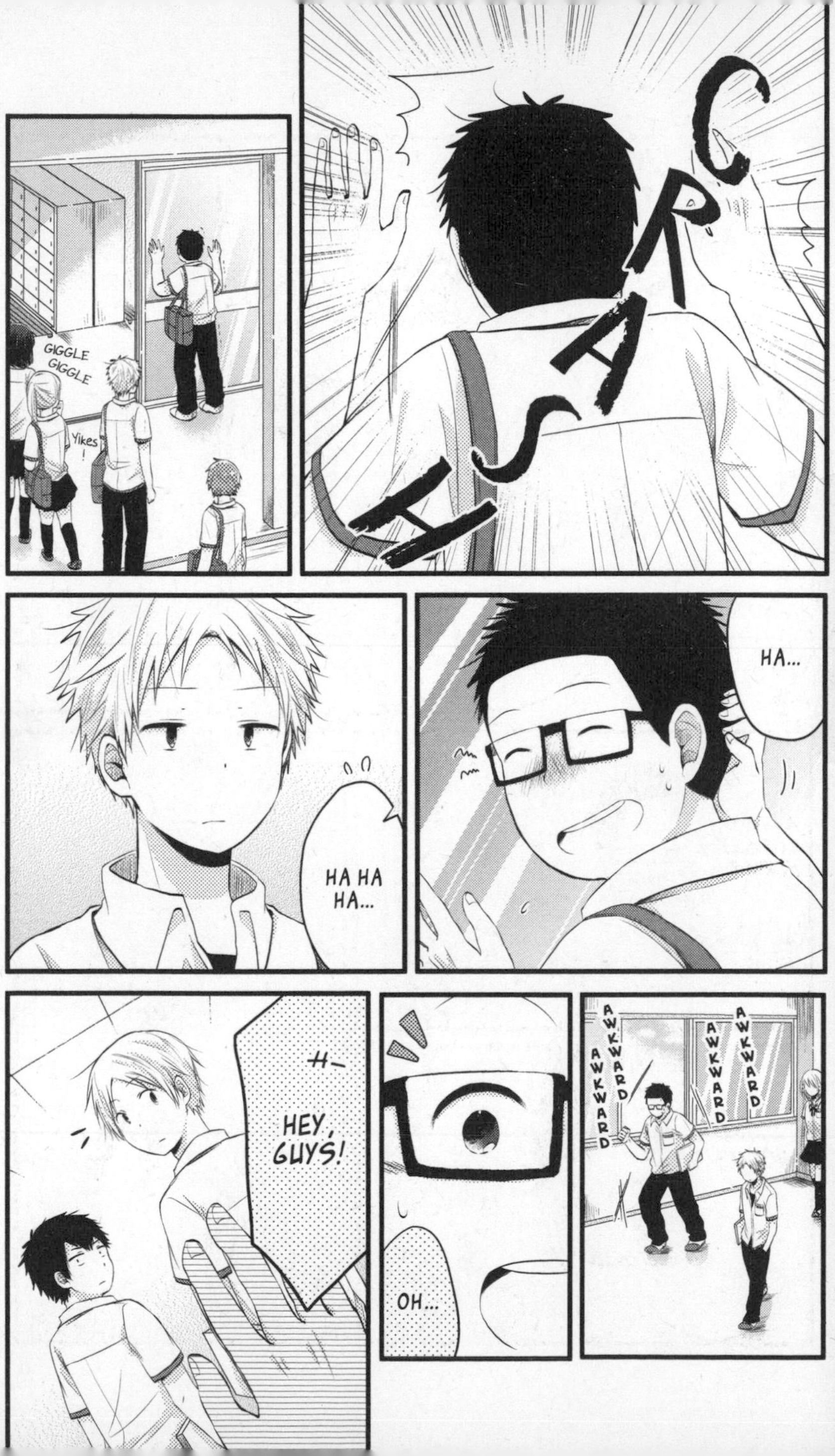
CRASH
GIGGLE GIGGLE
Yikes!
HA...
HA HA HA...
AWKWARD
AWKWARD
AWKWARD
OH...
H-
HEY, GUYS!

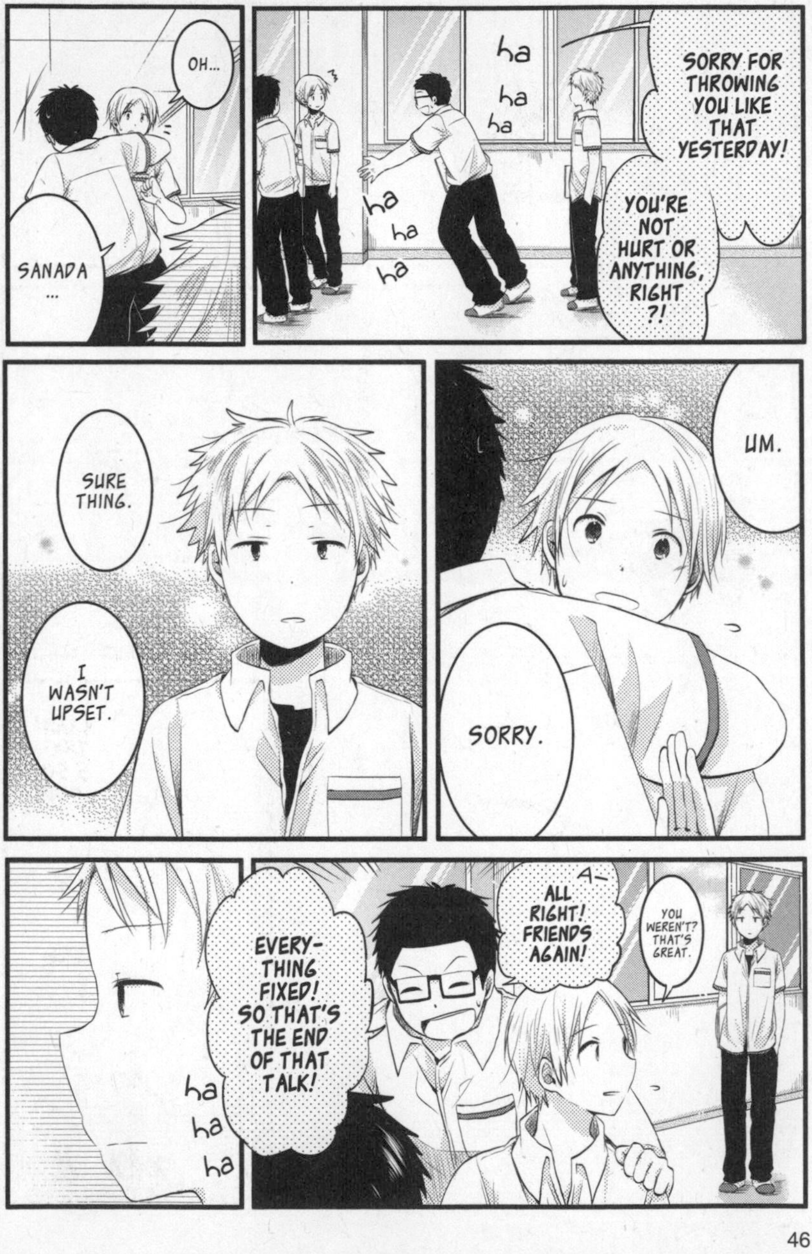
SORRY FOR THROWING YOU LIKE THAT YESTERDAY!
YOU'RE NOT HURT OR ANYTHING, RIGHT?!
ha ha ha
ha ha ha
OH...
SANADA ...
UM.
SORRY.
SURE THING.
I WASN'T UPSET.
YOU WEREN'T? THAT'S GREAT.
A- ALL RIGHT! FRIENDS AGAIN!
EVERY-THING FIXED! SO THAT'S THE END OF THAT TALK!
ha ha ha

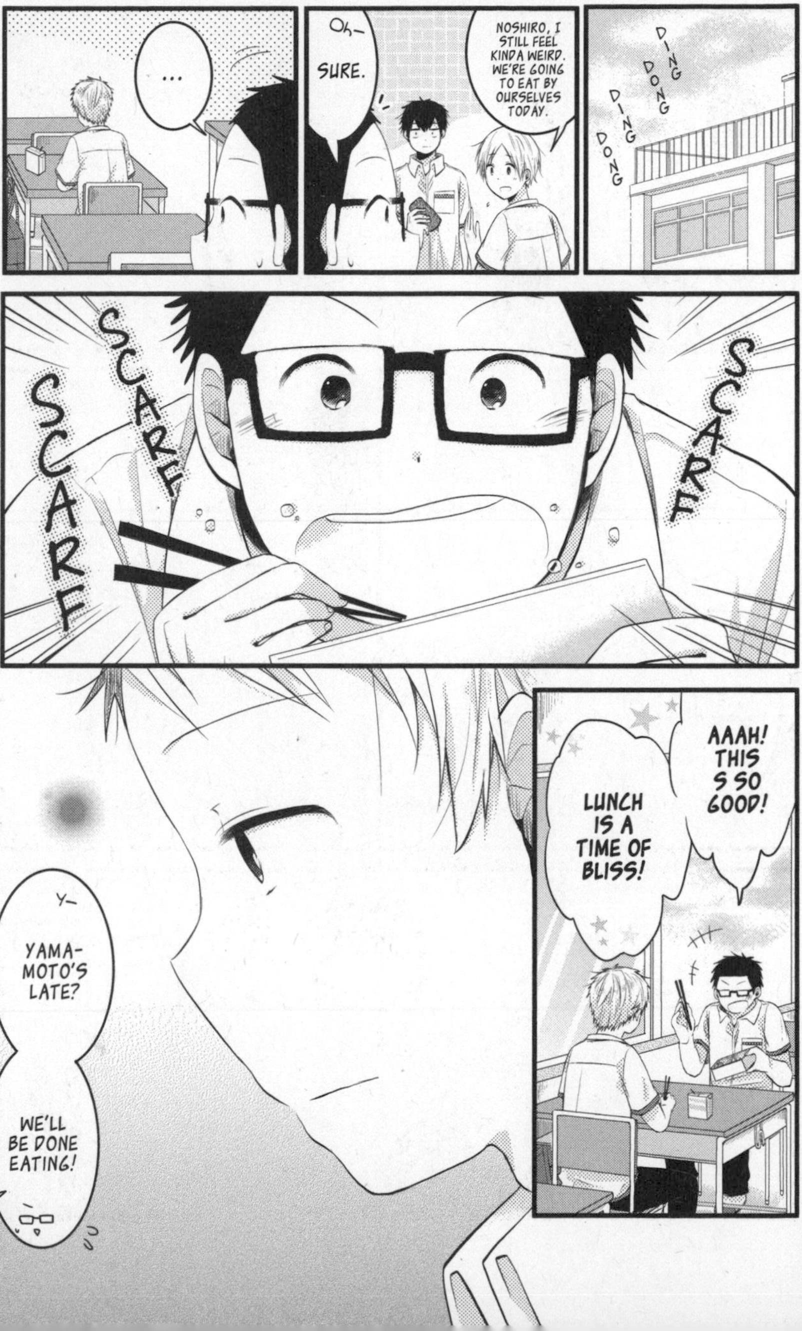
DING DONG DING DONG
NOSHIRO, I STILL FEEL KINDA WEIRD. WE'RE GOING TO EAT BY OURSELVES TODAY.
Oh— SURE.
...
SCARF
SCARF SCARF
AAAH! THIS S SO GOOD!
LUNCH IS A TIME OF BLISS!
Y— YAMA-MOTO'S LATE?
WE'LL BE DONE EATING!

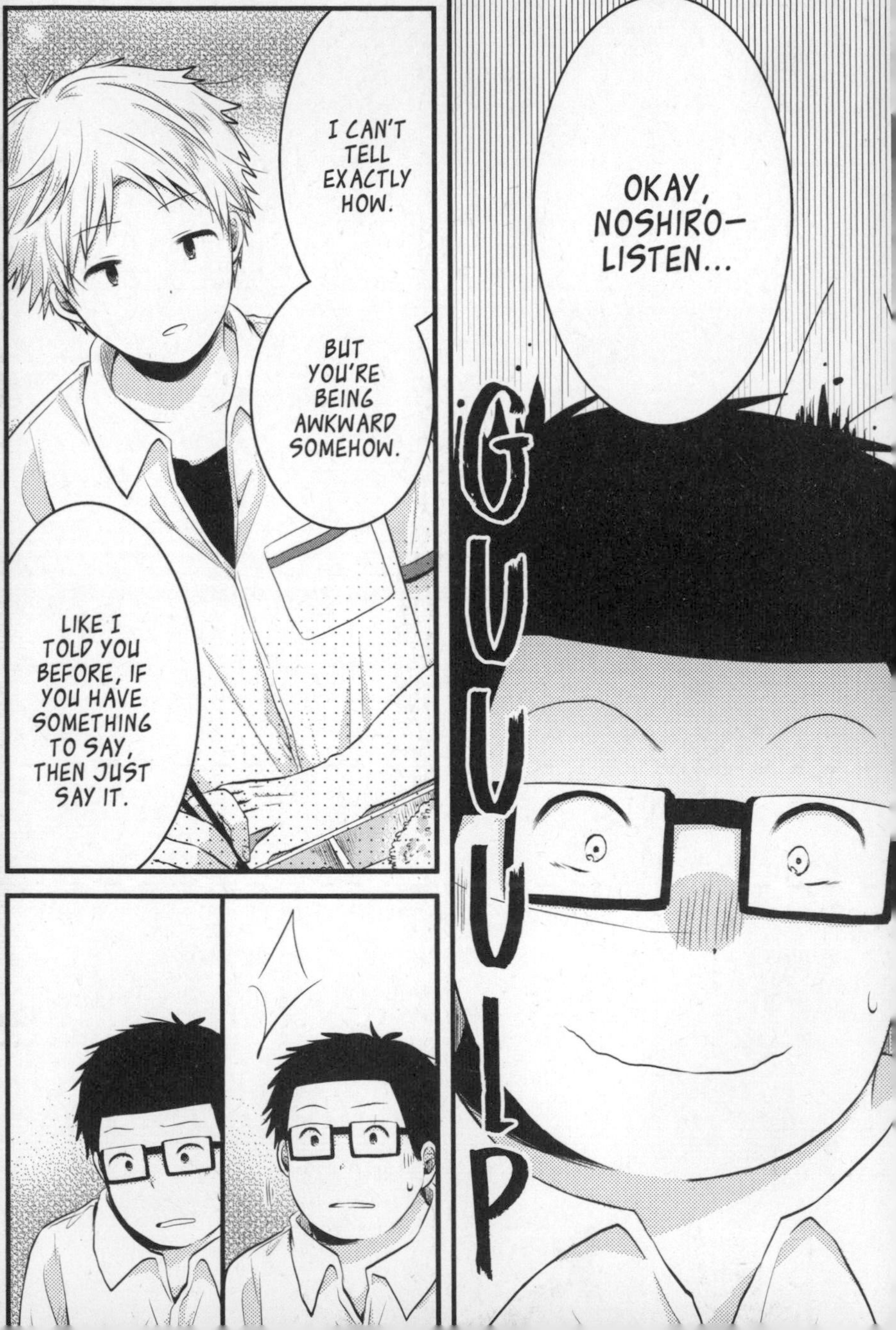
OKAY, NOSHIRO— LISTEN...
GULP
I CAN'T TELL EXACTLY HOW.
BUT YOU'RE BEING AWKWARD SOMEHOW.
LIKE I TOLD YOU BEFORE, IF YOU HAVE SOMETHING TO SAY, THEN JUST SAY IT.

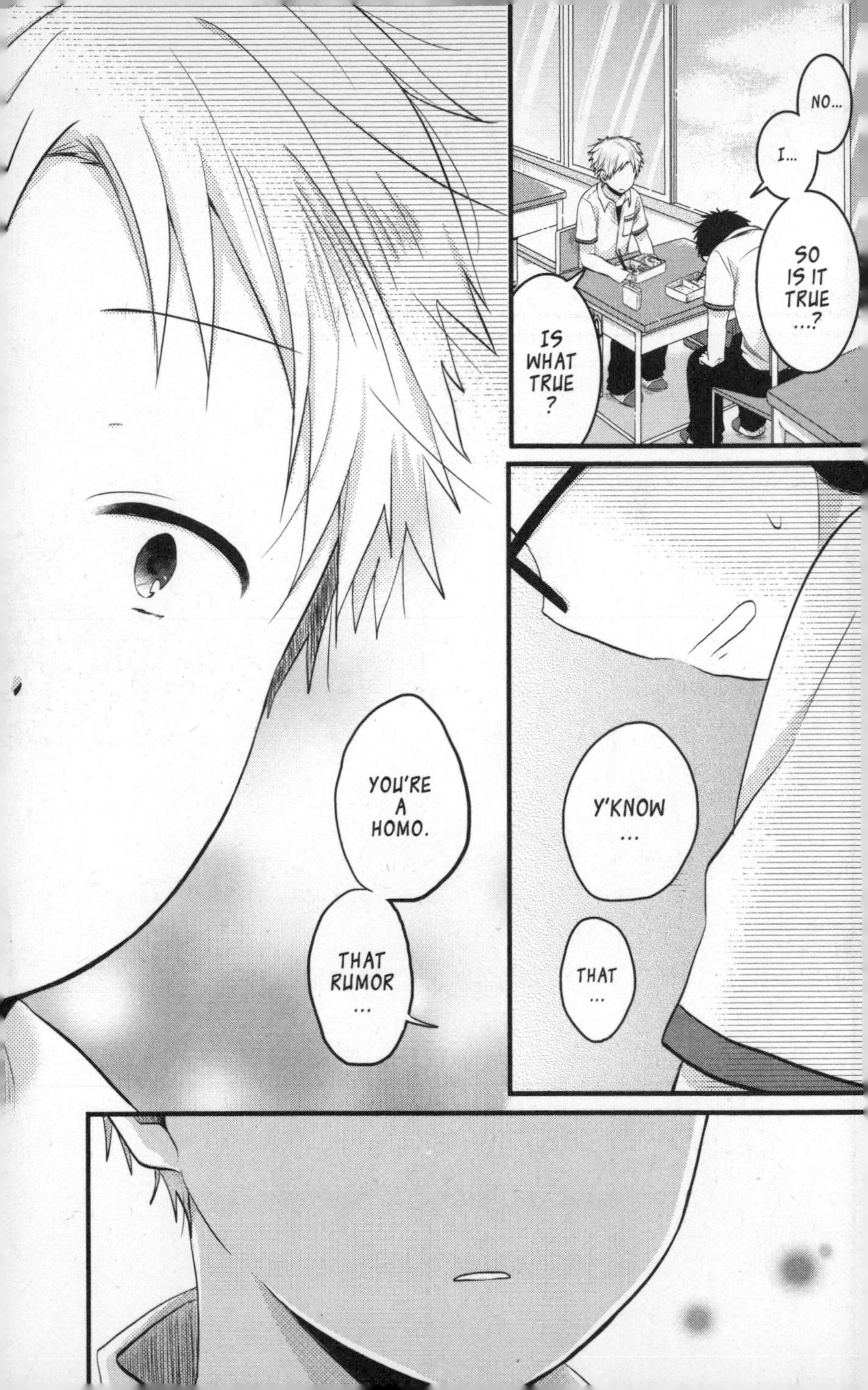
NO...
I...
SO IS IT TRUE ...?
IS WHAT TRUE ?
Y'KNOW ...
THAT ...
YOU'RE A HOMO.
THAT RUMOR ...

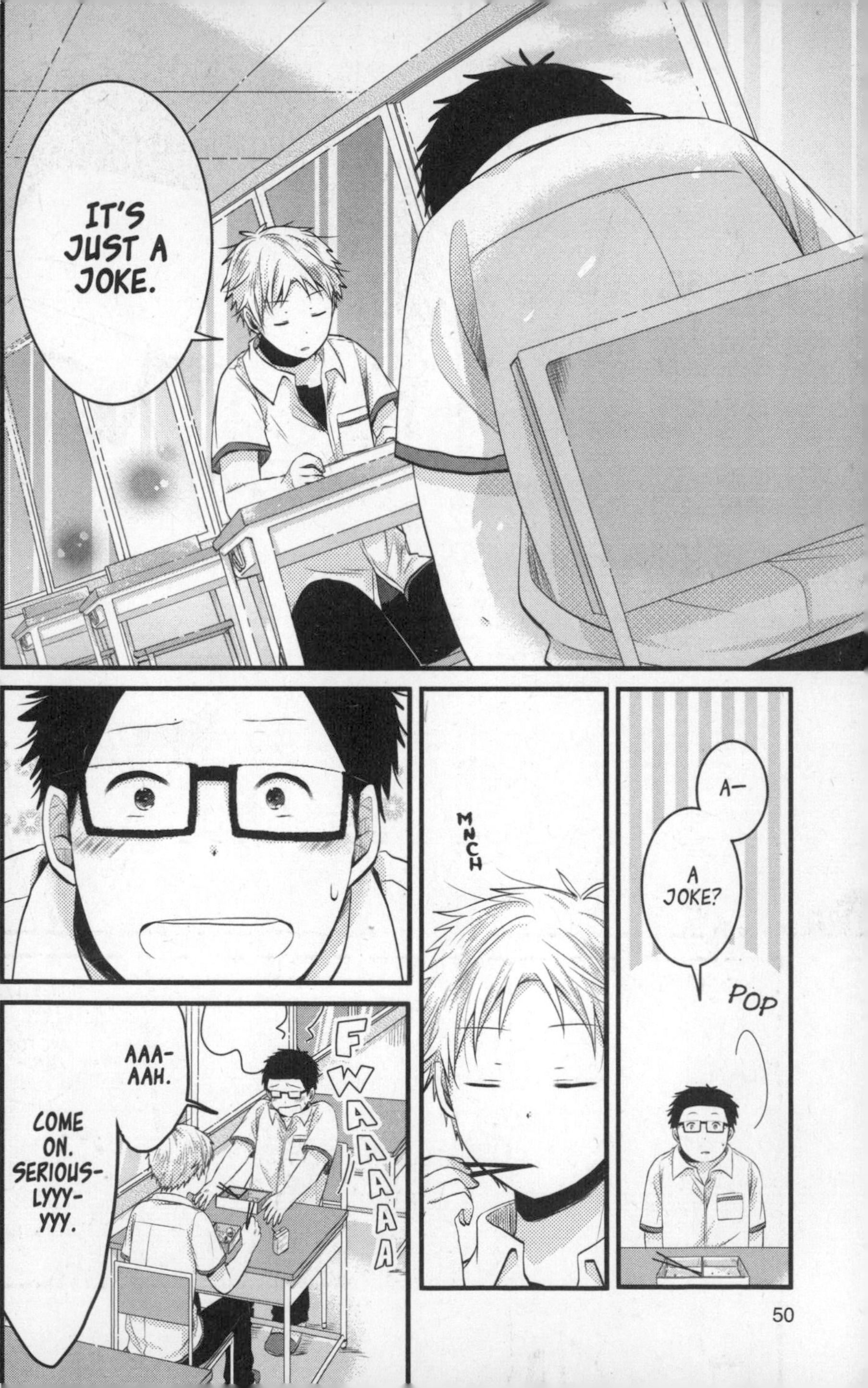
IT'S JUST A JOKE.
A—
A JOKE?
POP
MNCH
FWAAAAAA
AAA-AAH.
COME ON. SERIOUS-LYYY-YYY.

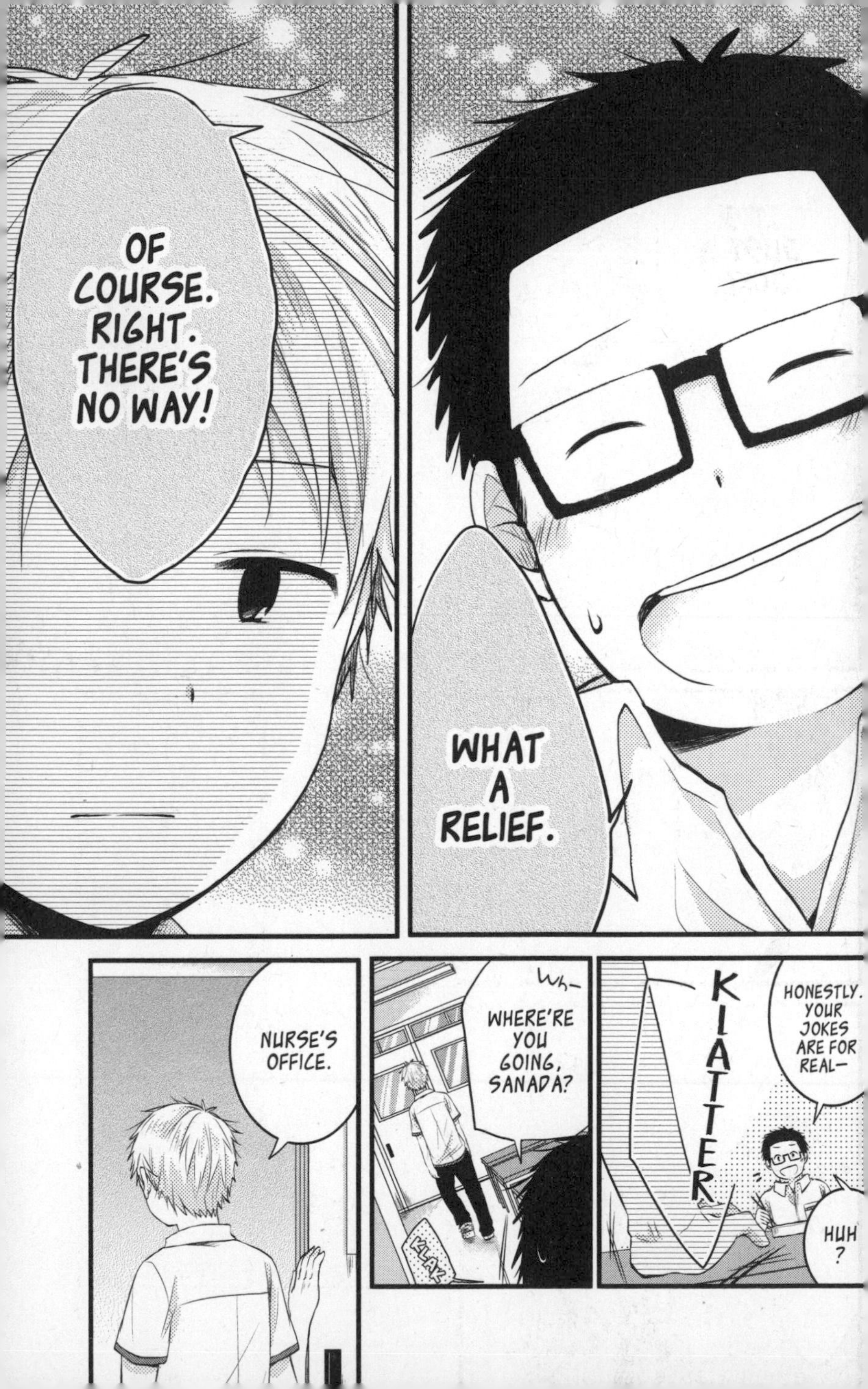
WHAT A RELIEF.
OF COURSE. RIGHT. THERE'S NO WAY!
HONESTLY. YOUR JOKES ARE FOR REAL—
KLATTER
HUH?
Wh-
WHERE'RE YOU GOING, SANADA?
KLAK
NURSE'S OFFICE.

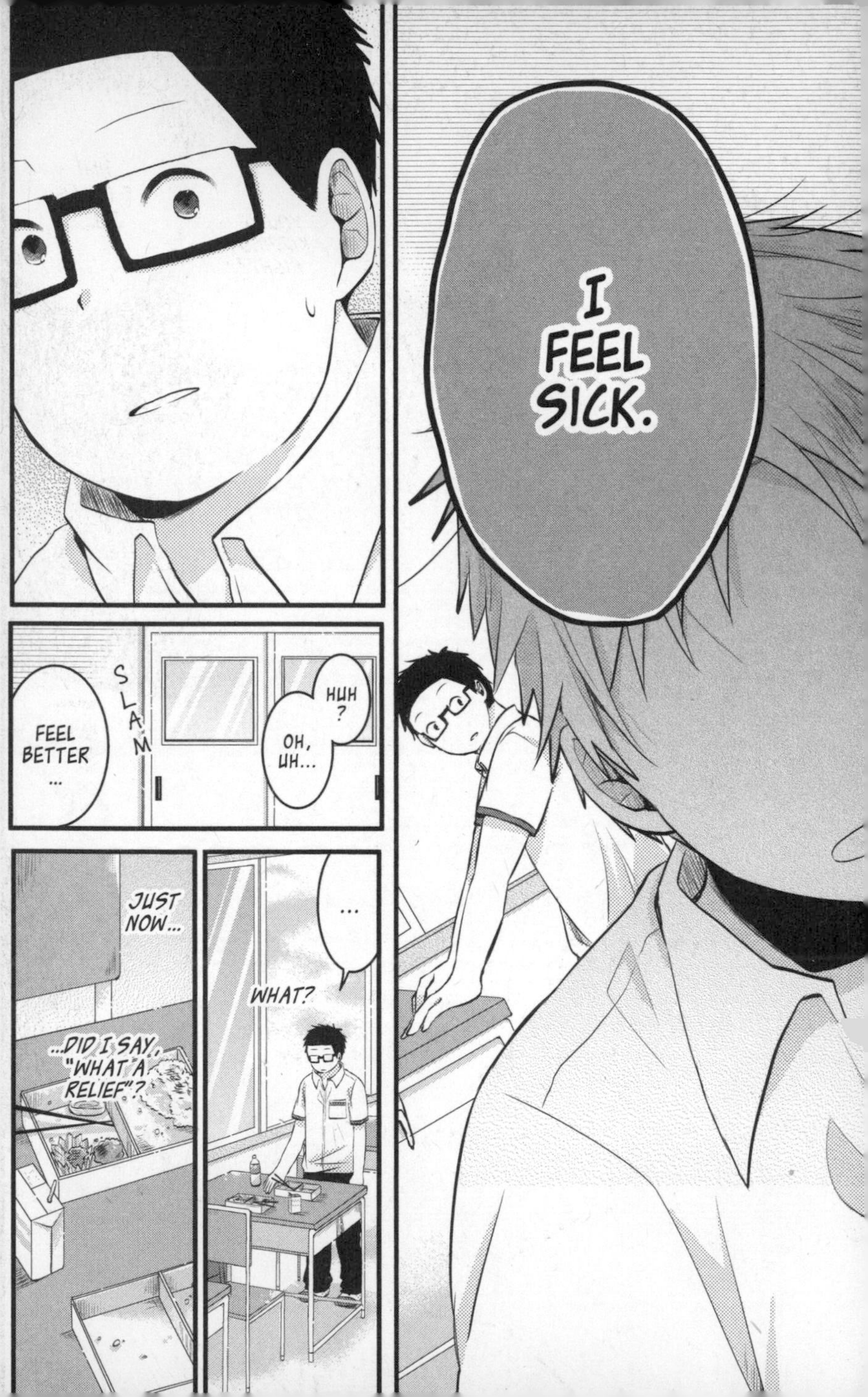
I FEEL SICK.
HUH? OH, UH...
SLAM
FEEL BETTER...
...
WHAT?
JUST NOW...
...DID I SAY, "WHAT A RELIEF"?

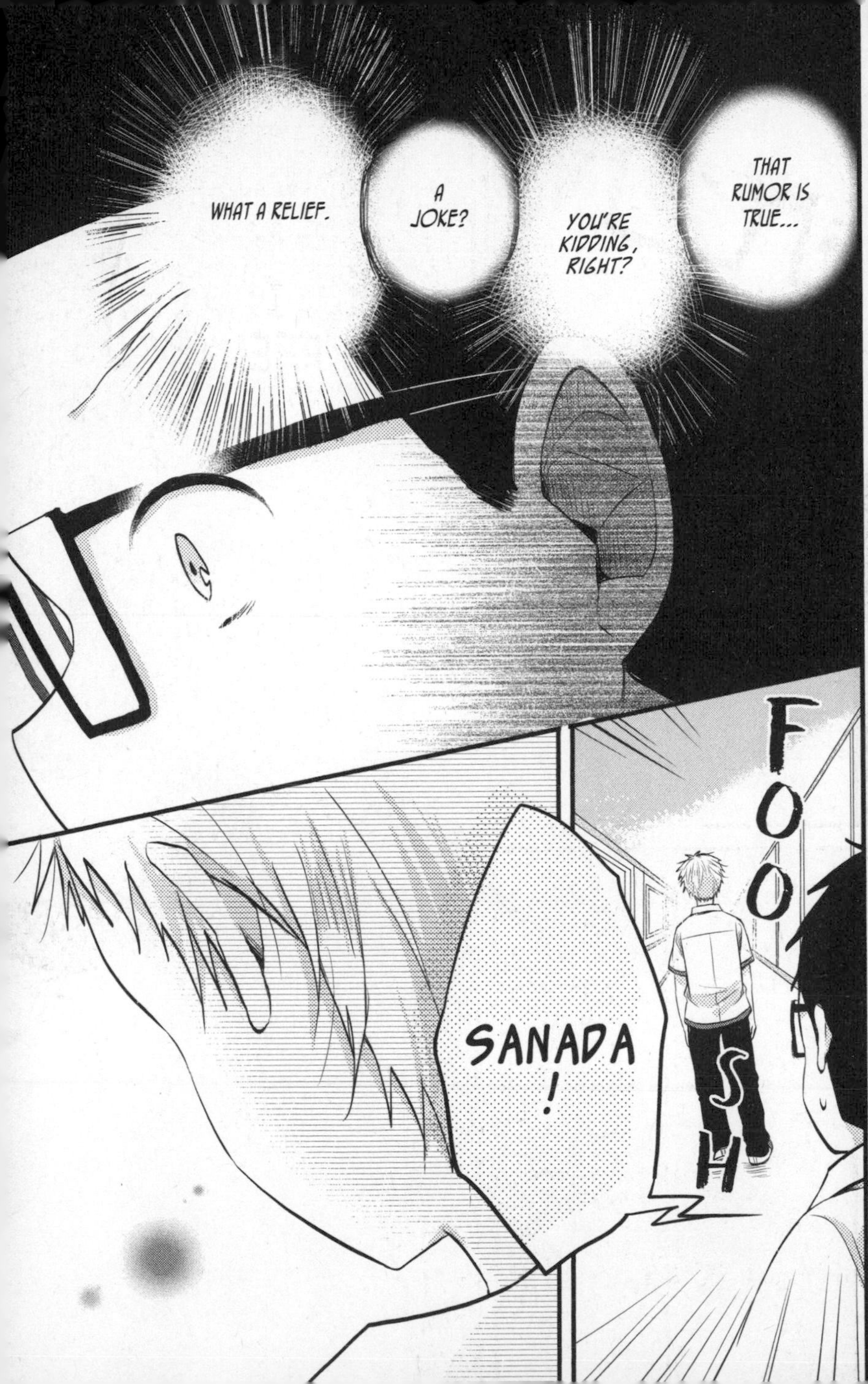
THAT RUMOR IS TRUE...
YOU'RE KIDDING, RIGHT?
A JOKE?
WHAT A RELIEF.
FOOSH
SANADA!

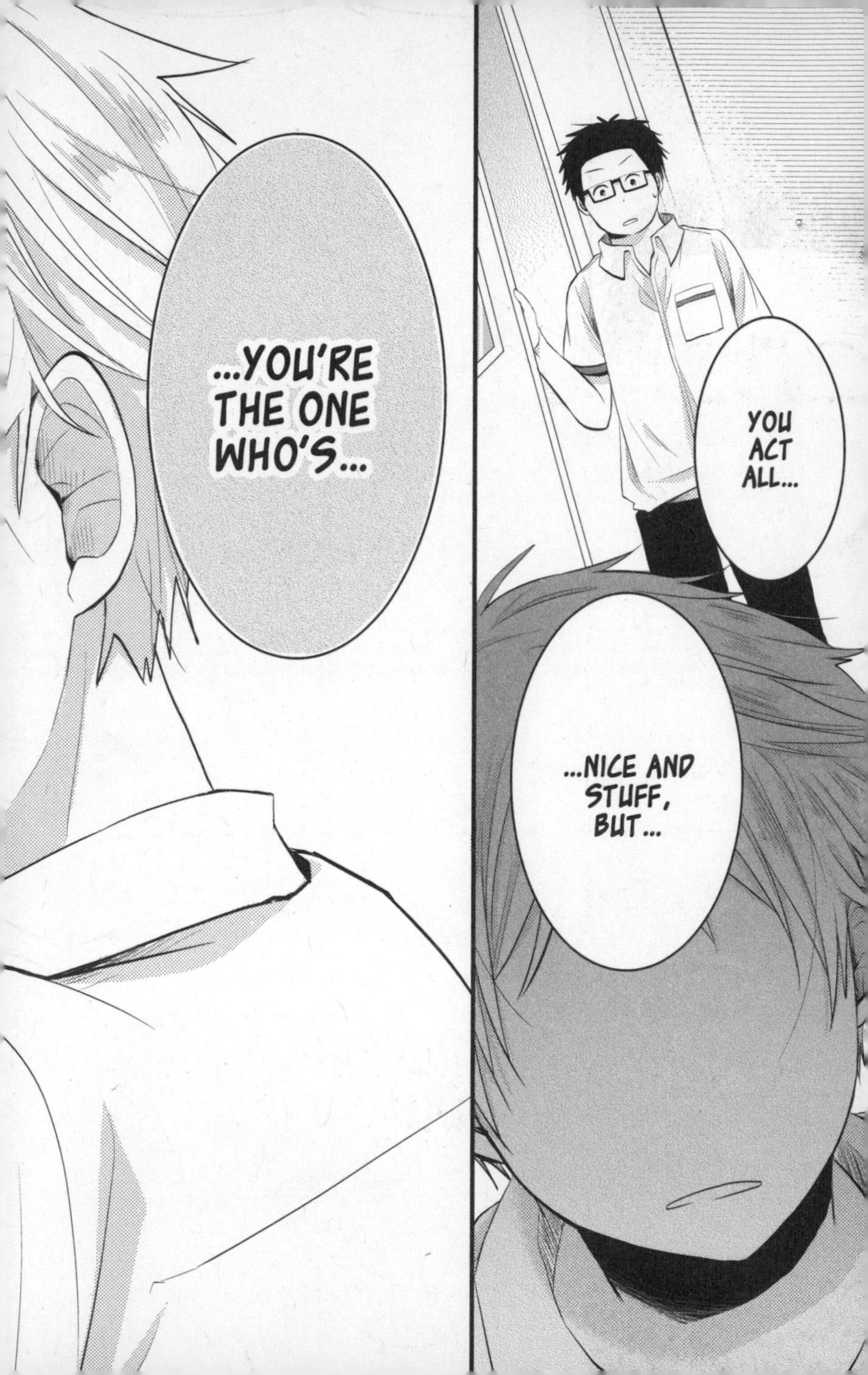
YOU ACT ALL...
...NICE AND STUFF, BUT...
...YOU'RE THE ONE WHO'S...

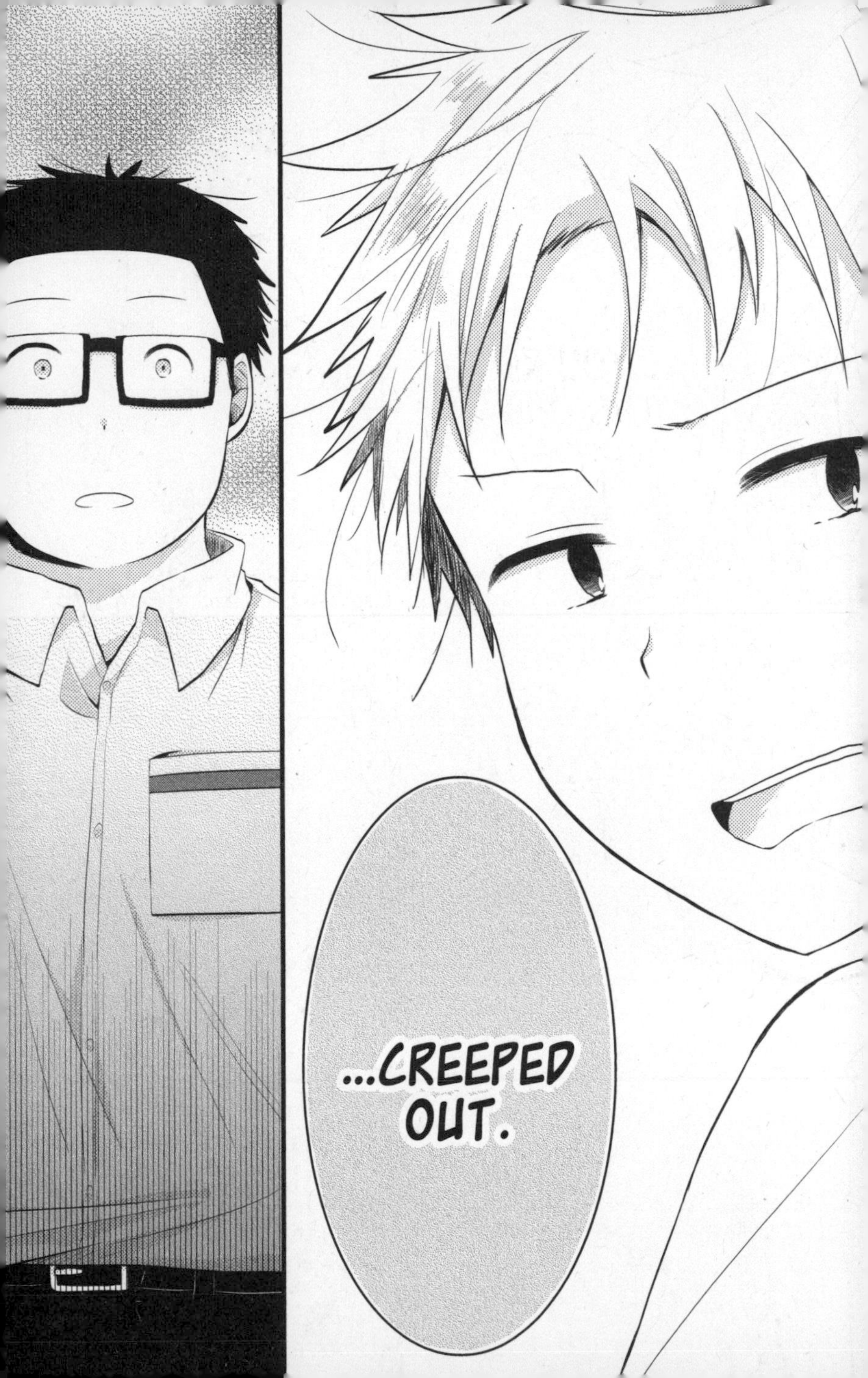
...CREEPED OUT.

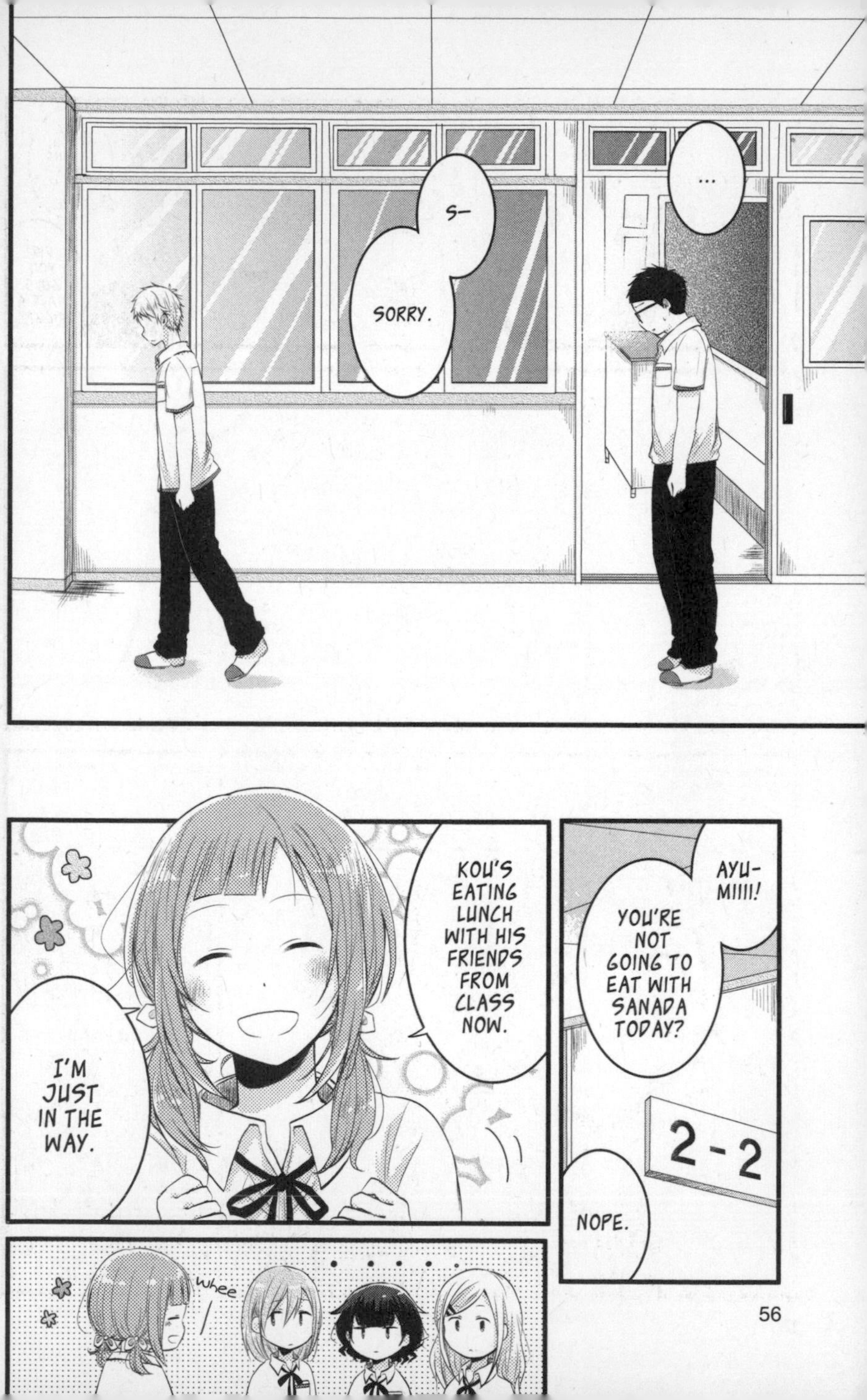
...
S—
SORRY.
AYU-MIIII!
YOU'RE NOT GOING TO EAT WITH SANADA TODAY?
2-2
NOPE.
KOU'S EATING LUNCH WITH HIS FRIENDS FROM CLASS NOW.
I'M JUST IN THE WAY.
. . . . .
whee

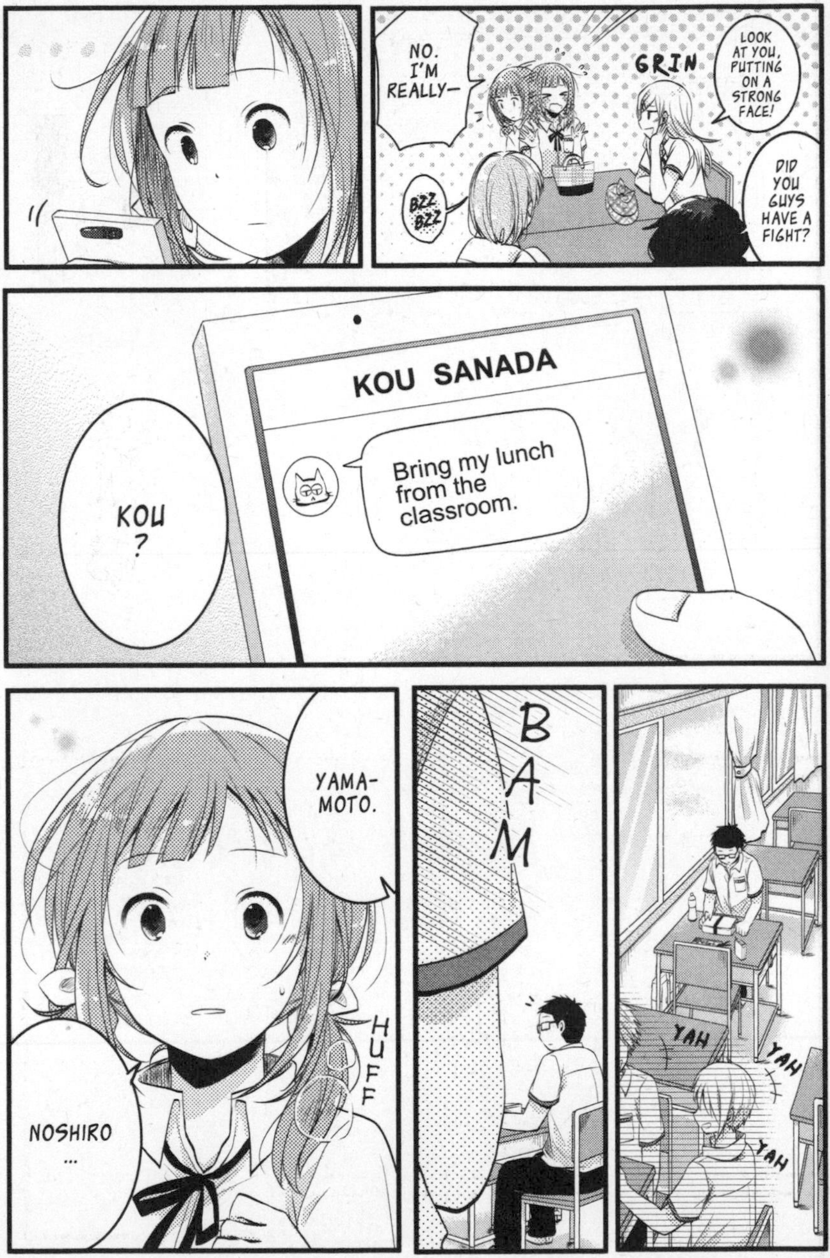
LOOK AT YOU, PUTTING ON A STRONG FACE!
GRIN
DID YOU GUYS HAVE A FIGHT?
NO. I'M REALLY—
BZZ BZZ
KOU SANADA
Bring my lunch from the classroom.
KOU?
YAH
YAH
YAH
BAM
YAMA-MOTO.
HUFF
NOSHIRO...

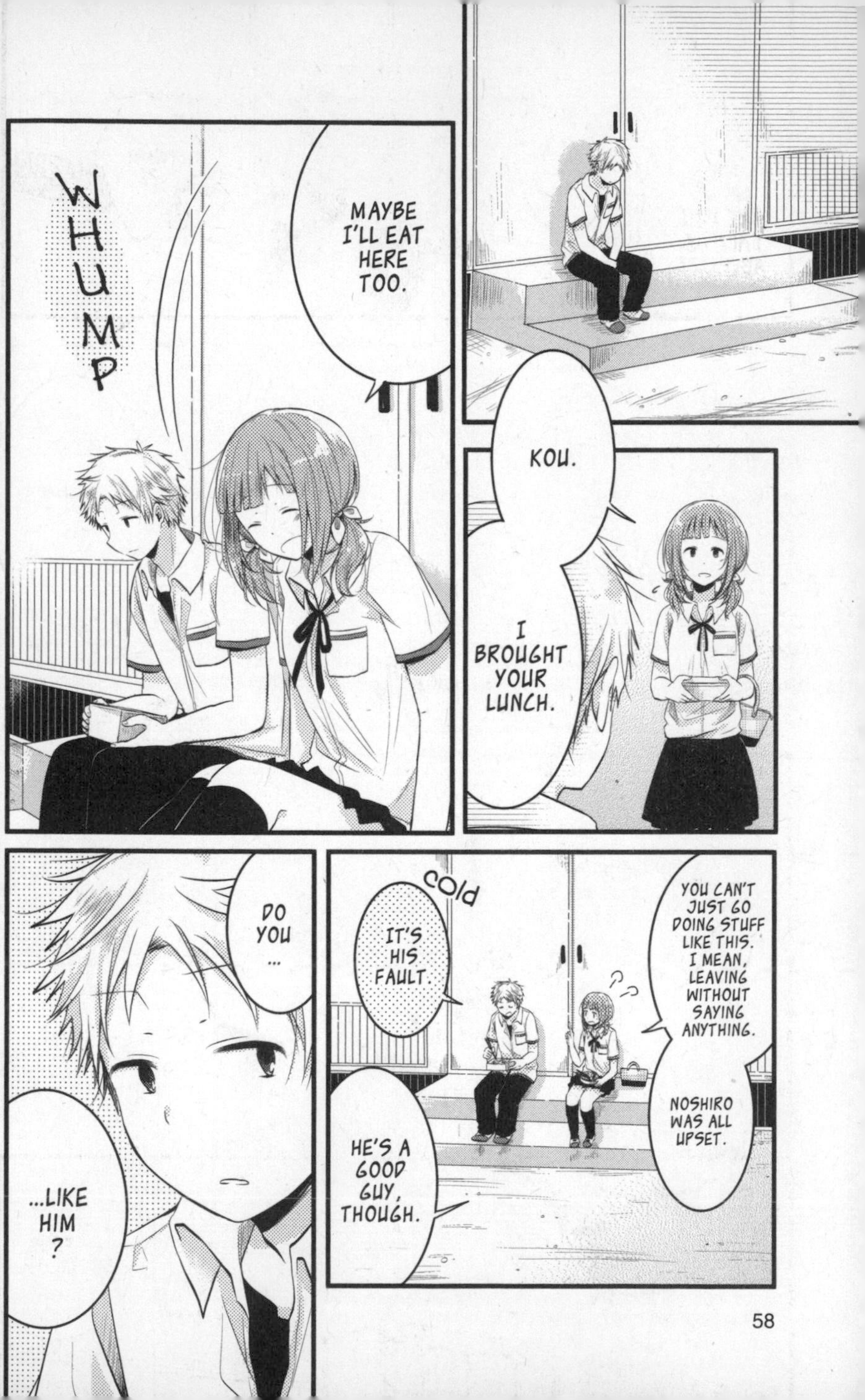
KOU.
I BROUGHT YOUR LUNCH.
MAYBE I'LL EAT HERE TOO.
WHUMP
YOU CAN'T JUST GO DOING STUFF LIKE THIS. I MEAN, LEAVING WITHOUT SAYING ANYTHING.
NOSHIRO WAS ALL UPSET.
COLD
IT'S HIS FAULT.
HE'S A GOOD GUY, THOUGH.
DO YOU ...
...LIKE HIM ?

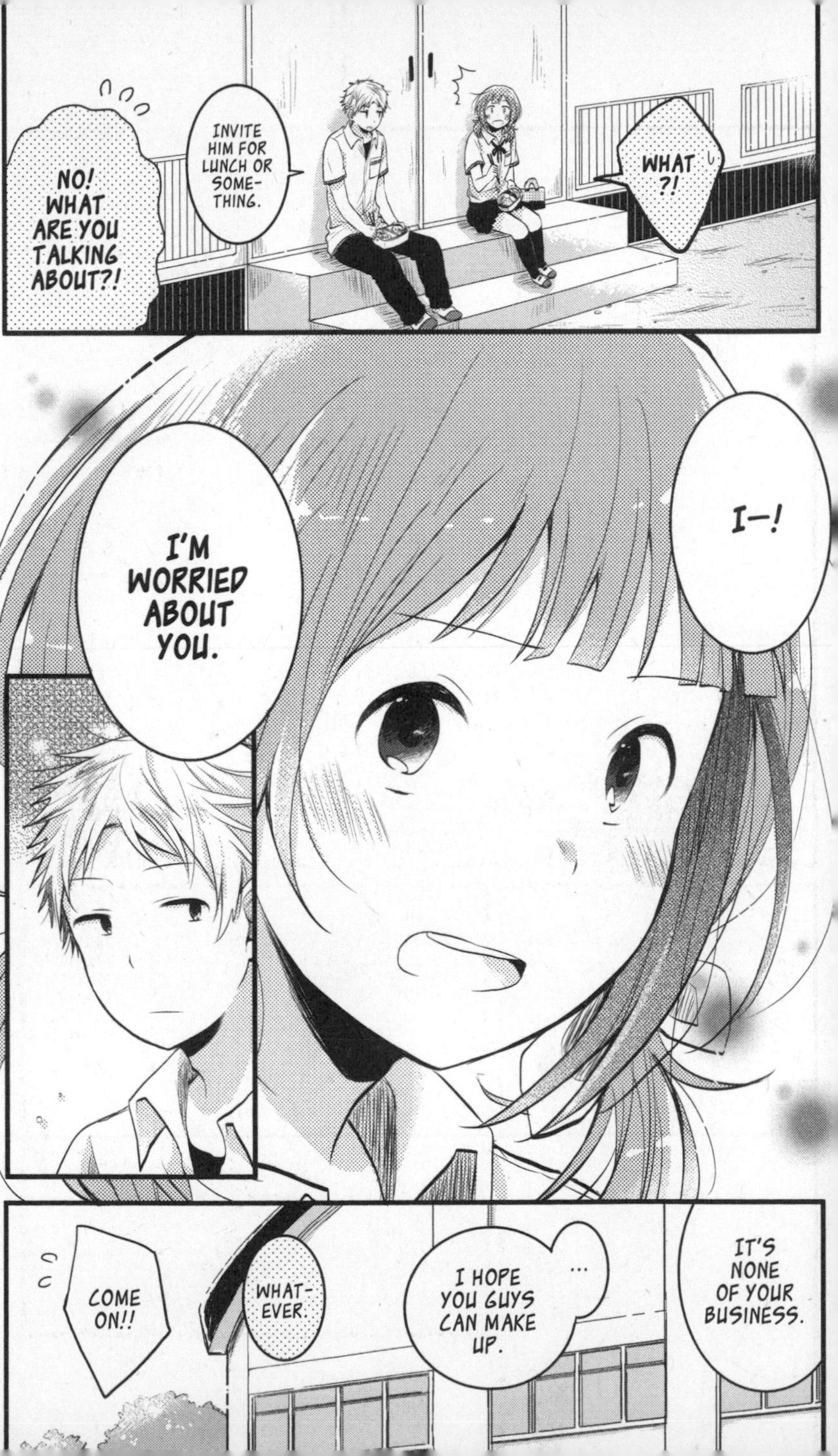
WHAT?!
INVITE HIM FOR LUNCH OR SOME-THING.
NO! WHAT ARE YOU TALKING ABOUT?!
I—!
I'M WORRIED ABOUT YOU.
IT'S NONE OF YOUR BUSINESS.
...
I HOPE YOU GUYS CAN MAKE UP.
WHAT-EVER.
COME ON!!

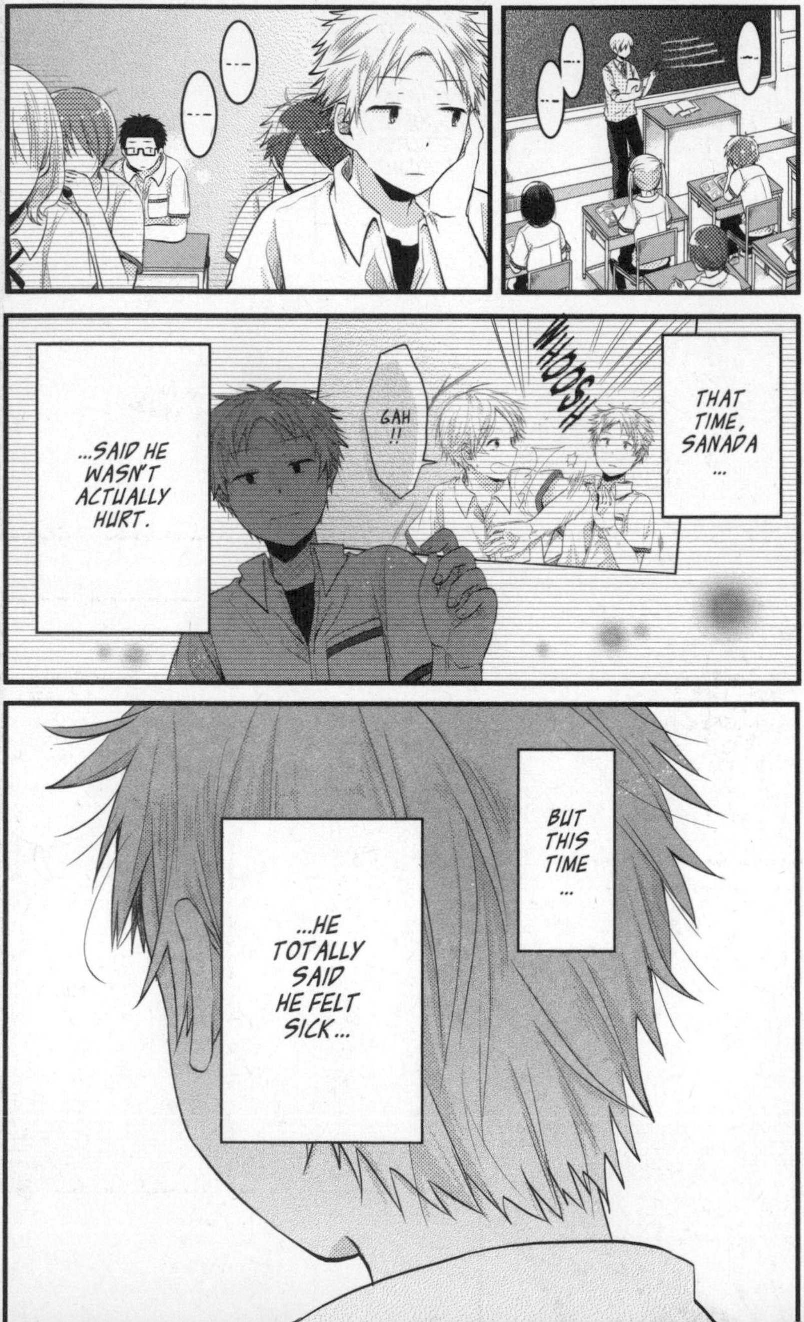
...
...
...
...
...
THAT TIME, SANADA...
WHOOSH
GAH!!
...SAID HE WASN'T ACTUALLY HURT.
BUT THIS TIME...
...HE TOTALLY SAID HE FELT SICK...

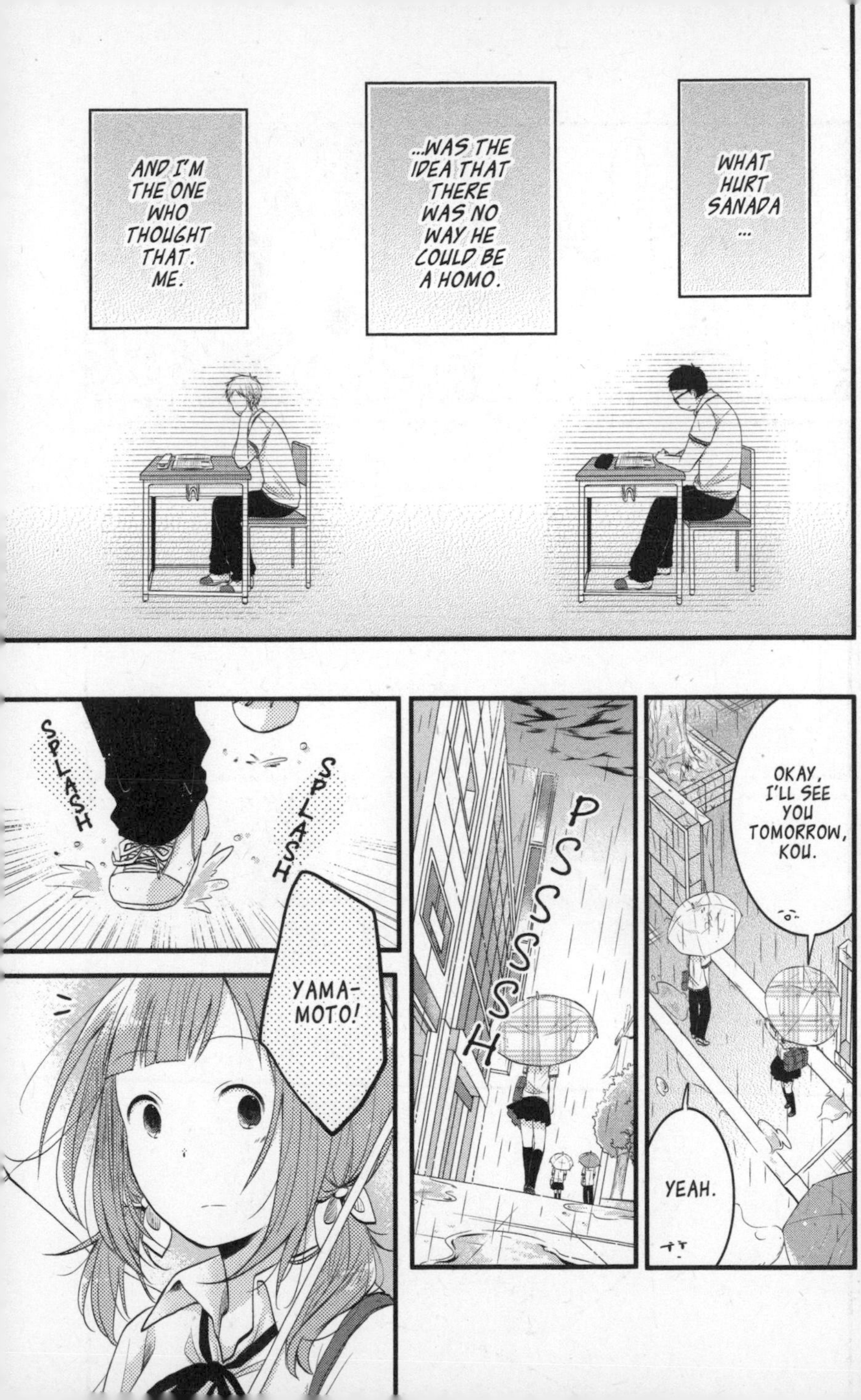
WHAT HURT SANADA ...
...WAS THE IDEA THAT THERE WAS NO WAY HE COULD BE A HOMO.
AND I'M THE ONE WHO THOUGHT THAT. ME.
OKAY, I'LL SEE YOU TOMORROW, KOU.
YEAH.
PSSSSH
SPLASH
SPLASH
YAMA-MOTO!

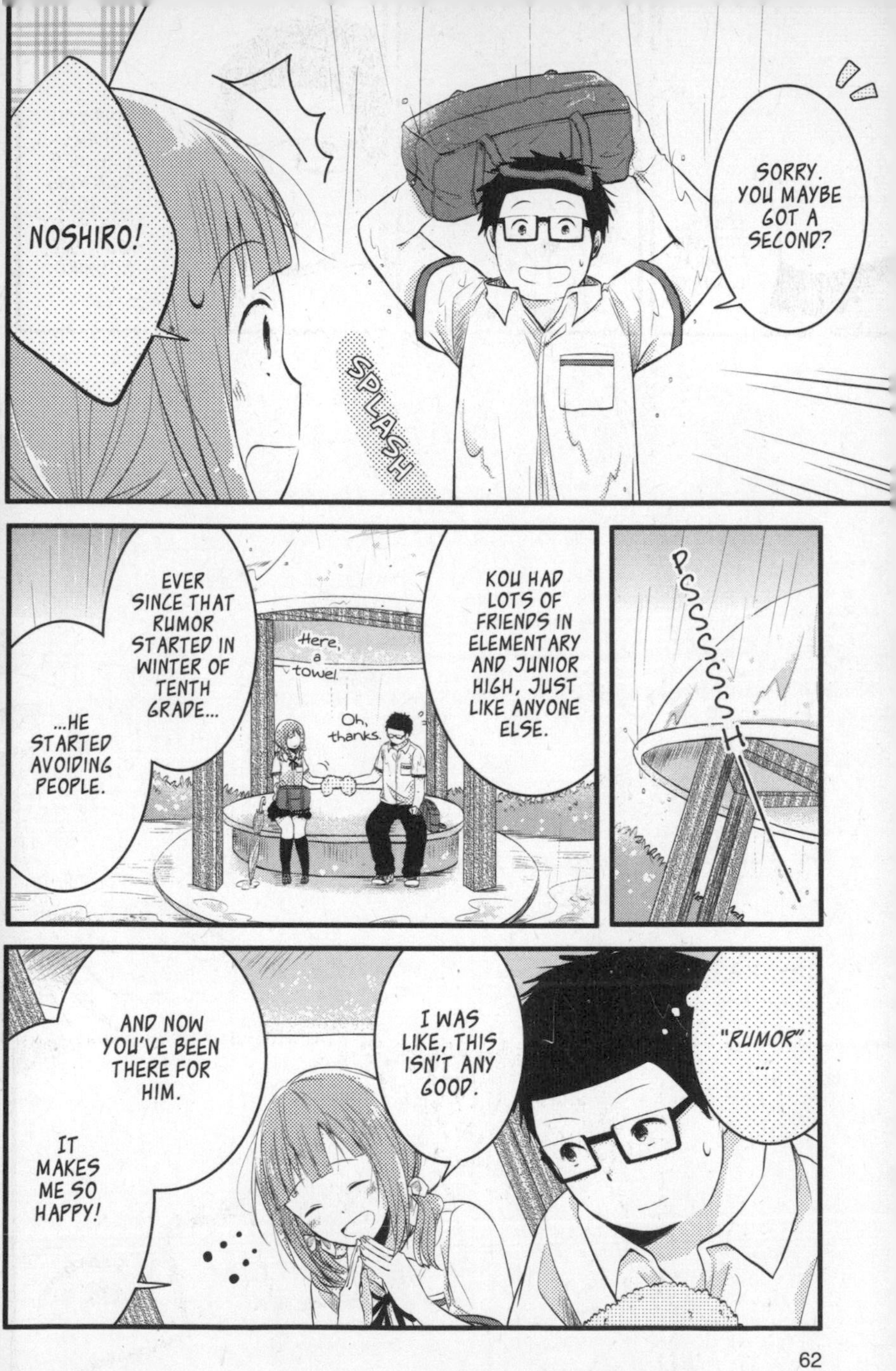
SORRY. YOU MAYBE GOT A SECOND?
SPLASH
NOSHIRO!
PSSSSSH
KOU HAD LOTS OF FRIENDS IN ELEMENTARY AND JUNIOR HIGH, JUST LIKE ANYONE ELSE.
Oh, thanks.
Here, a towel.
EVER SINCE THAT RUMOR STARTED IN WINTER OF TENTH GRADE...
...HE STARTED AVOIDING PEOPLE.
"RUMOR"...
I WAS LIKE, THIS ISN'T ANY GOOD.
AND NOW YOU'VE BEEN THERE FOR HIM.
IT MAKES ME SO HAPPY!

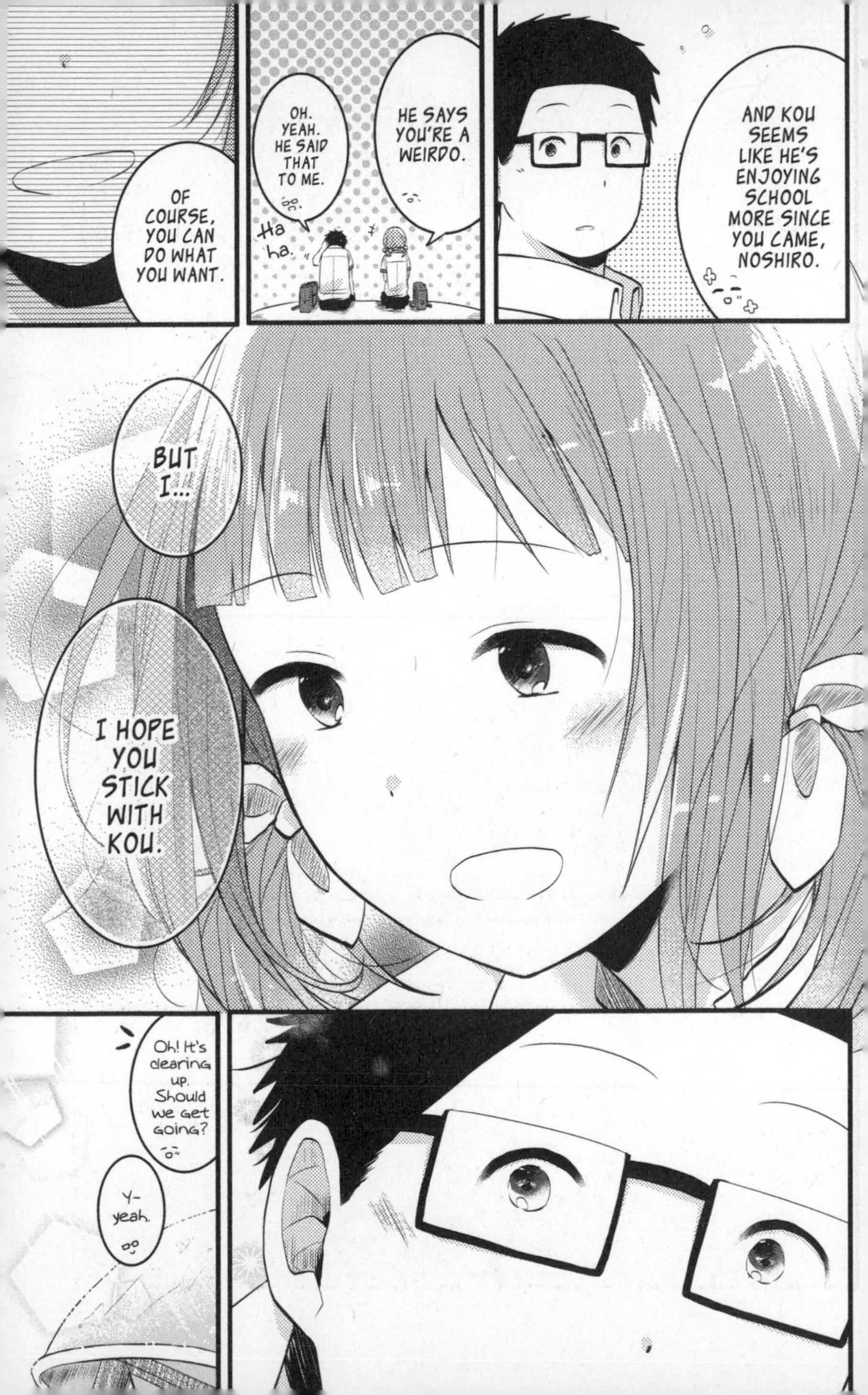
AND KOU SEEMS LIKE HE'S ENJOYING SCHOOL MORE SINCE YOU CAME, NOSHIRO.
HE SAYS YOU'RE A WEIRDO.
OH. YEAH. HE SAID THAT TO ME.
Ha ha.
OF COURSE, YOU CAN DO WHAT YOU WANT.
BUT I...
I HOPE YOU STICK WITH KOU.
Oh! It's clearing up. Should we get going?
Y-yeah.

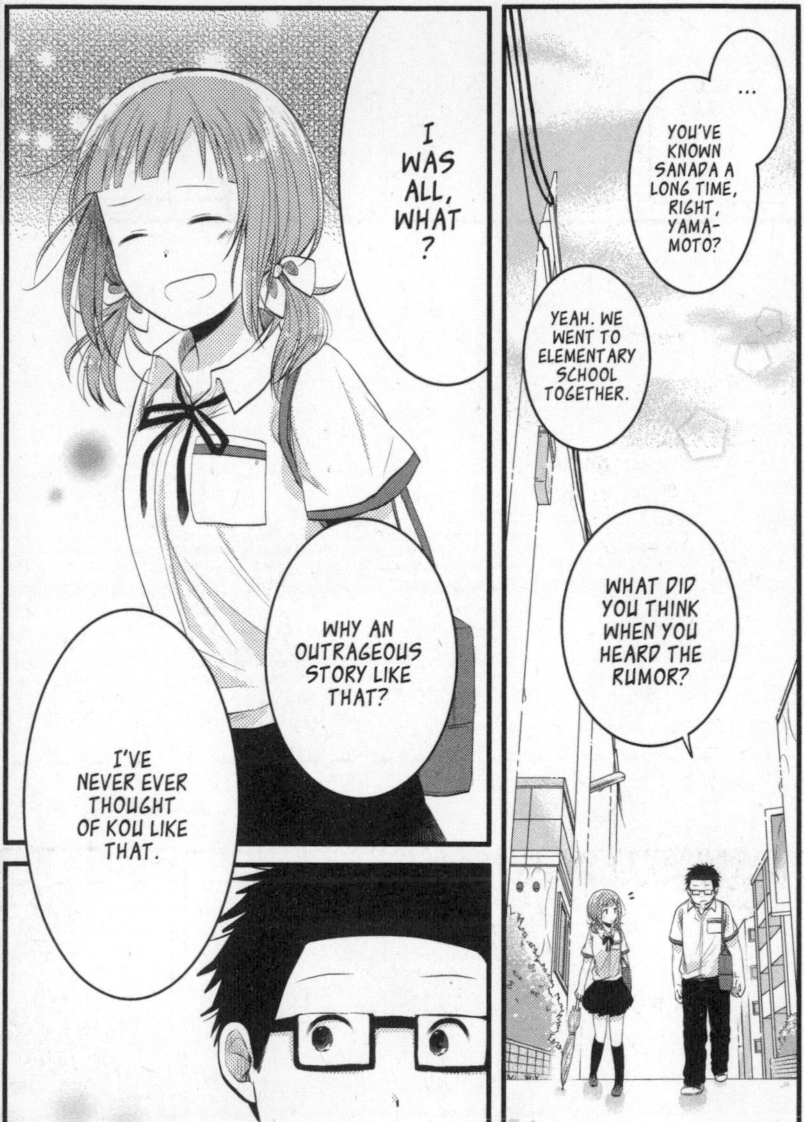
...
YOU'VE KNOWN SANADA A LONG TIME, RIGHT, YAMA-MOTO?
YEAH. WE WENT TO ELEMENTARY SCHOOL TOGETHER.
WHAT DID YOU THINK WHEN YOU HEARD THE RUMOR?
I WAS ALL, WHAT?
WHY AN OUTRAGEOUS STORY LIKE THAT?
I'VE NEVER EVER THOUGHT OF KOU LIKE THAT.

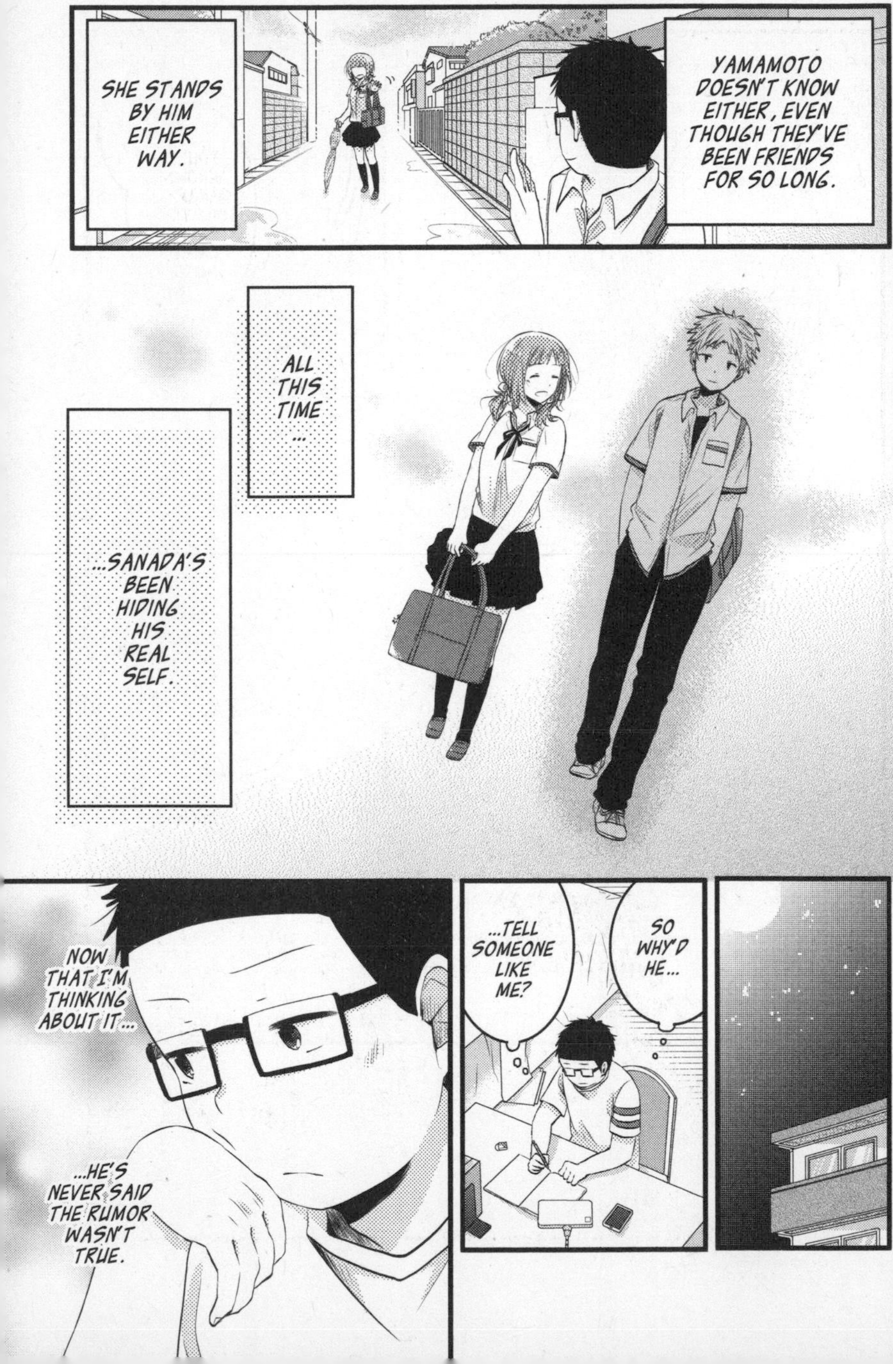
YAMAMOTO DOESN'T KNOW EITHER, EVEN THOUGH THEY'VE BEEN FRIENDS FOR SO LONG.
SHE STANDS BY HIM EITHER WAY.
ALL THIS TIME ...
...SANADA'S BEEN HIDING HIS REAL SELF.
SO WHY'D HE...
...TELL SOMEONE LIKE ME?
NOW THAT I'M THINKING ABOUT IT...
...HE'S NEVER SAID THE RUMOR WASN'T TRUE.

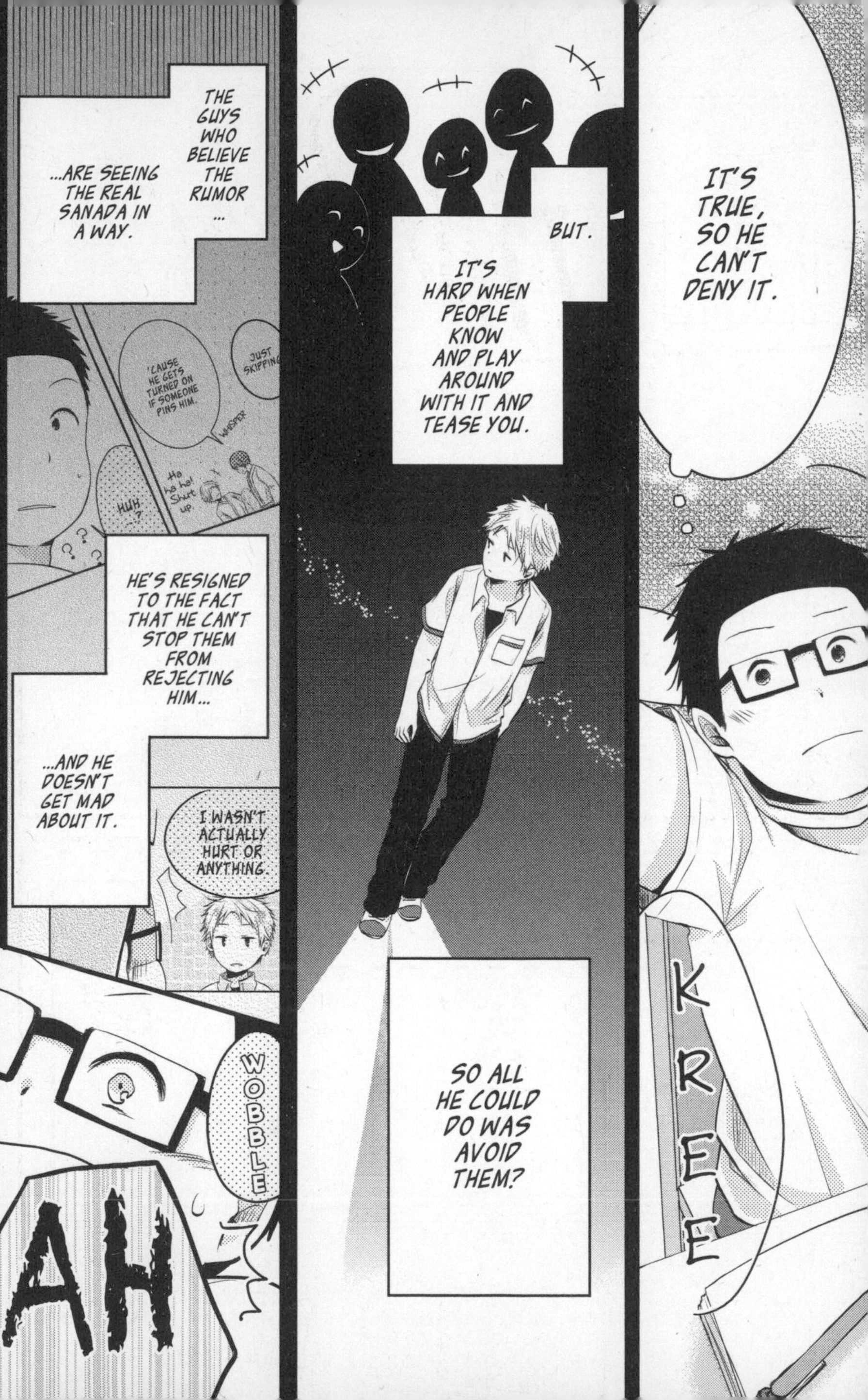
IT'S TRUE, SO HE CAN'T DENY IT.
KREE
BUT.
IT'S HARD WHEN PEOPLE KNOW AND PLAY AROUND WITH IT AND TEASE YOU.
SO ALL HE COULD DO WAS AVOID THEM?
THE GUYS WHO BELIEVE THE RUMOR...
...ARE SEEING THE REAL SANADA IN A WAY.
JUST SKIPPING
'CAUSE HE GETS TURNED ON IF SOMEONE PINS HIM.
WHISPER
Ha ha ha! Shut up.
HUH?
HE'S RESIGNED TO THE FACT THAT HE CAN'T STOP THEM FROM REJECTING HIM...
...AND HE DOESN'T GET MAD ABOUT IT.
I WASN'T ACTUALLY HURT OR ANYTHING.
WOBBLE
AH

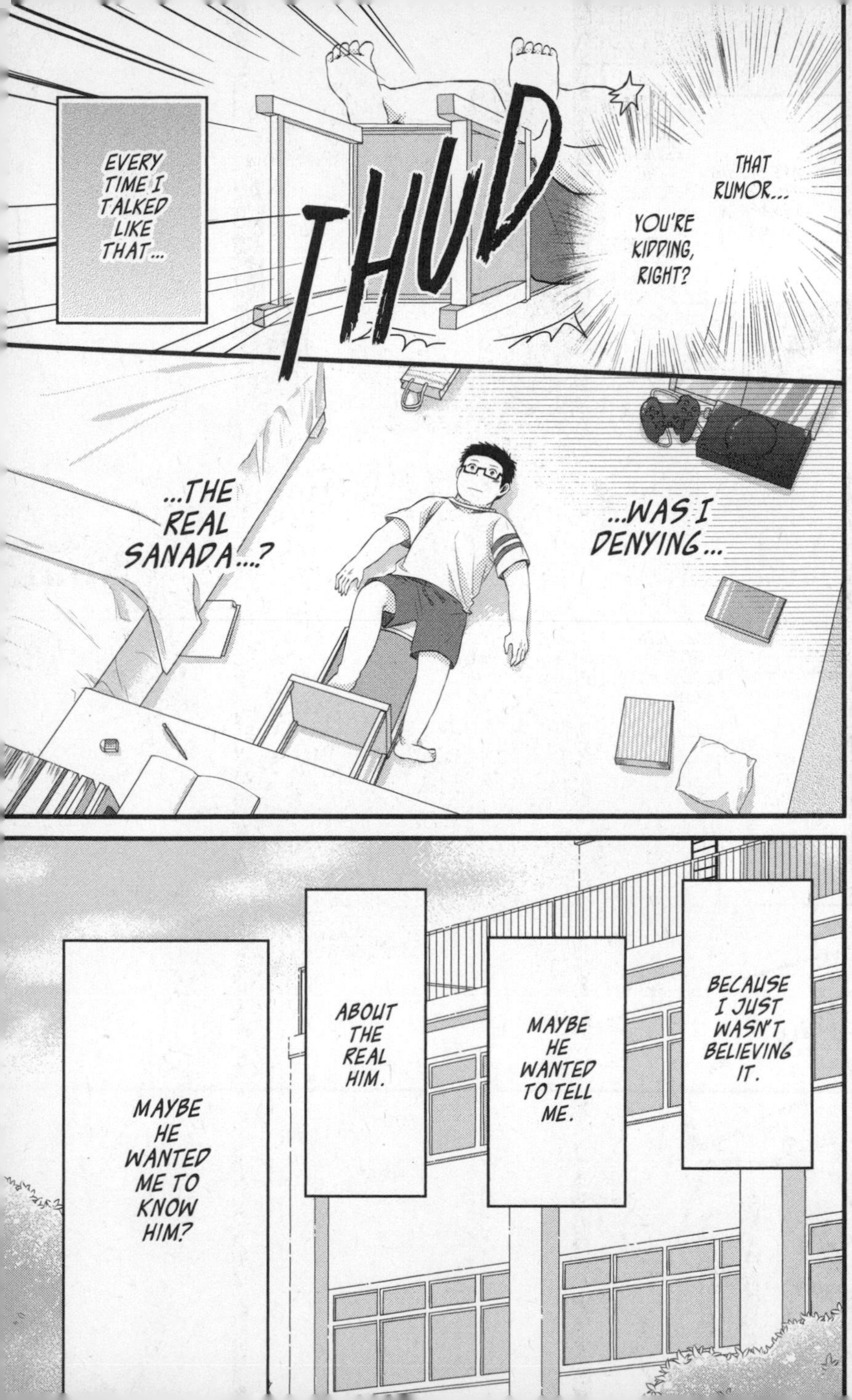
THAT RUMOR...
YOU'RE KIDDING, RIGHT?
THUD
EVERY TIME I TALKED LIKE THAT...
...WAS I DENYING...
...THE REAL SANADA...?
BECAUSE I JUST WASN'T BELIEVING IT.
MAYBE HE WANTED TO TELL ME.
ABOUT THE REAL HIM.
MAYBE HE WANTED ME TO KNOW HIM?

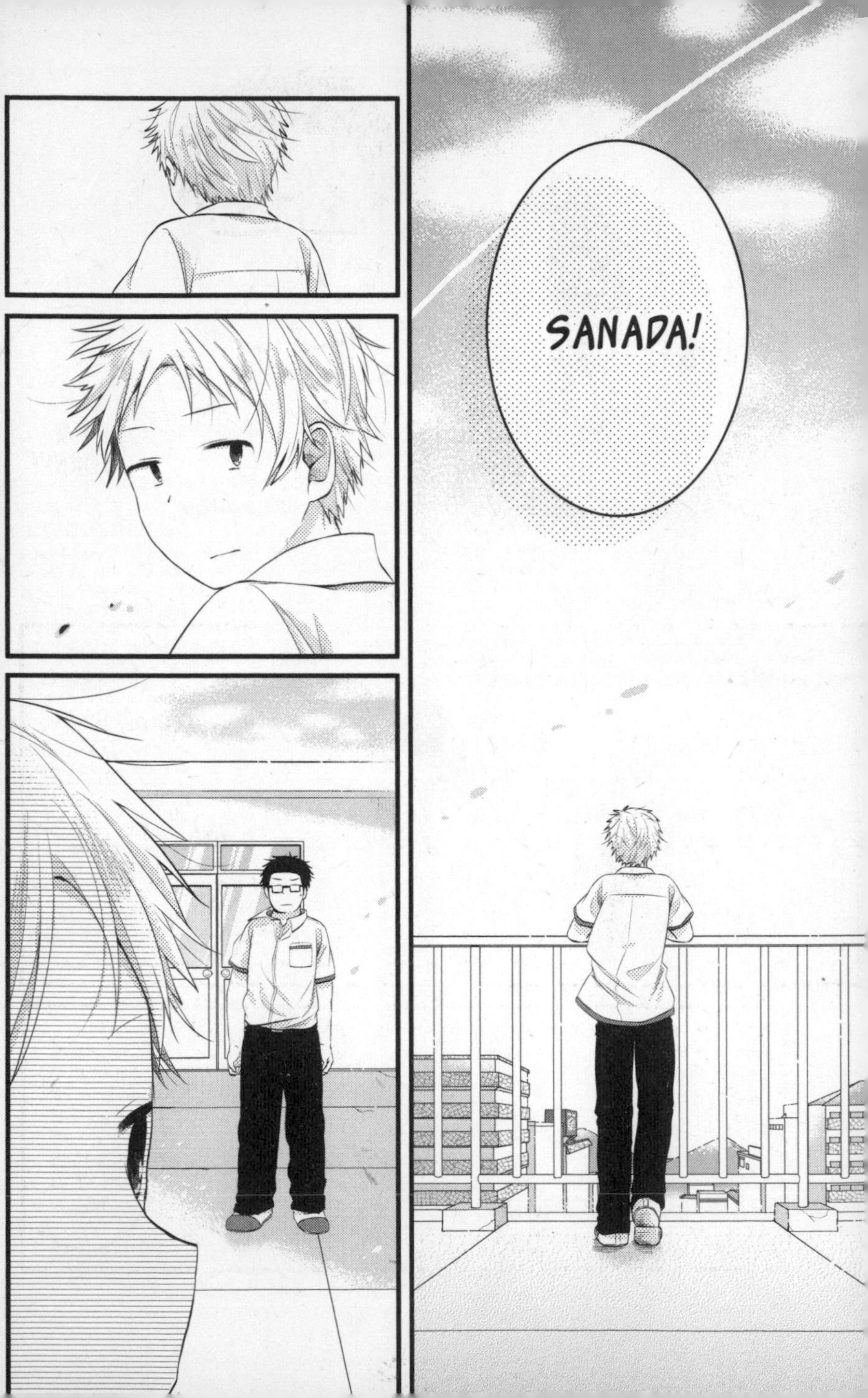
SANADA!

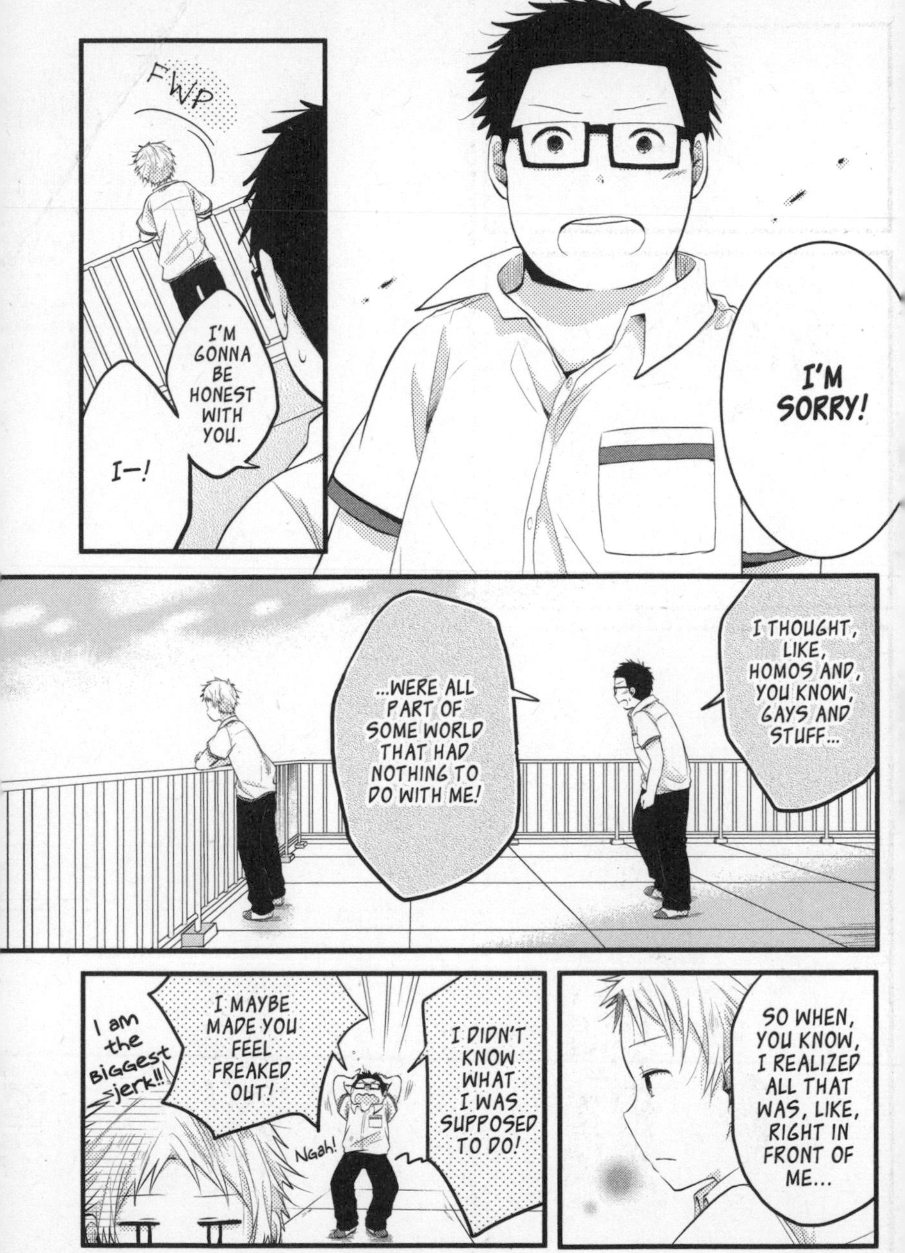
I'M SORRY!
FWP
I'M GONNA BE HONEST WITH YOU.
I—!
I THOUGHT, LIKE, HOMOS AND, YOU KNOW, GAYS AND STUFF...
...WERE ALL PART OF SOME WORLD THAT HAD NOTHING TO DO WITH ME!
SO WHEN, YOU KNOW, I REALIZED ALL THAT WAS, LIKE, RIGHT IN FRONT OF ME...
I DIDN'T KNOW WHAT I WAS SUPPOSED TO DO!
I MAYBE MADE YOU FEEL FREAKED OUT!
Ngah!
I am the biggest jerk!!

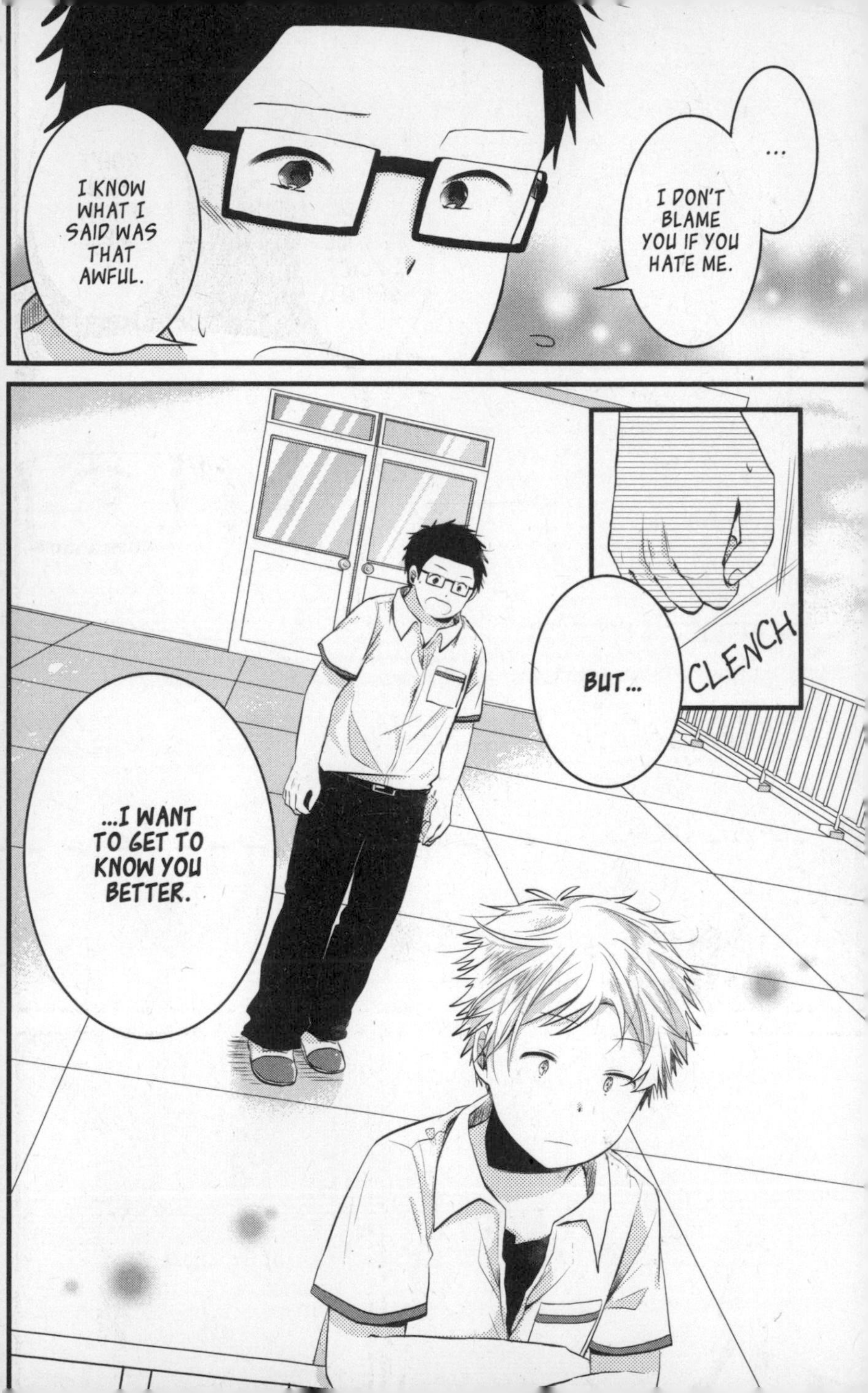
...
I DON'T BLAME YOU IF YOU HATE ME.
I KNOW WHAT I SAID WAS THAT AWFUL.
CLENCH
BUT...
...I WANT TO GET TO KNOW YOU BETTER.

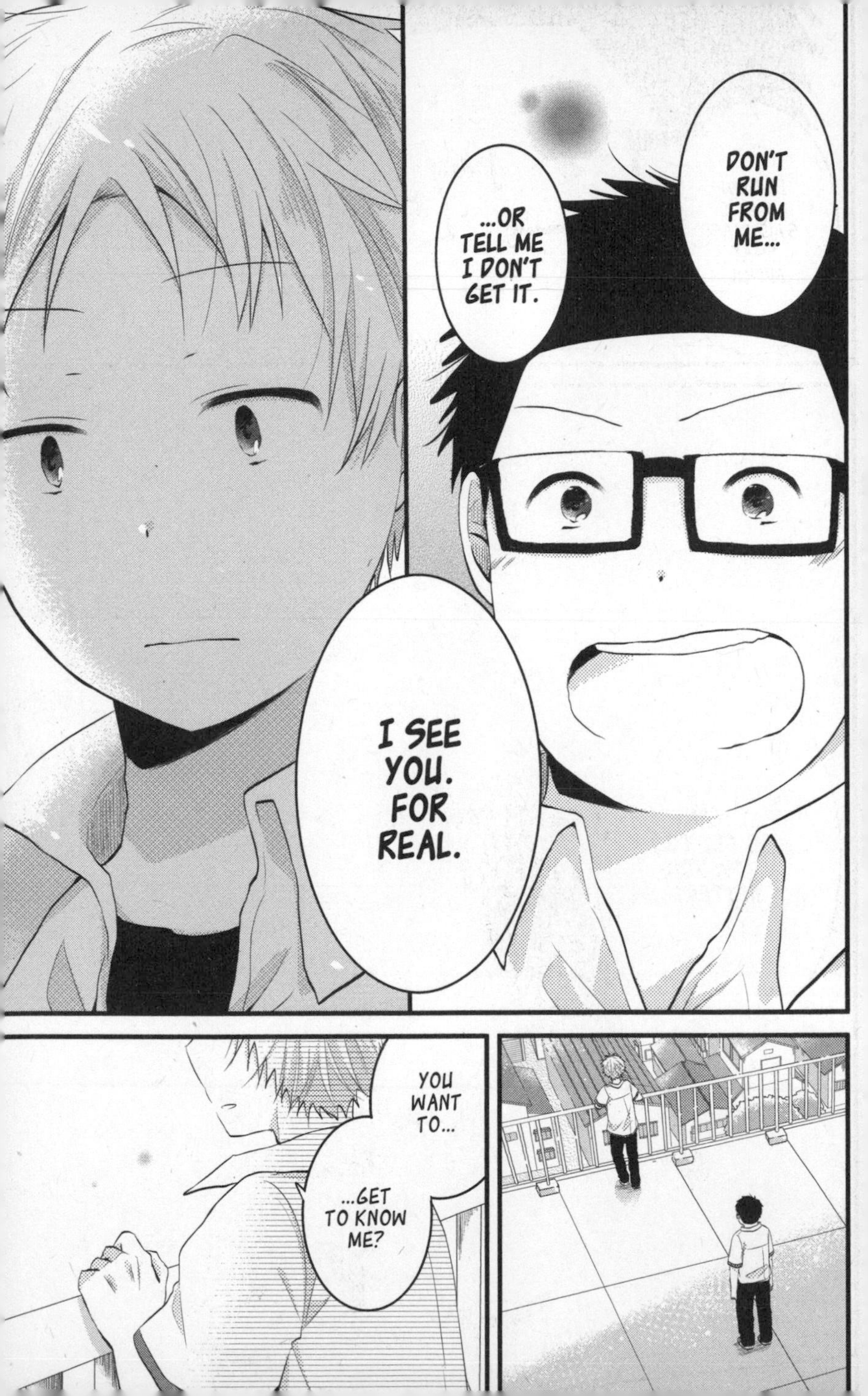
DON'T RUN FROM ME...
...OR TELL ME I DON'T GET IT.
I SEE YOU. FOR REAL.
YOU WANT TO...
...GET TO KNOW ME?

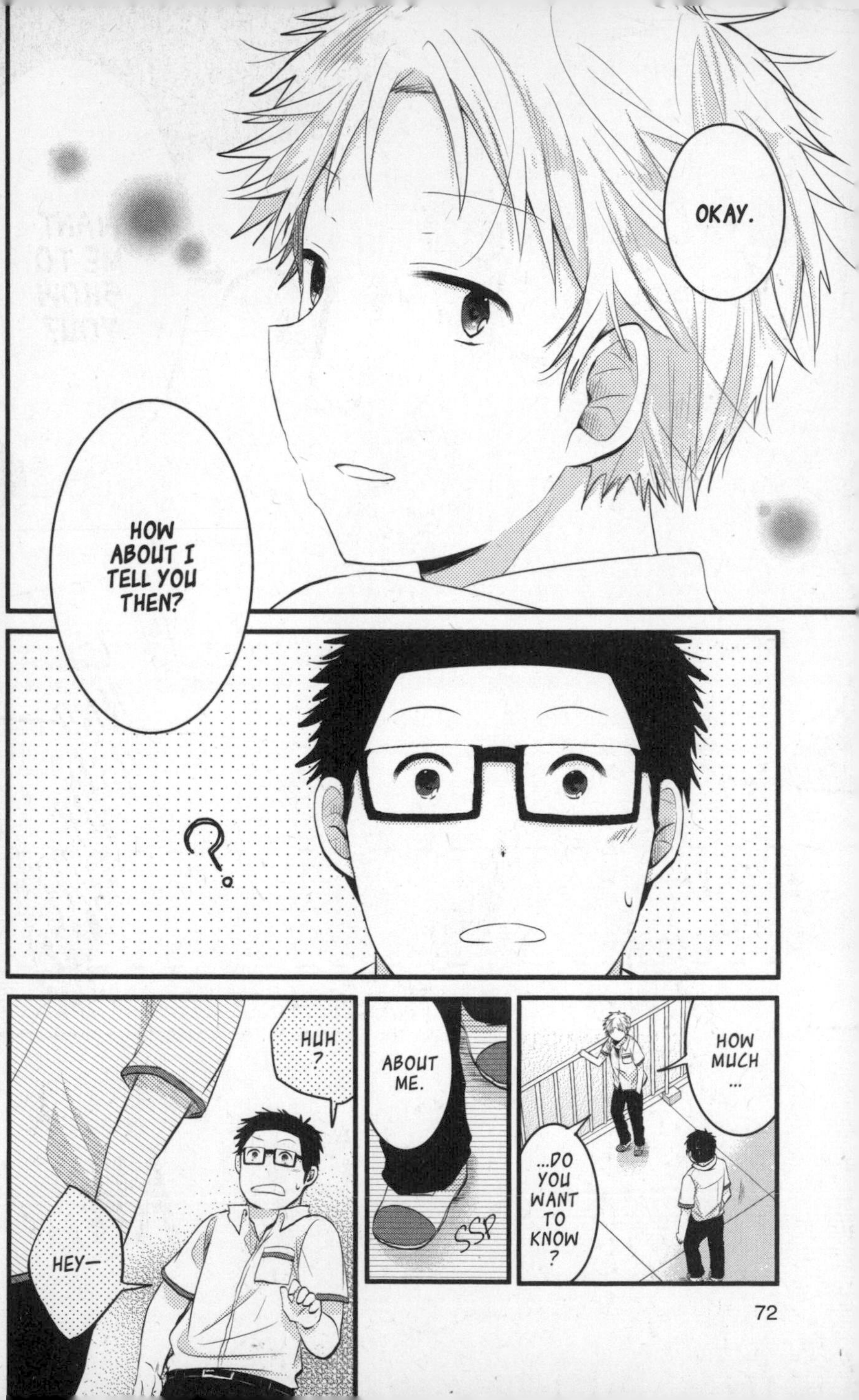
OKAY.
HOW ABOUT I TELL YOU THEN?
?
HOW MUCH ...
...DO YOU WANT TO KNOW?
ABOUT ME.
SSP
HUH?
HEY—

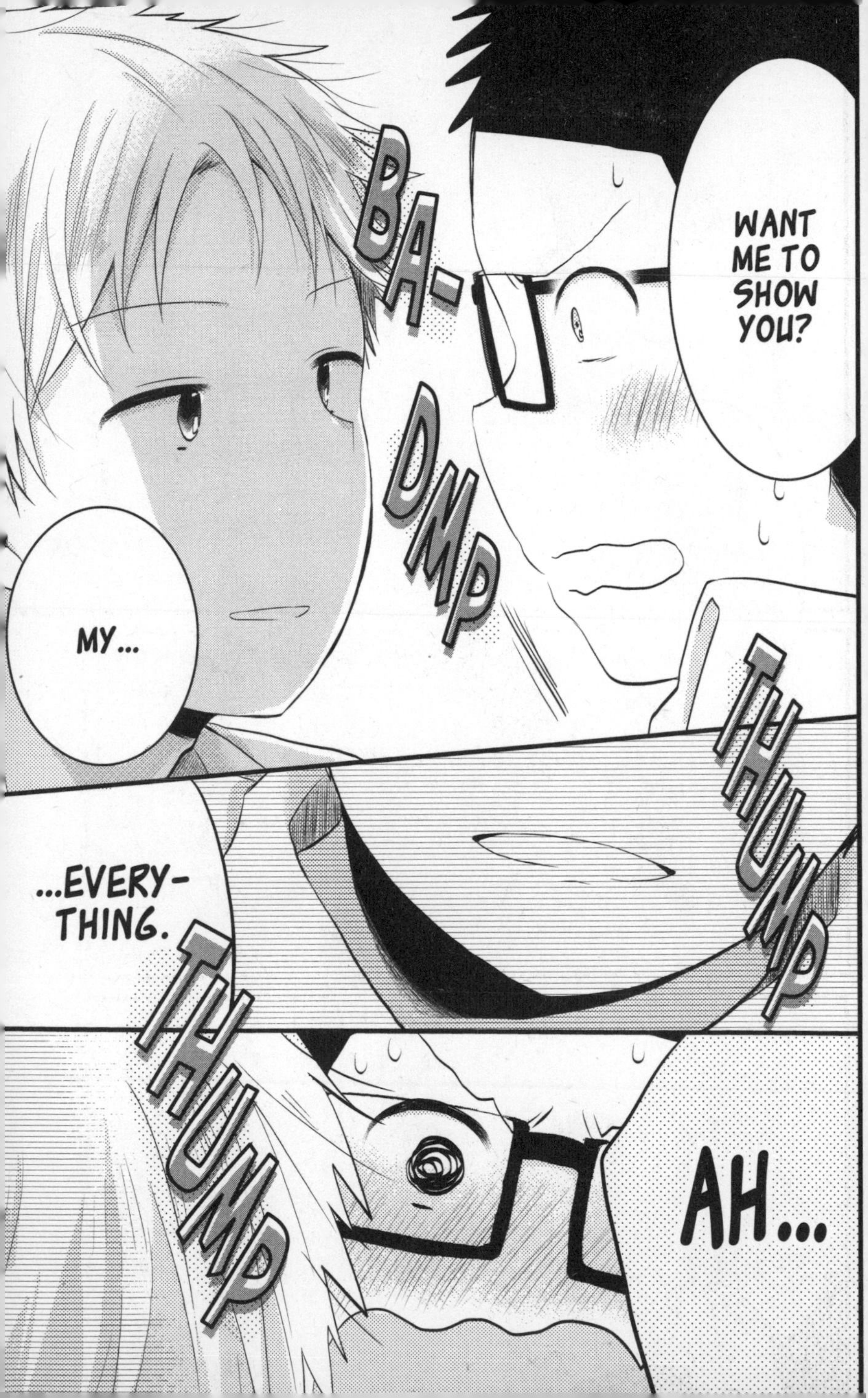
WANT ME TO SHOW YOU?
BA-DMP
MY...
THUMP
...EVERY-THING.
THUMP
AH...

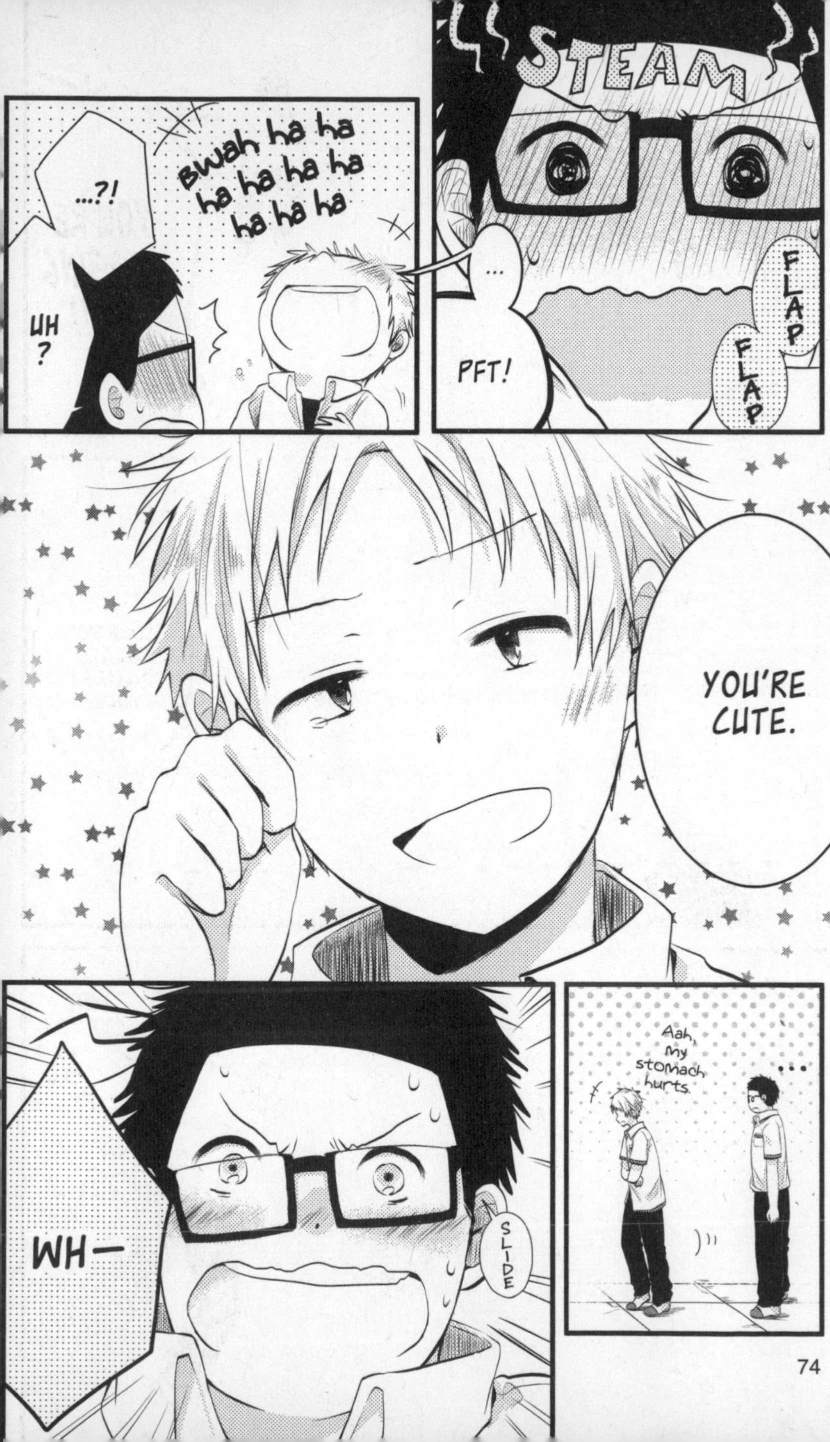
STEAM
FLAP FLAP
...
PFT!
Bwah ha ha ha ha ha ha ha ha ha
...?!
UH ?
YOU'RE CUTE.
Aah, my stomach hurts.
...
SLIDE
WH—

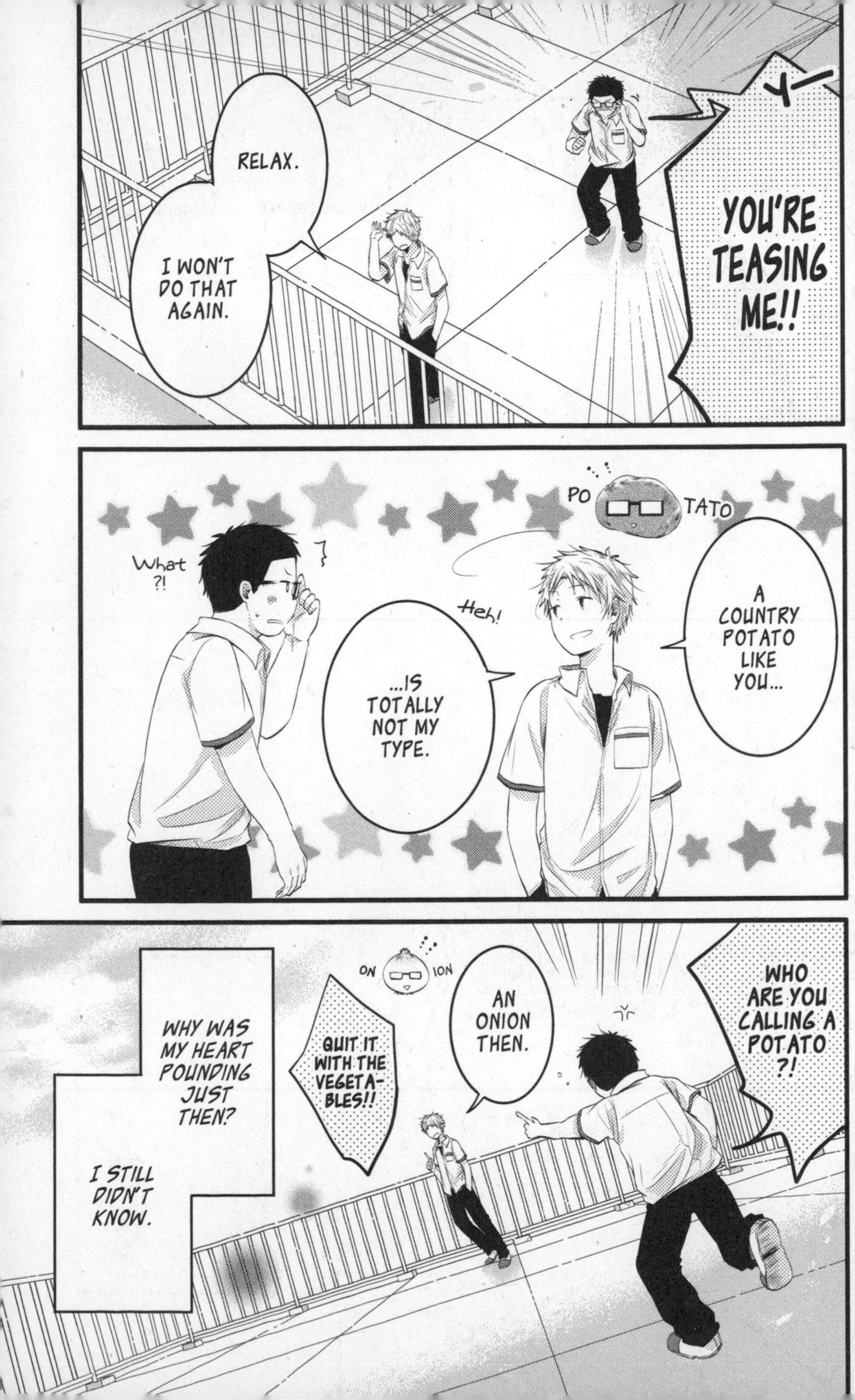
Y—
YOU'RE TEASING ME!!
RELAX.
I WON'T DO THAT AGAIN.
PO TATO
A COUNTRY POTATO LIKE YOU...
Heh!
...IS TOTALLY NOT MY TYPE.
What ?!
WHO ARE YOU CALLING A POTATO ?!
AN ONION THEN.
ON ION
QUIT IT WITH THE VEGETA-BLES!!
WHY WAS MY HEART POUNDING JUST THEN?
I STILL DIDN'T KNOW.

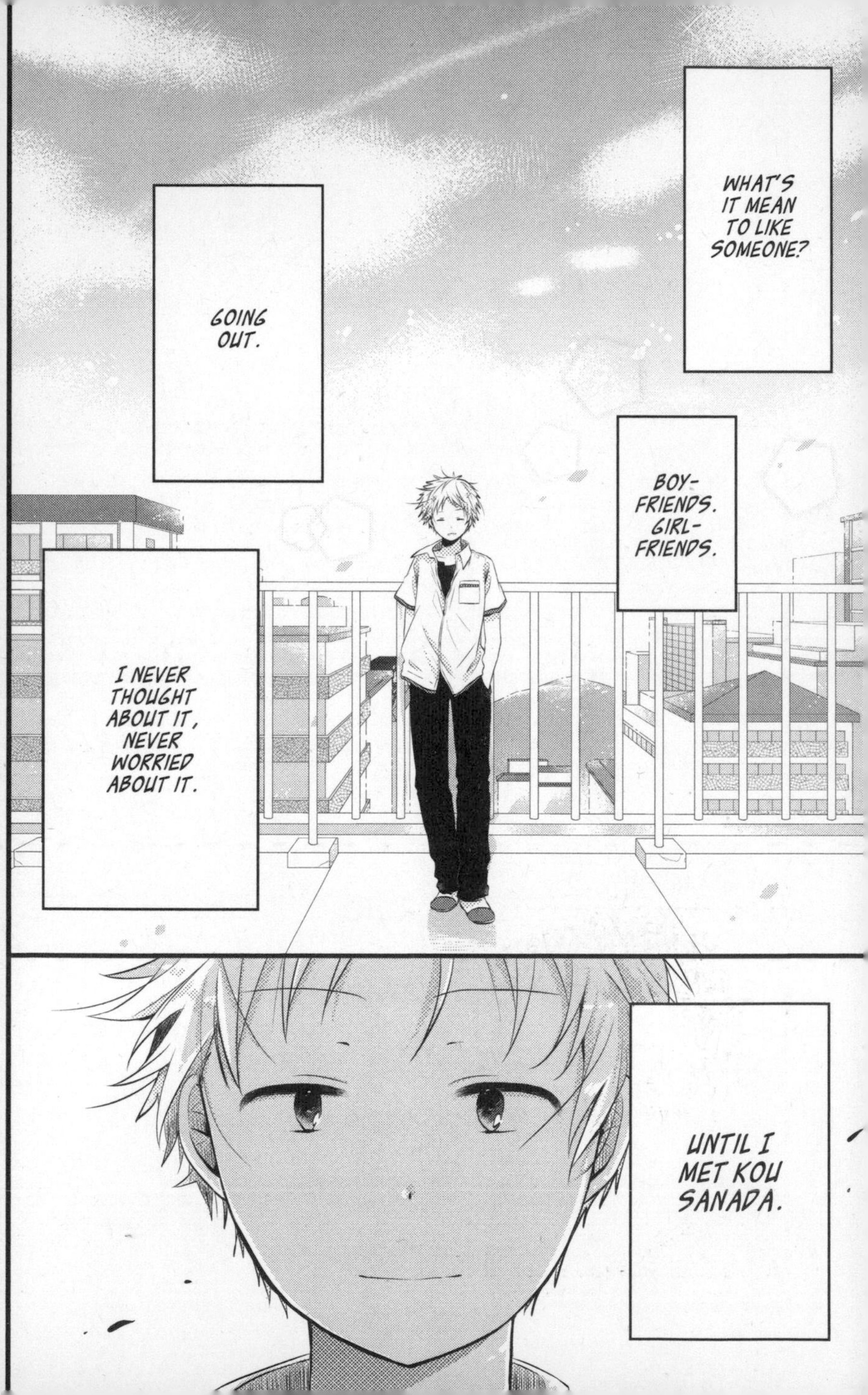
WHAT'S IT MEAN TO LIKE SOMEONE?
GOING OUT.
BOY-FRIENDS. GIRL-FRIENDS.
I NEVER THOUGHT ABOUT IT, NEVER WORRIED ABOUT IT.
UNTIL I MET KOU SANADA.

That Blue
Sky Feeling

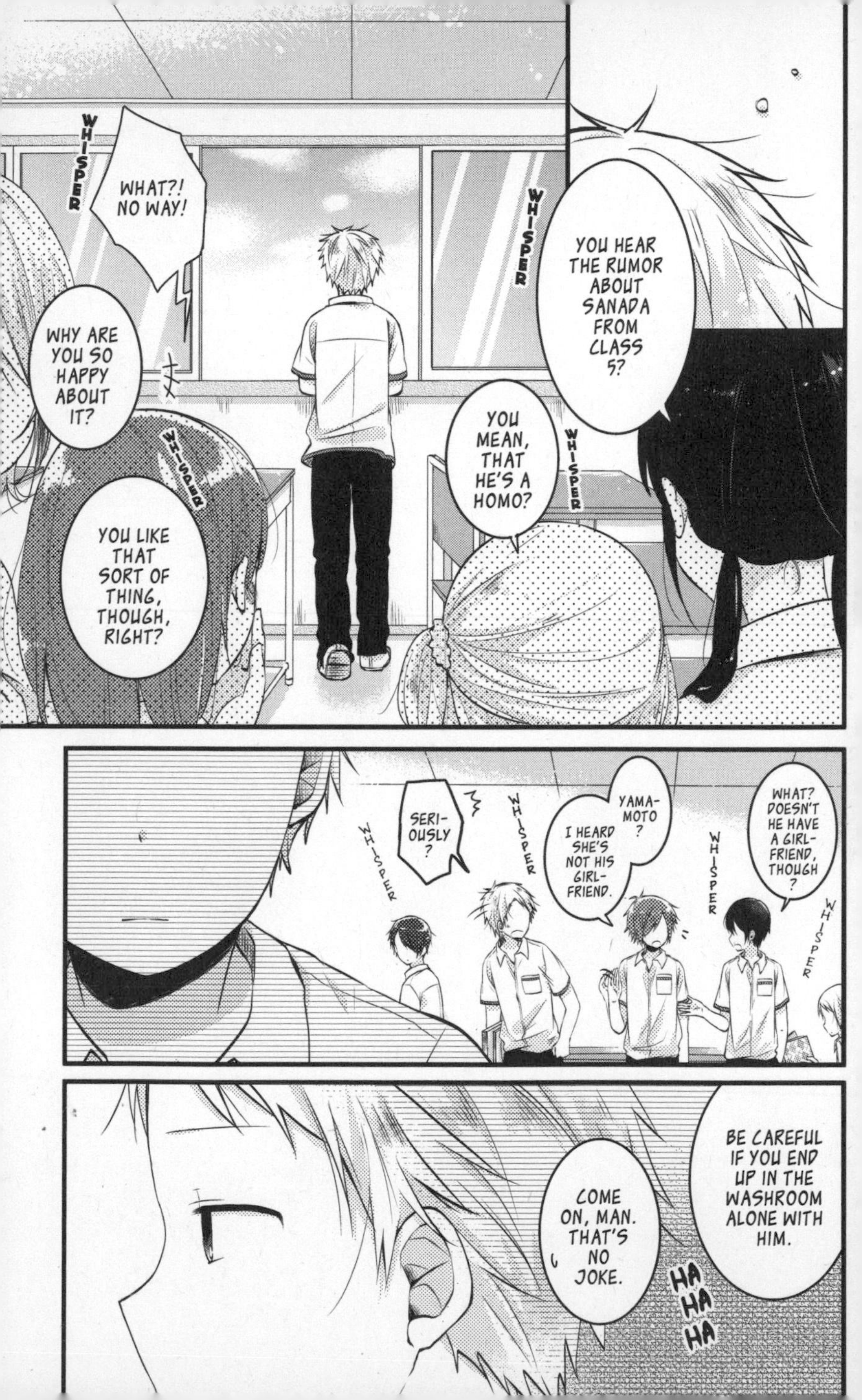
WHISPER
YOU HEAR THE RUMOR ABOUT SANADA FROM CLASS 5?
WHISPER
YOU MEAN, THAT HE'S A HOMO?
WHISPER
WHAT?! NO WAY!
WHY ARE YOU SO HAPPY ABOUT IT?
WHISPER
YOU LIKE THAT SORT OF THING, THOUGH, RIGHT?
WHISPER
WHAT? DOESN'T HE HAVE A GIRLFRIEND, THOUGH?
WHISPER
YAMAMOTO?
I HEARD SHE'S NOT HIS GIRLFRIEND.
WHISPER
SERIOUSLY?
WHISPER
BE CAREFUL IF YOU END UP IN THE WASHROOM ALONE WITH HIM.
HA HA HA
COME ON, MAN. THAT'S NO JOKE.

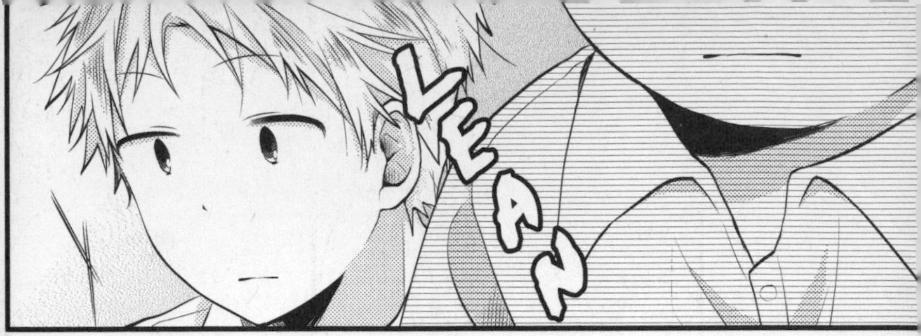
LEAN
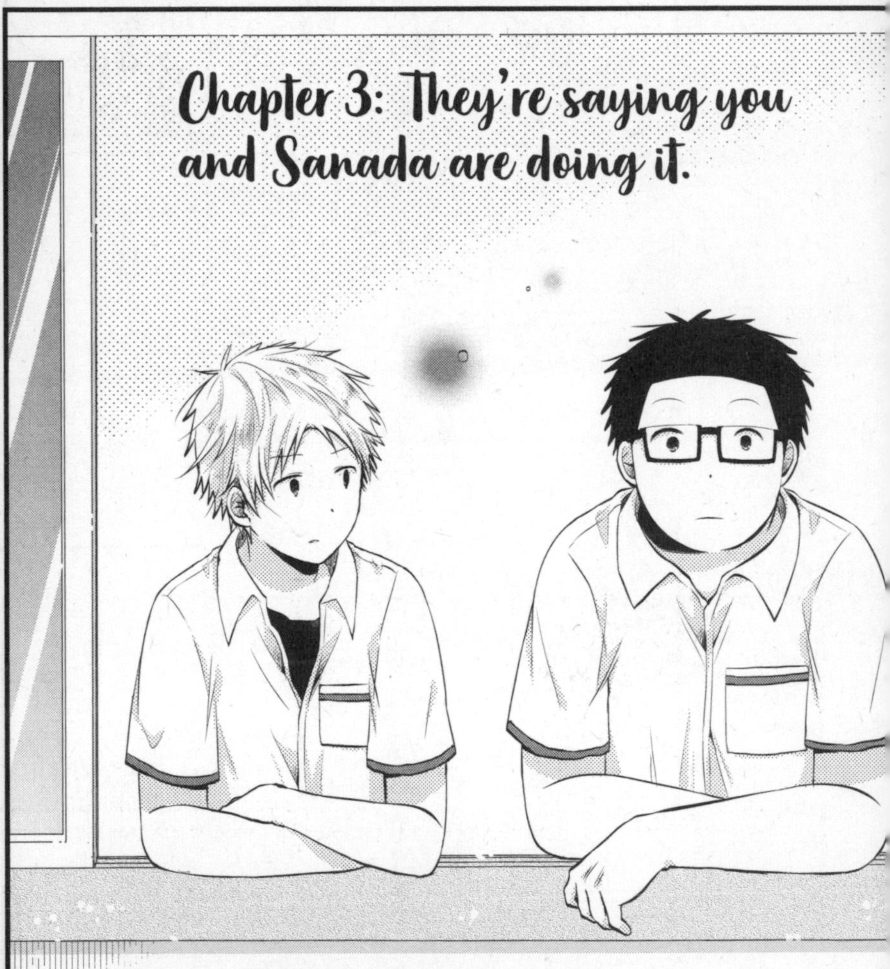
Chapter 3: They're saying you and Sanada are doing it.

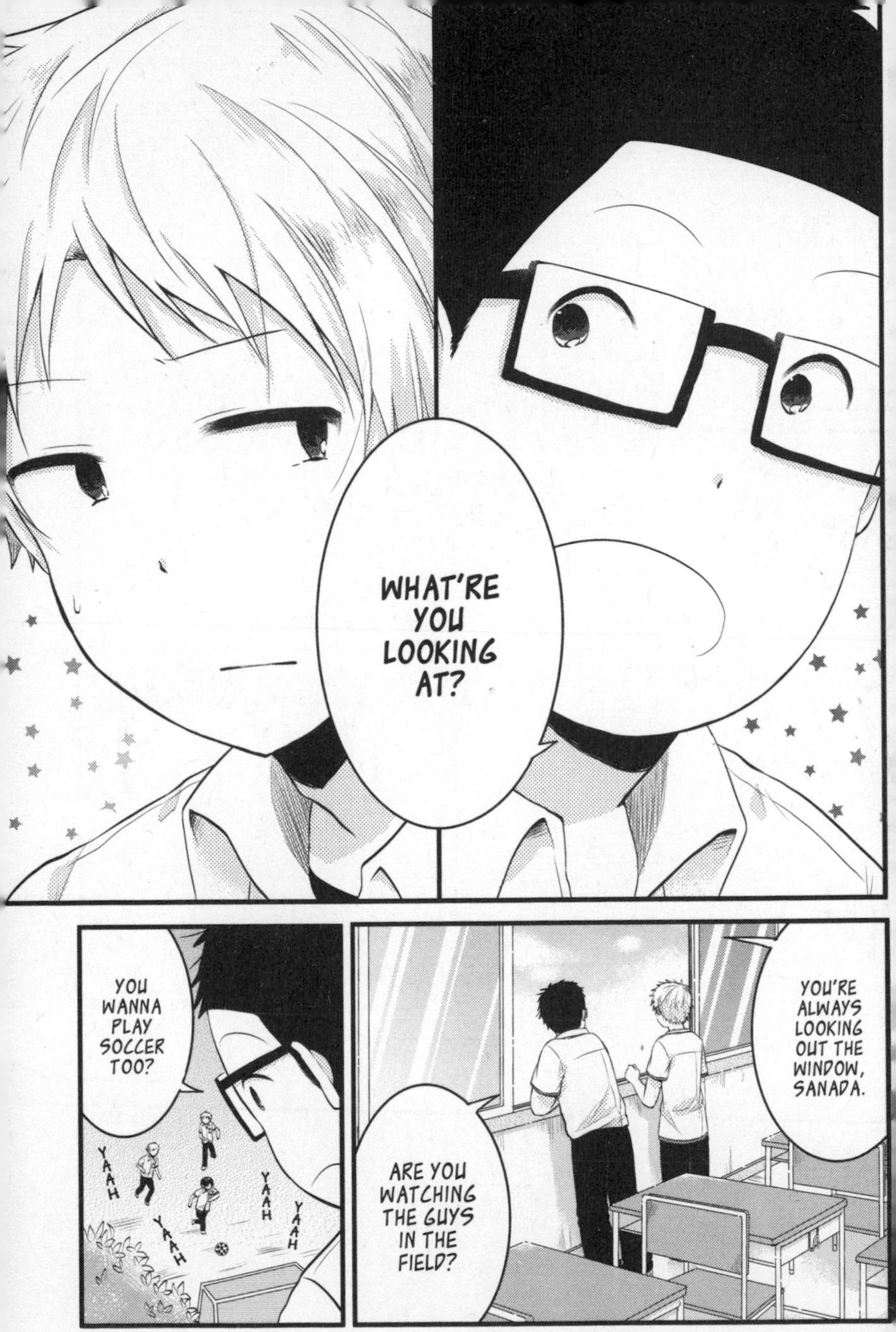
WHAT'RE YOU LOOKING AT?
YOU'RE ALWAYS LOOKING OUT THE WINDOW, SANADA.
ARE YOU WATCHING THE GUYS IN THE FIELD?
YOU WANNA PLAY SOCCER TOO?
YAAH
YAAH
YAAH
YAAH

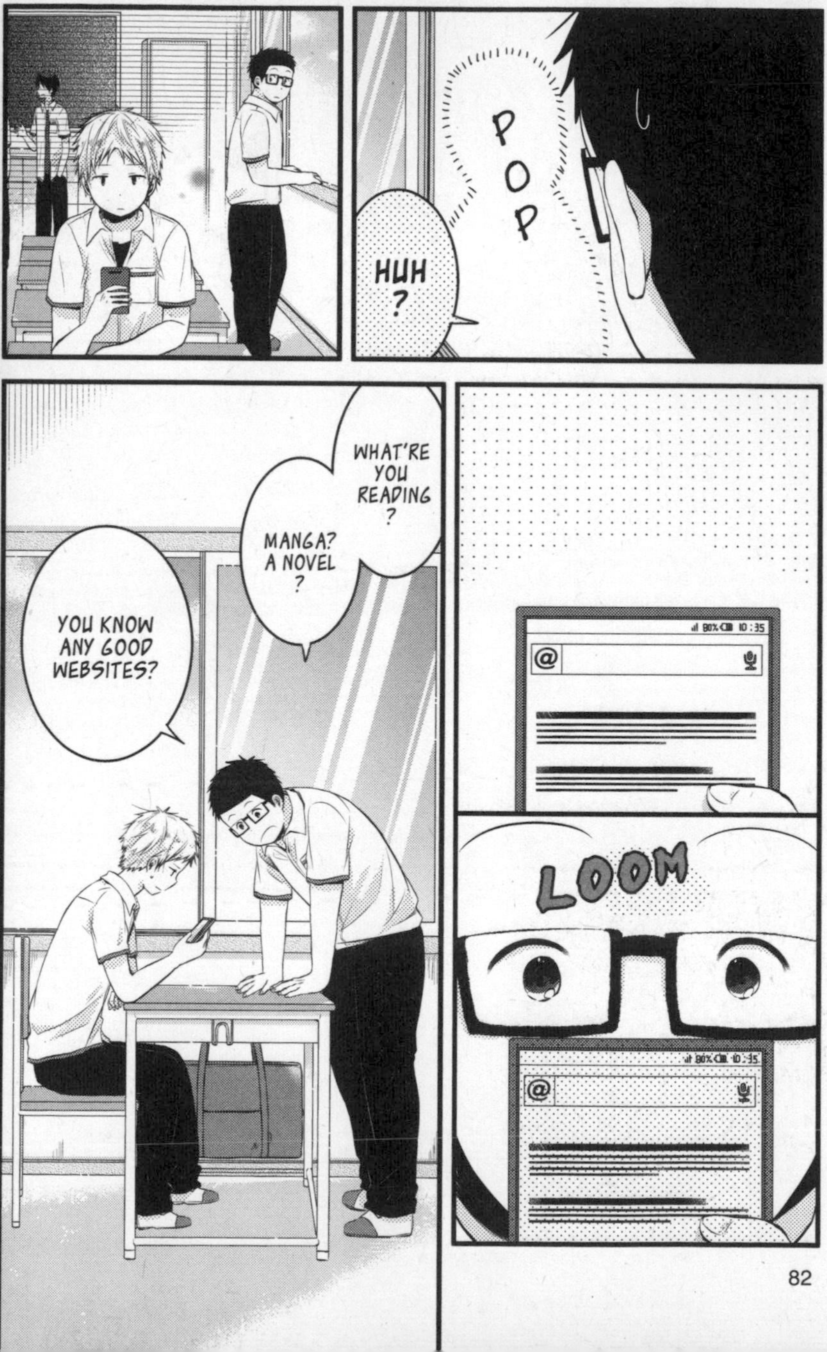
POP
HUH?
LOOM
WHAT'RE YOU READING?
MANGA? A NOVEL?
YOU KNOW ANY GOOD WEBSITES?

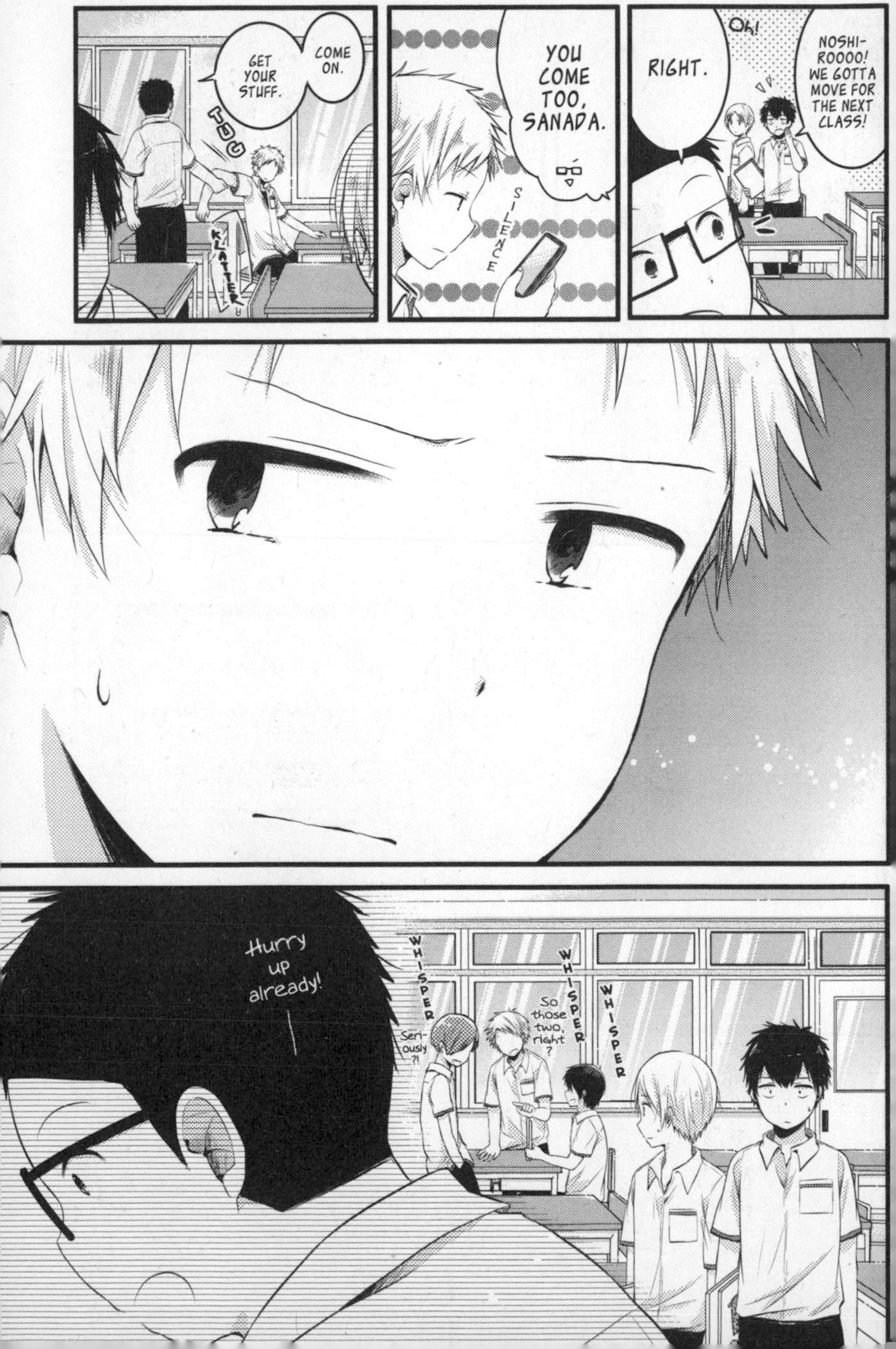
NOSHI-ROOOO! WE GOTTA MOVE FOR THE NEXT CLASS!
Oh!
RIGHT.
YOU COME TOO, SANADA.
SILENCE
COME ON.
GET YOUR STUFF.
TUG
KLATTER
WHISPER
So those two, right?
WHISPER
Seri-ously?!
WHISPER
Hurry up already!

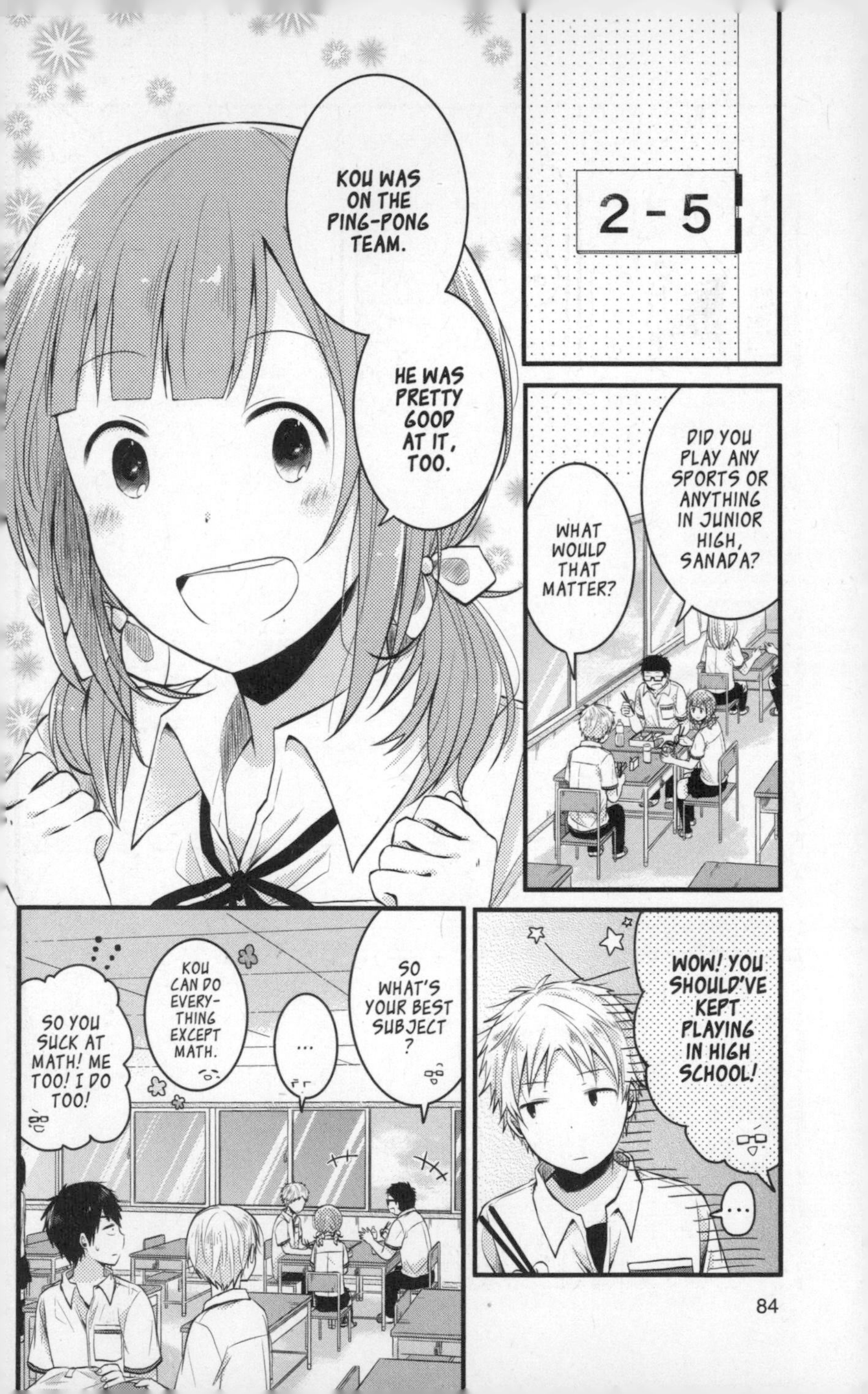
2 - 5
DID YOU PLAY ANY SPORTS OR ANYTHING IN JUNIOR HIGH, SANADA?
WHAT WOULD THAT MATTER?
KOU WAS ON THE PING-PONG TEAM.
HE WAS PRETTY GOOD AT IT, TOO.
WOW! YOU SHOULD'VE KEPT PLAYING IN HIGH SCHOOL!
...
SO WHAT'S YOUR BEST SUBJECT?
...
KOU CAN DO EVERY-THING EXCEPT MATH.
SO YOU SUCK AT MATH! ME TOO! I DO TOO!

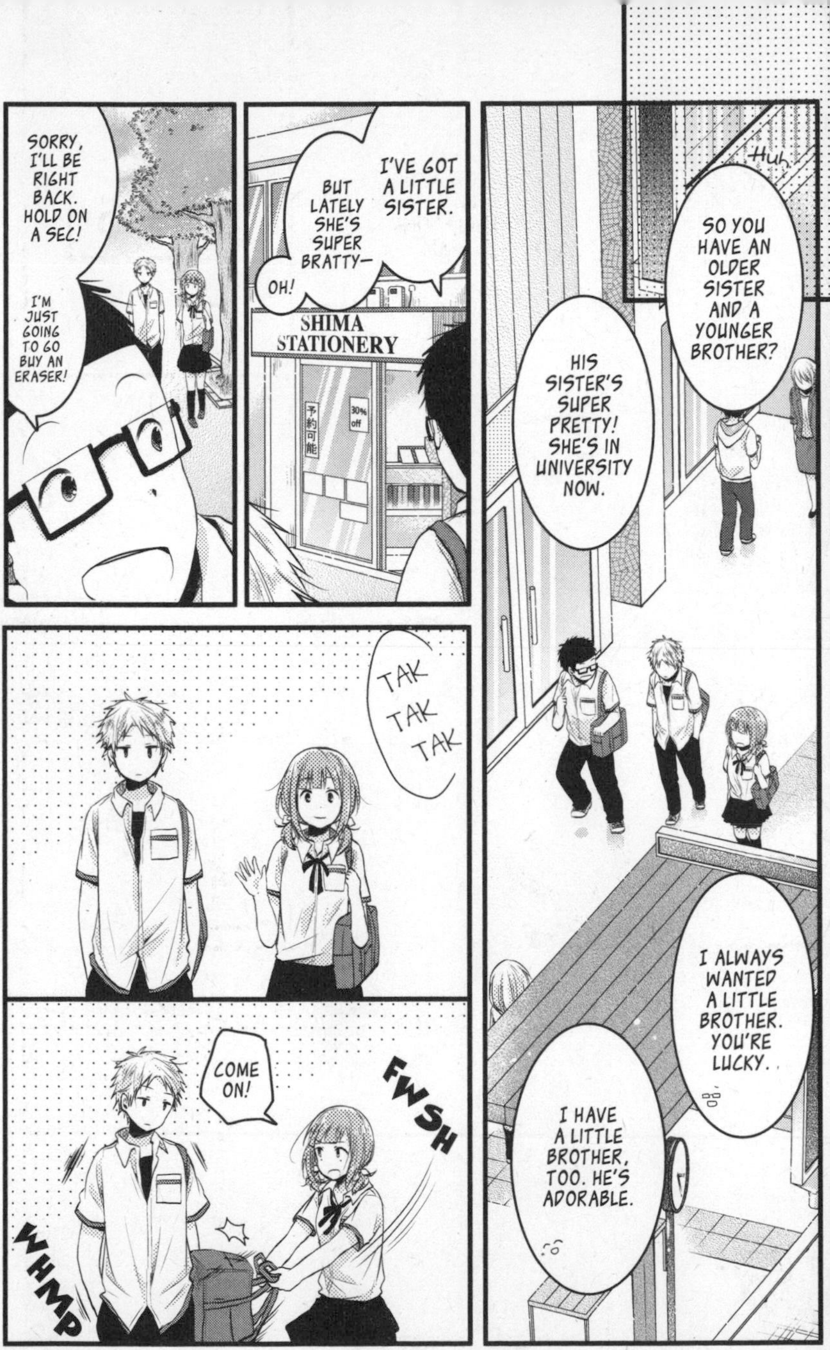
Huh.
SO YOU HAVE AN OLDER SISTER AND A YOUNGER BROTHER?
HIS SISTER'S SUPER PRETTY! SHE'S IN UNIVERSITY NOW.
I ALWAYS WANTED A LITTLE BROTHER. YOU'RE LUCKY.
I HAVE A LITTLE BROTHER, TOO. HE'S ADORABLE.
I'VE GOT A LITTLE SISTER.
BUT LATELY SHE'S SUPER BRATTY—
OH!
SHIMA STATIONERY
予約可能
30% off
SORRY, I'LL BE RIGHT BACK. HOLD ON A SEC!
I'M JUST GOING TO GO BUY AN ERASER!
TAK TAK TAK
COME ON!
FWSH
WHMP

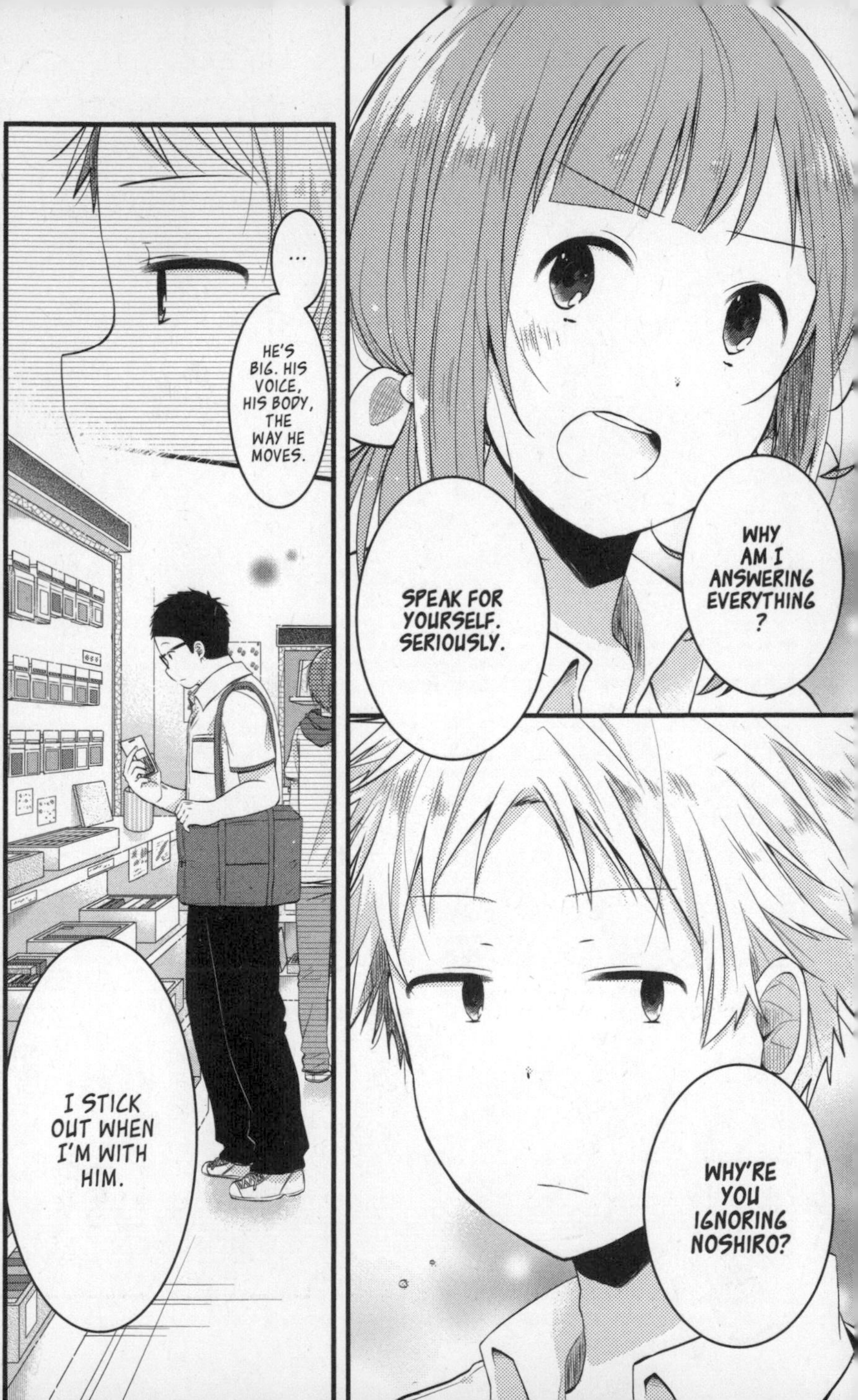
WHY AM I ANSWERING EVERYTHING?
SPEAK FOR YOURSELF. SERIOUSLY.
WHY'RE YOU IGNORING NOSHIRO?
...
HE'S BIG. HIS VOICE, HIS BODY, THE WAY HE MOVES.
I STICK OUT WHEN I'M WITH HIM.

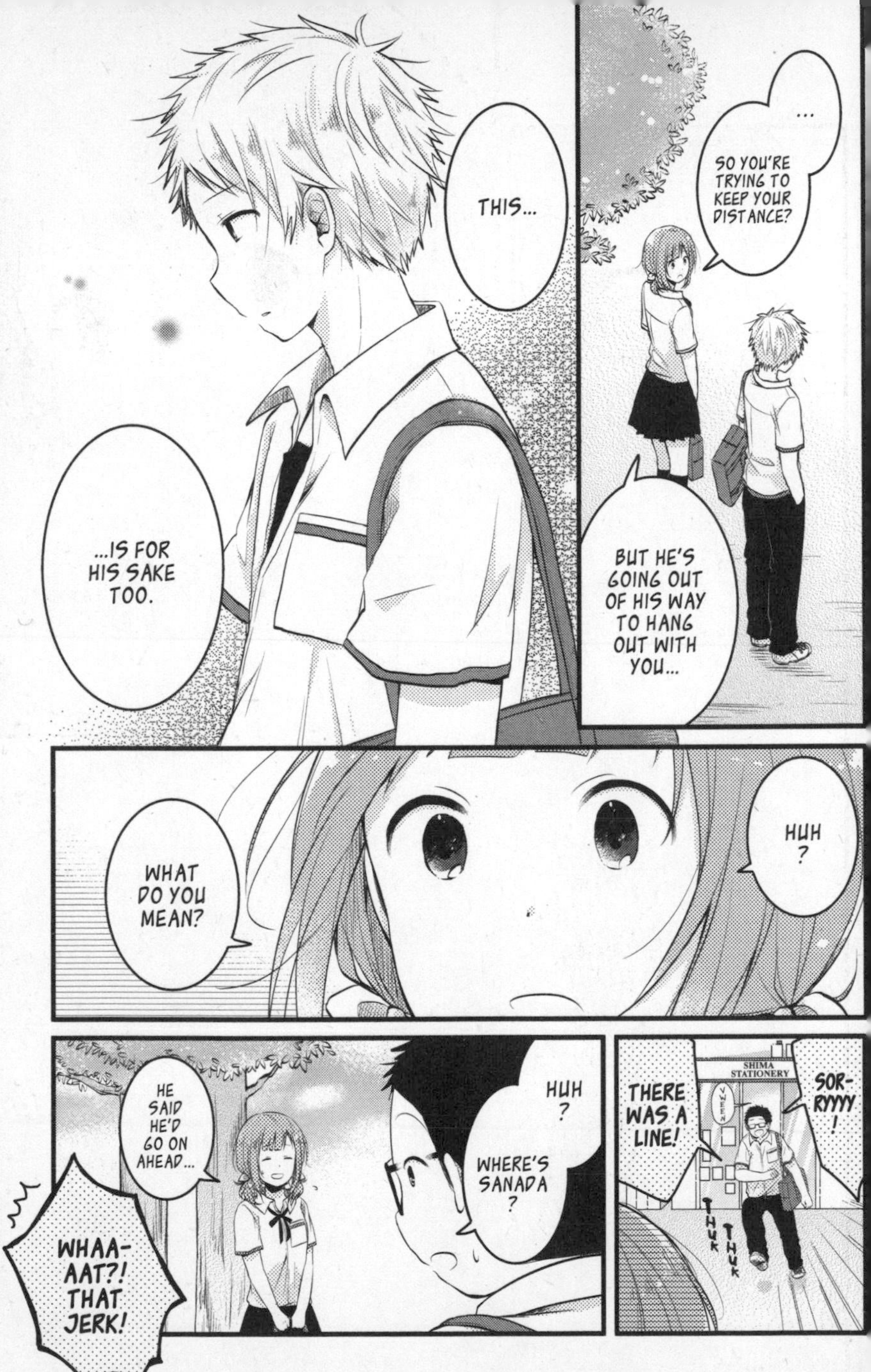
...
SO YOU'RE TRYING TO KEEP YOUR DISTANCE?
BUT HE'S GOING OUT OF HIS WAY TO HANG OUT WITH YOU...
THIS...
...IS FOR HIS SAKE TOO.
HUH?
WHAT DO YOU MEAN?
SHIMA STATIONERY
SOR-RYYYY!
VWEEN
THERE WAS A LINE!
THUK THUK
HUH?
WHERE'S SANADA?
HE SAID HE'D GO ON AHEAD...
WHAA-AAT?! THAT JERK!

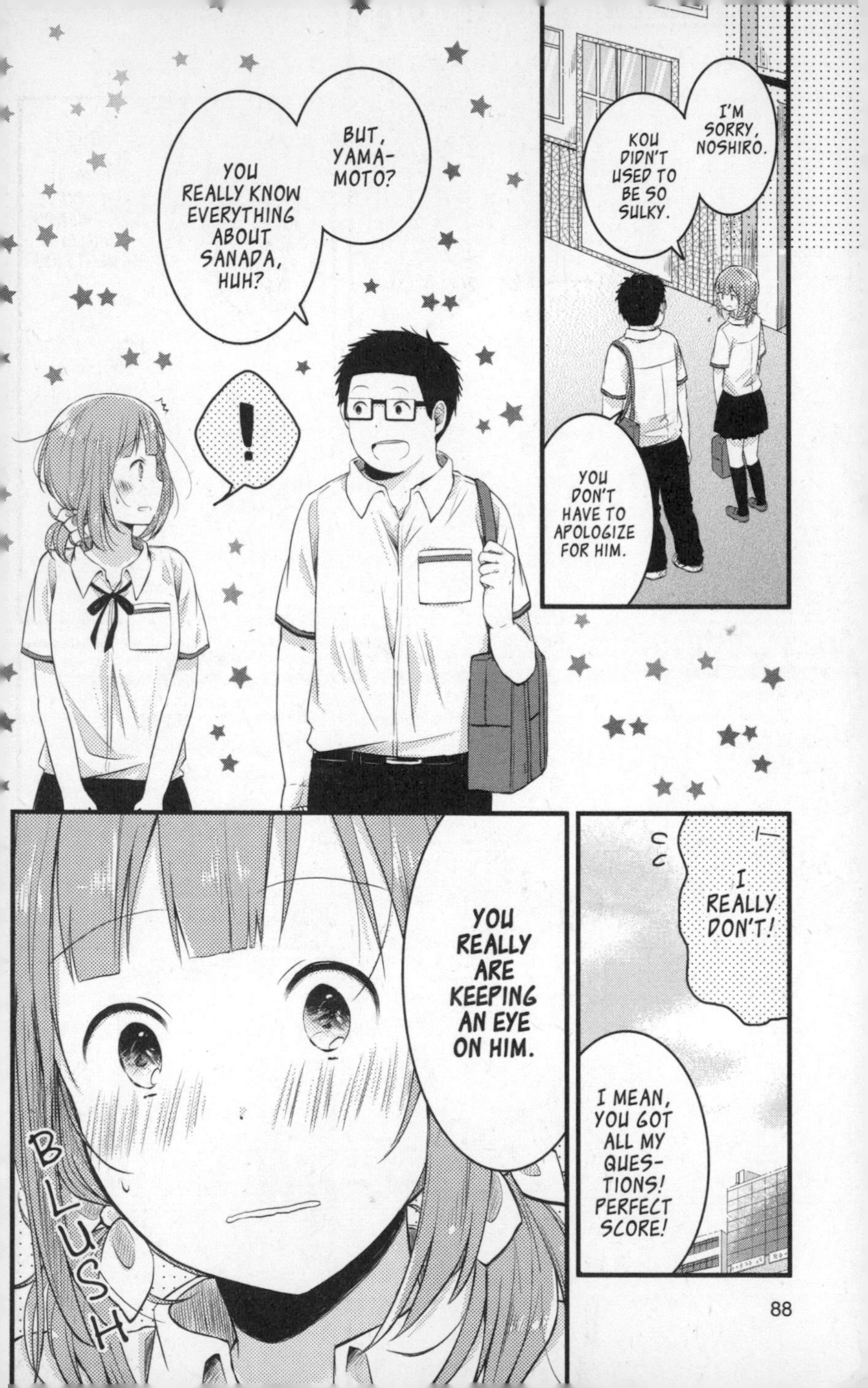
I'M SORRY, NOSHIRO.
KOU DIDN'T USED TO BE SO SULKY.
YOU DON'T HAVE TO APOLOGIZE FOR HIM.
BUT, YAMAMOTO?
YOU REALLY KNOW EVERYTHING ABOUT SANADA, HUH?
!
I— I REALLY DON'T!
I MEAN, YOU GOT ALL MY QUESTIONS! PERFECT SCORE!
YOU REALLY ARE KEEPING AN EYE ON HIM.
BLUSH

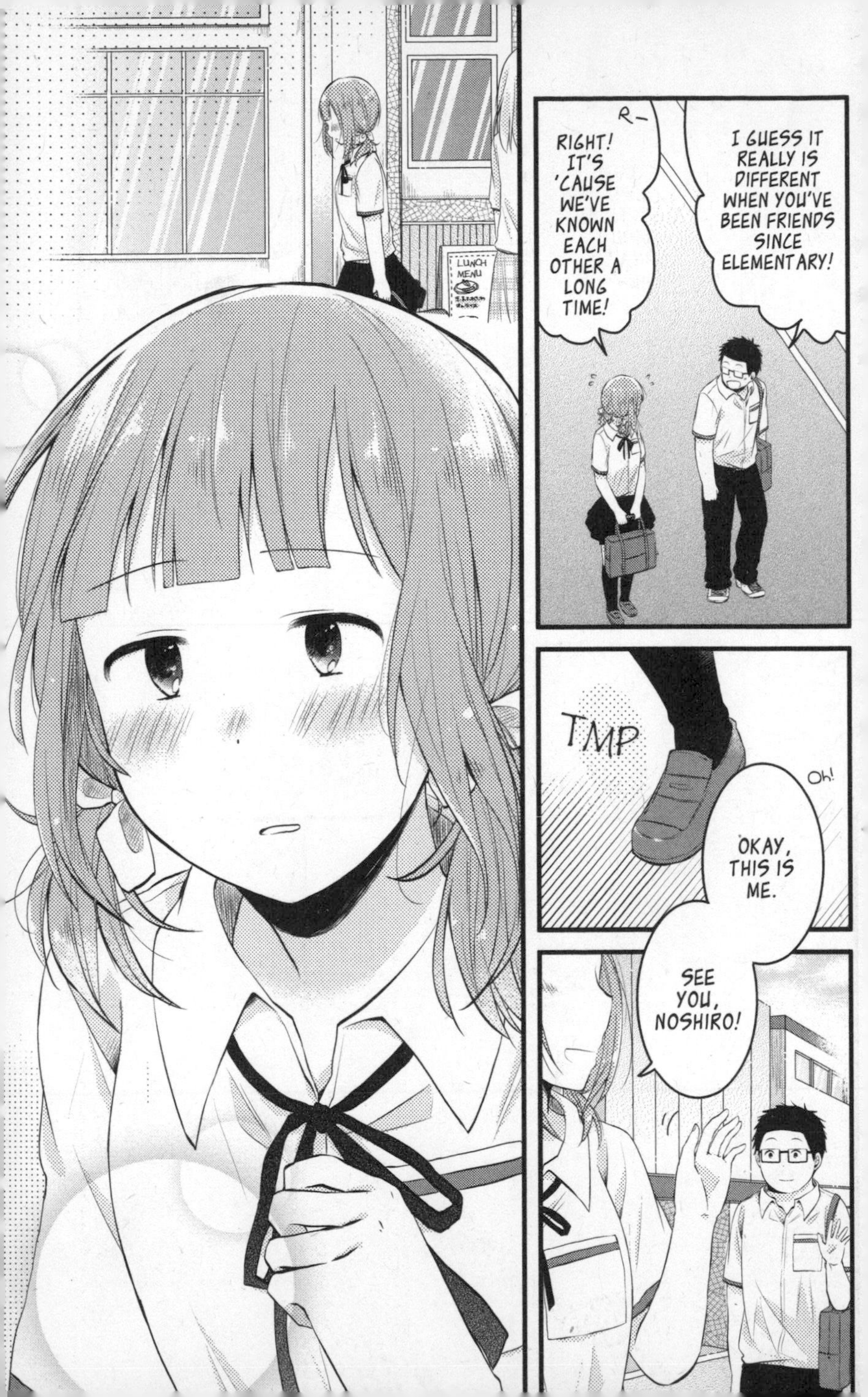
I GUESS IT REALLY IS DIFFERENT WHEN YOU'VE BEEN FRIENDS SINCE ELEMENTARY!
R—
RIGHT! IT'S 'CAUSE WE'VE KNOWN EACH OTHER A LONG TIME!
TMP
Oh!
OKAY, THIS IS ME.
SEE YOU, NOSHIRO!
LUNCH MENU

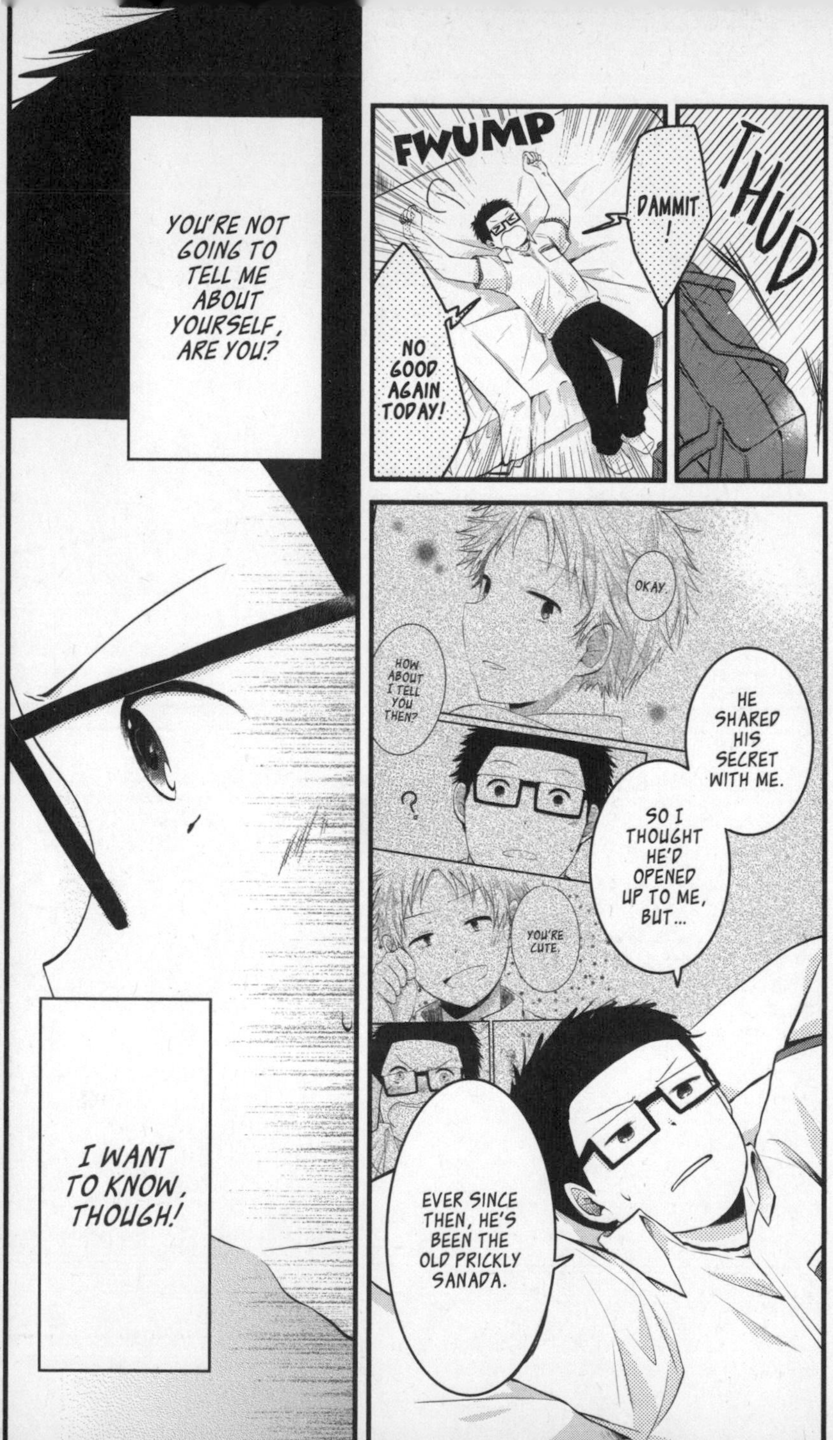
THUD
FWUMP
DAMMIT!
NO GOOD AGAIN TODAY!
OKAY.
HOW ABOUT I TELL YOU THEN?
HE SHARED HIS SECRET WITH ME.
SO I THOUGHT HE'D OPENED UP TO ME, BUT...
YOU'RE CUTE.
EVER SINCE THEN, HE'S BEEN THE OLD PRICKLY SANADA.
YOU'RE NOT GOING TO TELL ME ABOUT YOURSELF, ARE YOU?
I WANT TO KNOW, THOUGH!

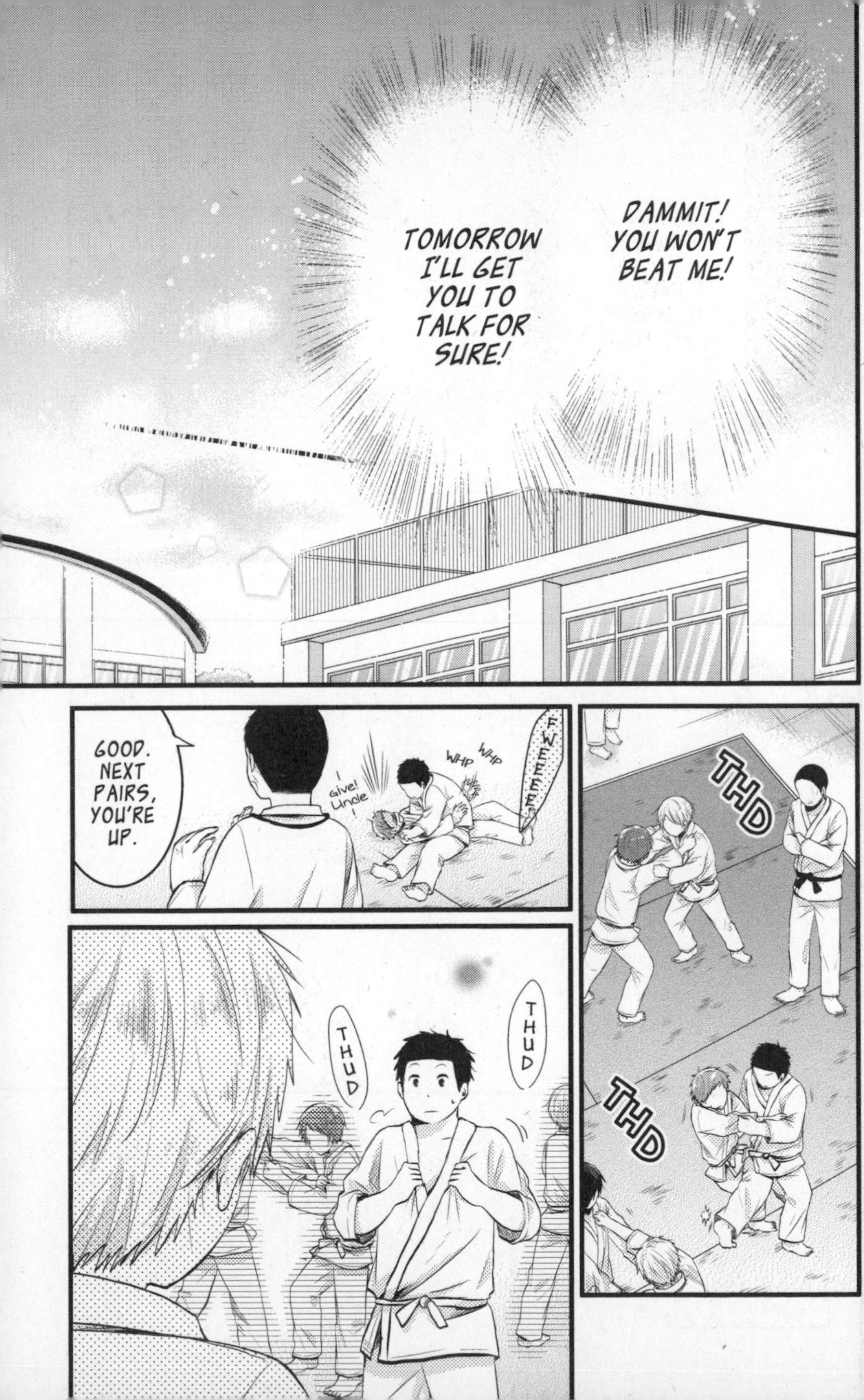
DAMMIT! YOU WON'T BEAT ME!
TOMORROW I'LL GET YOU TO TALK FOR SURE!
THD
THD
FWEEEE
WHP WHP
I give! Uncle!
GOOD. NEXT PAIRS, YOU'RE UP.
THUD
THUD

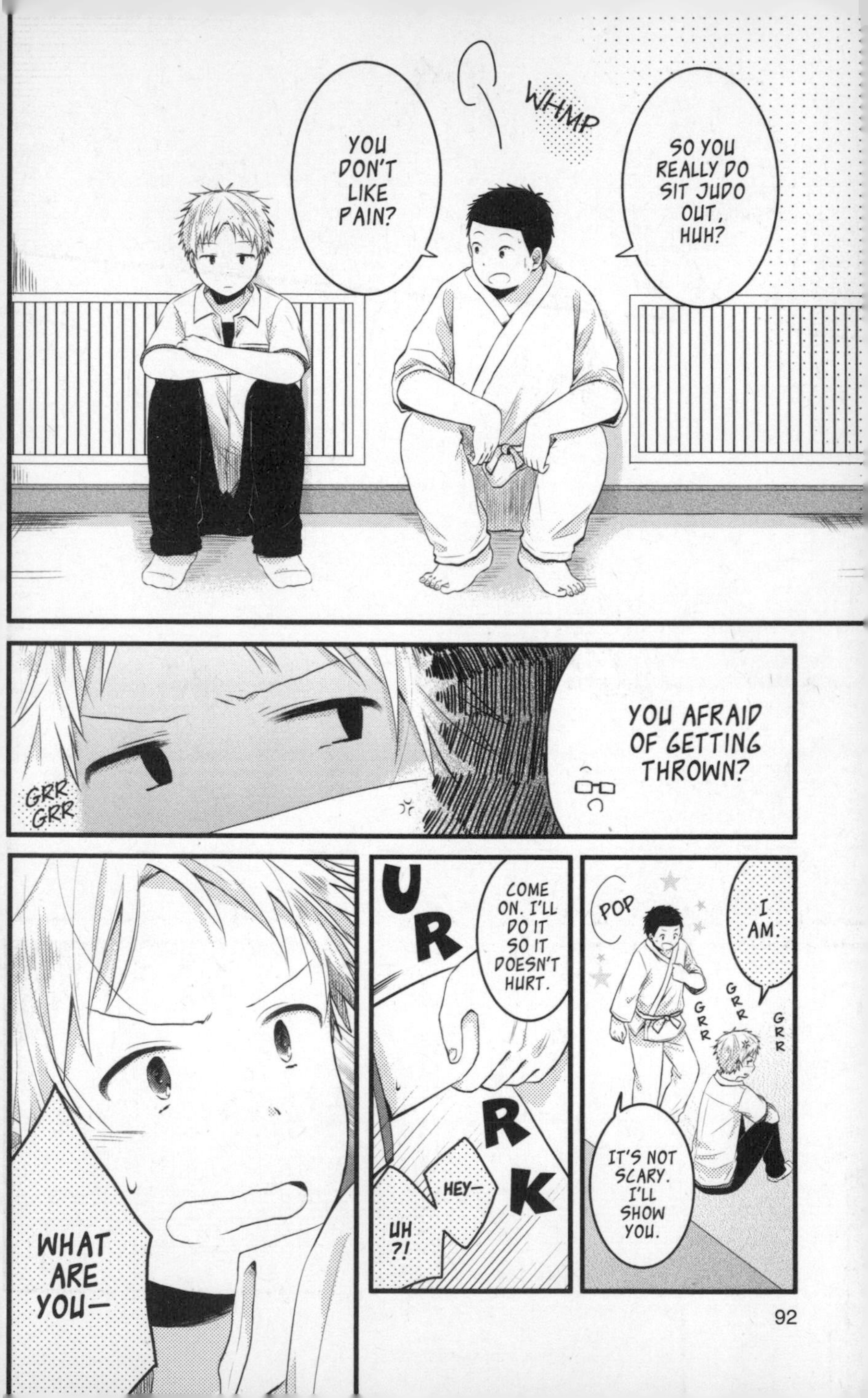
SO YOU REALLY DO SIT JUDO OUT, HUH?
WHMP
YOU DON'T LIKE PAIN?
YOU AFRAID OF GETTING THROWN?
GRR GRR
I AM.
POP
GRR GRR GRR
IT'S NOT SCARY. I'LL SHOW YOU.
COME ON. I'LL DO IT SO IT DOESN'T HURT.
URRK
HEY—
UH?!
WHAT ARE YOU—

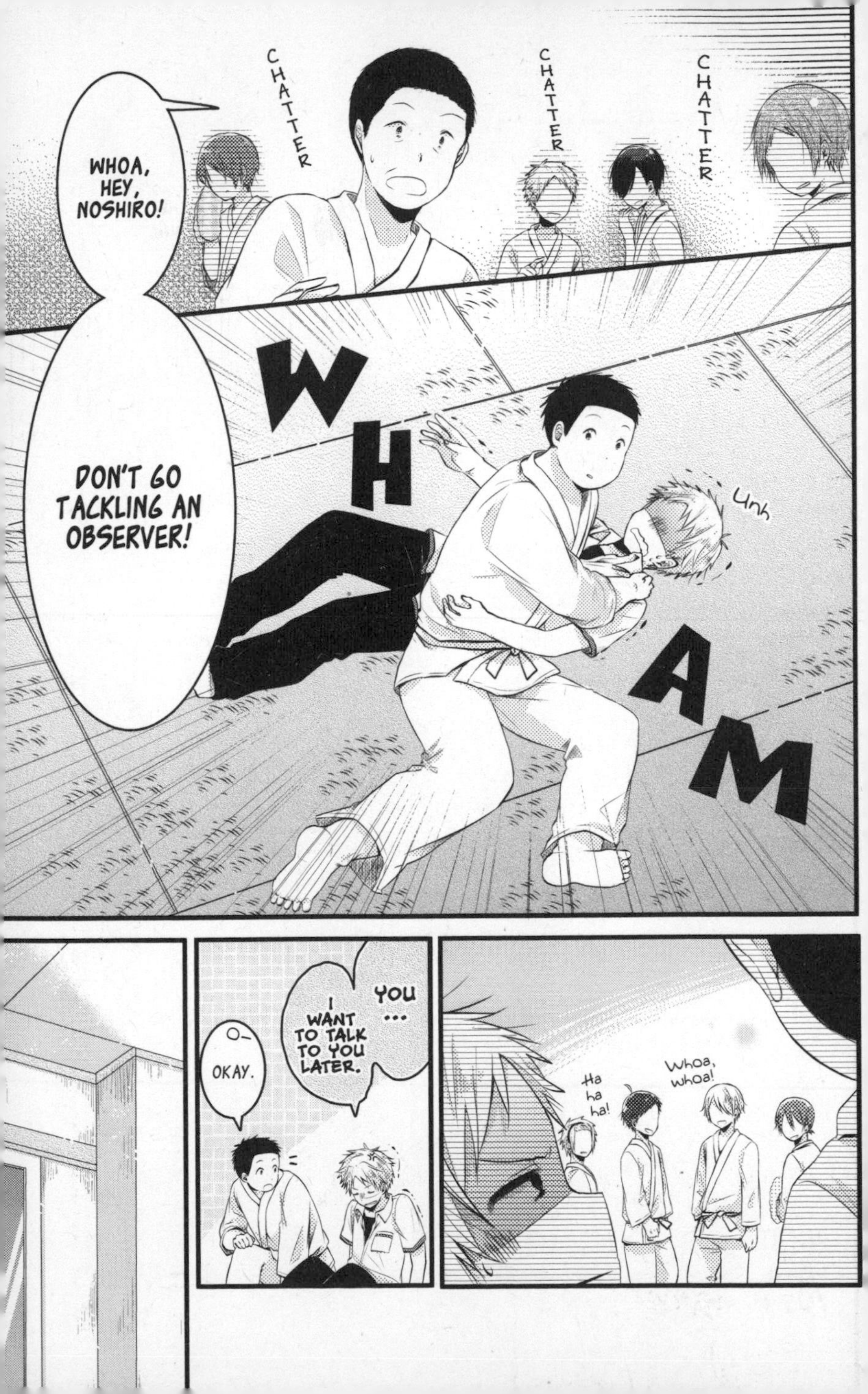
CHATTER
CHATTER
CHATTER
WHOA, HEY, NOSHIRO!
DON'T GO TACKLING AN OBSERVER!
WHAM
Unh
Whoa, whoa!
Ha ha ha!
YOU...
I WANT TO TALK TO YOU LATER.
O-OKAY.

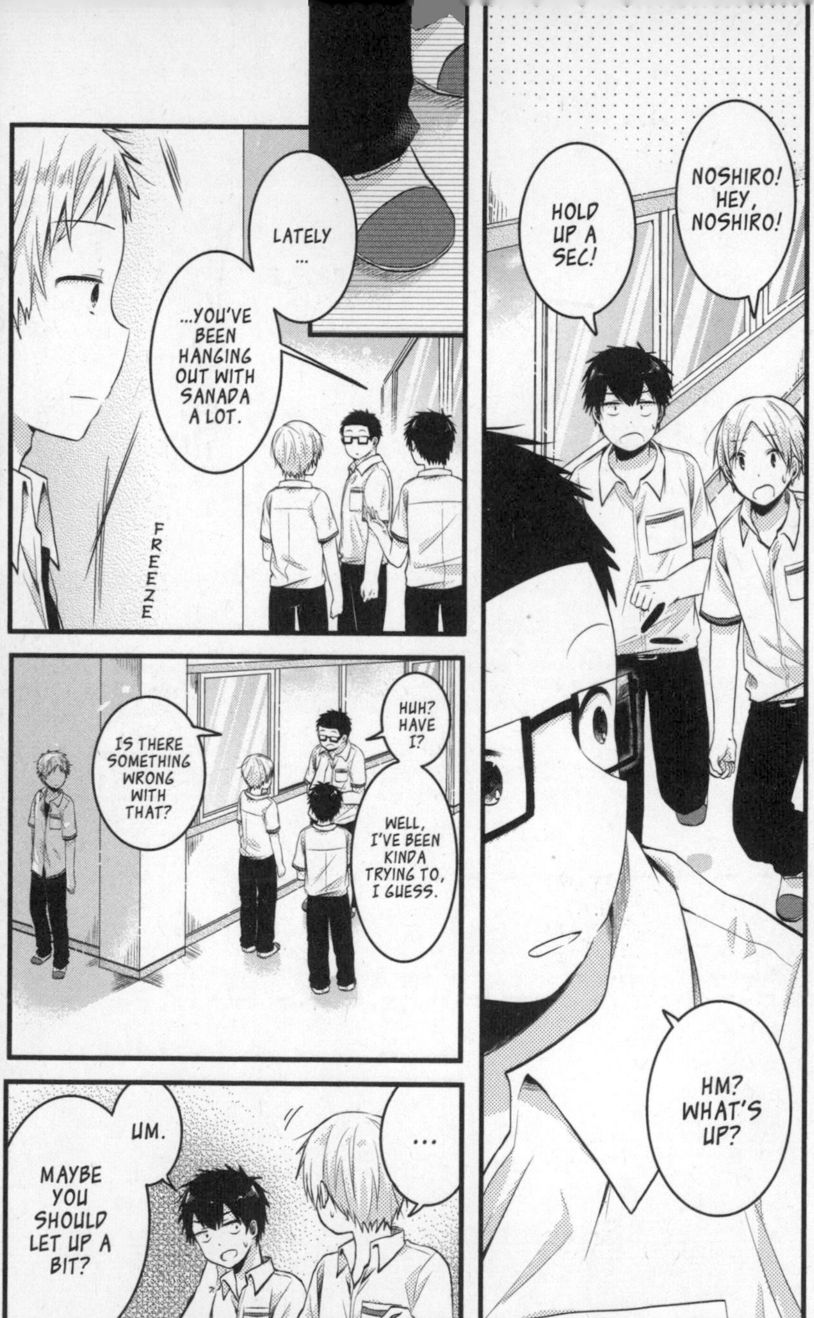
NOSHIRO! HEY, NOSHIRO!
HOLD UP A SEC!
HM? WHAT'S UP?
LATELY ...
...YOU'VE BEEN HANGING OUT WITH SANADA A LOT.
FREEZE
HUH? HAVE I?
WELL, I'VE BEEN KINDA TRYING TO, I GUESS.
IS THERE SOMETHING WRONG WITH THAT?
...
UM.
MAYBE YOU SHOULD LET UP A BIT?

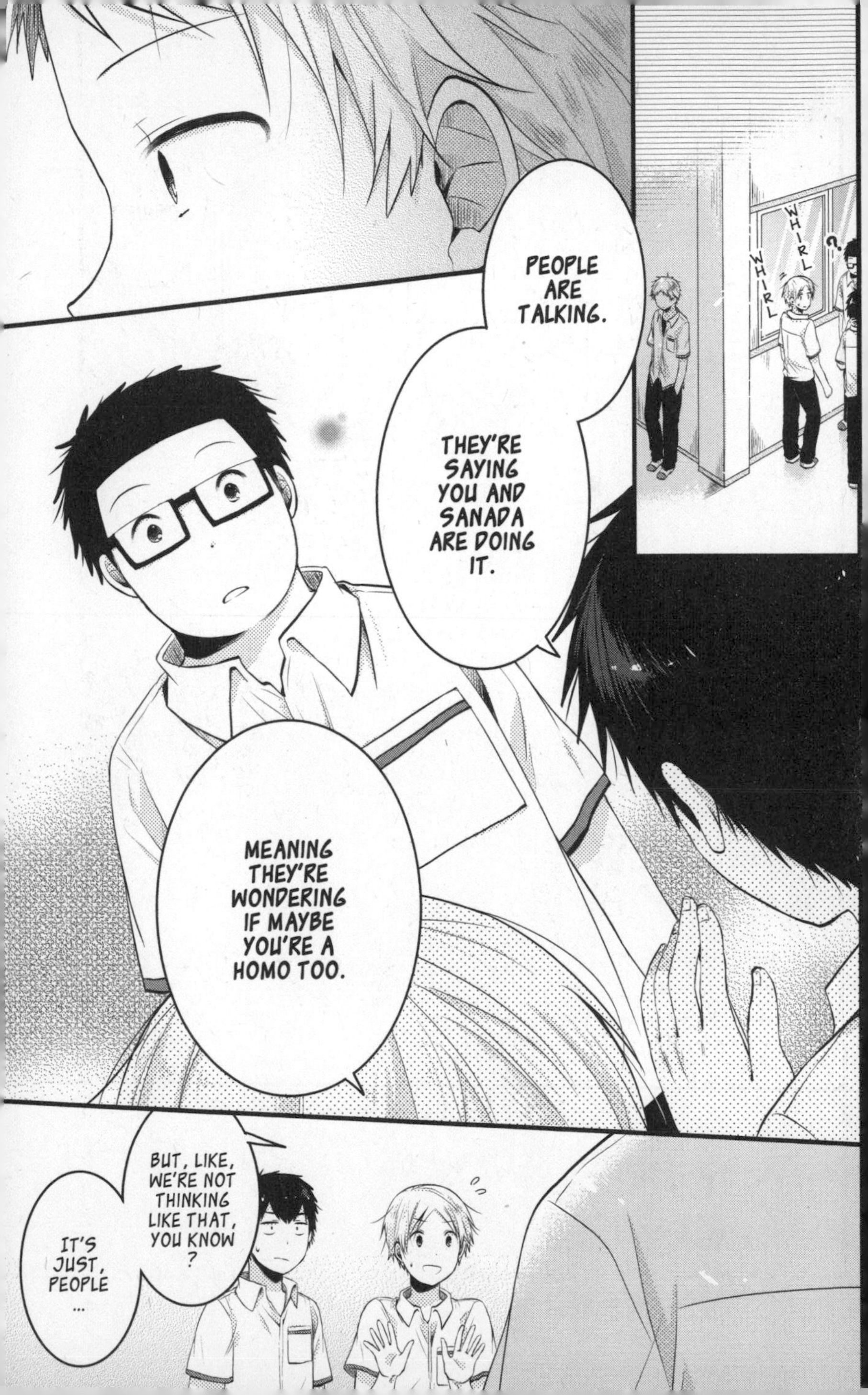
WHIRL
WHIRL
?
PEOPLE ARE TALKING.
THEY'RE SAYING YOU AND SANADA ARE DOING IT.
MEANING THEY'RE WONDERING IF MAYBE YOU'RE A HOMO TOO.
BUT, LIKE, WE'RE NOT THINKING LIKE THAT, YOU KNOW?
IT'S JUST, PEOPLE...

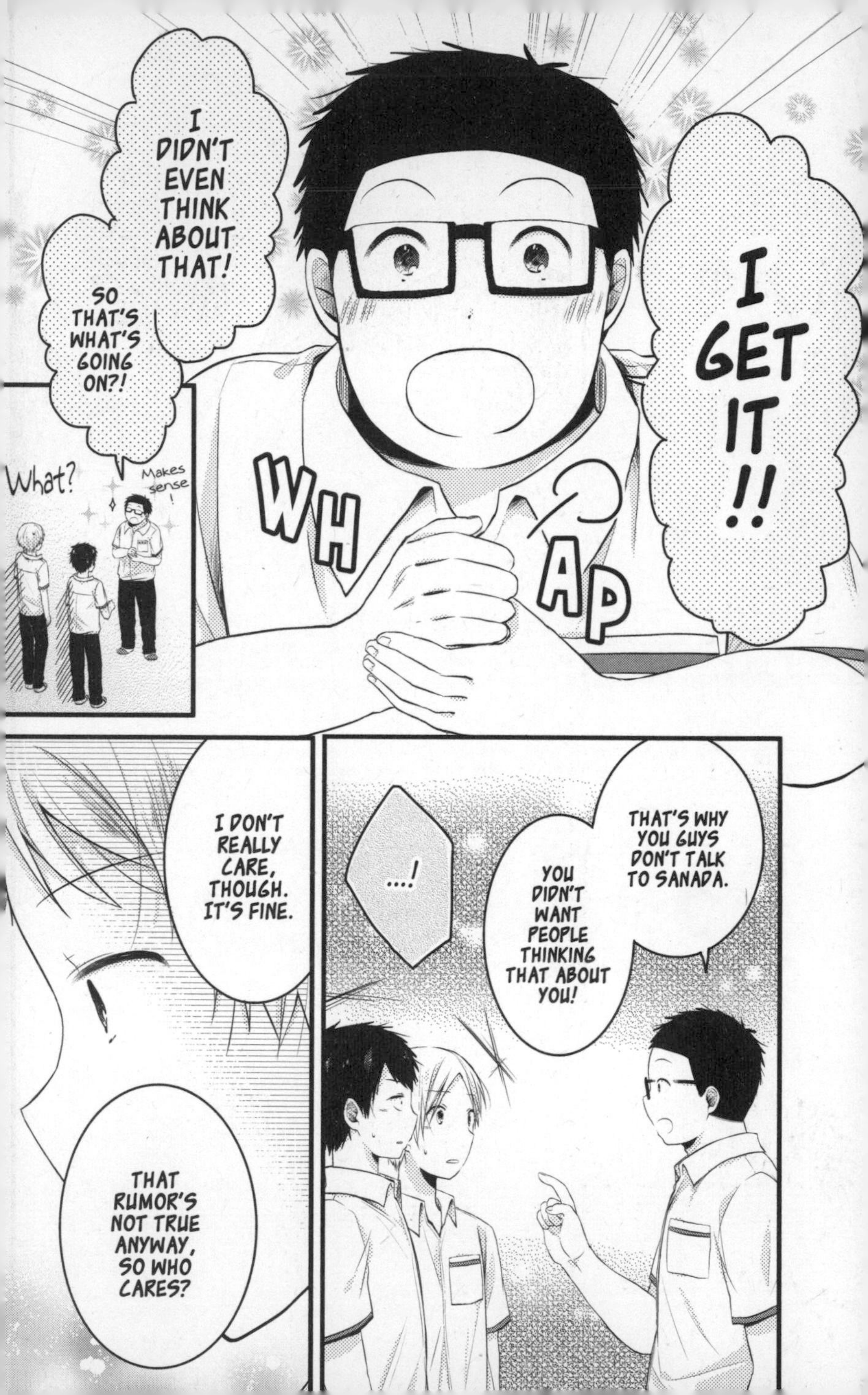
I GET IT!!
WHAP
I DIDN'T EVEN THINK ABOUT THAT!
SO THAT'S WHAT'S GOING ON?!
Makes sense!
What?
THAT'S WHY YOU GUYS DON'T TALK TO SANADA.
YOU DIDN'T WANT PEOPLE THINKING THAT ABOUT YOU!
...!
I DON'T REALLY CARE, THOUGH. IT'S FINE.
THAT RUMOR'S NOT TRUE ANYWAY, SO WHO CARES?

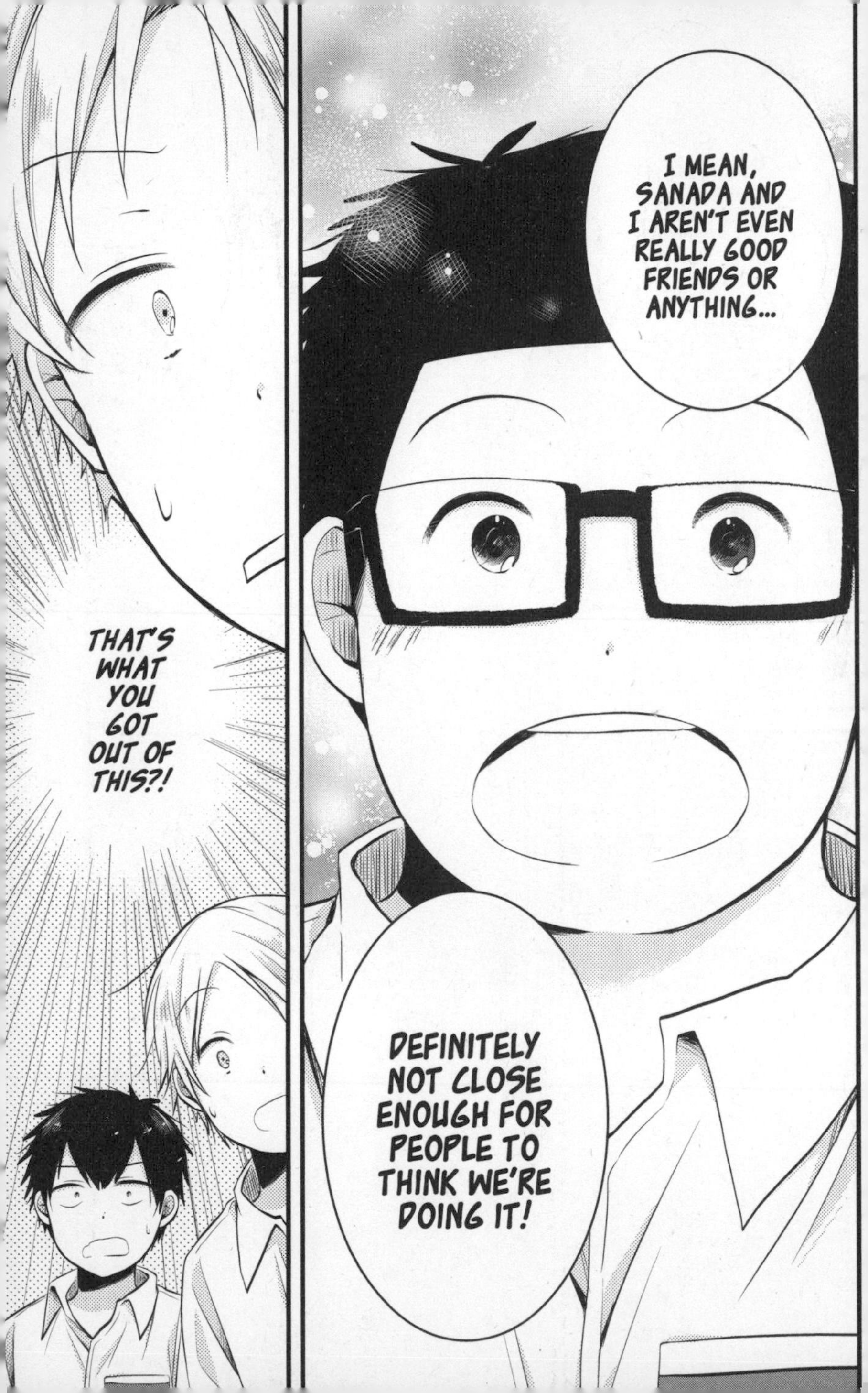
I MEAN, SANADA AND I AREN'T EVEN REALLY GOOD FRIENDS OR ANYTHING...
DEFINITELY NOT CLOSE ENOUGH FOR PEOPLE TO THINK WE'RE DOING IT!
THAT'S WHAT YOU GOT OUT OF THIS?!

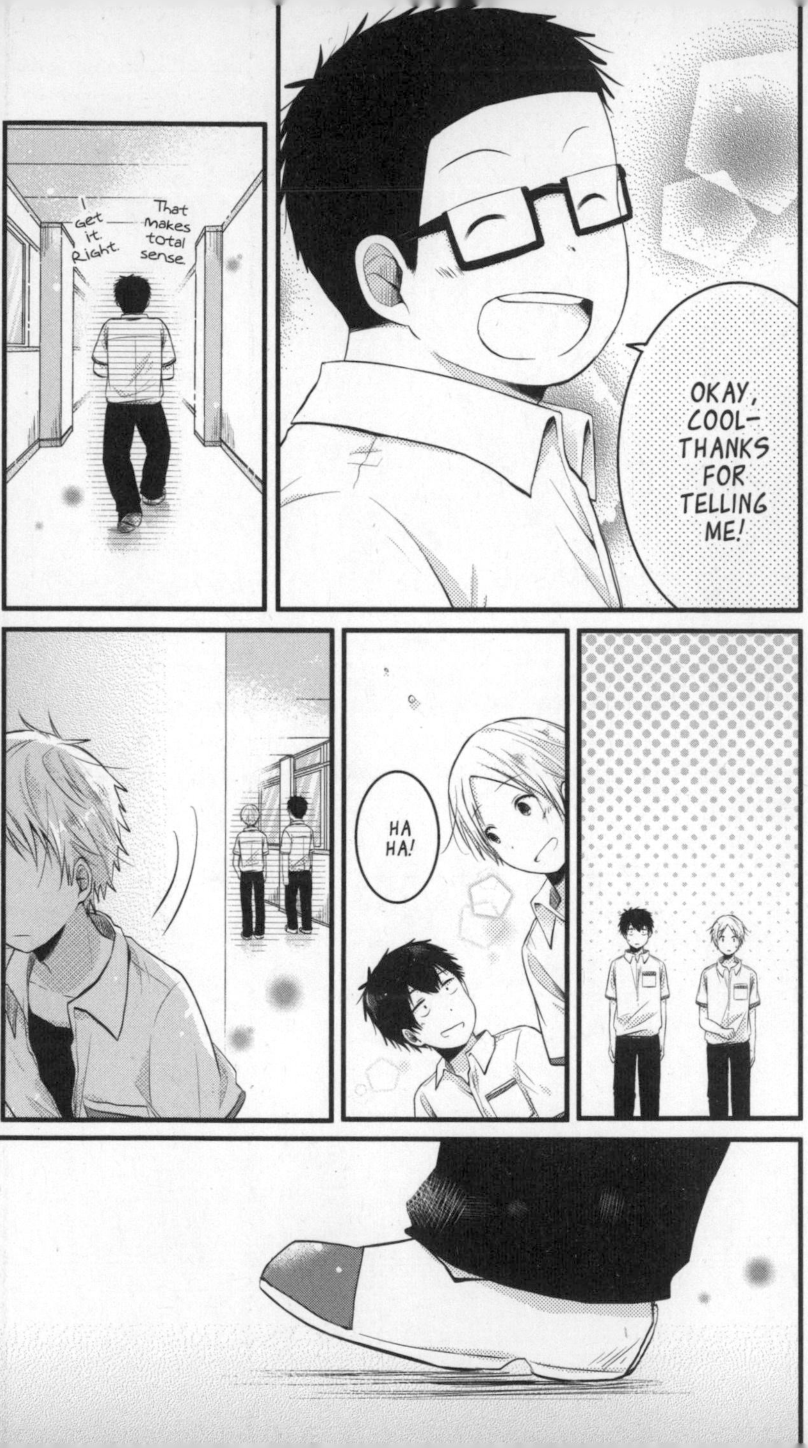
OKAY, COOL— THANKS FOR TELLING ME!
That makes total sense.
I get it. Right.
HA HA!

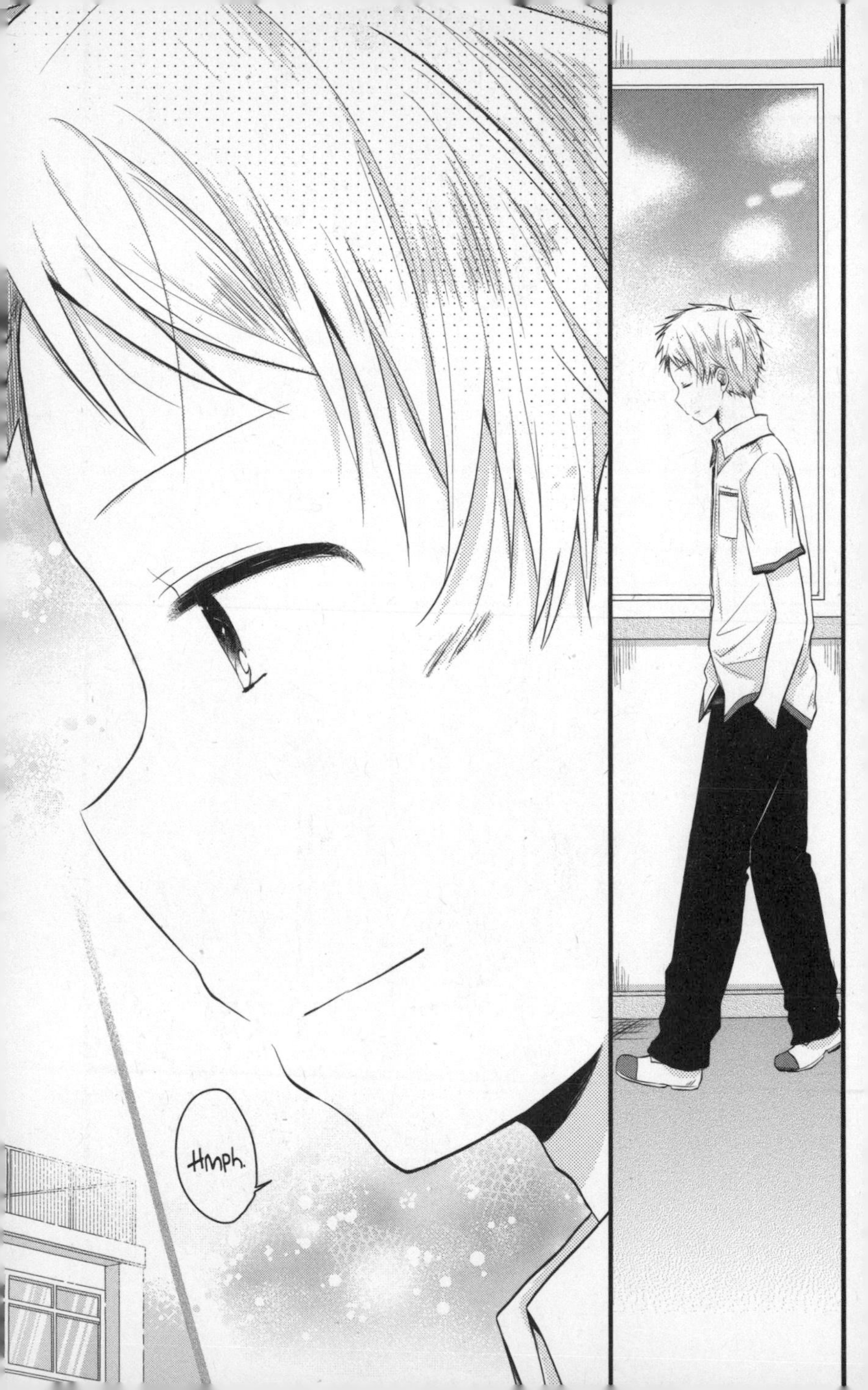
Hmph.

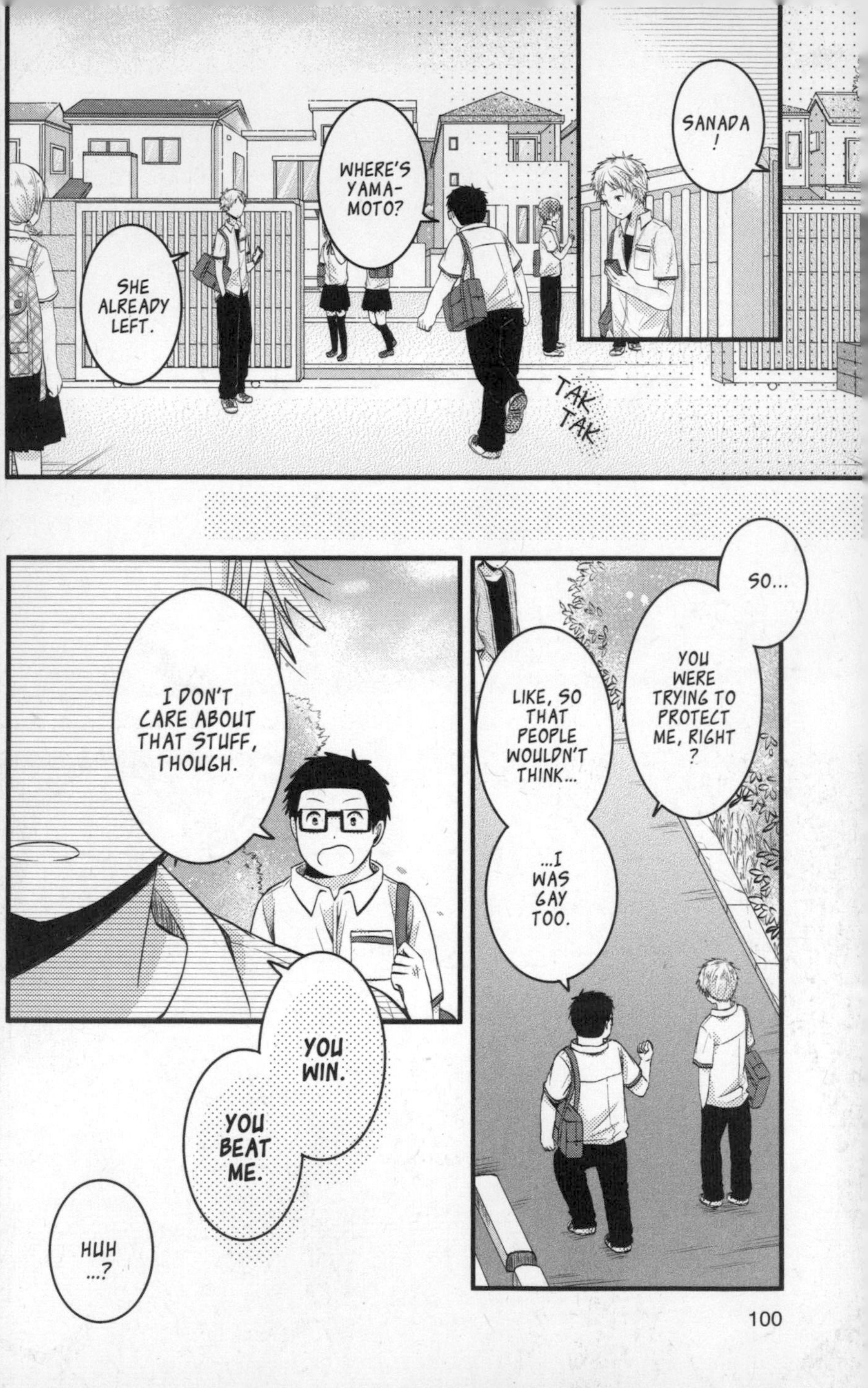
SANADA!
WHERE'S YAMAMOTO?
SHE ALREADY LEFT.
TAK TAK
SO...
YOU WERE TRYING TO PROTECT ME, RIGHT?
LIKE, SO THAT PEOPLE WOULDN'T THINK...
...I WAS GAY TOO.
I DON'T CARE ABOUT THAT STUFF, THOUGH.
YOU WIN.
YOU BEAT ME.
HUH...?

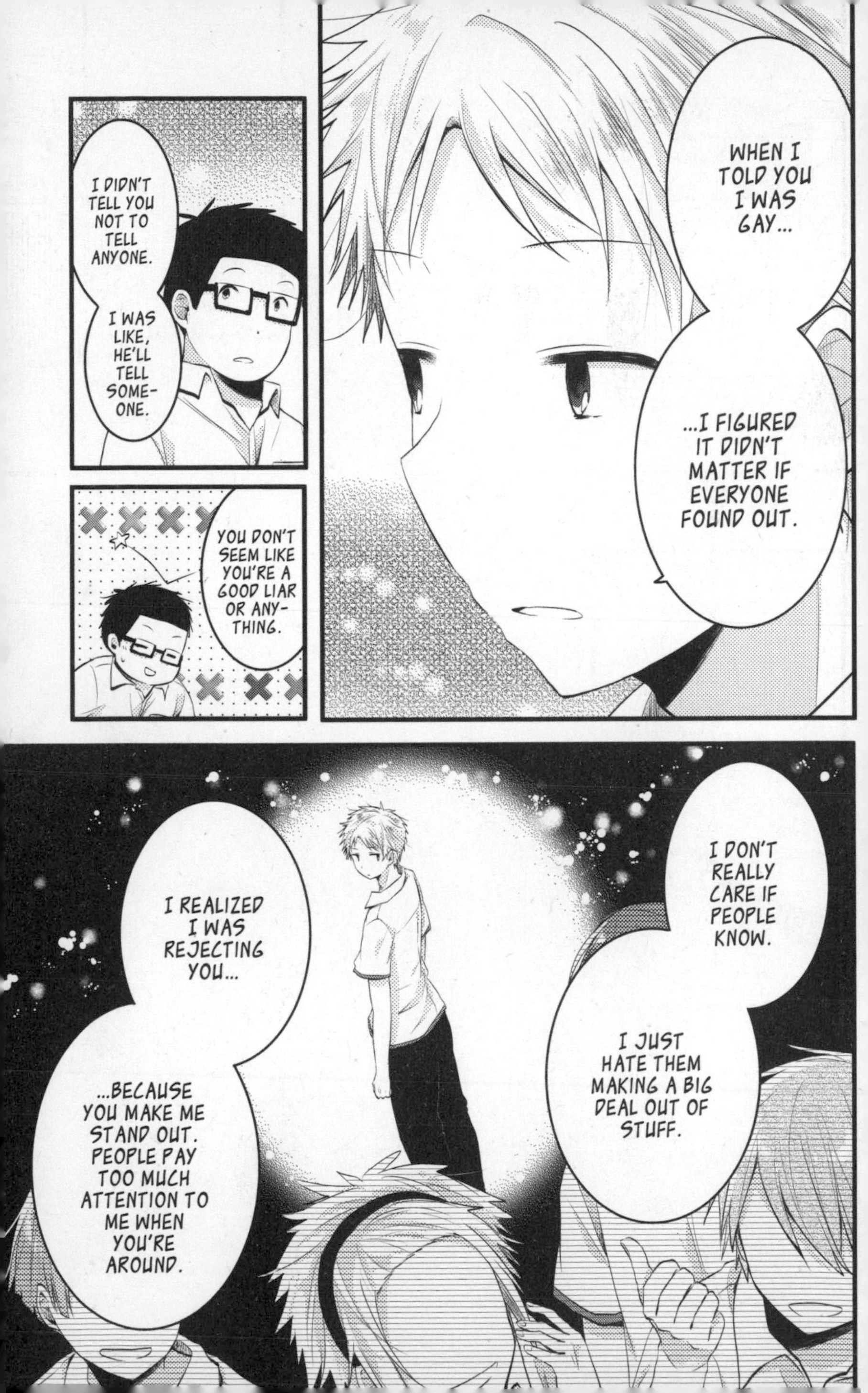
WHEN I TOLD YOU I WAS GAY...
...I FIGURED IT DIDN'T MATTER IF EVERYONE FOUND OUT.
I DIDN'T TELL YOU NOT TO TELL ANYONE.
I WAS LIKE, HE'LL TELL SOME-ONE.
YOU DON'T SEEM LIKE YOU'RE A GOOD LIAR OR ANY-THING.
I DON'T REALLY CARE IF PEOPLE KNOW.
I JUST HATE THEM MAKING A BIG DEAL OUT OF STUFF.
I REALIZED I WAS REJECTING YOU...
...BECAUSE YOU MAKE ME STAND OUT. PEOPLE PAY TOO MUCH ATTENTION TO ME WHEN YOU'RE AROUND.

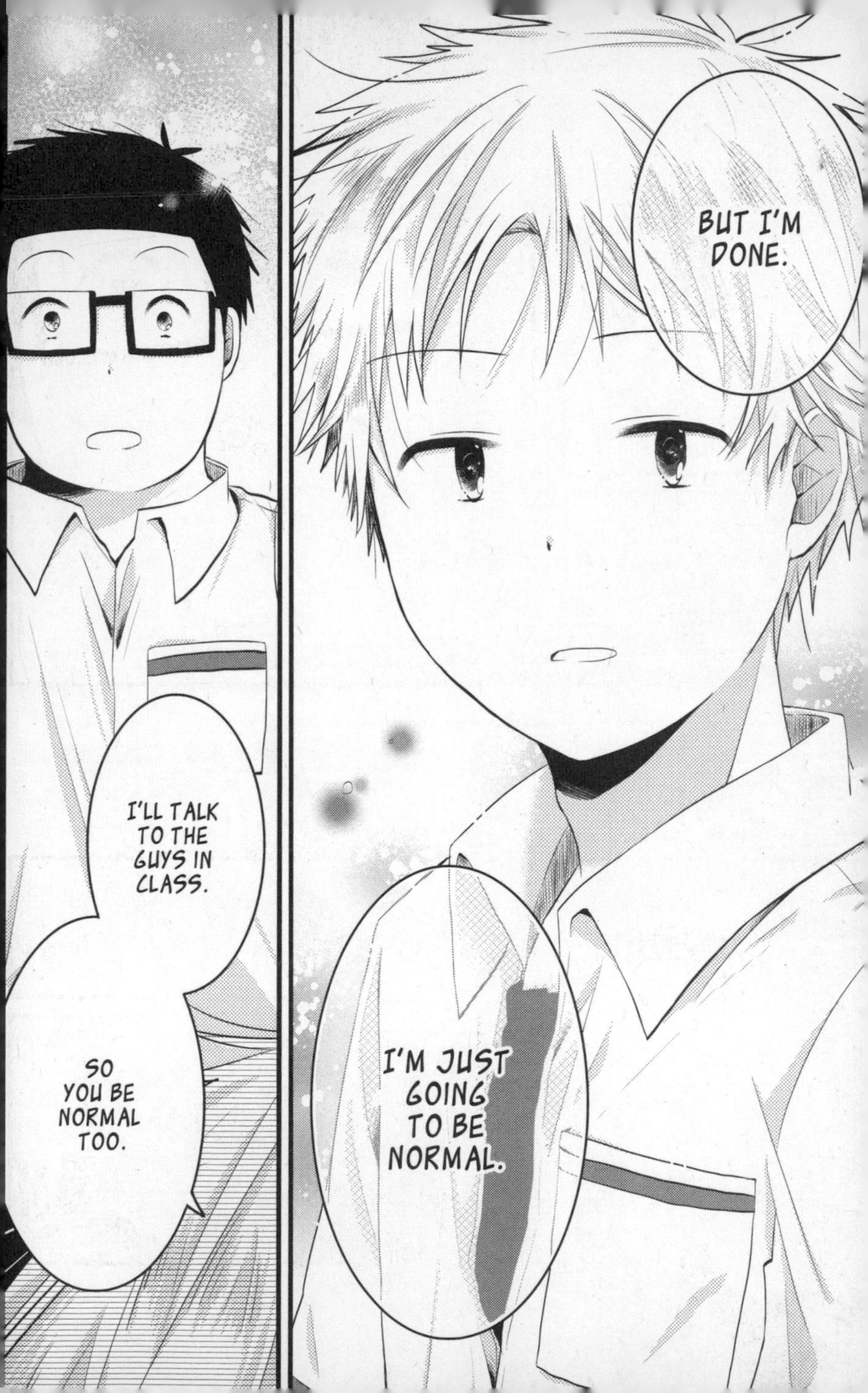
BUT I'M DONE.
I'M JUST GOING TO BE NORMAL.
I'LL TALK TO THE GUYS IN CLASS.
SO YOU BE NORMAL TOO.

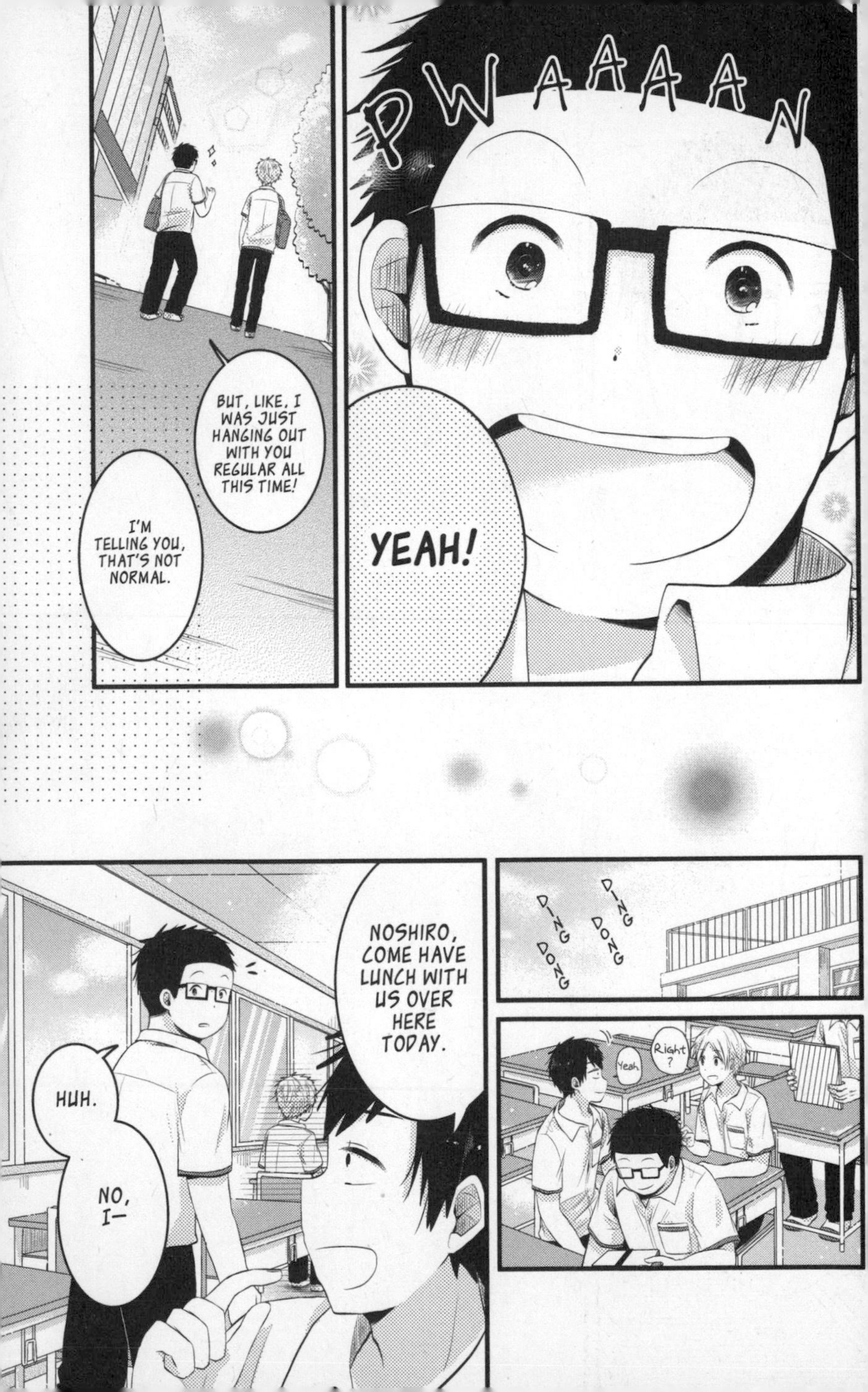
PWAAAAN
YEAH!
BUT, LIKE, I WAS JUST HANGING OUT WITH YOU REGULAR ALL THIS TIME!
I'M TELLING YOU, THAT'S NOT NORMAL.
DING DONG
DING DONG
Right?
Yeah
NOSHIRO, COME HAVE LUNCH WITH US OVER HERE TODAY.
HUH.
NO, I—

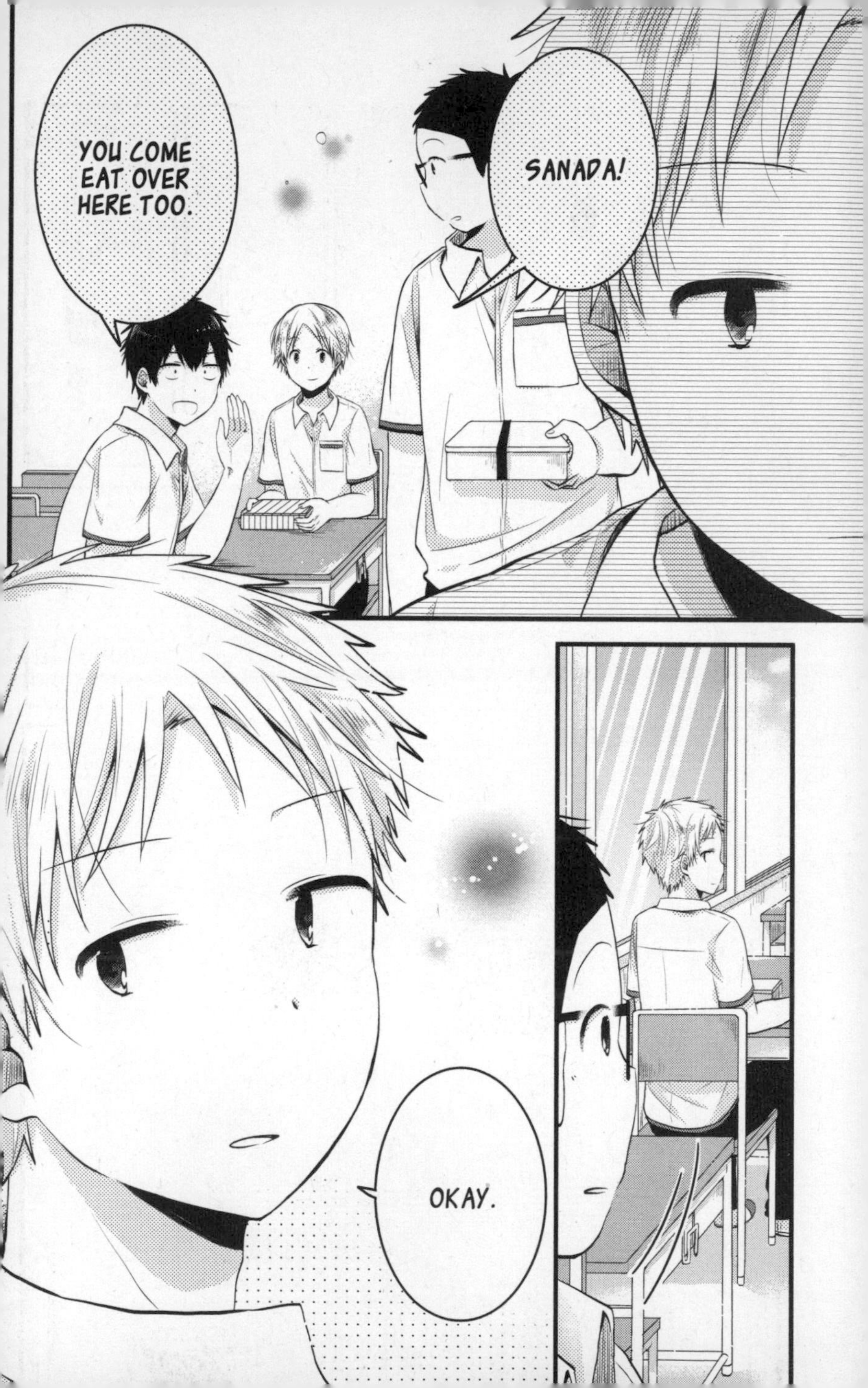
SANADA!
YOU COME EAT OVER HERE TOO.
OKAY.

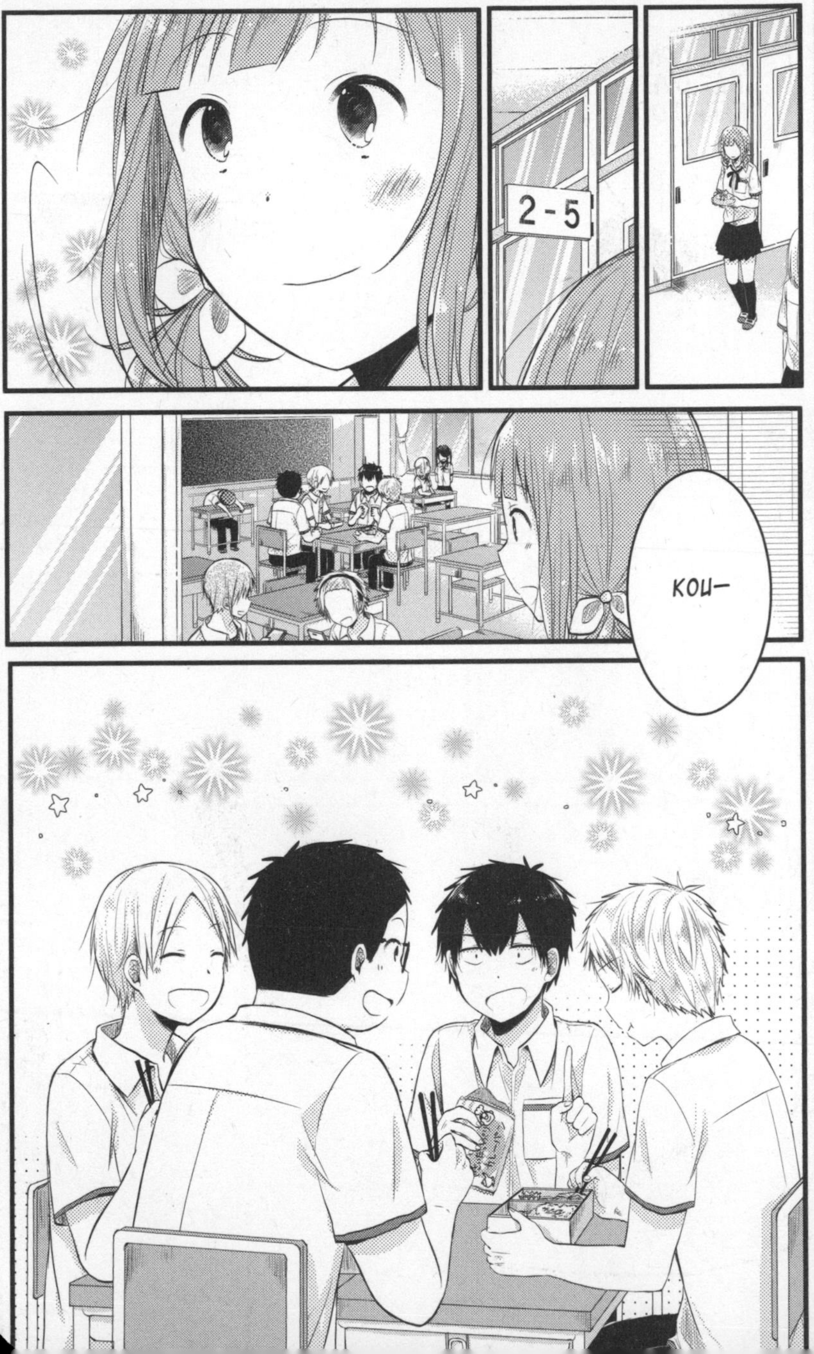
2-5
KOU—

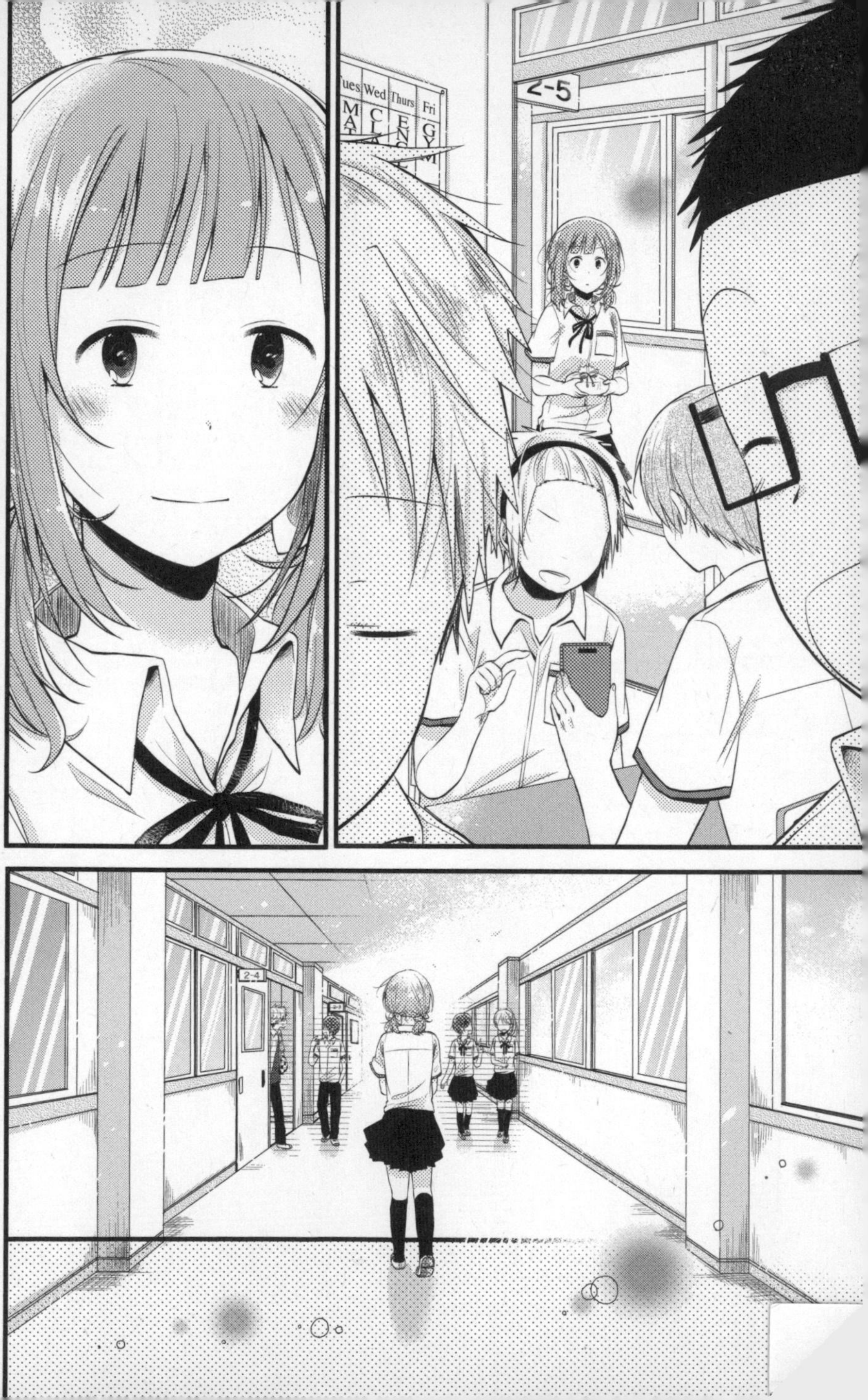
Tues Wed Thurs Fri
2-5
2-4

That Blue
Sky Feeling

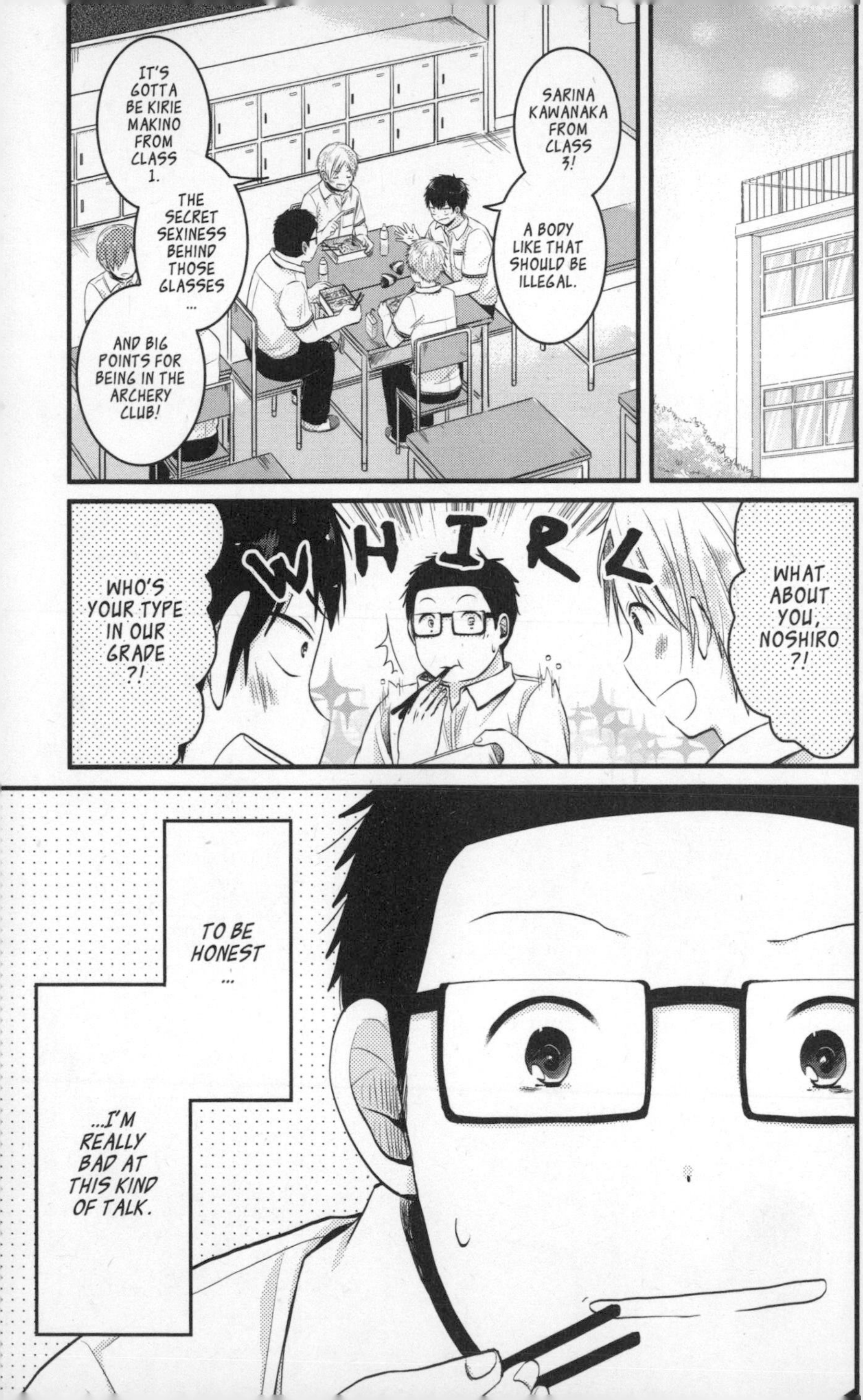
SARINA KAWANAKA FROM CLASS 3!
A BODY LIKE THAT SHOULD BE ILLEGAL.
IT'S GOTTA BE KIRIE MAKINO FROM CLASS 1.
THE SECRET SEXINESS BEHIND THOSE GLASSES...
AND BIG POINTS FOR BEING IN THE ARCHERY CLUB!
WHAT ABOUT YOU, NOSHIRO?!
WHIRL
WHO'S YOUR TYPE IN OUR GRADE?!
TO BE HONEST...
...I'M REALLY BAD AT THIS KIND OF TALK.

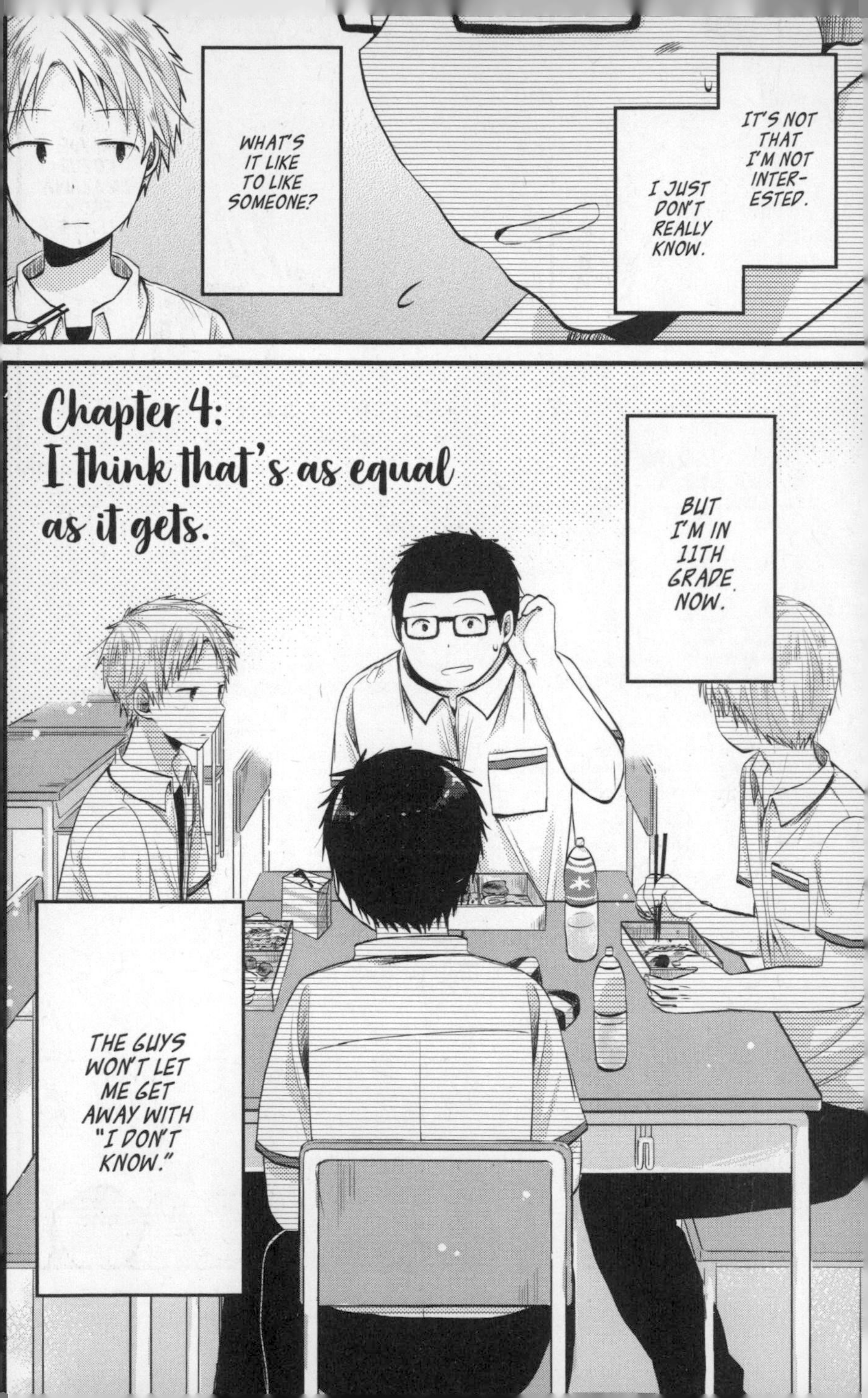
IT'S NOT THAT I'M NOT INTER-ESTED.
I JUST DON'T REALLY KNOW.
WHAT'S IT LIKE TO LIKE SOMEONE?
Chapter 4: I think that's as equal as it gets.
BUT I'M IN 11TH GRADE NOW.
THE GUYS WON'T LET ME GET AWAY WITH "I DON'T KNOW."

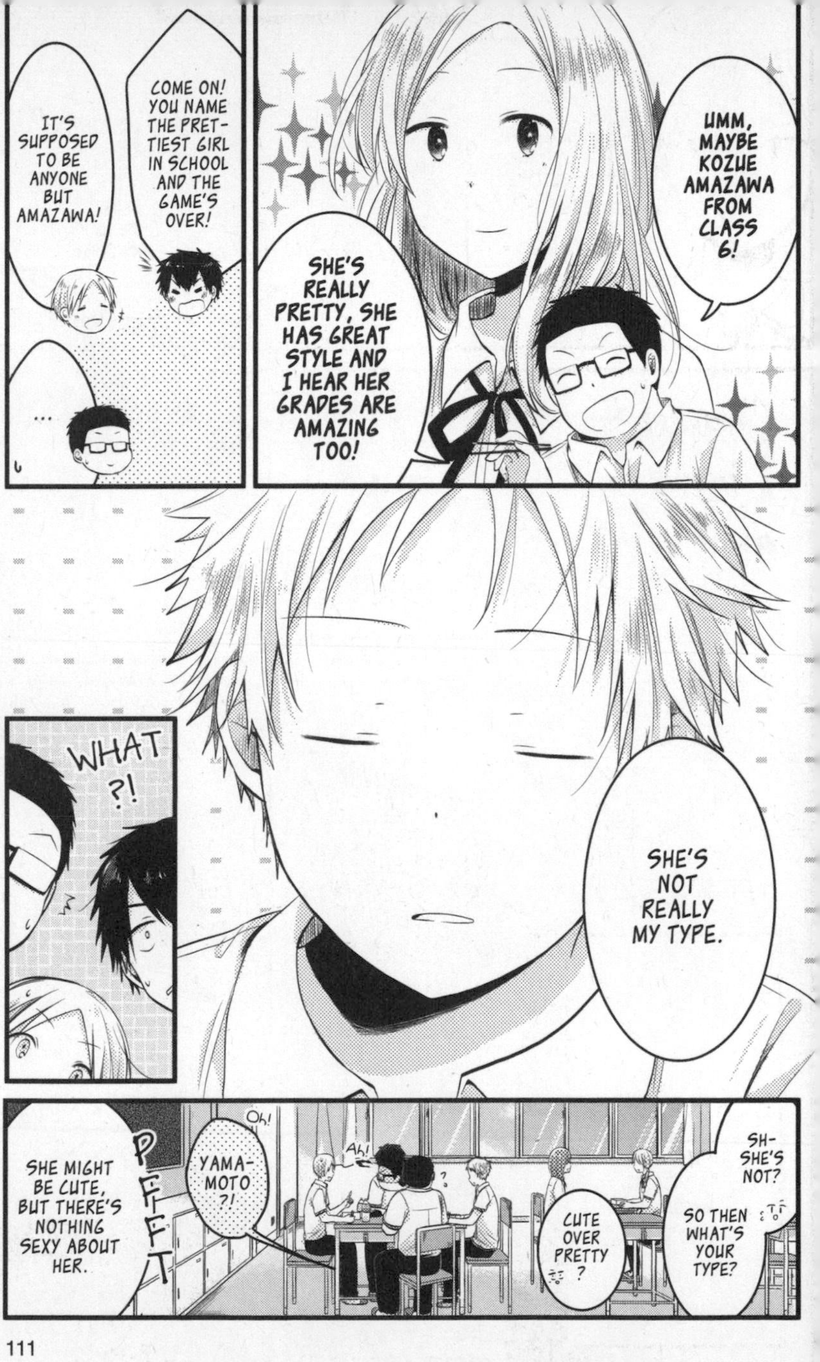
UMM, MAYBE KOZUE AMAZAWA FROM CLASS 6!
SHE'S REALLY PRETTY, SHE HAS GREAT STYLE AND I HEAR HER GRADES ARE AMAZING TOO!
COME ON! YOU NAME THE PRET-TIEST GIRL IN SCHOOL AND THE GAME'S OVER!
IT'S SUPPOSED TO BE ANYONE BUT AMAZAWA!
...
SHE'S NOT REALLY MY TYPE.
WHAT?!
SH-SHE'S NOT?
SO THEN WHAT'S YOUR TYPE?
CUTE OVER PRETTY?
Oh!
Ah!
YAMA-MOTO?!
PFFFT
SHE MIGHT BE CUTE, BUT THERE'S NOTHING SEXY ABOUT HER.

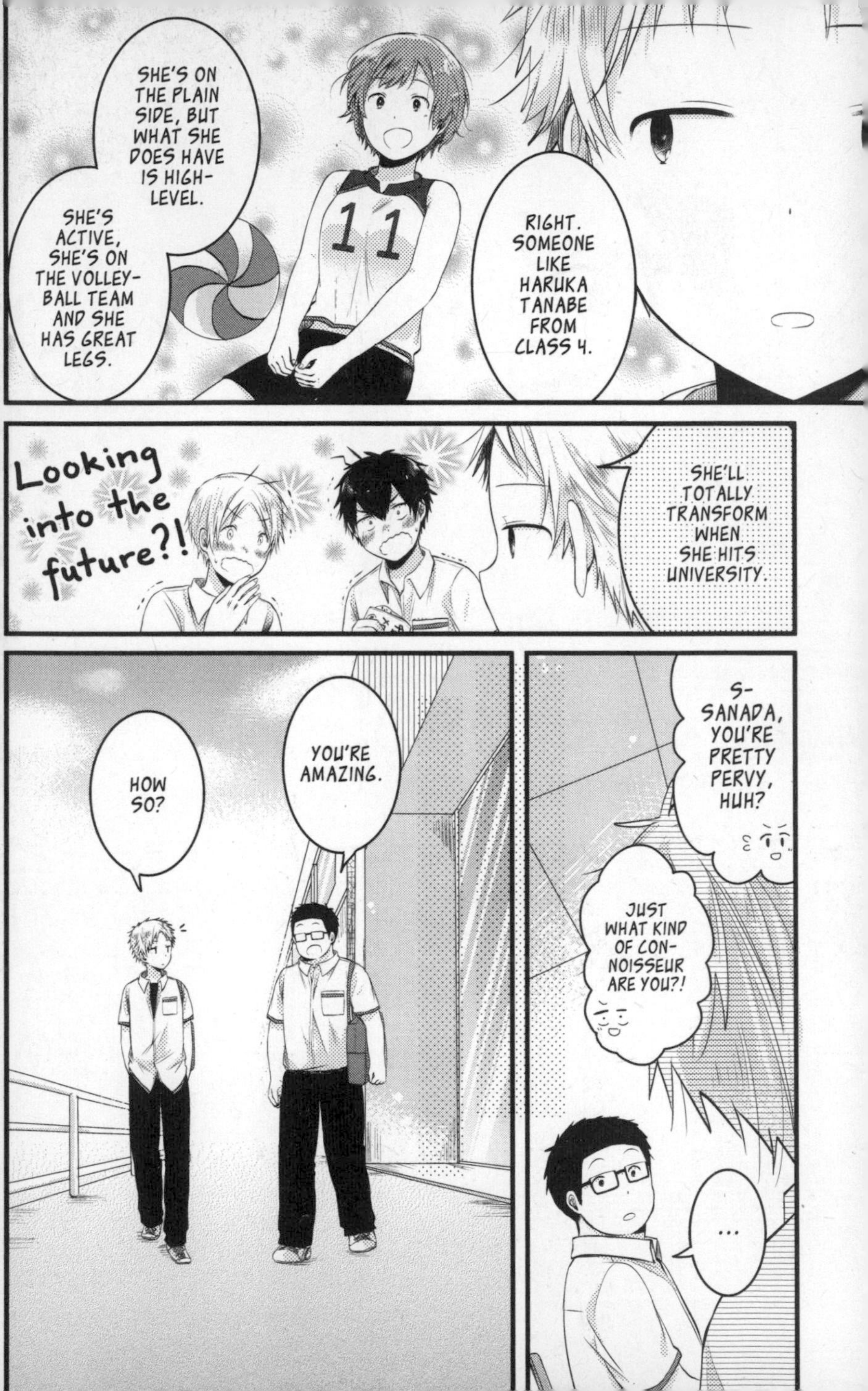
RIGHT. SOMEONE LIKE HARUKA TANABE FROM CLASS 4.
SHE'S ON THE PLAIN SIDE, BUT WHAT SHE DOES HAVE IS HIGH-LEVEL.
SHE'S ACTIVE, SHE'S ON THE VOLLEY-BALL TEAM AND SHE HAS GREAT LEGS.
SHE'LL TOTALLY TRANSFORM WHEN SHE HITS UNIVERSITY.
Looking into the future?!
S-SANADA, YOU'RE PRETTY PERVY, HUH?
JUST WHAT KIND OF CON-NOISSEUR ARE YOU?!
...
YOU'RE AMAZING.
HOW SO?

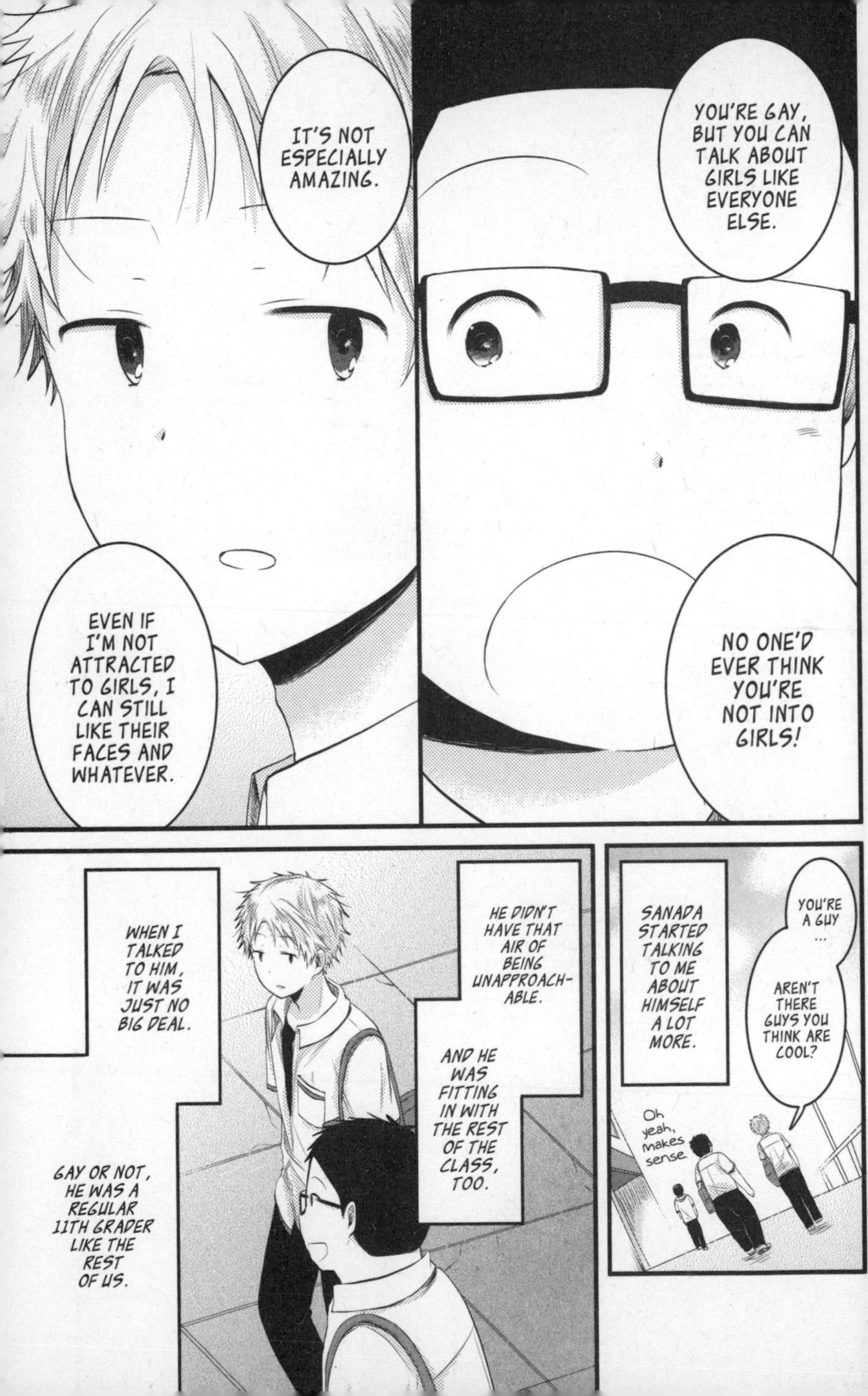
YOU'RE GAY, BUT YOU CAN TALK ABOUT GIRLS LIKE EVERYONE ELSE.
NO ONE'D EVER THINK YOU'RE NOT INTO GIRLS!
IT'S NOT ESPECIALLY AMAZING.
EVEN IF I'M NOT ATTRACTED TO GIRLS, I CAN STILL LIKE THEIR FACES AND WHATEVER.
YOU'RE A GUY ...
AREN'T THERE GUYS YOU THINK ARE COOL?
SANADA STARTED TALKING TO ME ABOUT HIMSELF A LOT MORE.
Oh yeah, makes sense.
HE DIDN'T HAVE THAT AIR OF BEING UNAPPROACH-ABLE.
AND HE WAS FITTING IN WITH THE REST OF THE CLASS, TOO.
WHEN I TALKED TO HIM, IT WAS JUST NO BIG DEAL.
GAY OR NOT, HE WAS A REGULAR 11TH GRADER LIKE THE REST OF US.

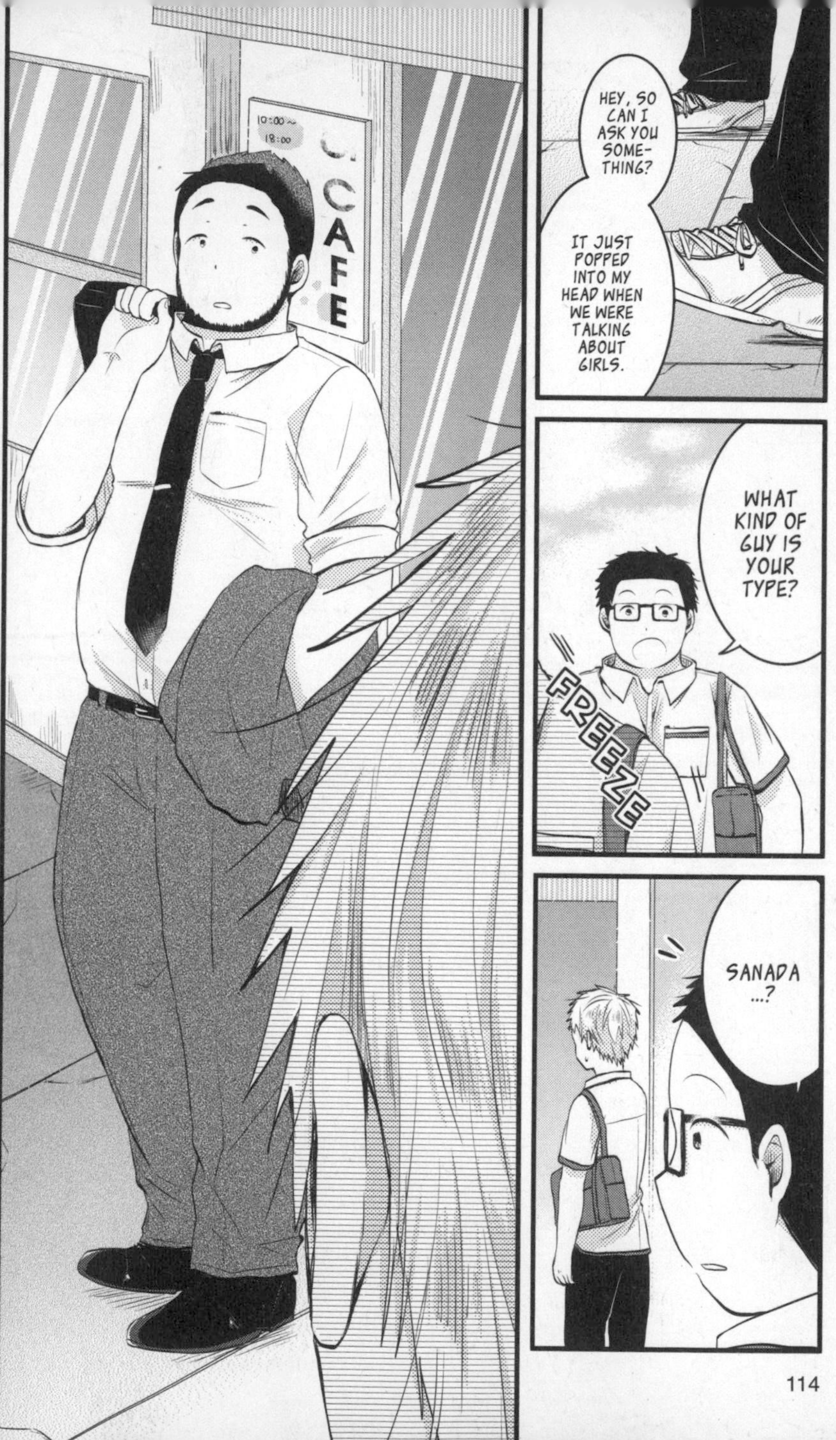
HEY, SO CAN I ASK YOU SOME-THING?
IT JUST POPPED INTO MY HEAD WHEN WE WERE TALKING ABOUT GIRLS.
WHAT KIND OF GUY IS YOUR TYPE?
FREEZE
SANADA ...?
10:00 ~ 18:00
CAFE

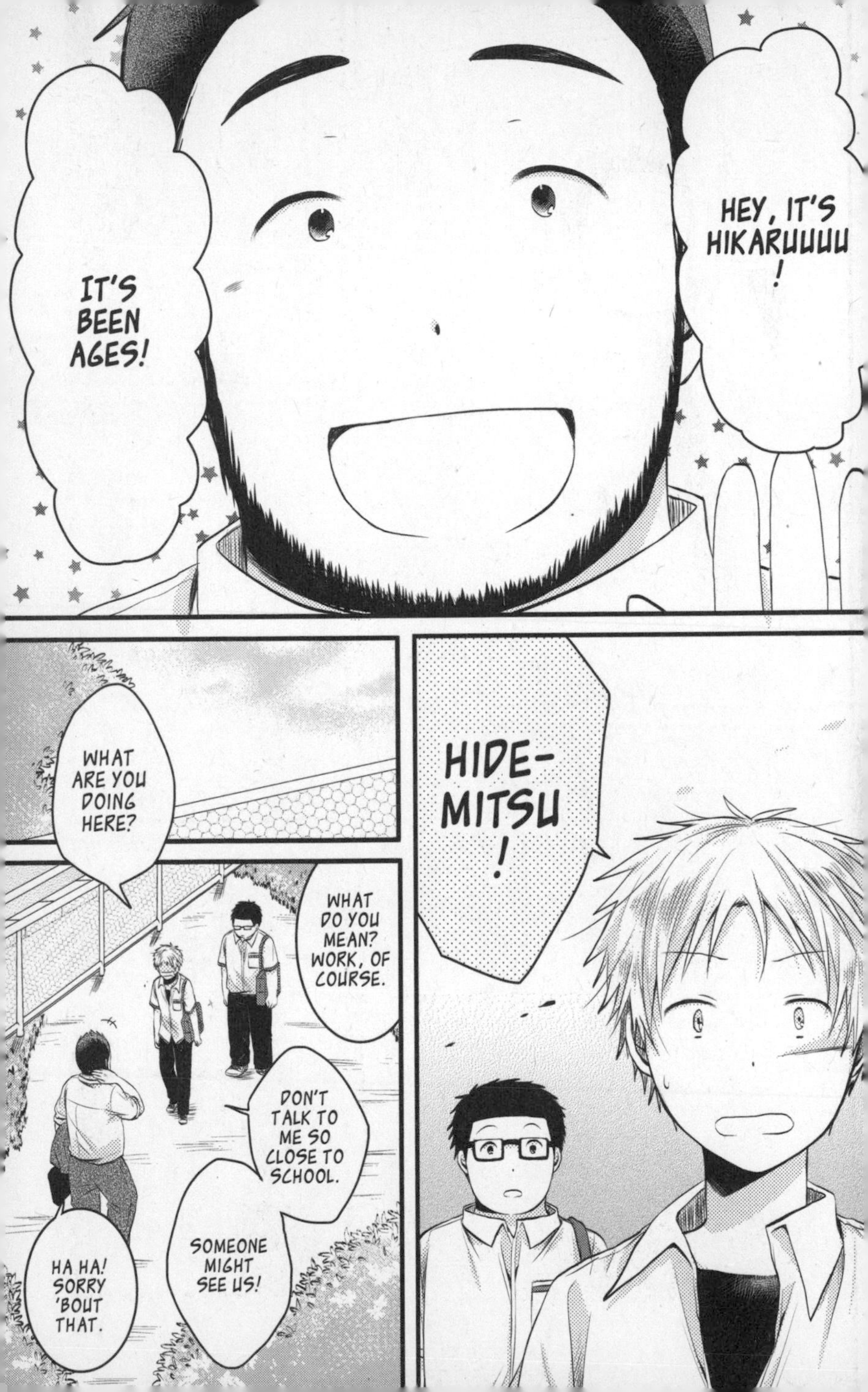
HEY, IT'S HIKARUUUU!
IT'S BEEN AGES!
HIDE-MITSU!
WHAT ARE YOU DOING HERE?
WHAT DO YOU MEAN? WORK, OF COURSE.
DON'T TALK TO ME SO CLOSE TO SCHOOL.
SOMEONE MIGHT SEE US!
HA HA! SORRY 'BOUT THAT.

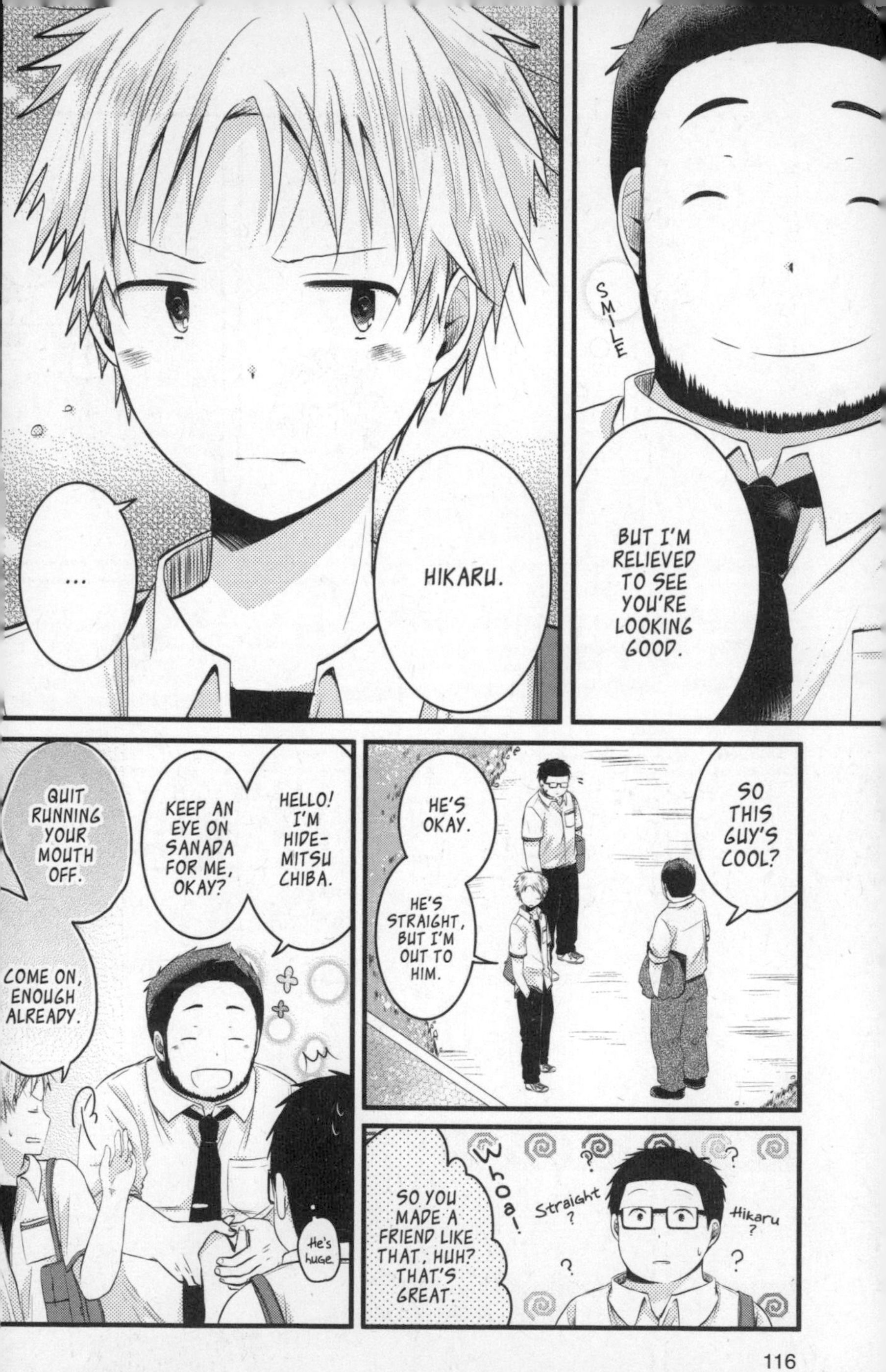
SMILE
BUT I'M RELIEVED TO SEE YOU'RE LOOKING GOOD.
HIKARU.
...
SO THIS GUY'S COOL?
HE'S OKAY.
HE'S STRAIGHT, BUT I'M OUT TO HIM.
Hikaru?
Straight?
Whoa!
SO YOU MADE A FRIEND LIKE THAT, HUH? THAT'S GREAT.
HELLO! I'M HIDE-MITSU CHIBA.
KEEP AN EYE ON SANADA FOR ME, OKAY?
QUIT RUNNING YOUR MOUTH OFF.
COME ON, ENOUGH ALREADY.
He's huge.

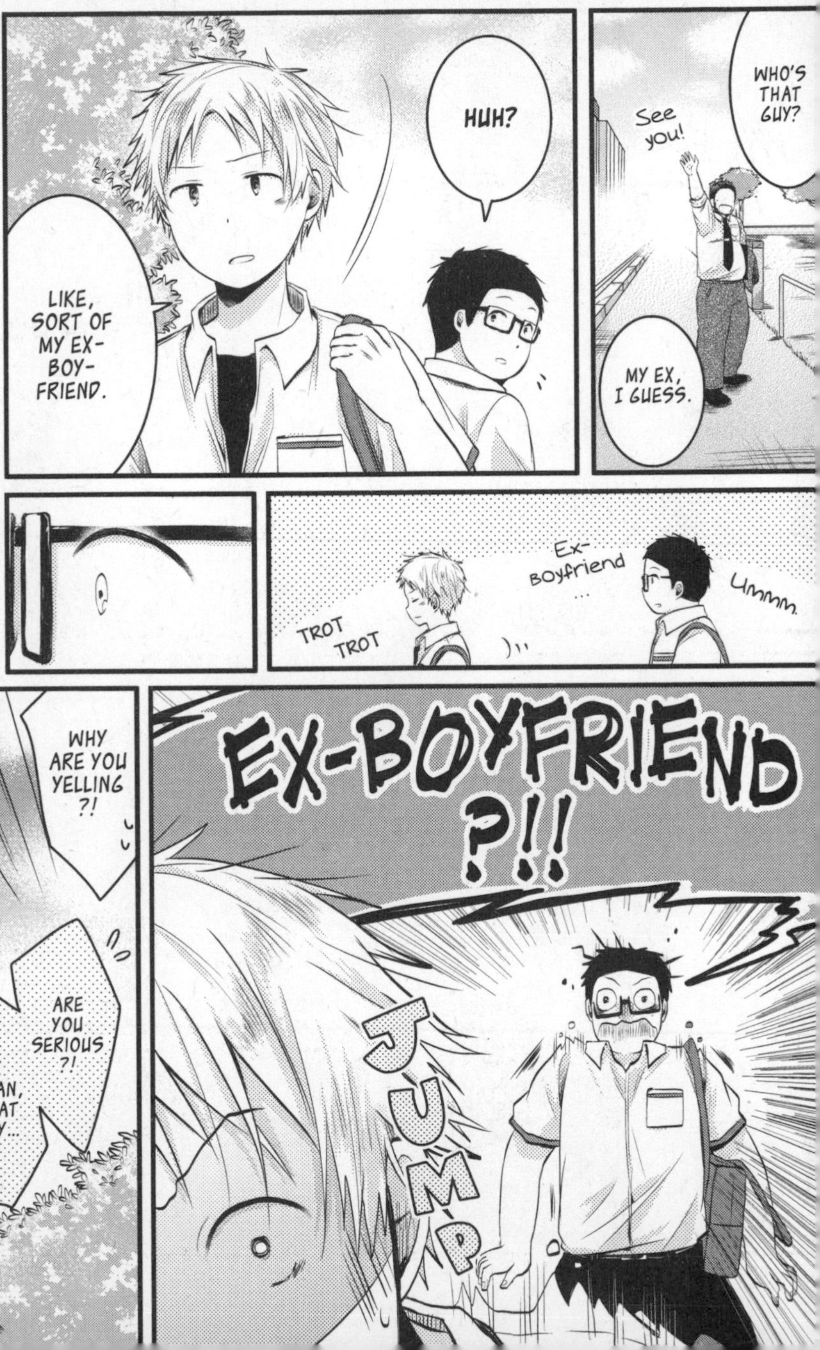
WHO'S THAT GUY?
See you!
MY EX, I GUESS.
HUH?
LIKE, SORT OF MY EX-BOYFRIEND.
Ex-boyfriend ...
Ummm.
TROT TROT
EX-BOYFRIEND ?!!
JUMP
WHY ARE YOU YELLING ?!
ARE YOU SERIOUS ?!
I MEAN, THAT GUY...

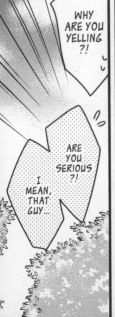

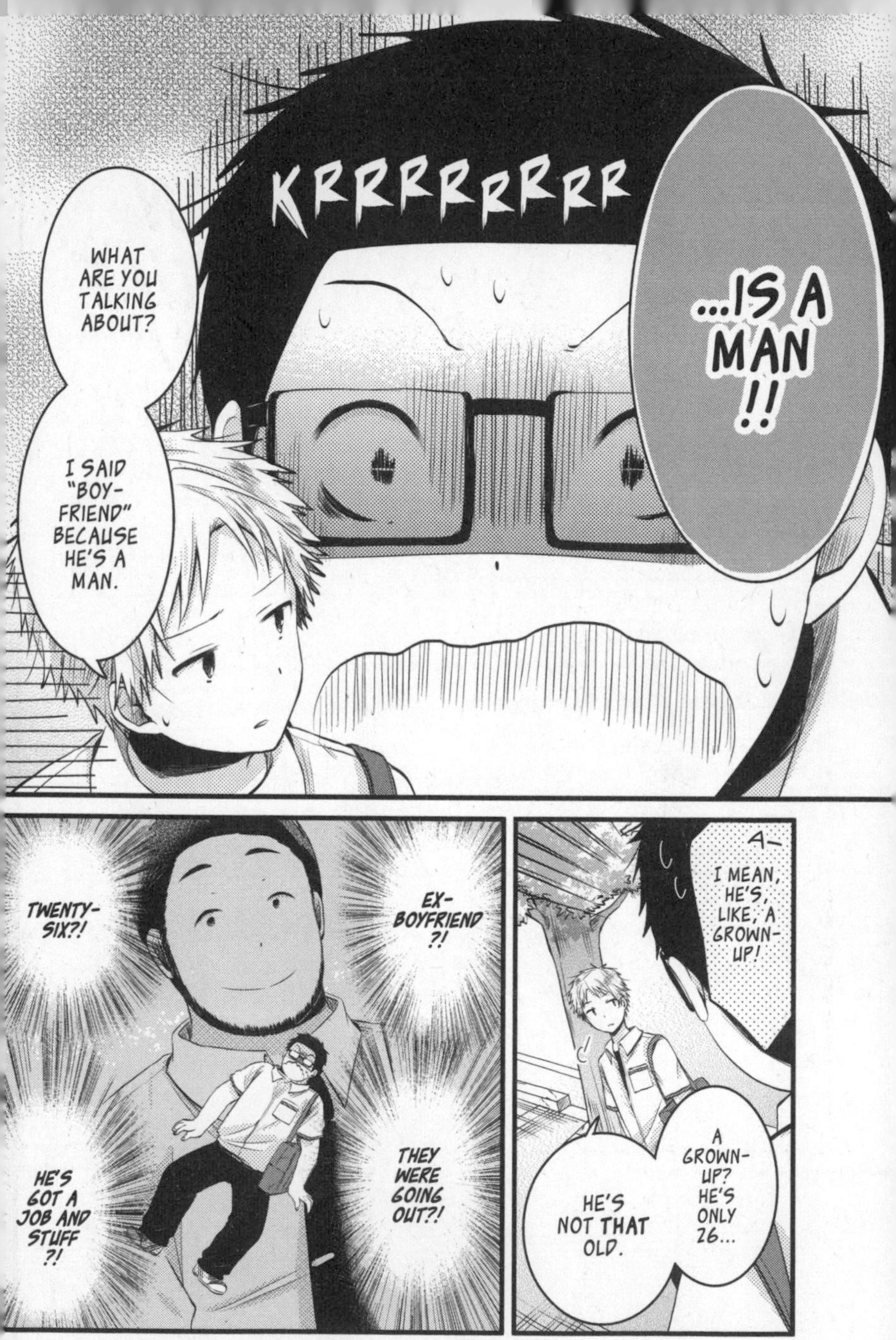
...IS A MAN!!
KRRRRRRRR
WHAT ARE YOU TALKING ABOUT?
I SAID "BOY-FRIEND" BECAUSE HE'S A MAN.
A— I MEAN, HE'S, LIKE, A GROWN-UP!
A GROWN-UP? HE'S ONLY 26...
HE'S NOT THAT OLD.
EX-BOYFRIEND?!
TWENTY-SIX?!
THEY WERE GOING OUT?!
HE'S GOT A JOB AND STUFF?!

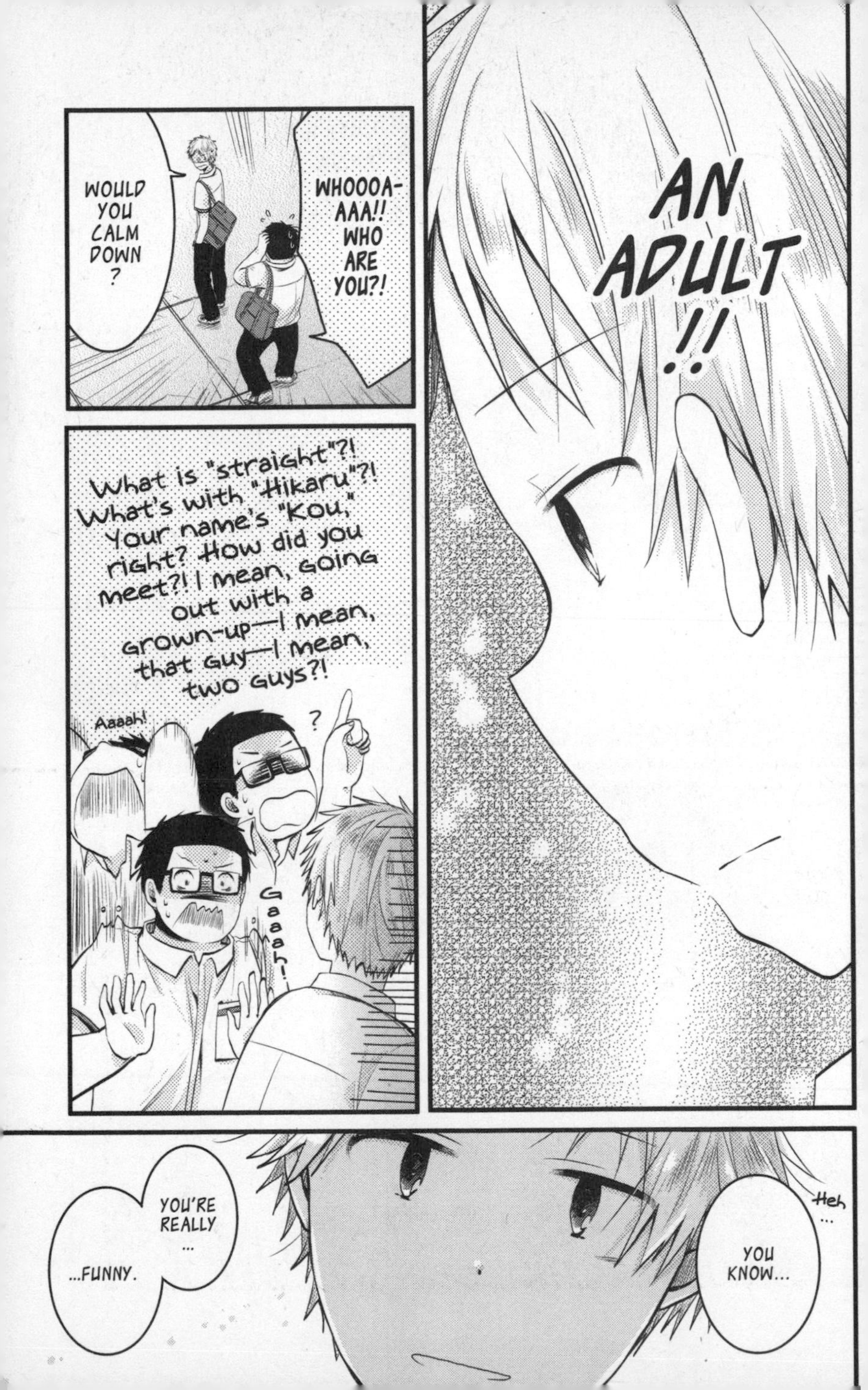
AN ADULT!!
WHOOOA-AAA!! WHO ARE YOU?!
WOULD YOU CALM DOWN?
What is "straight"?! What's with "Hikaru"?! Your name's "Kou," right? How did you meet?! I mean, going out with a grown-up—I mean, that guy—I mean, two guys?!
?
Aaaah!
Gaaaah!
Heh...
YOU KNOW...
YOU'RE REALLY...
...FUNNY.

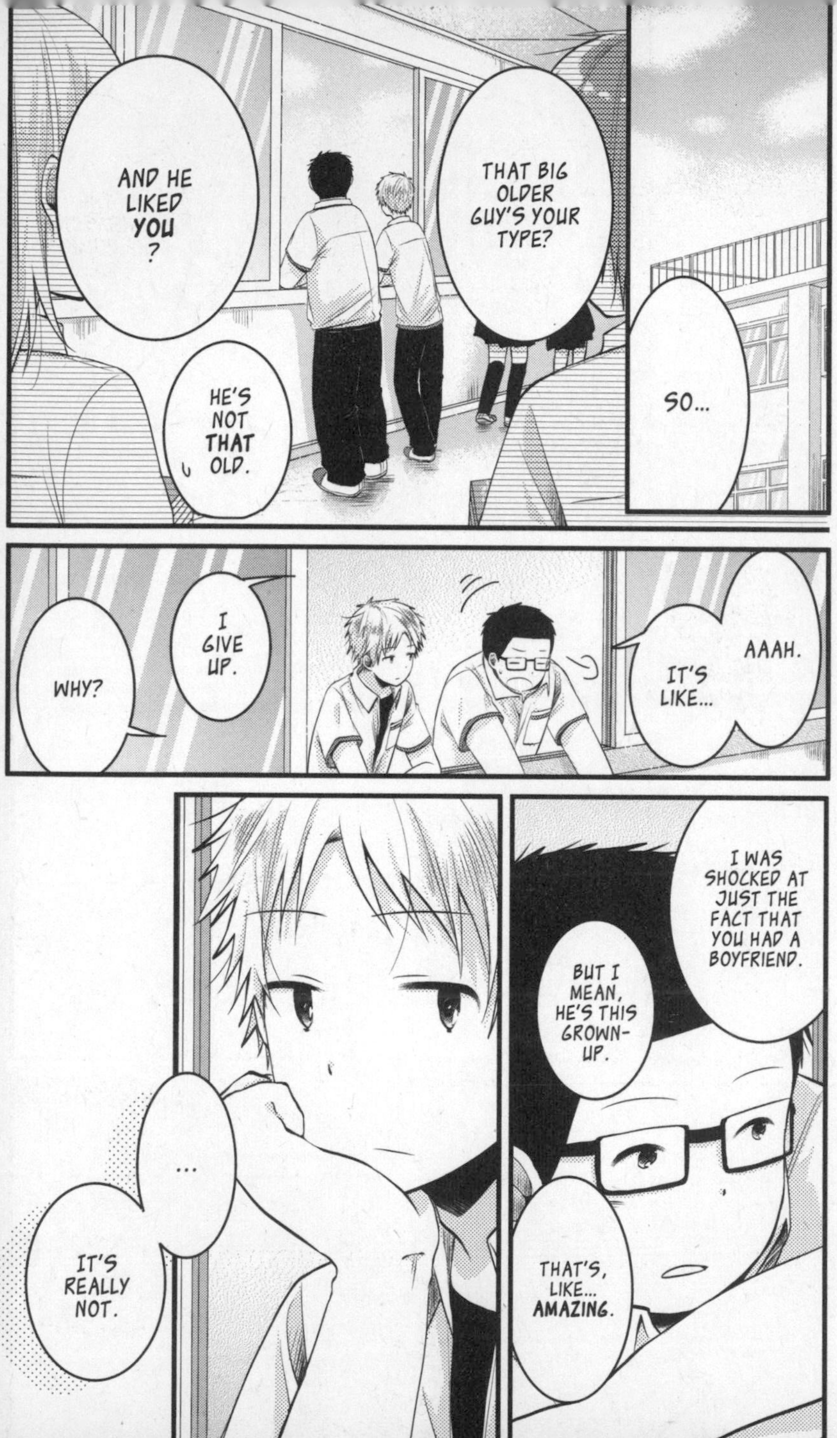
SO...
THAT BIG OLDER GUY'S YOUR TYPE?
AND HE LIKED YOU?
HE'S NOT THAT OLD.
AAAH. IT'S LIKE...
I GIVE UP.
WHY?
I WAS SHOCKED AT JUST THE FACT THAT YOU HAD A BOYFRIEND.
BUT I MEAN, HE'S THIS GROWN-UP.
THAT'S, LIKE... AMAZING.
...
IT'S REALLY NOT.

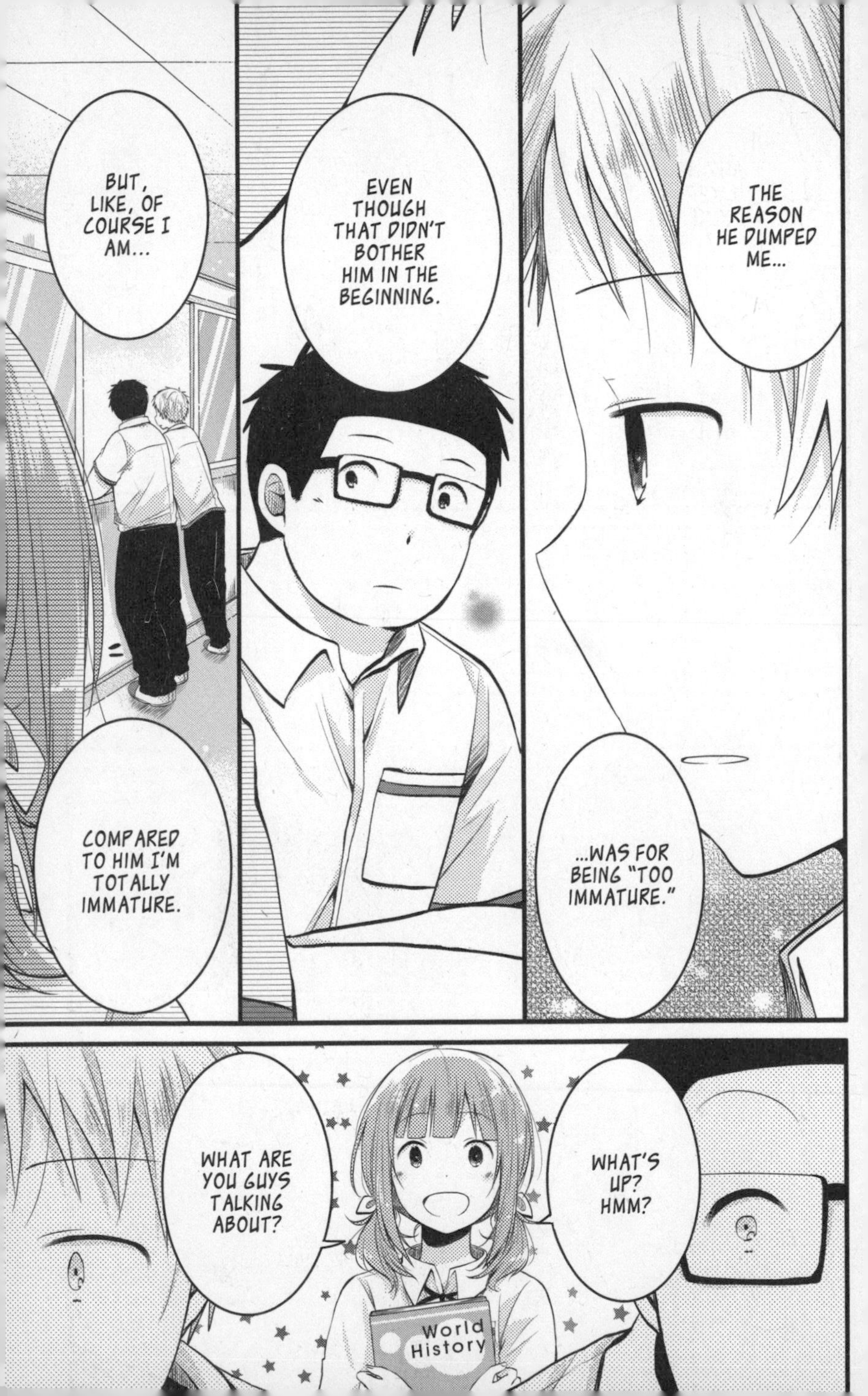
THE REASON HE DUMPED ME...
...WAS FOR BEING "TOO IMMATURE."
EVEN THOUGH THAT DIDN'T BOTHER HIM IN THE BEGINNING.
BUT, LIKE, OF COURSE I AM...
COMPARED TO HIM I'M TOTALLY IMMATURE.
WHAT'S UP? HMM?
WHAT ARE YOU GUYS TALKING ABOUT?
World History

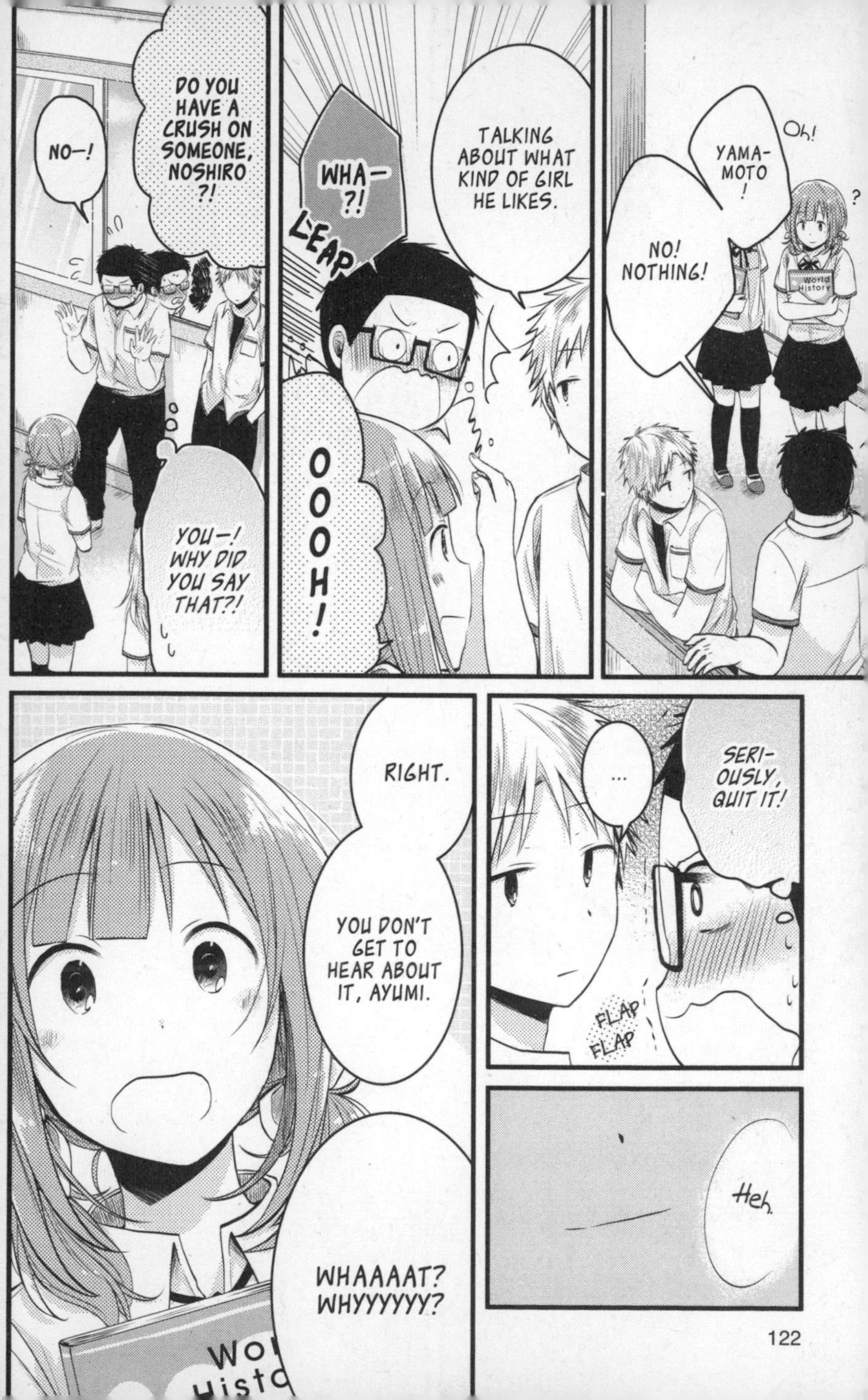
Oh!
YAMA-MOTO!
?
World History
NO! NOTHING!
TALKING ABOUT WHAT KIND OF GIRL HE LIKES.
WHA—?!
LEAP
OOOOH!
DO YOU HAVE A CRUSH ON SOMEONE, NOSHIRO?!
NO—!
YOU—! WHY DID YOU SAY THAT?!
SERI-OUSLY, QUIT IT!
...
FLAP FLAP
Heh.
RIGHT.
YOU DON'T GET TO HEAR ABOUT IT, AYUMI.
WHAAAAT? WHYYYYYY?

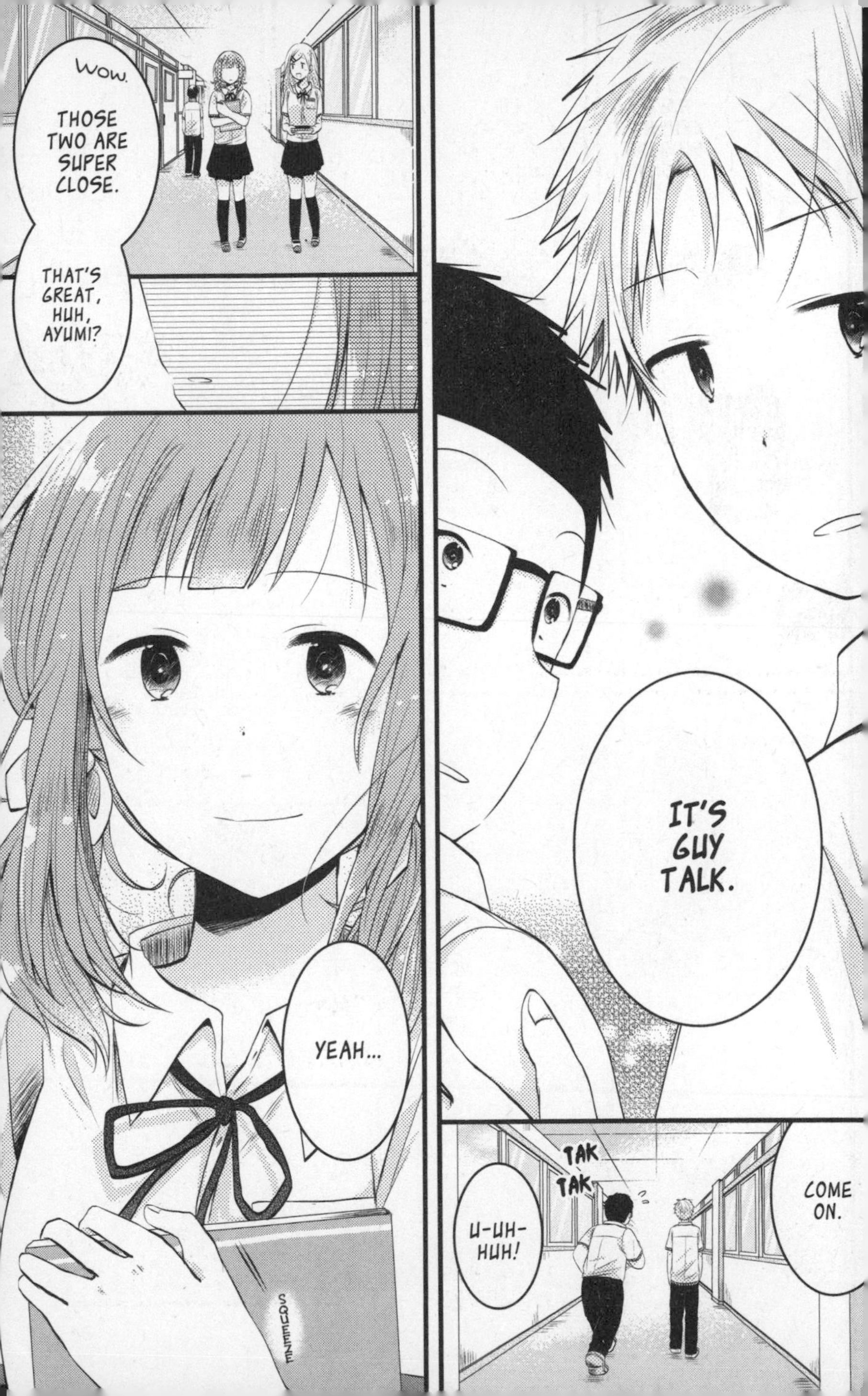
IT'S GUY TALK.
COME ON.
TAK TAK
U-UH-HUH!
WOW.
THOSE TWO ARE SUPER CLOSE.
THAT'S GREAT, HUH, AYUMI?
YEAH...
SQUEEZE

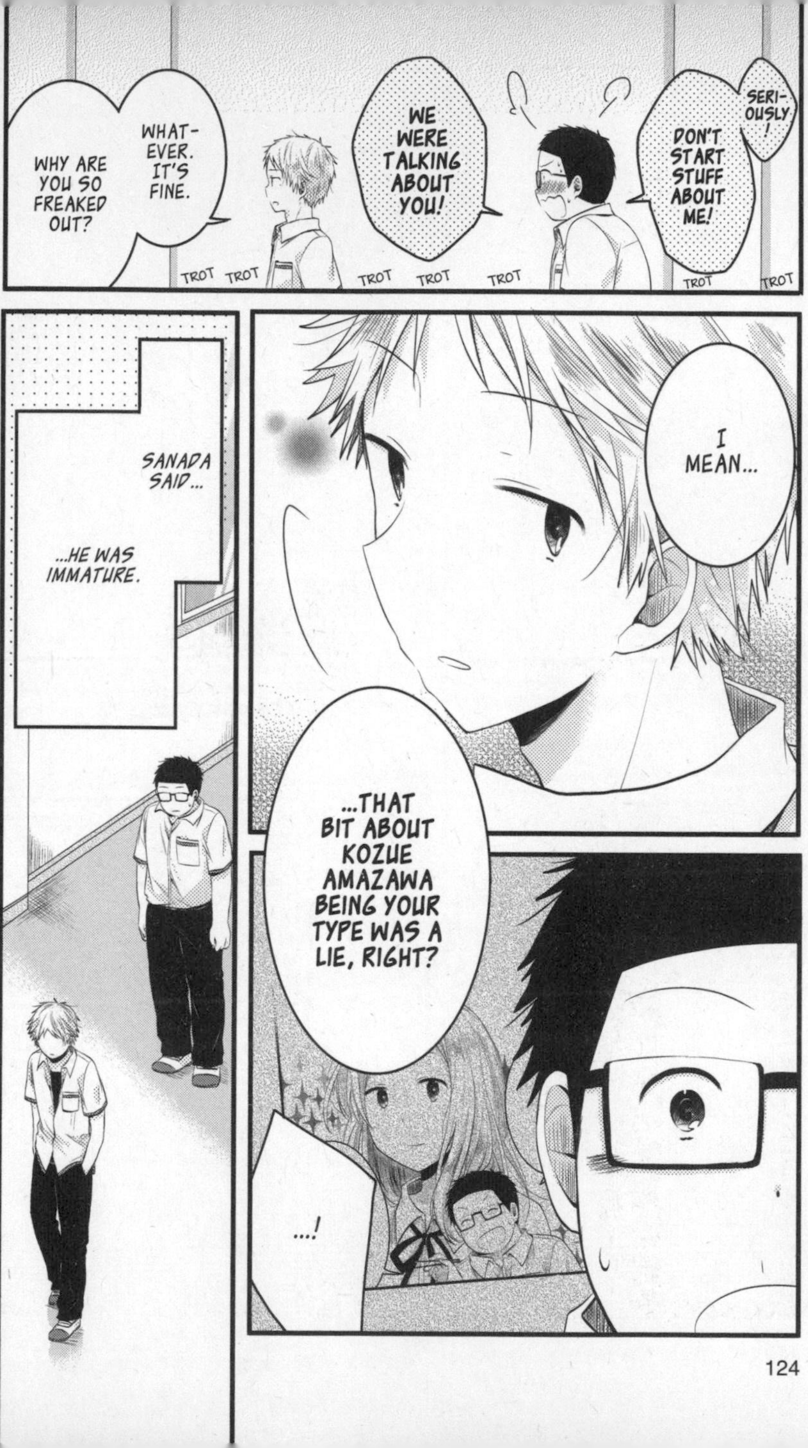
SERI-OUSLY!
DON'T START STUFF ABOUT ME!
TROT TROT
WE WERE TALKING ABOUT YOU!
TROT TROT TROT
WHAT-EVER. IT'S FINE.
WHY ARE YOU SO FREAKED OUT?
TROT TROT
I MEAN...
...THAT BIT ABOUT KOZUE AMAZAWA BEING YOUR TYPE WAS A LIE, RIGHT?
...!
SANADA SAID...
...HE WAS IMMATURE.

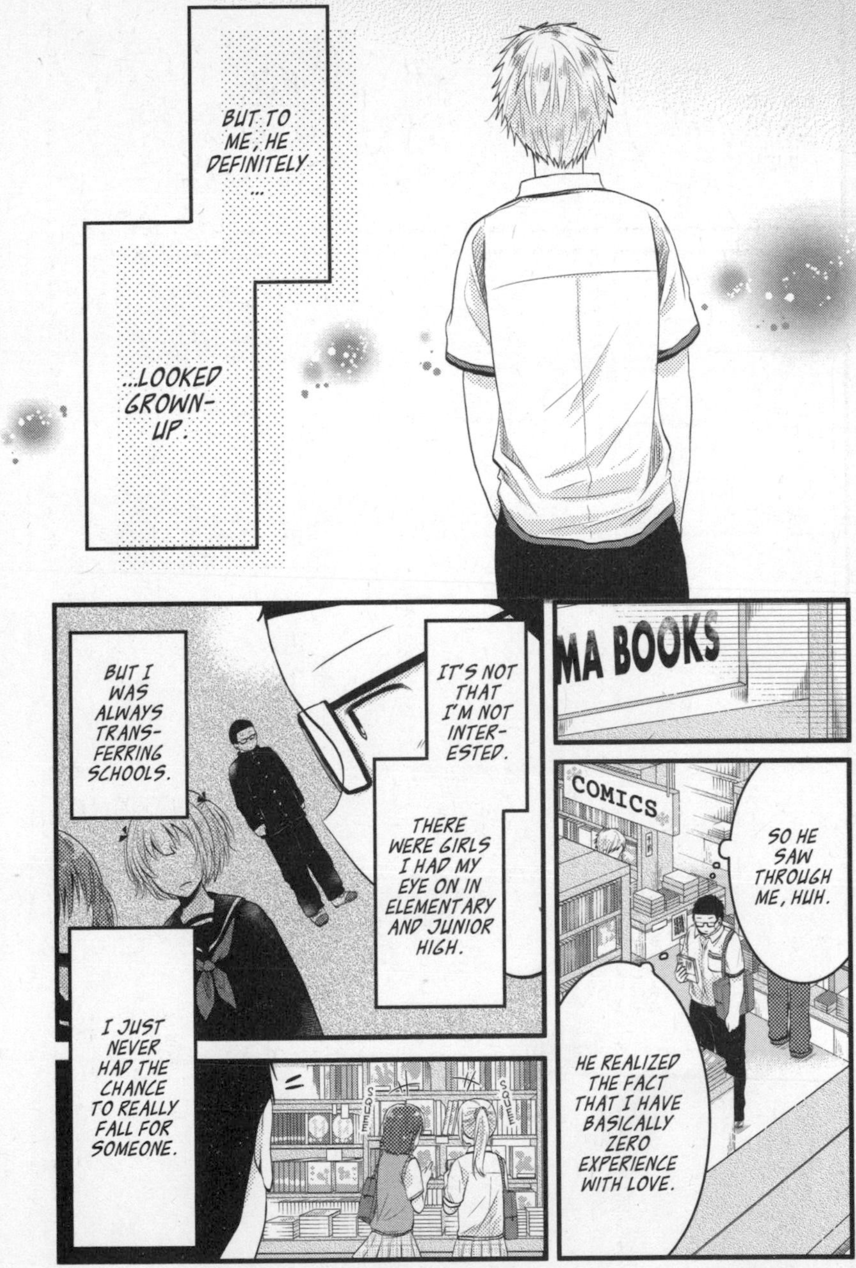
BUT TO ME, HE DEFINITELY ...
...LOOKED GROWN-UP.
MA BOOKS
COMICS
SO HE SAW THROUGH ME, HUH.
HE REALIZED THE FACT THAT I HAVE BASICALLY ZERO EXPERIENCE WITH LOVE.
IT'S NOT THAT I'M NOT INTERESTED.
THERE WERE GIRLS I HAD MY EYE ON IN ELEMENTARY AND JUNIOR HIGH.
BUT I WAS ALWAYS TRANSFERRING SCHOOLS.
I JUST NEVER HAD THE CHANCE TO REALLY FALL FOR SOMEONE.
SQUEE
SQUEE

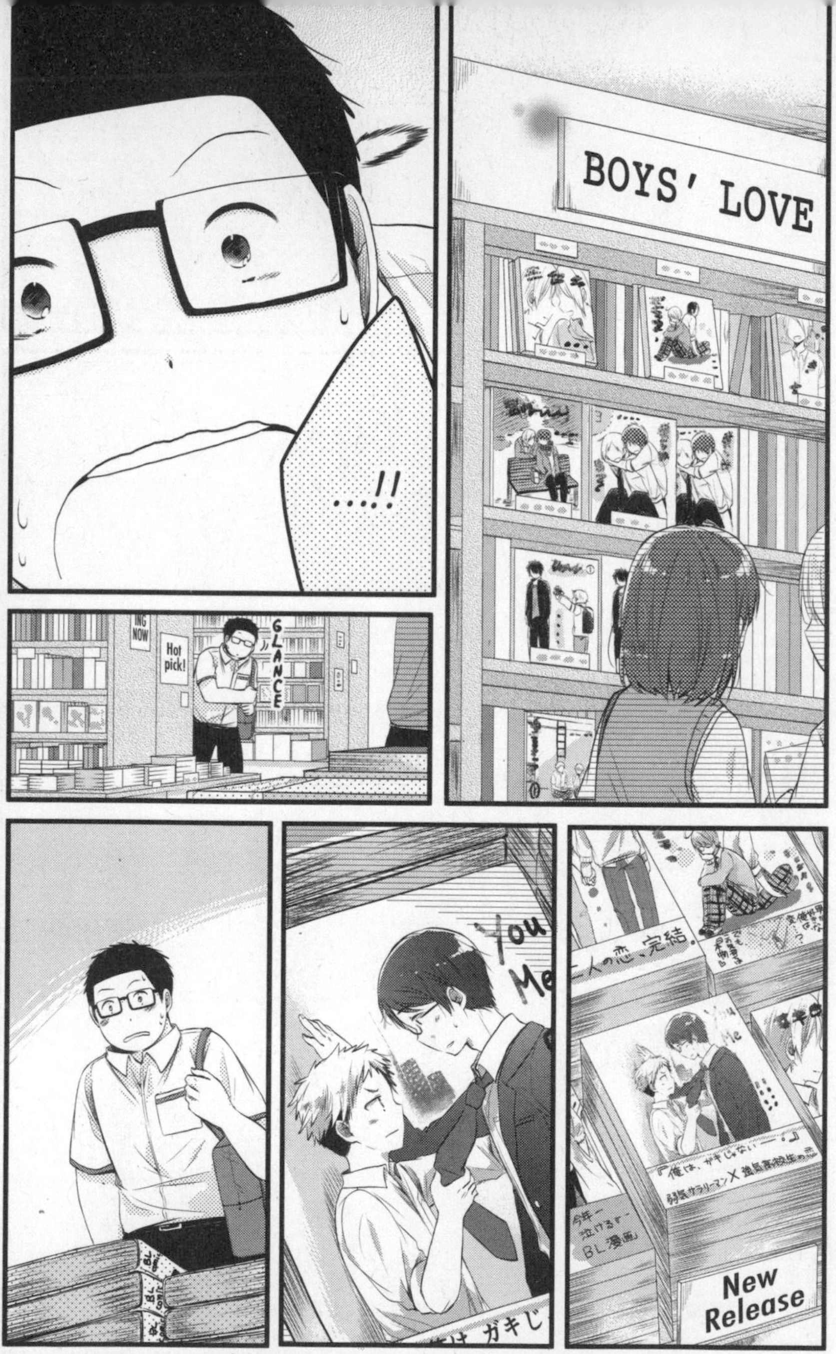
BOYS' LOVE
...!!
ING NOW
Hot pick!
GLANCE
二人の恋、完結。
『俺は、ガキじゃない――。』
弱気サラリーマン×強気高校生の恋
今年一泣ける BL漫画
New Release
You
Me
ガキじ

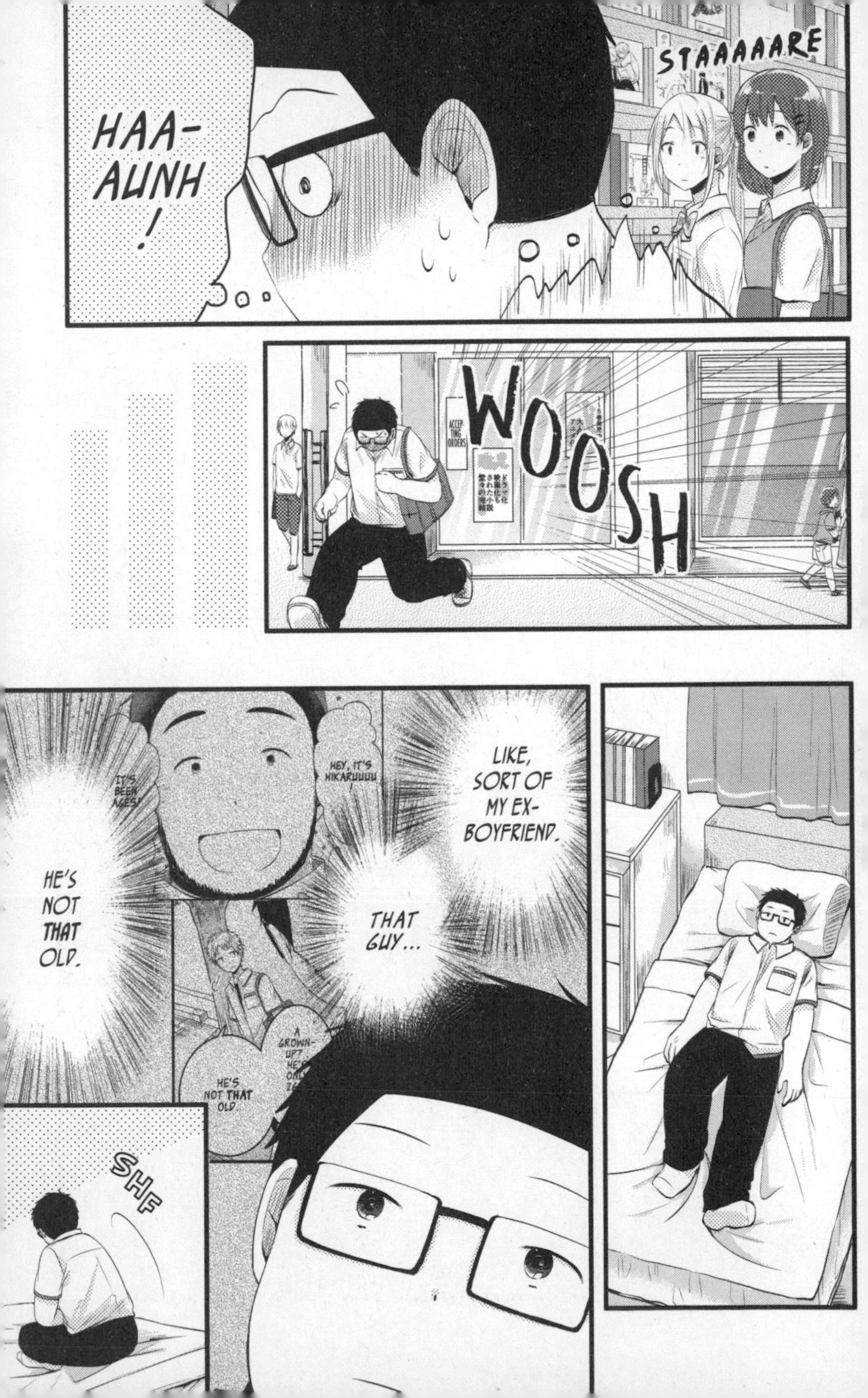
STAAAAARE
HAA-AUNH!
WOOSH
ACCEP-TING ORDERS
LIKE, SORT OF MY EX-BOYFRIEND.
HEY, IT'S HIKARUUUU!
IT'S BEEN AGES!
THAT GUY...
HE'S NOT THAT OLD.
A GROWN-UP? HE'S
HE'S NOT THAT OLD.
SHF

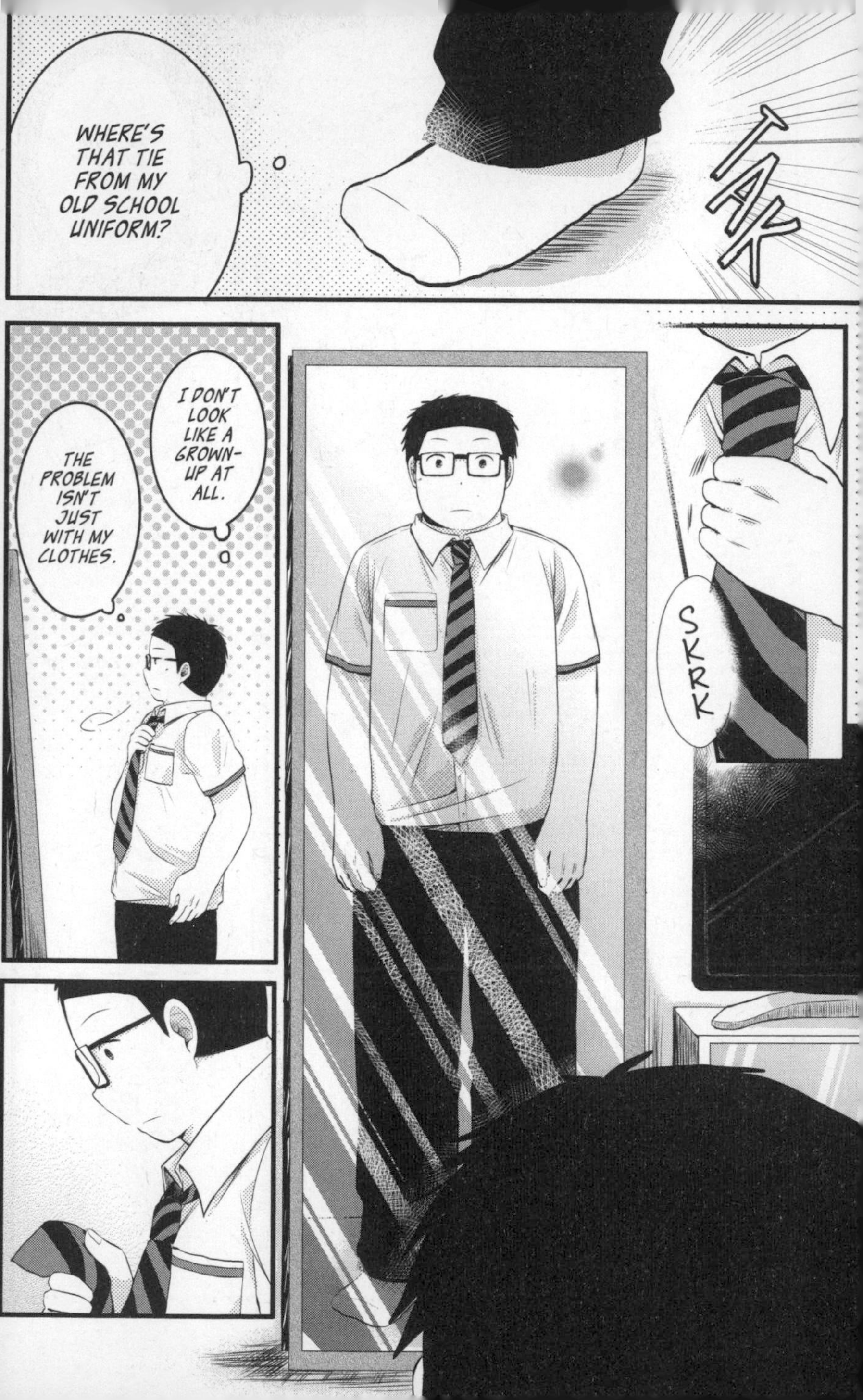
TAK
WHERE'S THAT TIE FROM MY OLD SCHOOL UNIFORM?
SKRK
I DON'T LOOK LIKE A GROWN-UP AT ALL.
THE PROBLEM ISN'T JUST WITH MY CLOTHES.

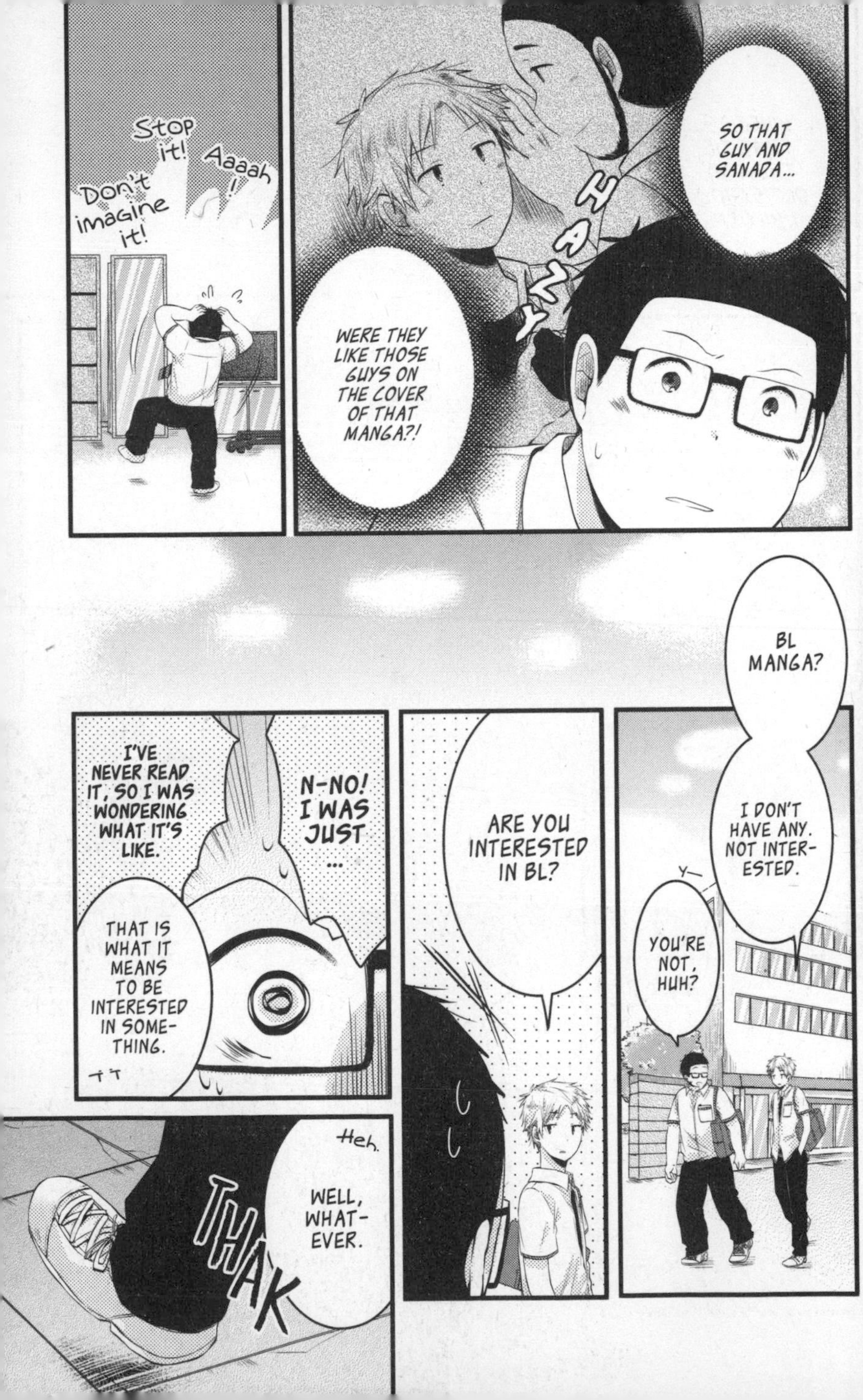
SO THAT GUY AND SANADA...
HAZY
WERE THEY LIKE THOSE GUYS ON THE COVER OF THAT MANGA?!
Stop it! Don't imagine it!
Aaaah!
BL MANGA?
I DON'T HAVE ANY. NOT INTER-ESTED.
Y—
YOU'RE NOT, HUH?
ARE YOU INTERESTED IN BL?
N-NO! I WAS JUST ...
I'VE NEVER READ IT, SO I WAS WONDERING WHAT IT'S LIKE.
THAT IS WHAT IT MEANS TO BE INTERESTED IN SOME-THING.
Heh.
WELL, WHAT-EVER.
THAK

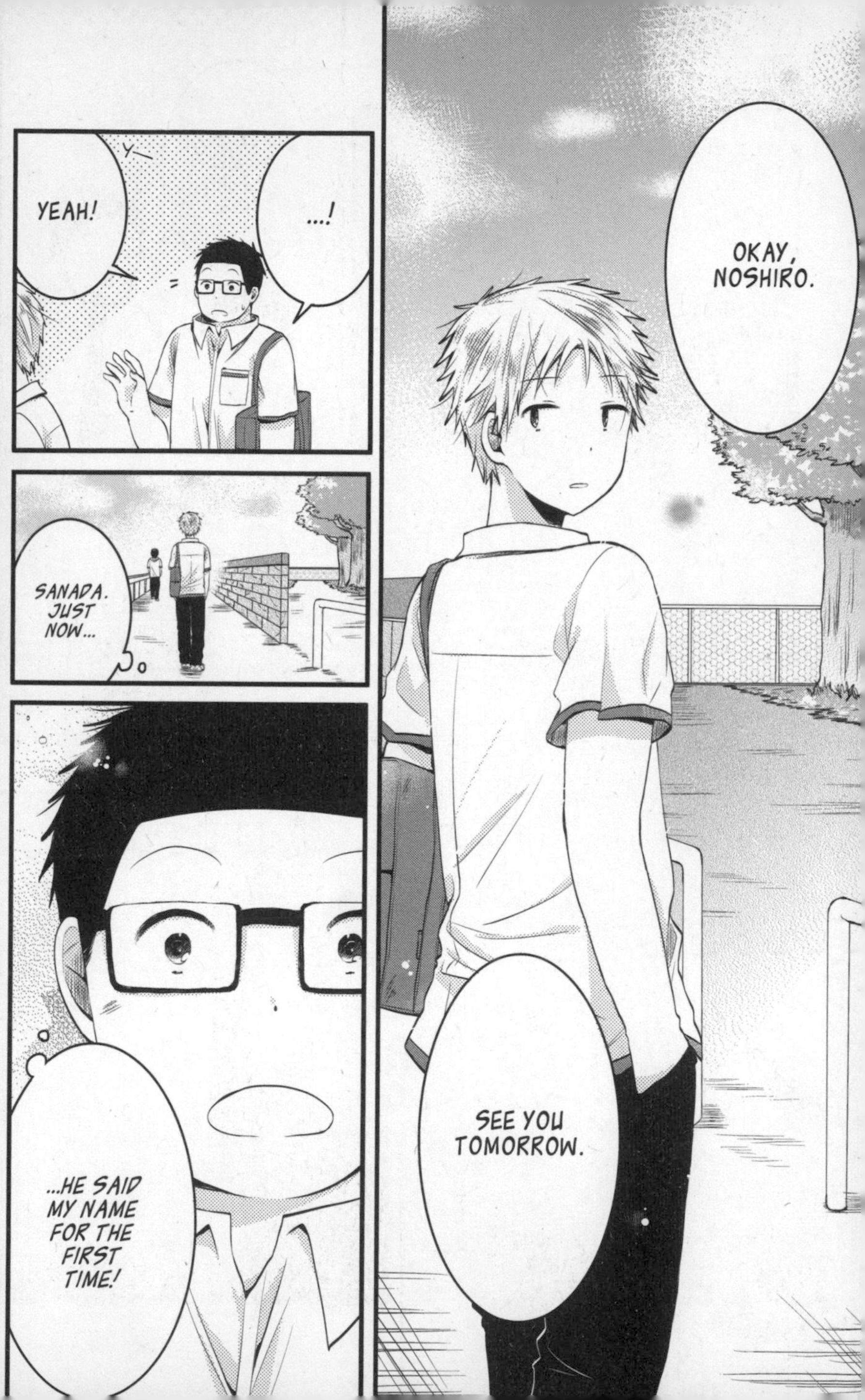
OKAY, NOSHIRO.
SEE YOU TOMORROW.
...!
YEAH!
SANADA. JUST NOW...
...HE SAID MY NAME FOR THE FIRST TIME!

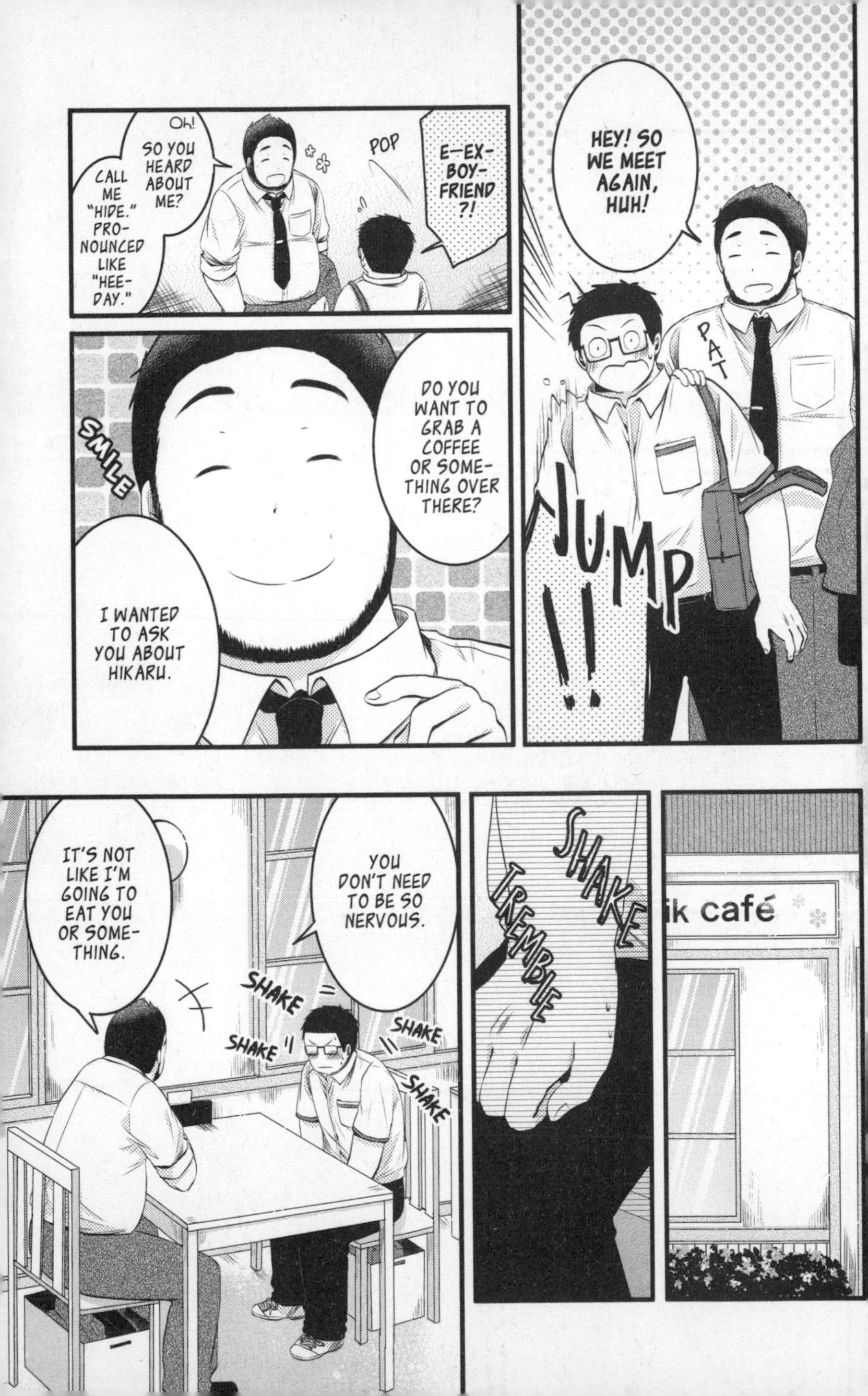
HEY! SO WE MEET AGAIN, HUH!
PAT
JUMP!!!
E-EX-BOYFRIEND?!
POP
Oh! SO YOU HEARD ABOUT ME?
CALL ME "HIDE." PRONOUNCED LIKE "HEE-DAY."
DO YOU WANT TO GRAB A COFFEE OR SOMETHING OVER THERE?
SMILE
I WANTED TO ASK YOU ABOUT HIKARU.
ik café
SHAKE
TREMBLE
YOU DON'T NEED TO BE SO NERVOUS.
IT'S NOT LIKE I'M GOING TO EAT YOU OR SOMETHING.
SHAKE
SHAKE
SHAKE
SHAKE

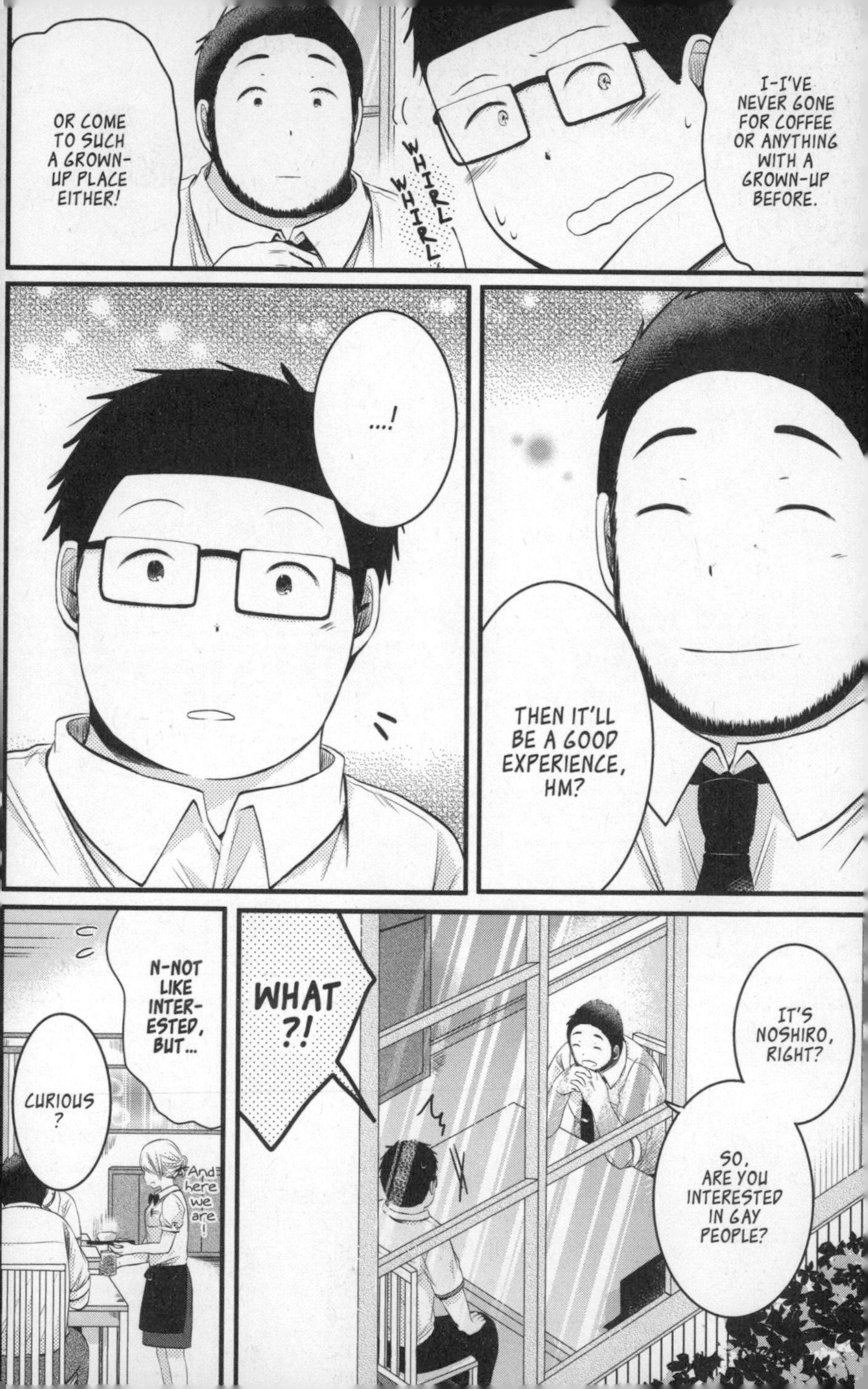
I-I'VE NEVER GONE FOR COFFEE OR ANYTHING WITH A GROWN-UP BEFORE.
WHIRL WHIRL
OR COME TO SUCH A GROWN-UP PLACE EITHER!
THEN IT'LL BE A GOOD EXPERIENCE, HM?
...!
IT'S NOSHIRO, RIGHT?
SO, ARE YOU INTERESTED IN GAY PEOPLE?
WHAT?!
N-NOT LIKE INTER-ESTED, BUT...
CURIOUS?
And here we are!

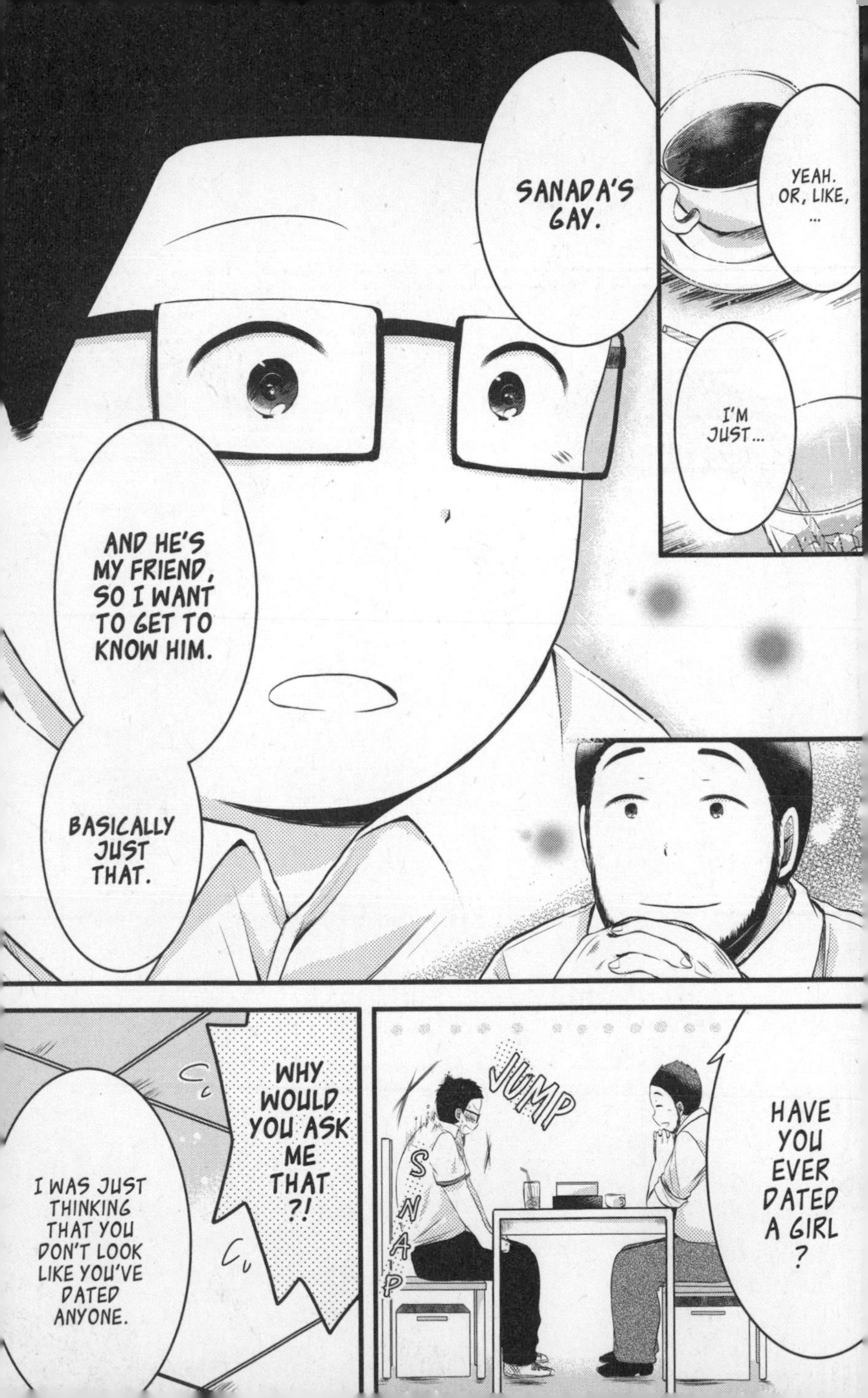
YEAH. OR, LIKE, ...
I'M JUST...
SANADA'S GAY.
AND HE'S MY FRIEND, SO I WANT TO GET TO KNOW HIM.
BASICALLY JUST THAT.
HAVE YOU EVER DATED A GIRL?
JUMP
SNAP
WHY WOULD YOU ASK ME THAT?!
I WAS JUST THINKING THAT YOU DON'T LOOK LIKE YOU'VE DATED ANYONE.

I HAVEN'T! IS THAT SO WRONG?! I—

YOU'RE CUTE.

HA HA HA! SORRY, SORRY.

I WASN'T TRYING TO TEASE YOU.

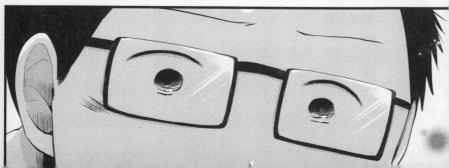

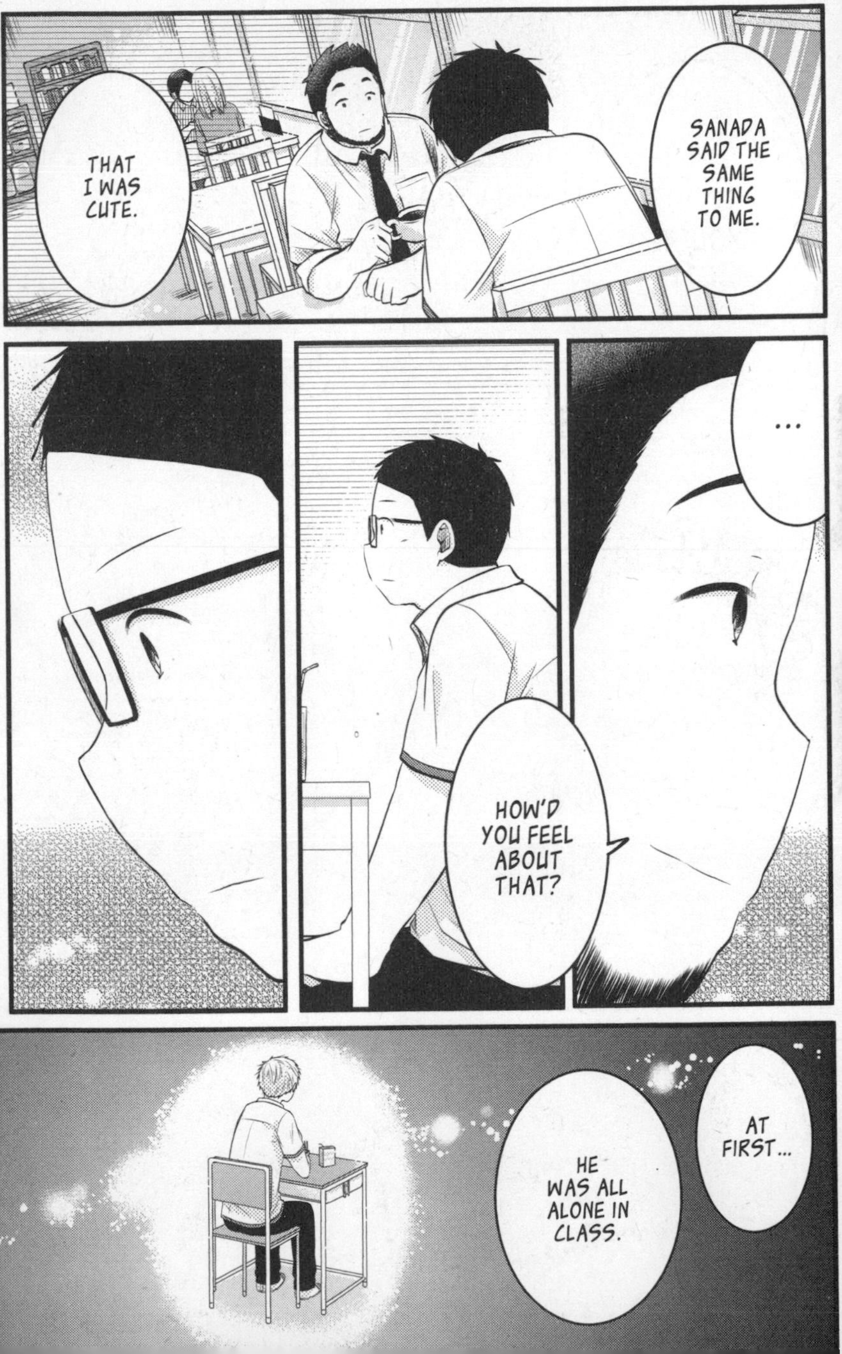
SANADA SAID THE SAME THING TO ME.
THAT I WAS CUTE.
...
HOW'D YOU FEEL ABOUT THAT?
AT FIRST...
HE WAS ALL ALONE IN CLASS.

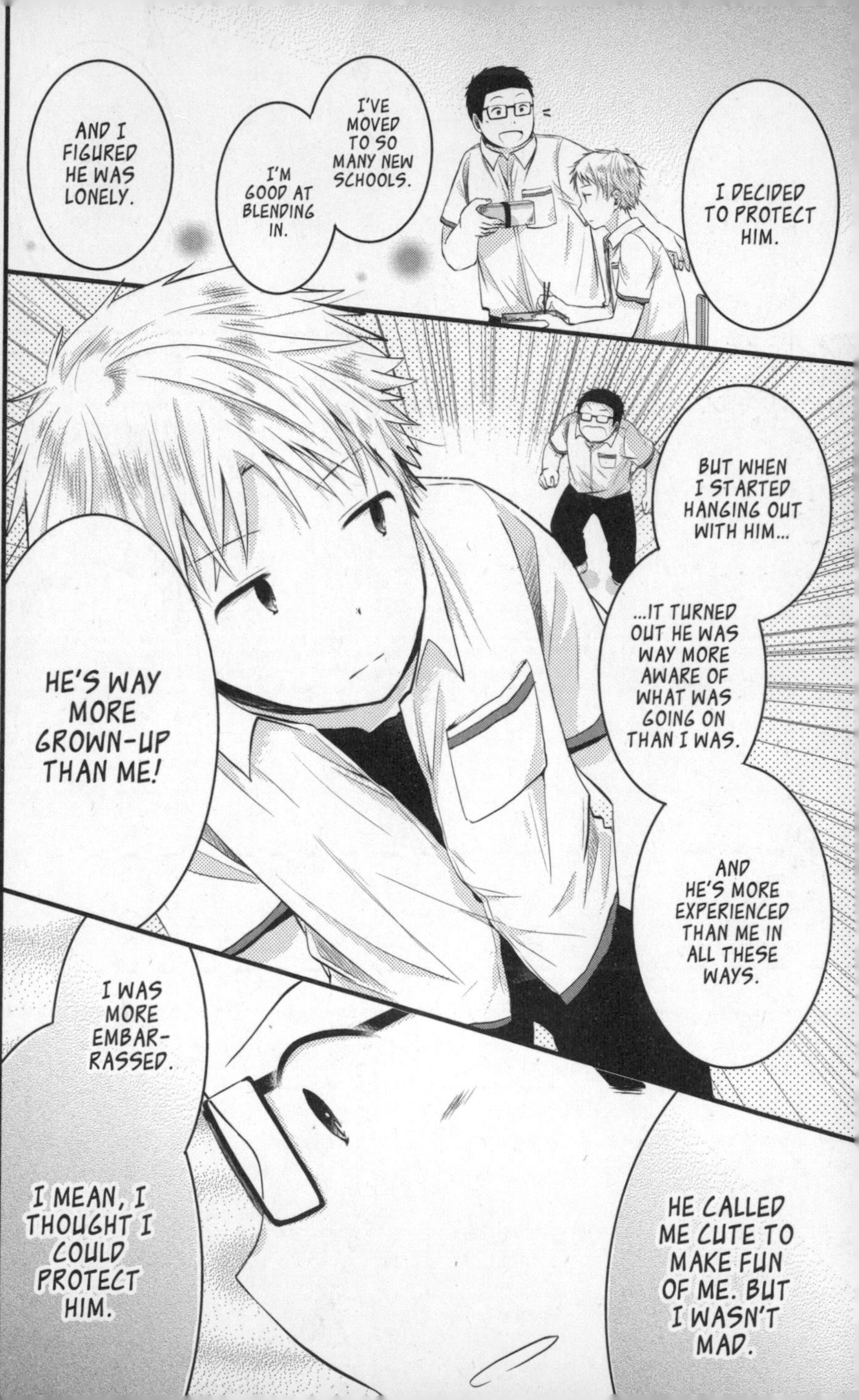
I DECIDED TO PROTECT HIM.
I'VE MOVED TO SO MANY NEW SCHOOLS.
I'M GOOD AT BLENDING IN.
AND I FIGURED HE WAS LONELY.
BUT WHEN I STARTED HANGING OUT WITH HIM...
...IT TURNED OUT HE WAS WAY MORE AWARE OF WHAT WAS GOING ON THAN I WAS.
AND HE'S MORE EXPERIENCED THAN ME IN ALL THESE WAYS.
HE'S WAY MORE GROWN-UP THAN ME!
HE CALLED ME CUTE TO MAKE FUN OF ME. BUT I WASN'T MAD.
I WAS MORE EMBARRASSED.
I MEAN, I THOUGHT I COULD PROTECT HIM.

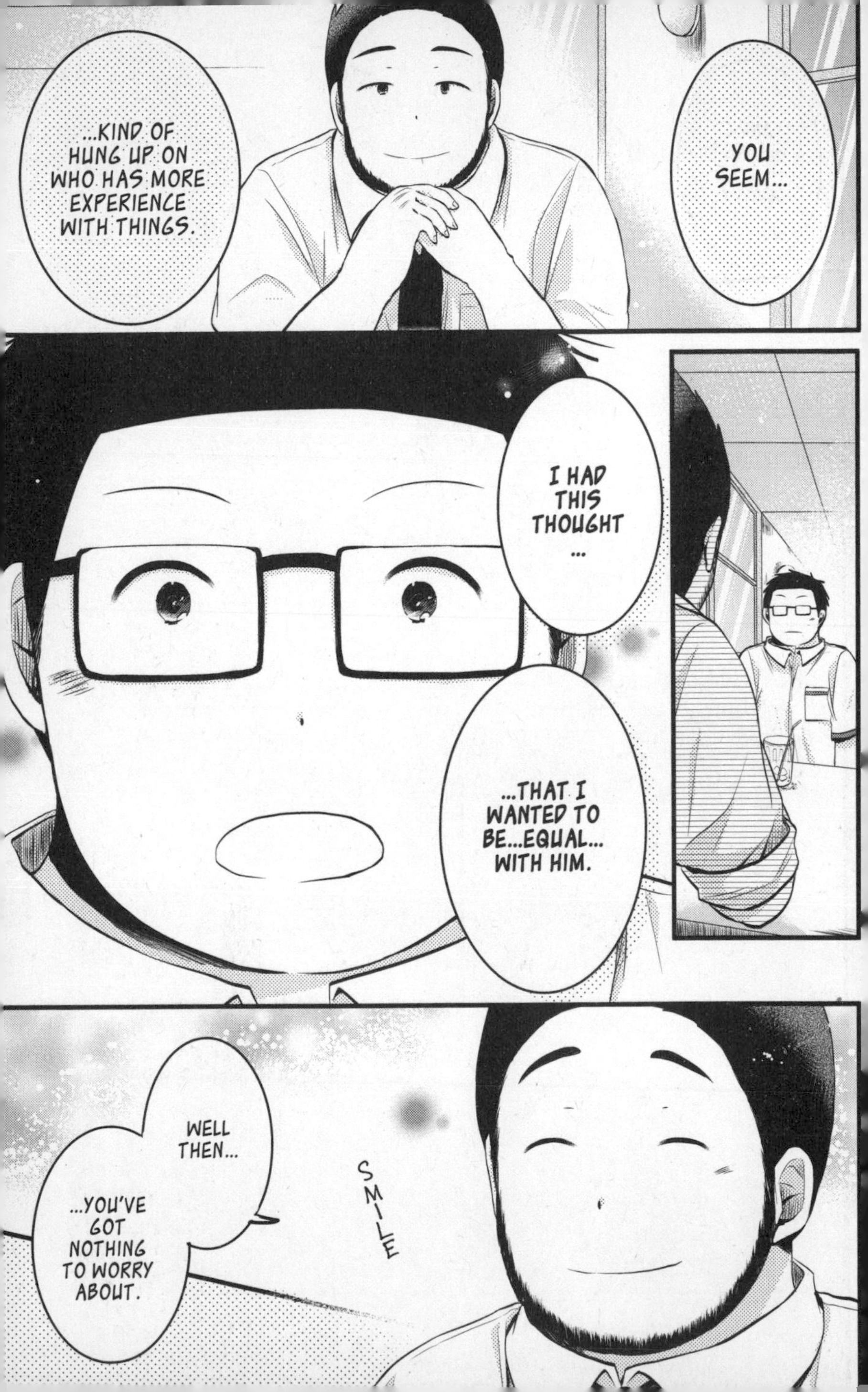
YOU SEEM...
...KIND OF HUNG UP ON WHO HAS MORE EXPERIENCE WITH THINGS.
I HAD THIS THOUGHT ...
...THAT I WANTED TO BE...EQUAL... WITH HIM.
SMILE
WELL THEN...
...YOU'VE GOT NOTHING TO WORRY ABOUT.

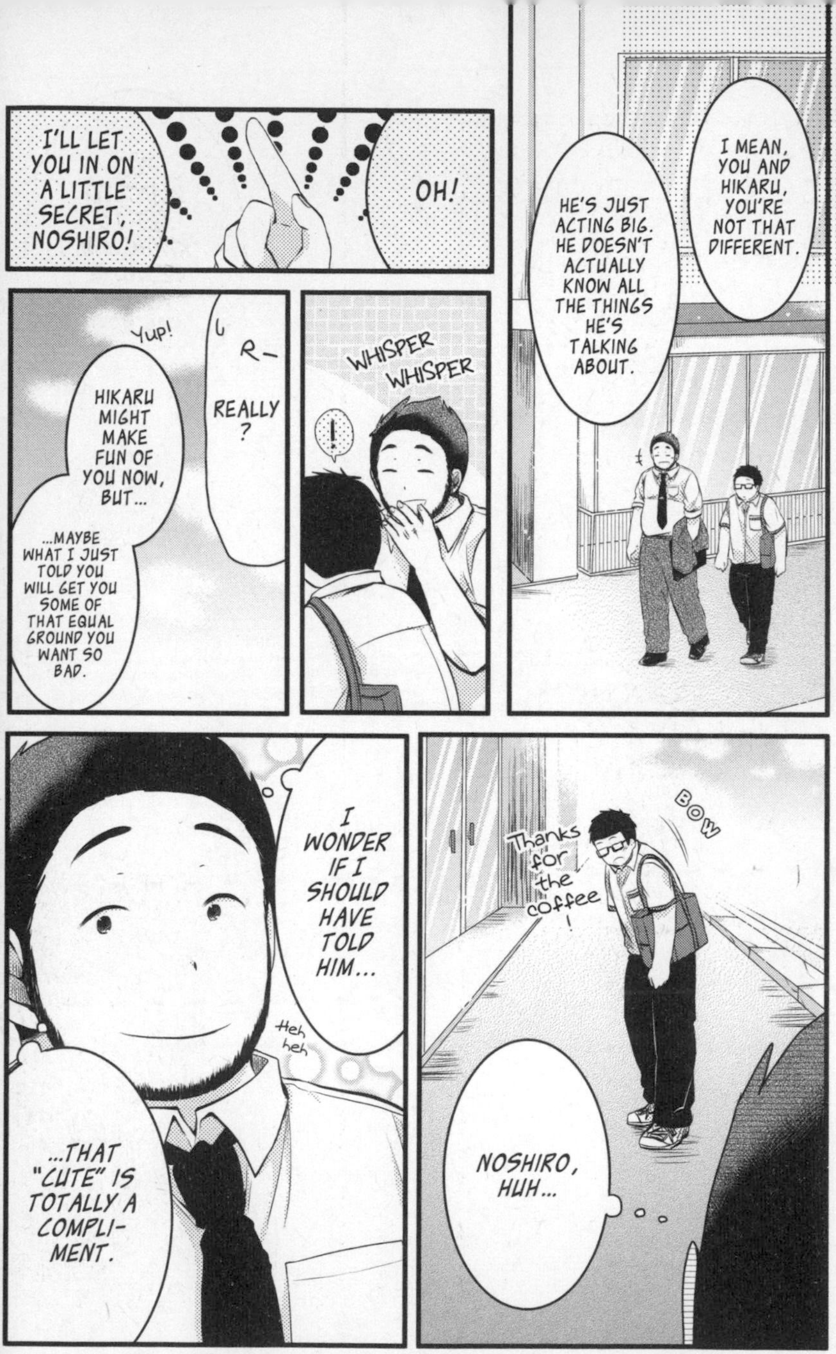
I MEAN, YOU AND HIKARU, YOU'RE NOT THAT DIFFERENT.
HE'S JUST ACTING BIG. HE DOESN'T ACTUALLY KNOW ALL THE THINGS HE'S TALKING ABOUT.
OH!
I'LL LET YOU IN ON A LITTLE SECRET, NOSHIRO!
WHISPER WHISPER
!
R– REALLY?
Yup!
HIKARU MIGHT MAKE FUN OF YOU NOW, BUT...
...MAYBE WHAT I JUST TOLD YOU WILL GET YOU SOME OF THAT EQUAL GROUND YOU WANT SO BAD.
BOW
Thanks for the coffee!
NOSHIRO, HUH...
I WONDER IF I SHOULD HAVE TOLD HIM...
Heh heh
...THAT "CUTE" IS TOTALLY A COMPLIMENT.

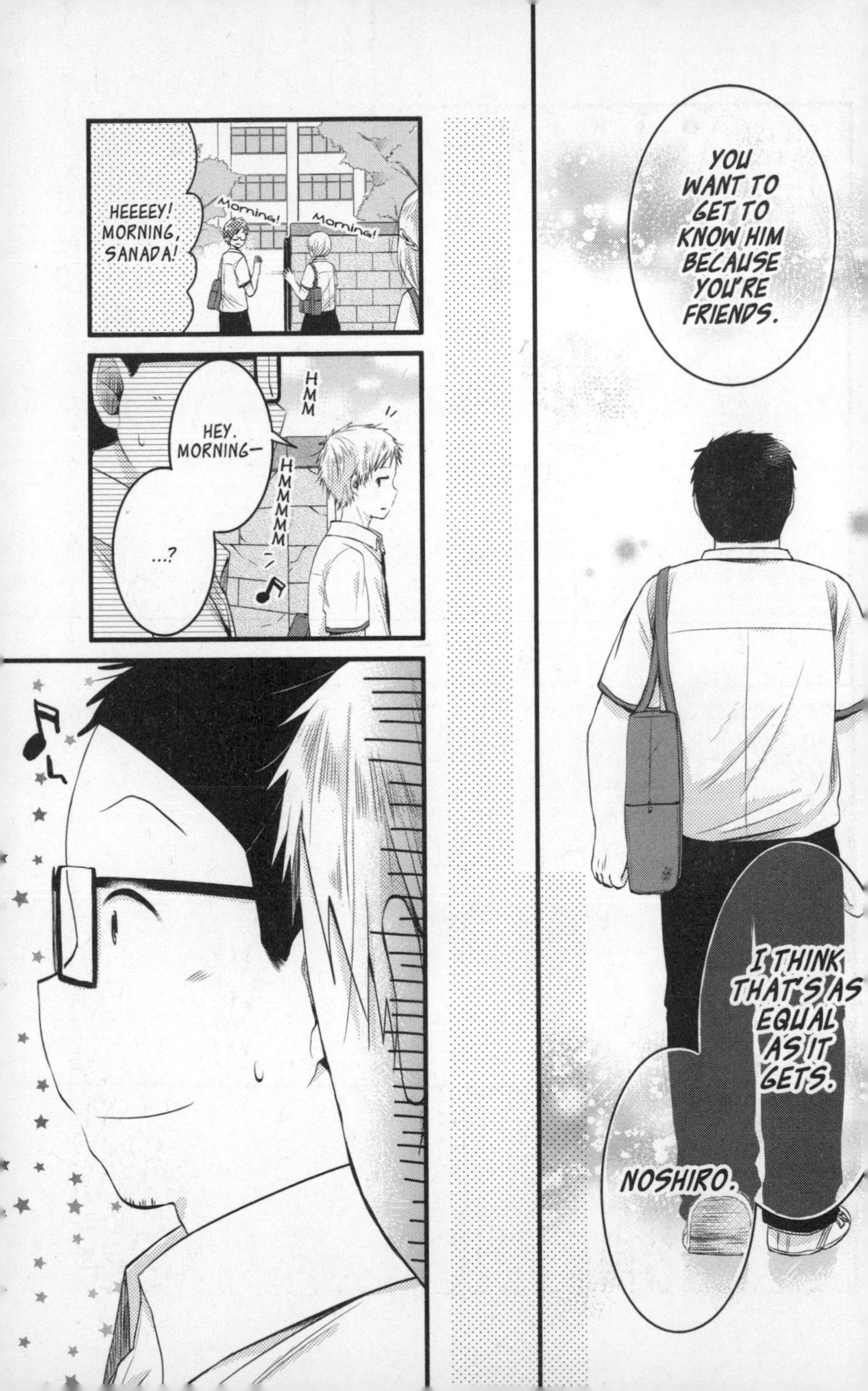
YOU WANT TO GET TO KNOW HIM BECAUSE YOU'RE FRIENDS.
I THINK THAT'S AS EQUAL AS IT GETS.
NOSHIRO.
Morning!
Morning!
HEEEEY! MORNING, SANADA!
HMM
HMMMMM
HEY. MORNING—
...?

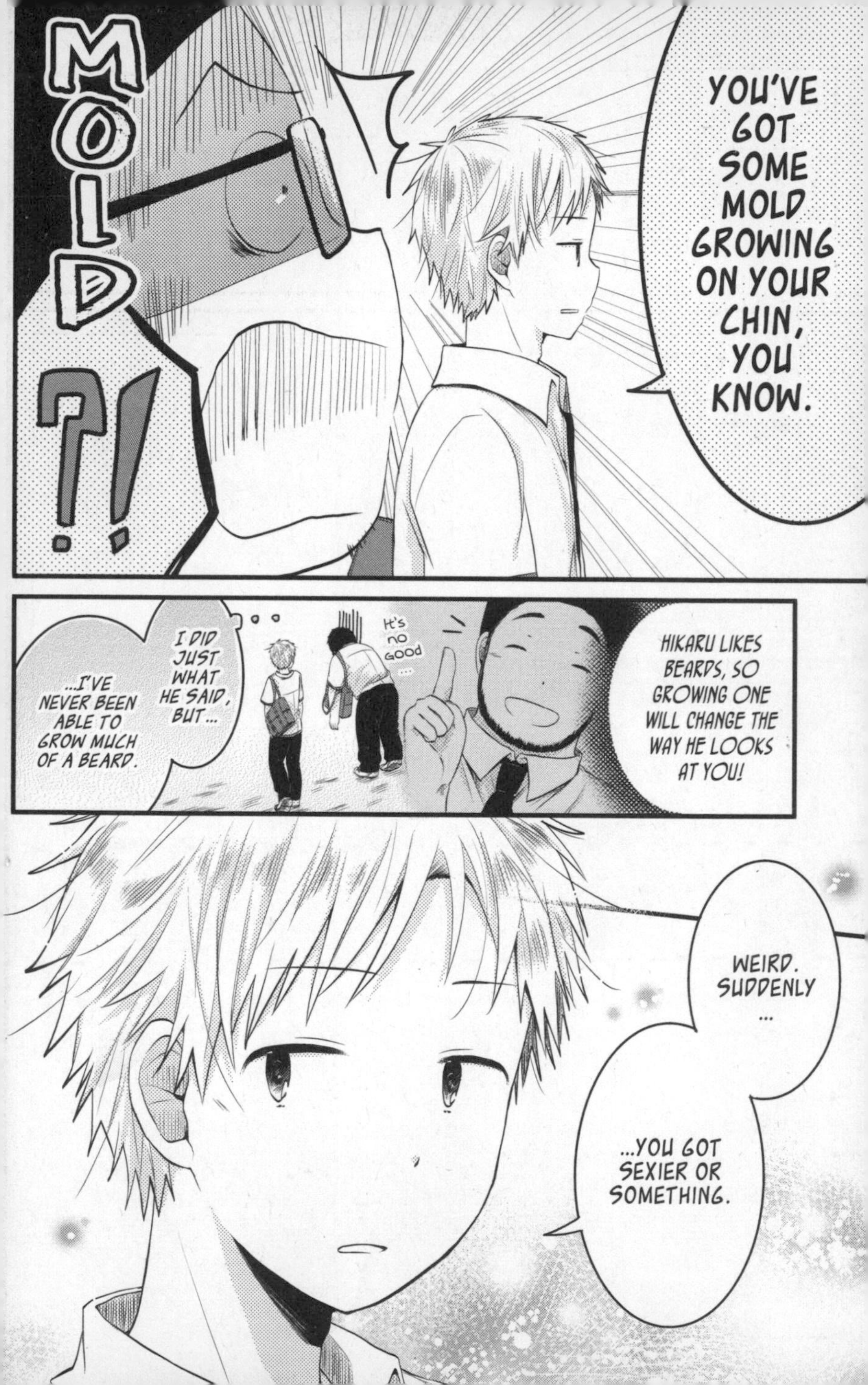
YOU'VE GOT SOME MOLD GROWING ON YOUR CHIN, YOU KNOW.
MOLD?!
HIKARU LIKES BEARDS, SO GROWING ONE WILL CHANGE THE WAY HE LOOKS AT YOU!
It's no good...
I DID JUST WHAT HE SAID, BUT...
...I'VE NEVER BEEN ABLE TO GROW MUCH OF A BEARD.
WEIRD. SUDDENLY...
...YOU GOT SEXIER OR SOMETHING.

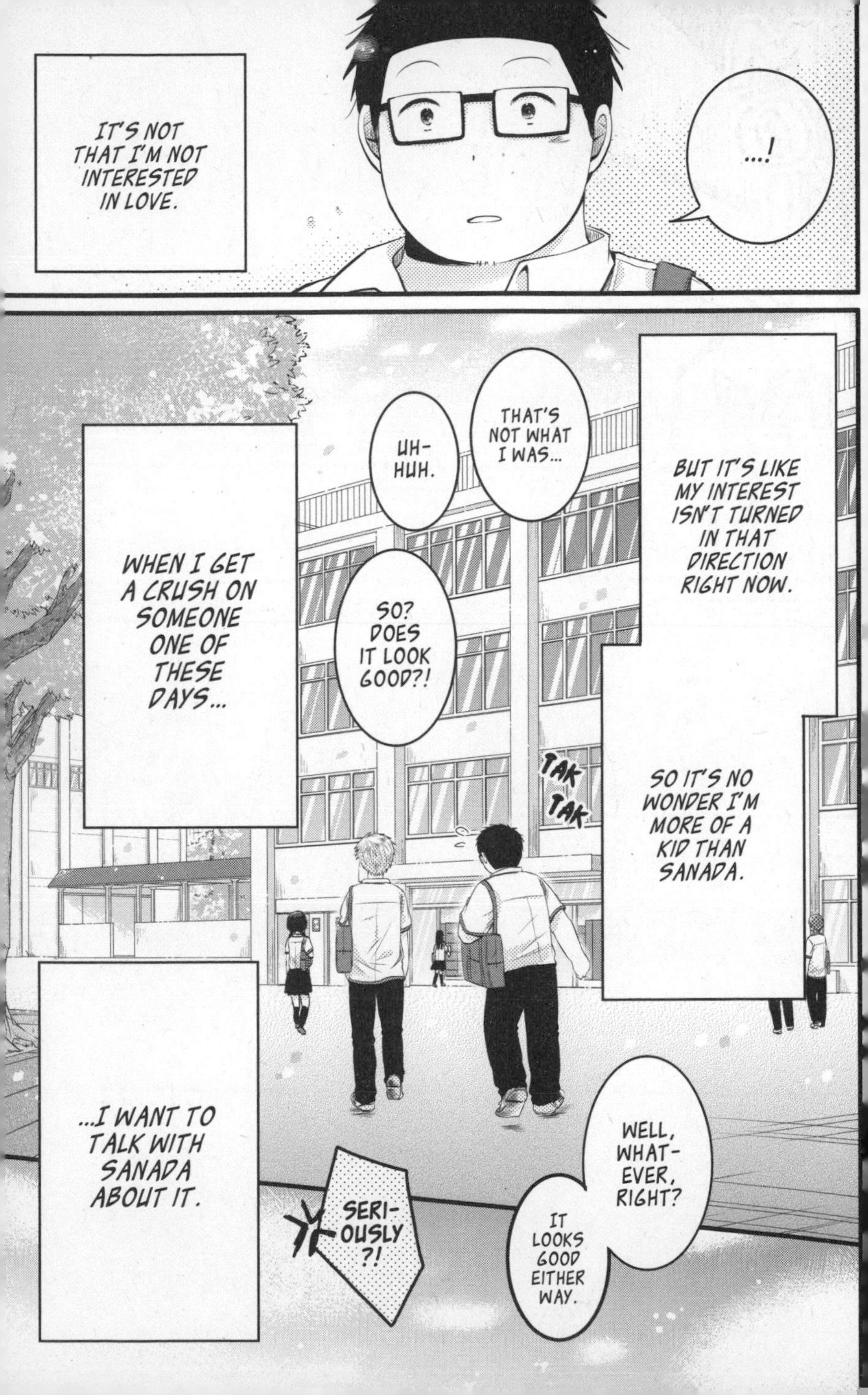
...!
IT'S NOT THAT I'M NOT INTERESTED IN LOVE.
BUT IT'S LIKE MY INTEREST ISN'T TURNED IN THAT DIRECTION RIGHT NOW.
THAT'S NOT WHAT I WAS...
UH-HUH.
SO? DOES IT LOOK GOOD?!
TAK TAK
SO IT'S NO WONDER I'M MORE OF A KID THAN SANADA.
WHEN I GET A CRUSH ON SOMEONE ONE OF THESE DAYS...
WELL, WHATEVER, RIGHT?
IT LOOKS GOOD EITHER WAY.
SERIOUSLY?!
...I WANT TO TALK WITH SANADA ABOUT IT.

That Blue
Sky Feeling

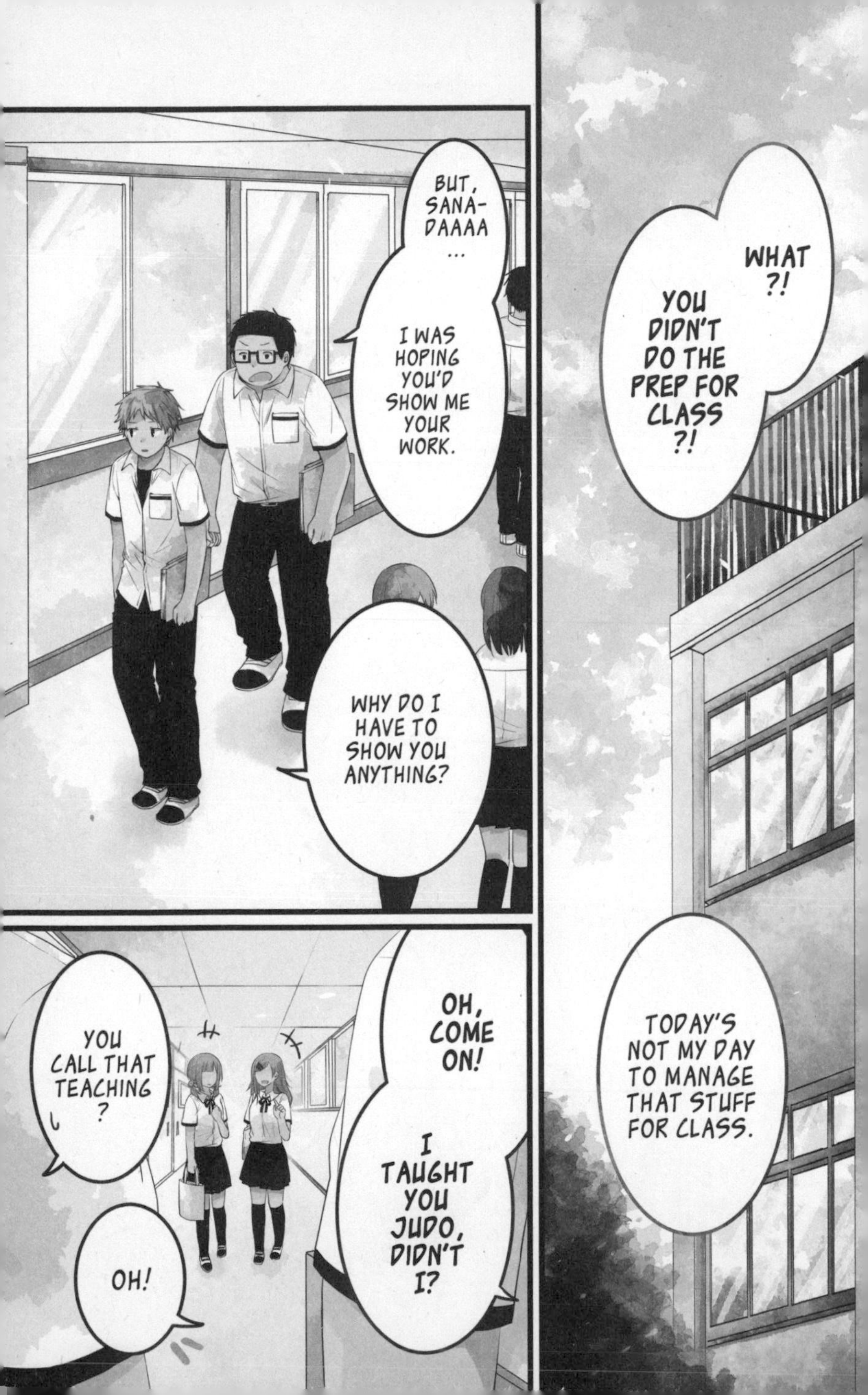
WHAT ?!
YOU DIDN'T DO THE PREP FOR CLASS ?!
TODAY'S NOT MY DAY TO MANAGE THAT STUFF FOR CLASS.
BUT, SANA-DAAAA ...
I WAS HOPING YOU'D SHOW ME YOUR WORK.
WHY DO I HAVE TO SHOW YOU ANYTHING?
OH, COME ON!
I TAUGHT YOU JUDO, DIDN'T I?
YOU CALL THAT TEACHING?
OH!

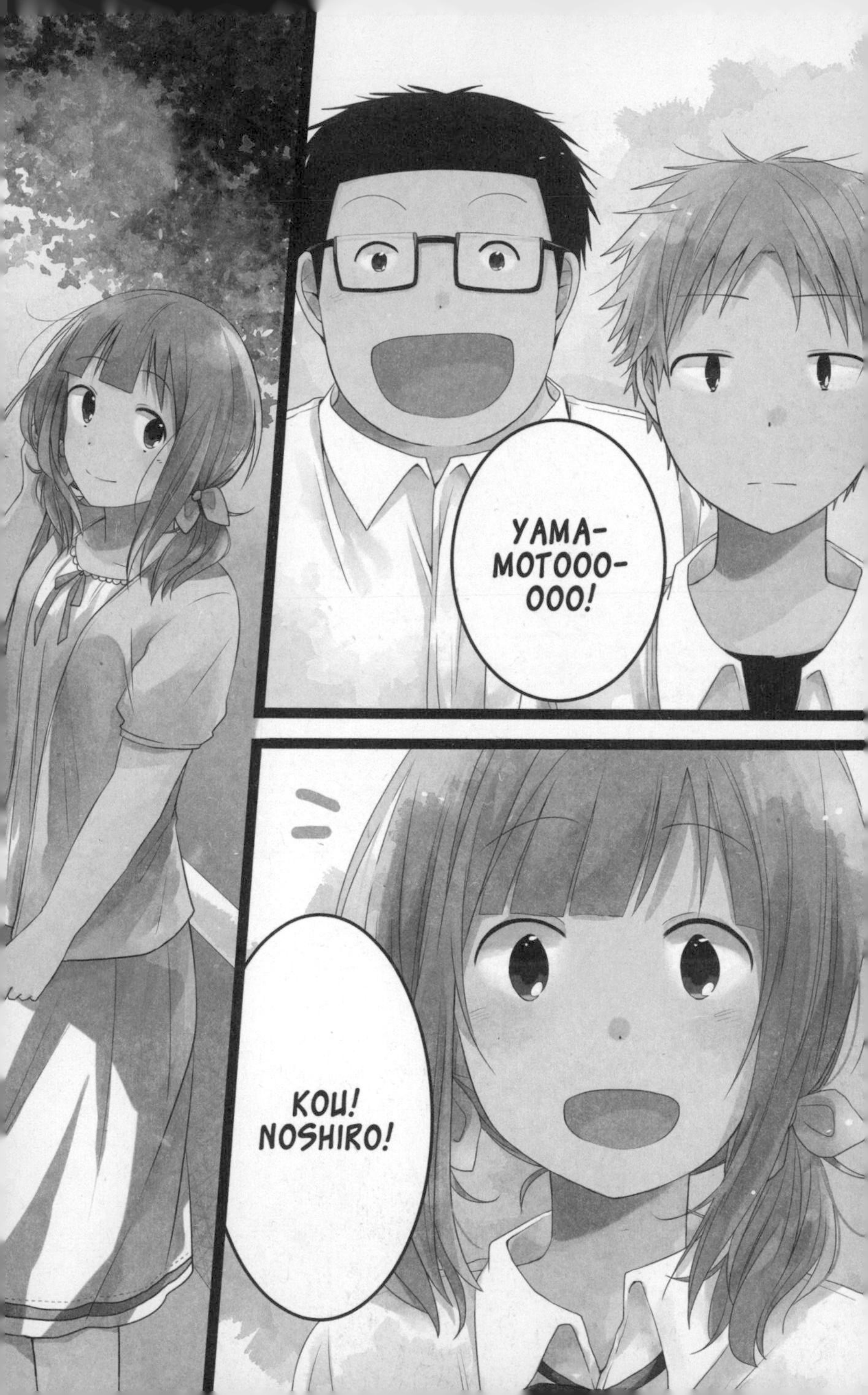
YAMA-MOTOOO-OOO!
KOU! NOSHIRO!

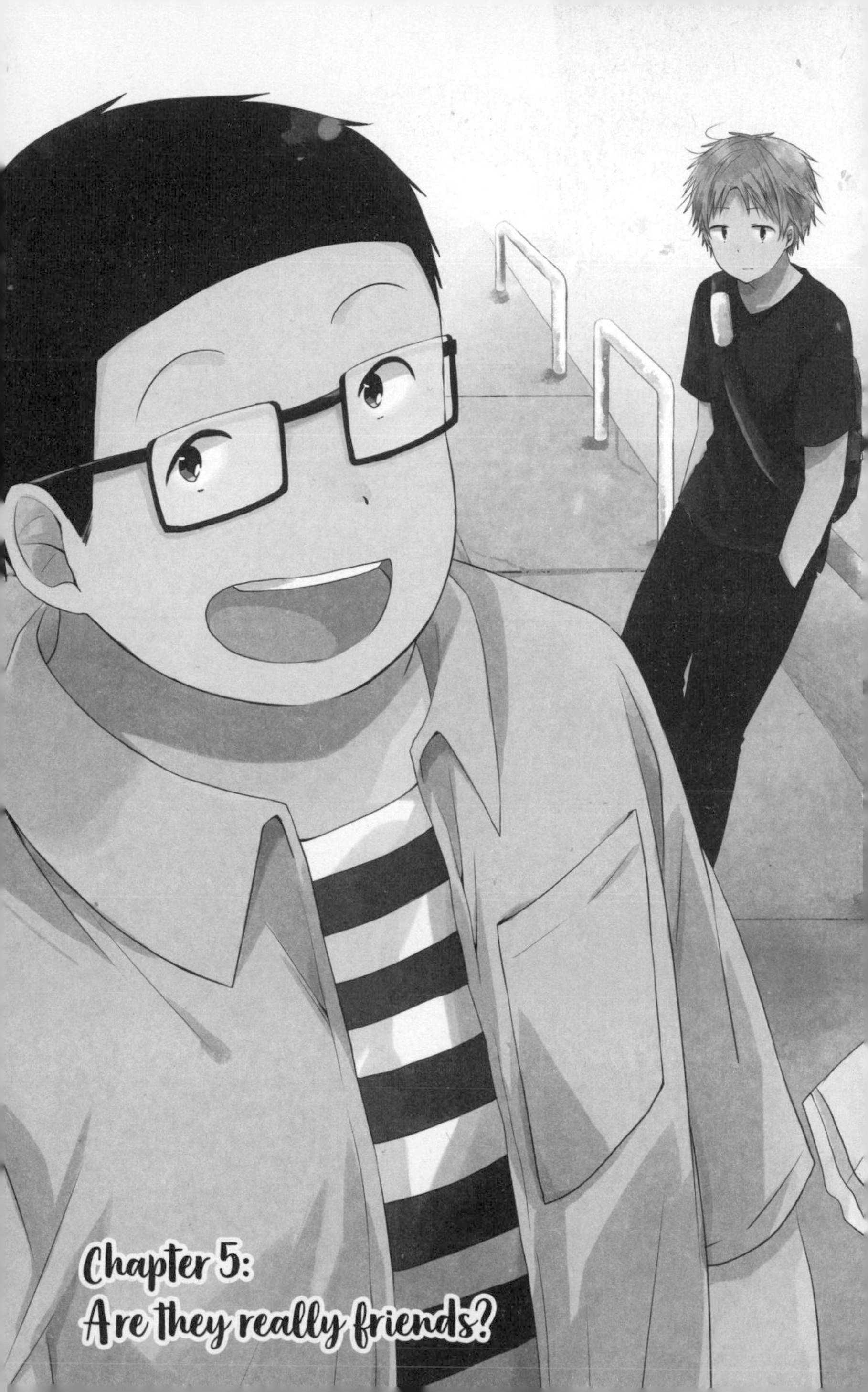
Chapter 5:
Are they really friends?

That Blue
Sky Feeling

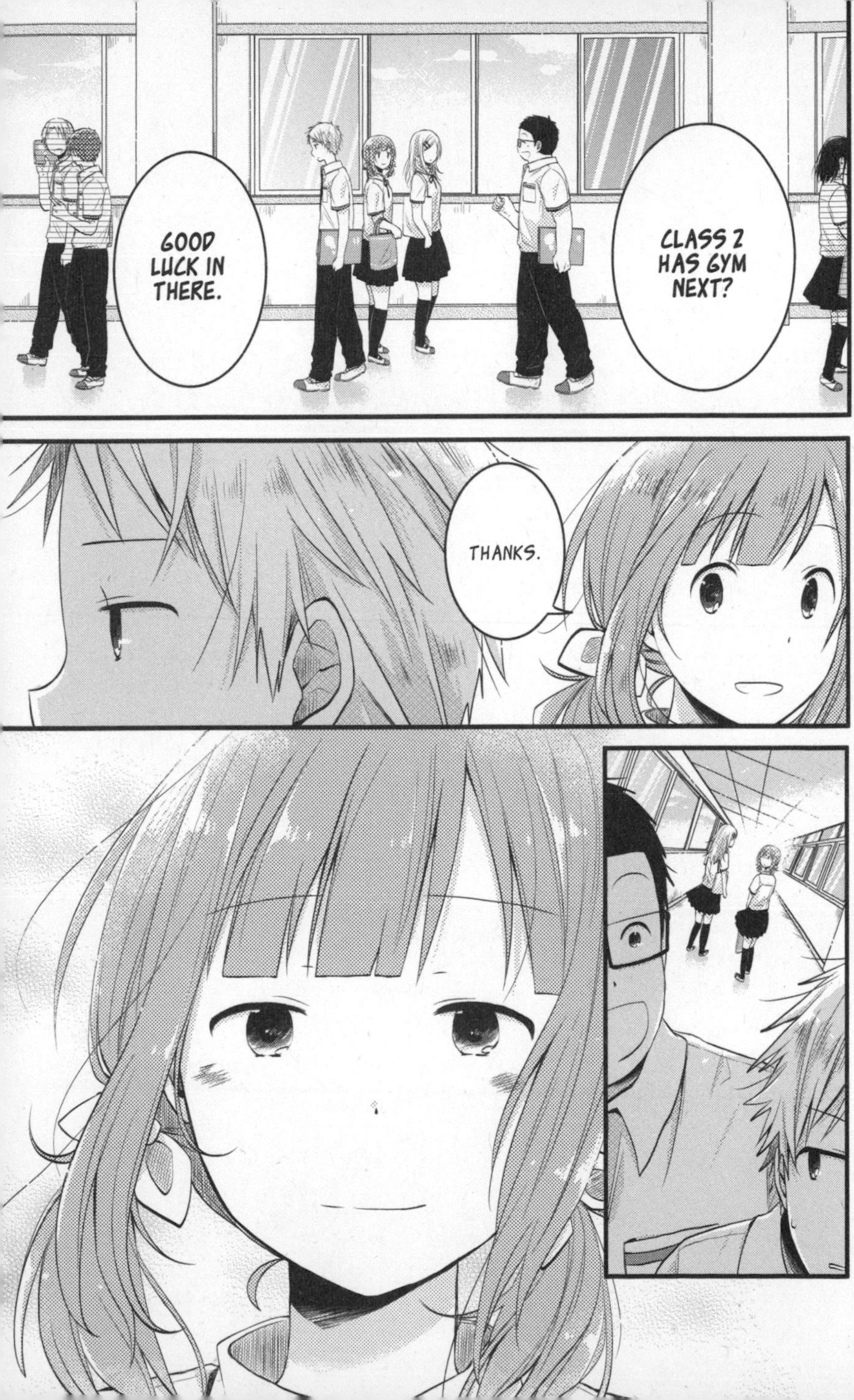
CLASS 2 HAS GYM NEXT?
GOOD LUCK IN THERE.
THANKS.

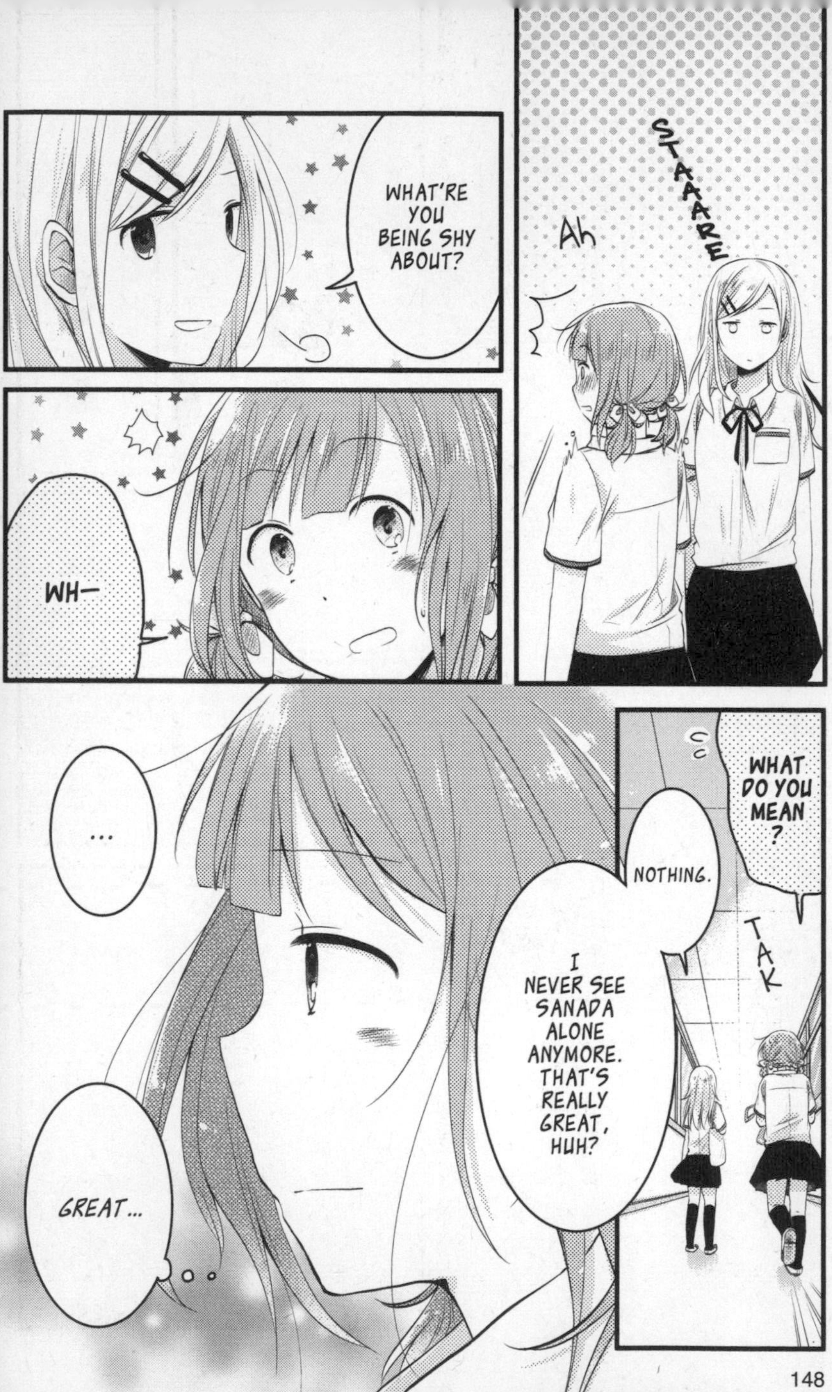
STAAARE
Ah
WHAT'RE YOU BEING SHY ABOUT?
WH–
WHAT DO YOU MEAN?
NOTHING.
I NEVER SEE SANADA ALONE ANYMORE. THAT'S REALLY GREAT, HUH?
TAK
...
GREAT...

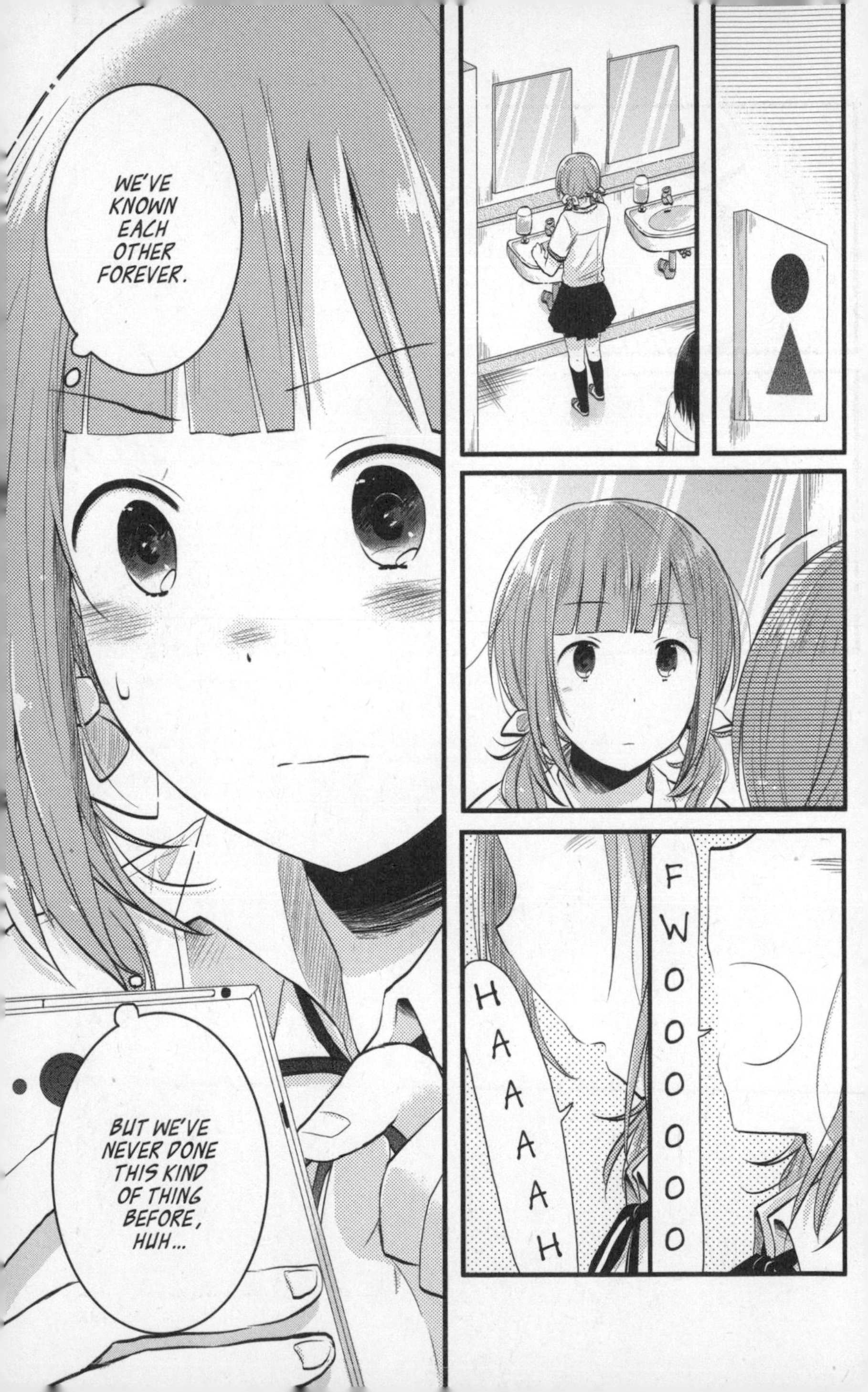
FWOOOOOOO
HAAAAH
WE'VE KNOWN EACH OTHER FOREVER.
BUT WE'VE NEVER DONE THIS KIND OF THING BEFORE, HUH...

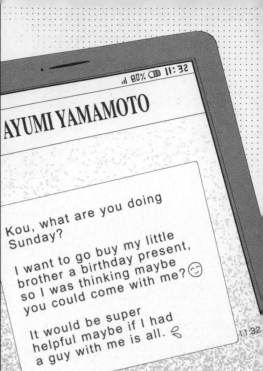

AYUMI YAMAMOTO

Kou, what are you doing Sunday?

I want to go buy my little brother a birthday present, so I was thinking maybe you could come with me? 😊

It would be super helpful maybe if I had a guy with me is all. ♪

11:32

NOSHIRO?

YOU FREE ON SUNDAY?

┬.┬

HUH?

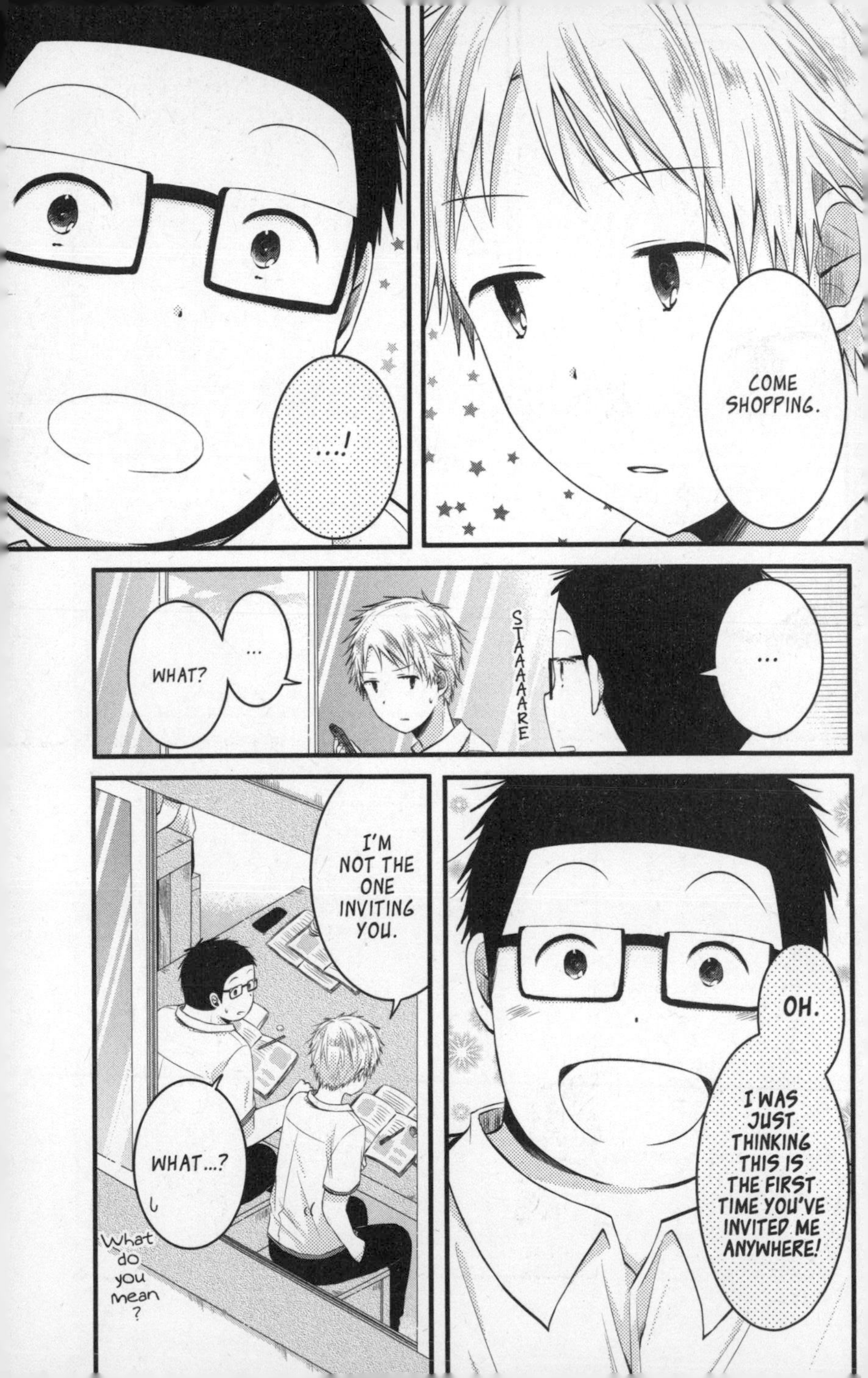
COME SHOPPING.
...!
...
STAAAAARE
...
WHAT?
OH.
I WAS JUST THINKING THIS IS THE FIRST TIME YOU'VE INVITED ME ANYWHERE!
I'M NOT THE ONE INVITING YOU.
WHAT...?
What do you mean?

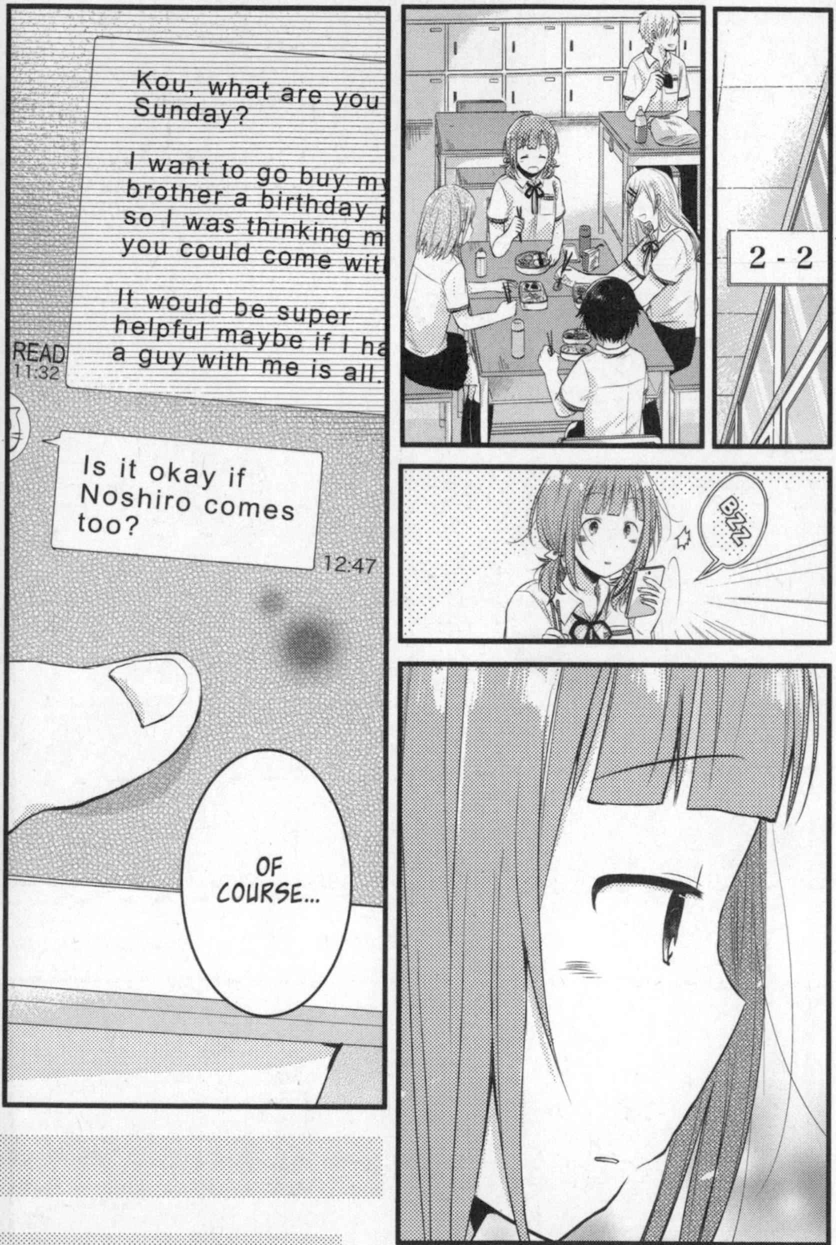
2 - 2
BZZ
Kou, what are you Sunday?
I want to go buy brother a birthday so I was thinking you could come
It would be super helpful maybe if I a guy with me is all.
READ 11:32
Is it okay if Noshiro comes too?
12:47
OF COURSE...

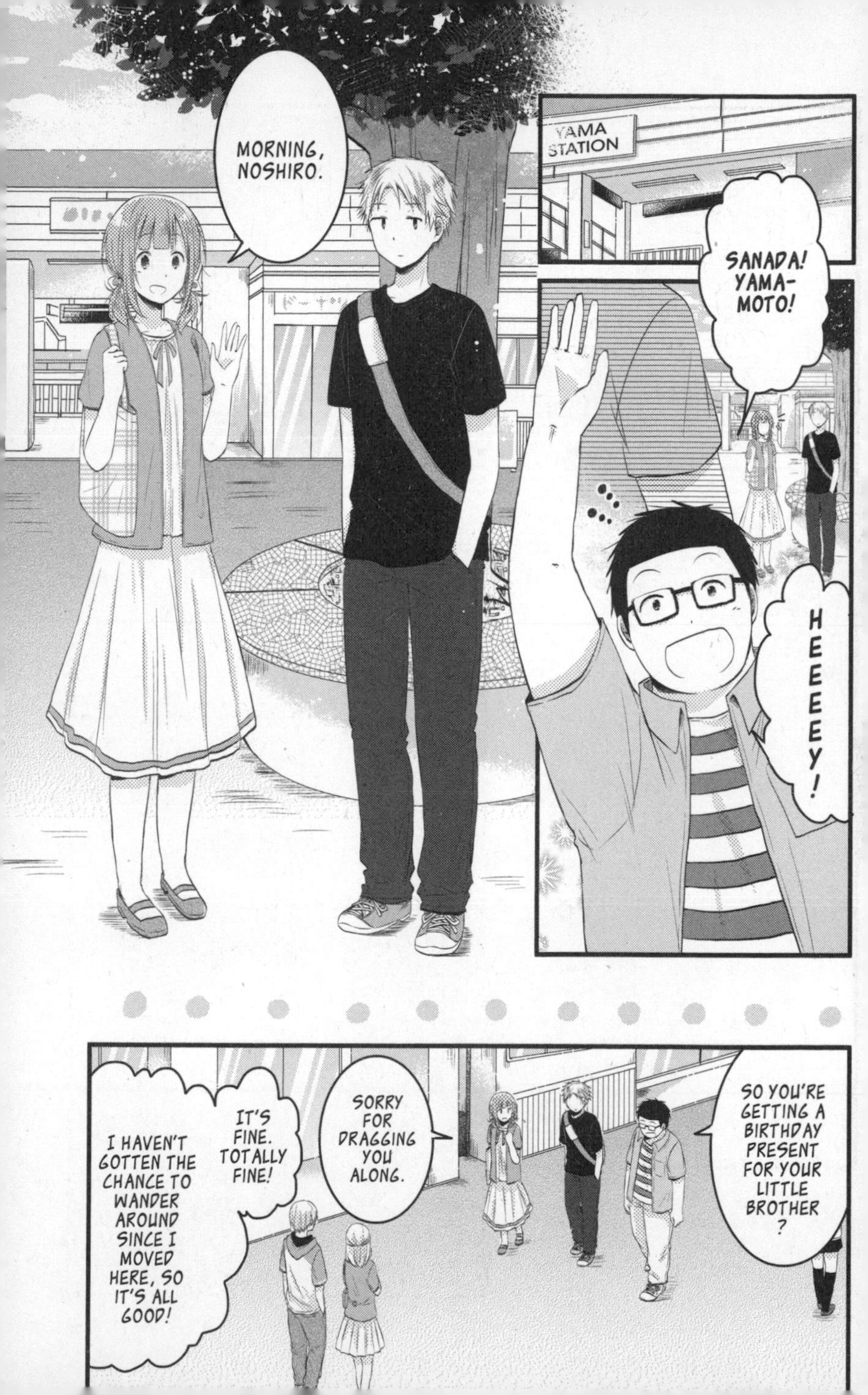
YAMA STATION
SANADA! YAMA-MOTO!
HEEEEY!
...
MORNING, NOSHIRO.
SO YOU'RE GETTING A BIRTHDAY PRESENT FOR YOUR LITTLE BROTHER?
SORRY FOR DRAGGING YOU ALONG.
IT'S FINE. TOTALLY FINE!
I HAVEN'T GOTTEN THE CHANCE TO WANDER AROUND SINCE I MOVED HERE, SO IT'S ALL GOOD!

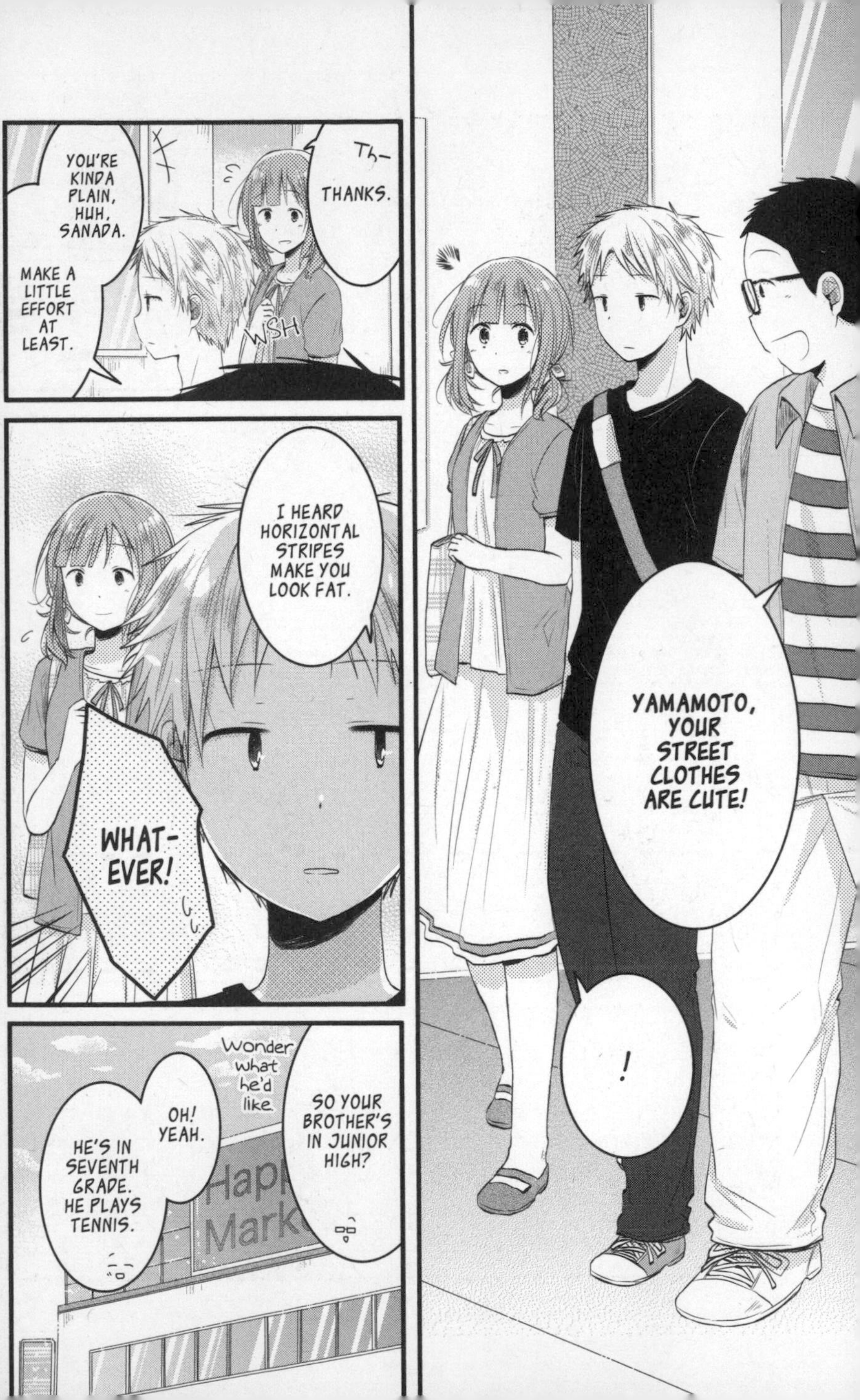
YAMAMOTO, YOUR STREET CLOTHES ARE CUTE!
!
Th-
THANKS.
YOU'RE KINDA PLAIN, HUH, SANADA.
MAKE A LITTLE EFFORT AT LEAST.
WSH
I HEARD HORIZONTAL STRIPES MAKE YOU LOOK FAT.
WHAT-EVER!
SO YOUR BROTHER'S IN JUNIOR HIGH?
Wonder what he'd like.
OH! YEAH.
HE'S IN SEVENTH GRADE. HE PLAYS TENNIS.

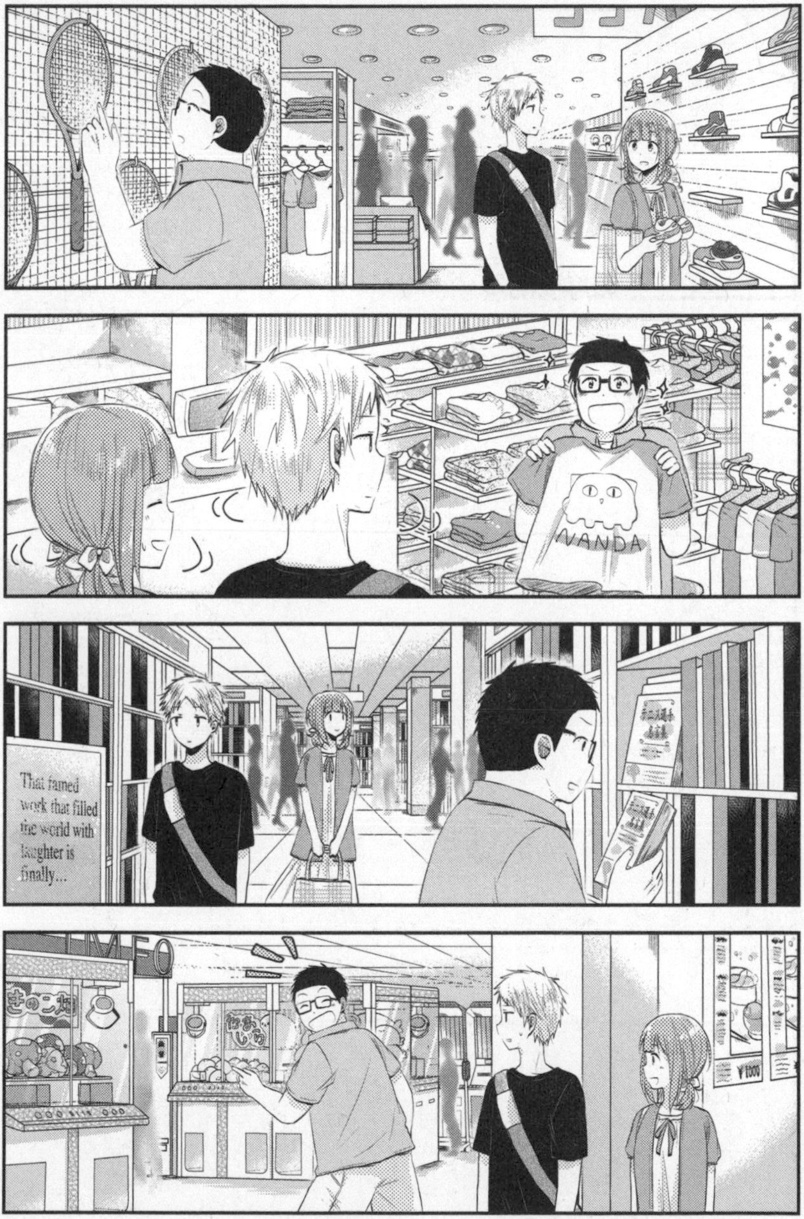
NANDA
That famed work that filled the world with laughter is finally...
¥1000

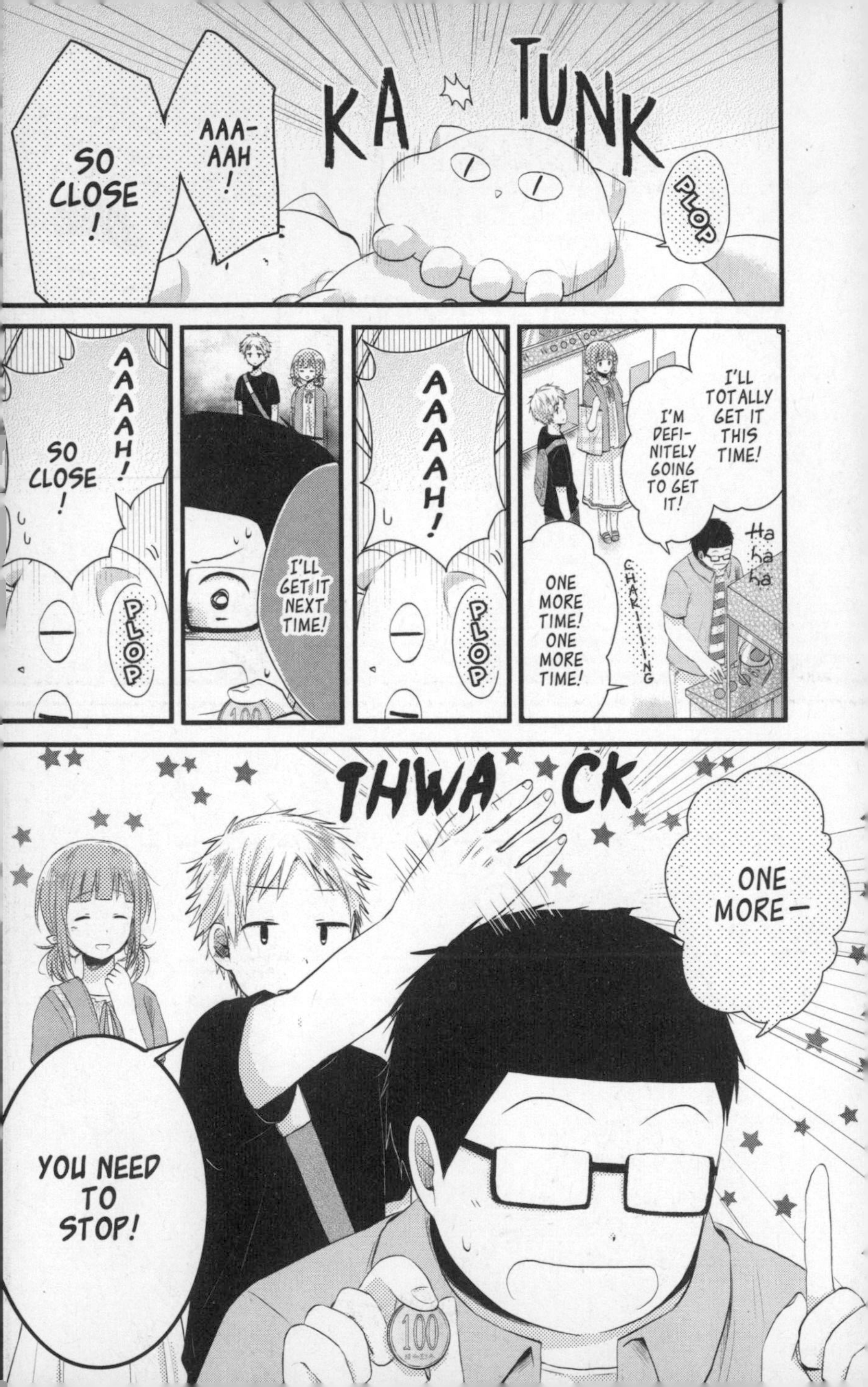
PLOP
KA TUNK
AAA-AAH!
SO CLOSE!
I'LL TOTALLY GET IT THIS TIME!
I'M DEFINITELY GOING TO GET IT!
Ha ha ha
CHAKIIIING
ONE MORE TIME! ONE MORE TIME!
AAAAAH!
PLOP
I'LL GET IT NEXT TIME!
AAAAAH!
SO CLOSE!
PLOP
THWACK
ONE MORE—
YOU NEED TO STOP!

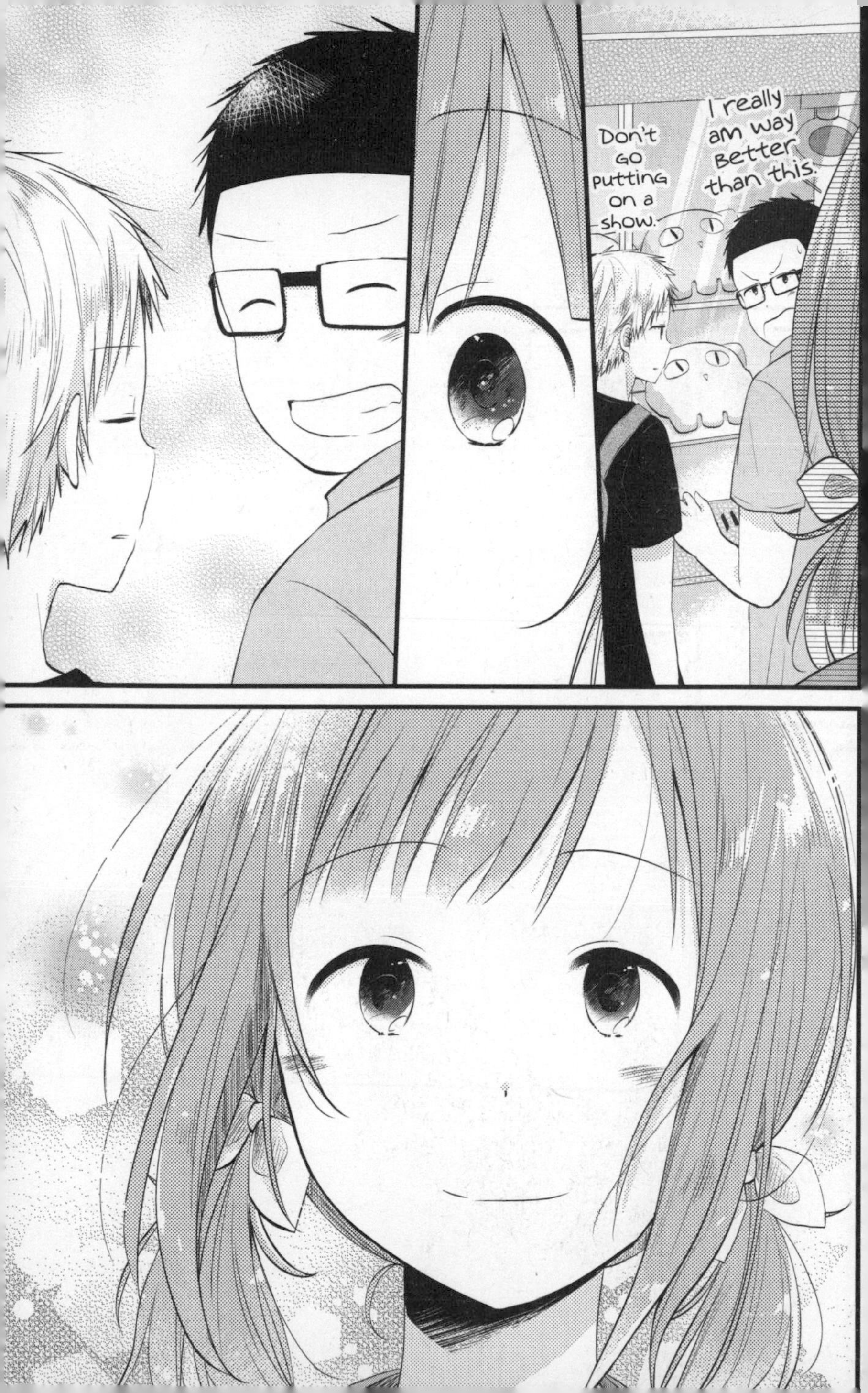
I really am way better than this.
Don't go putting on a show.

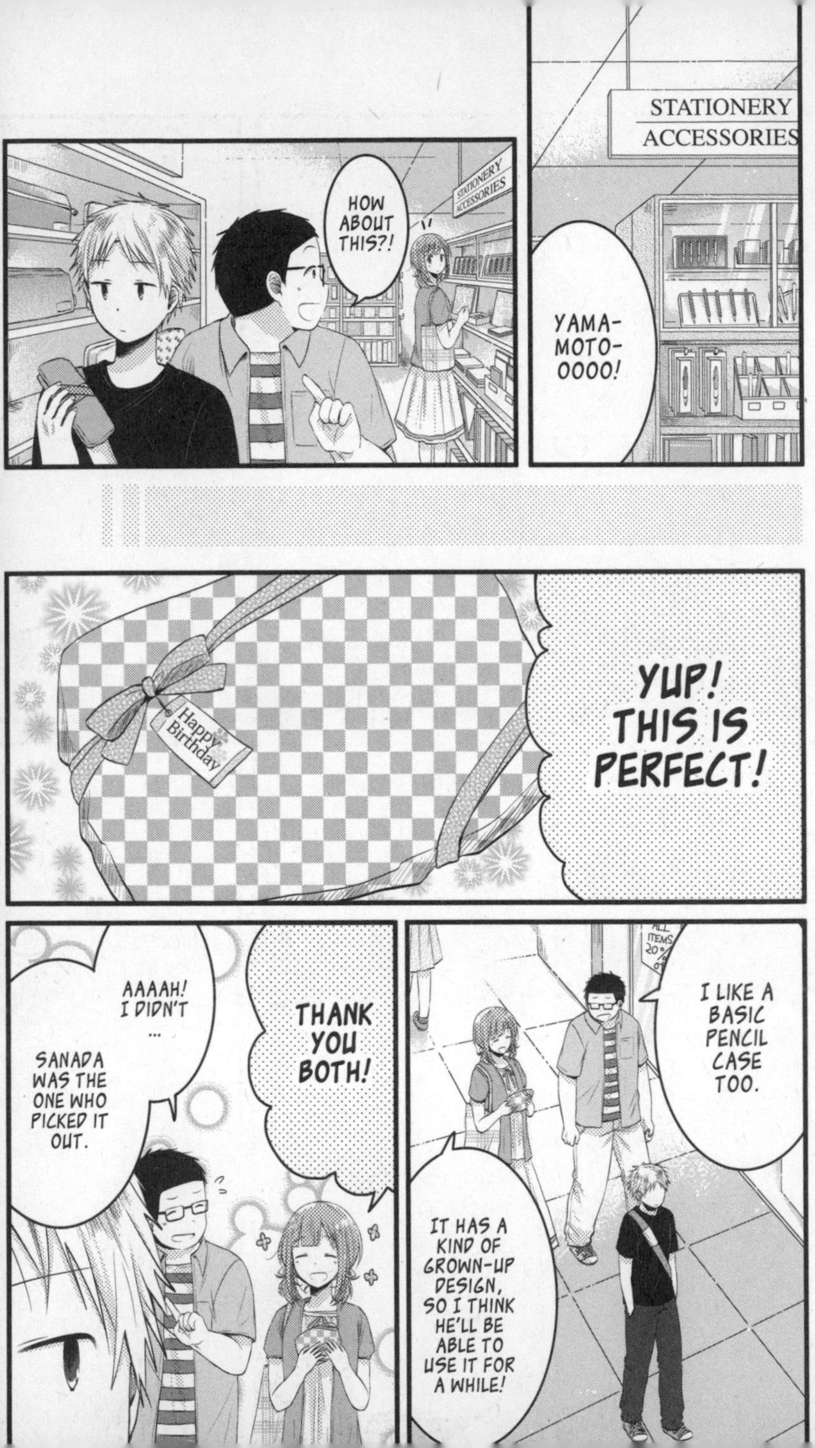
STATIONERY ACCESSORIES
YAMA-MOTO-OOOO!
HOW ABOUT THIS?!
STATIONERY ACCESSORIES
YUP! THIS IS PERFECT!
Happy Birthday
ALL ITEMS 20%
I LIKE A BASIC PENCIL CASE TOO.
IT HAS A KIND OF GROWN-UP DESIGN, SO I THINK HE'LL BE ABLE TO USE IT FOR A WHILE!
THANK YOU BOTH!
AAAAH! I DIDN'T ...
SANADA WAS THE ONE WHO PICKED IT OUT.

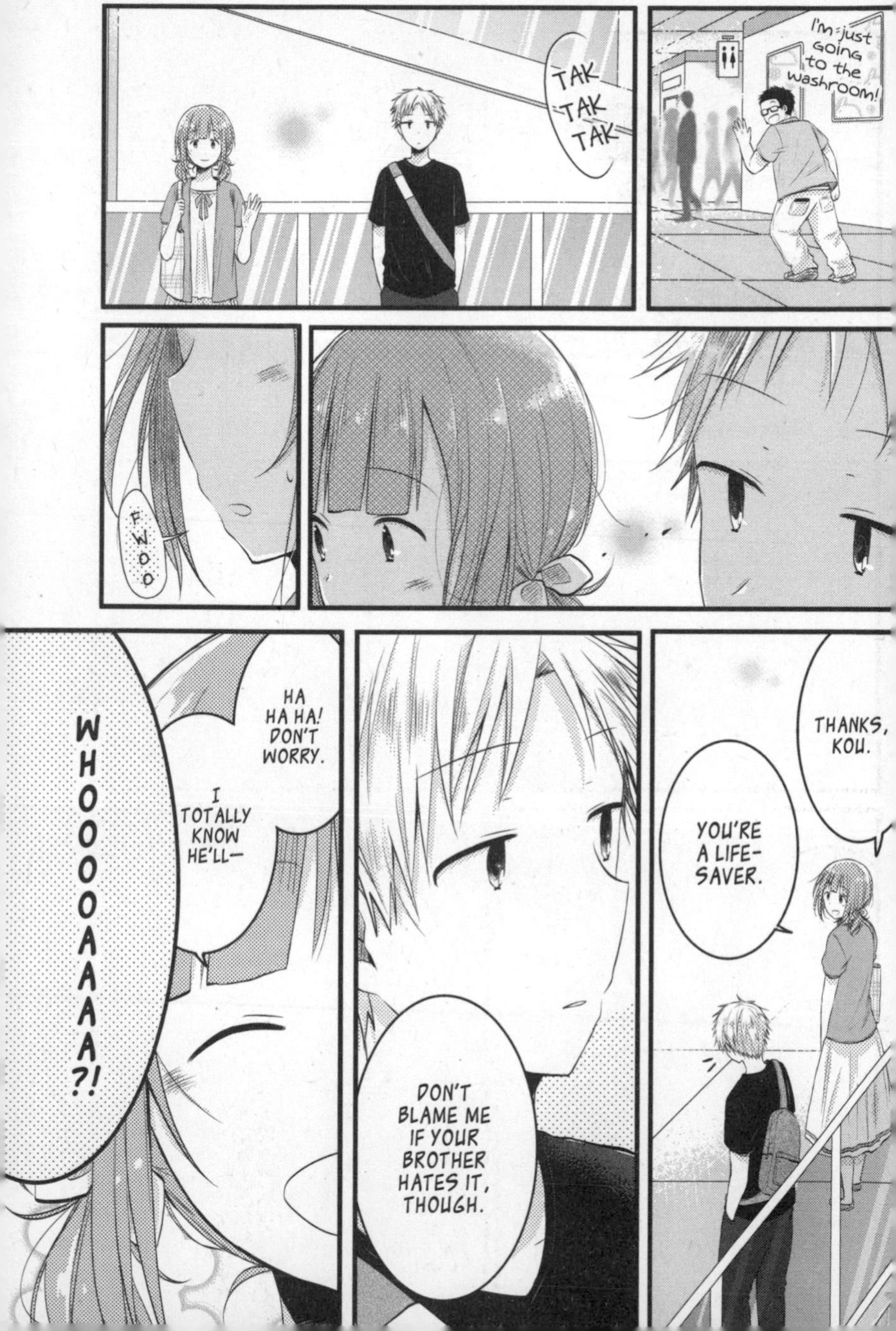
I'm just going to the washroom!
TAK TAK TAK
FWOO
THANKS, KOU.
YOU'RE A LIFE-SAVER.
DON'T BLAME ME IF YOUR BROTHER HATES IT, THOUGH.
HA HA HA! DON'T WORRY.
I TOTALLY KNOW HE'LL—
WHOOOOOAAAAAA?!

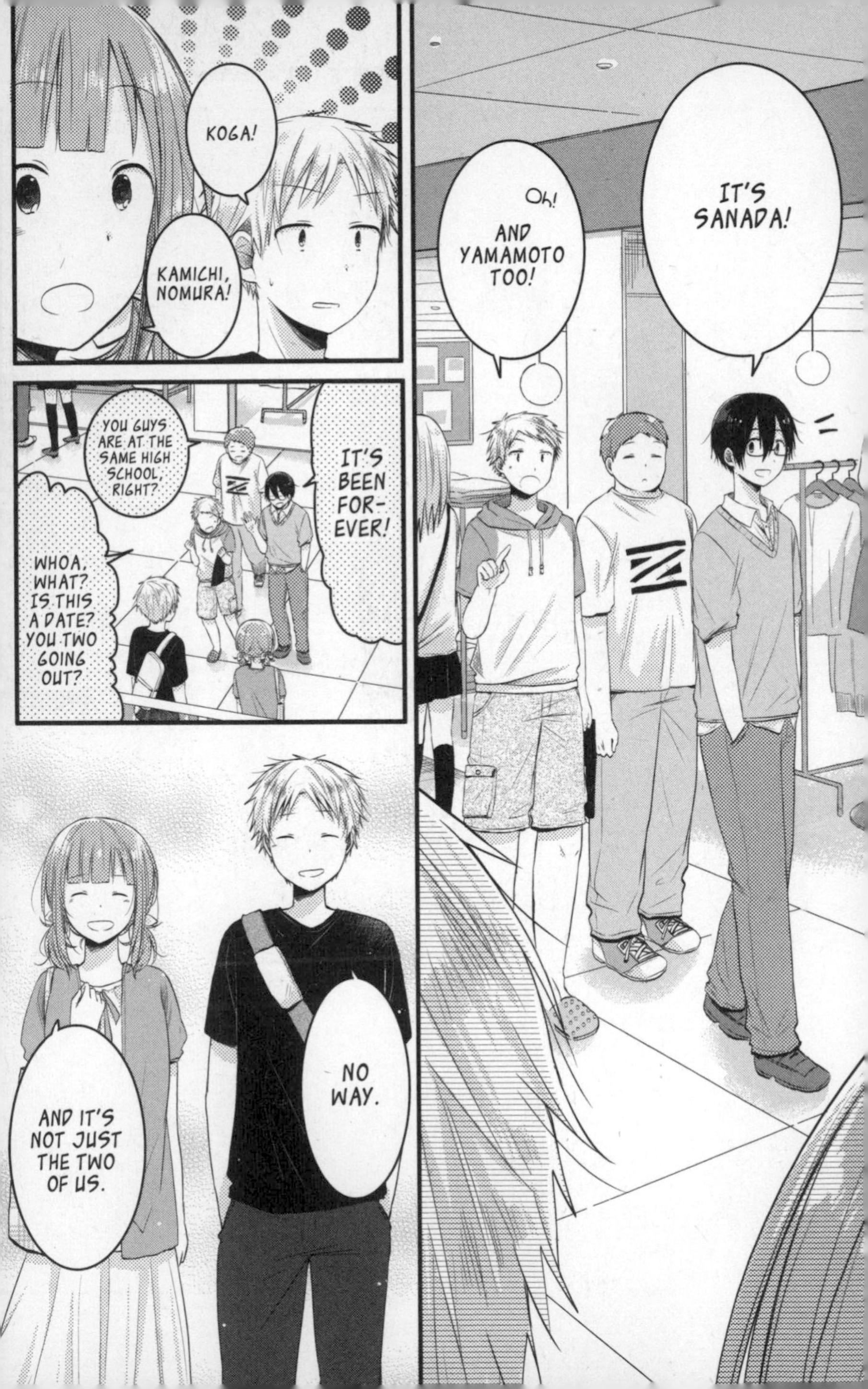
IT'S SANADA!
Oh! AND YAMAMOTO TOO!
KOGA!
KAMICHI, NOMURA!
IT'S BEEN FOR-EVER!
YOU GUYS ARE AT THE SAME HIGH SCHOOL, RIGHT?
WHOA, WHAT? IS THIS A DATE? YOU TWO GOING OUT?
NO WAY.
AND IT'S NOT JUST THE TWO OF US.

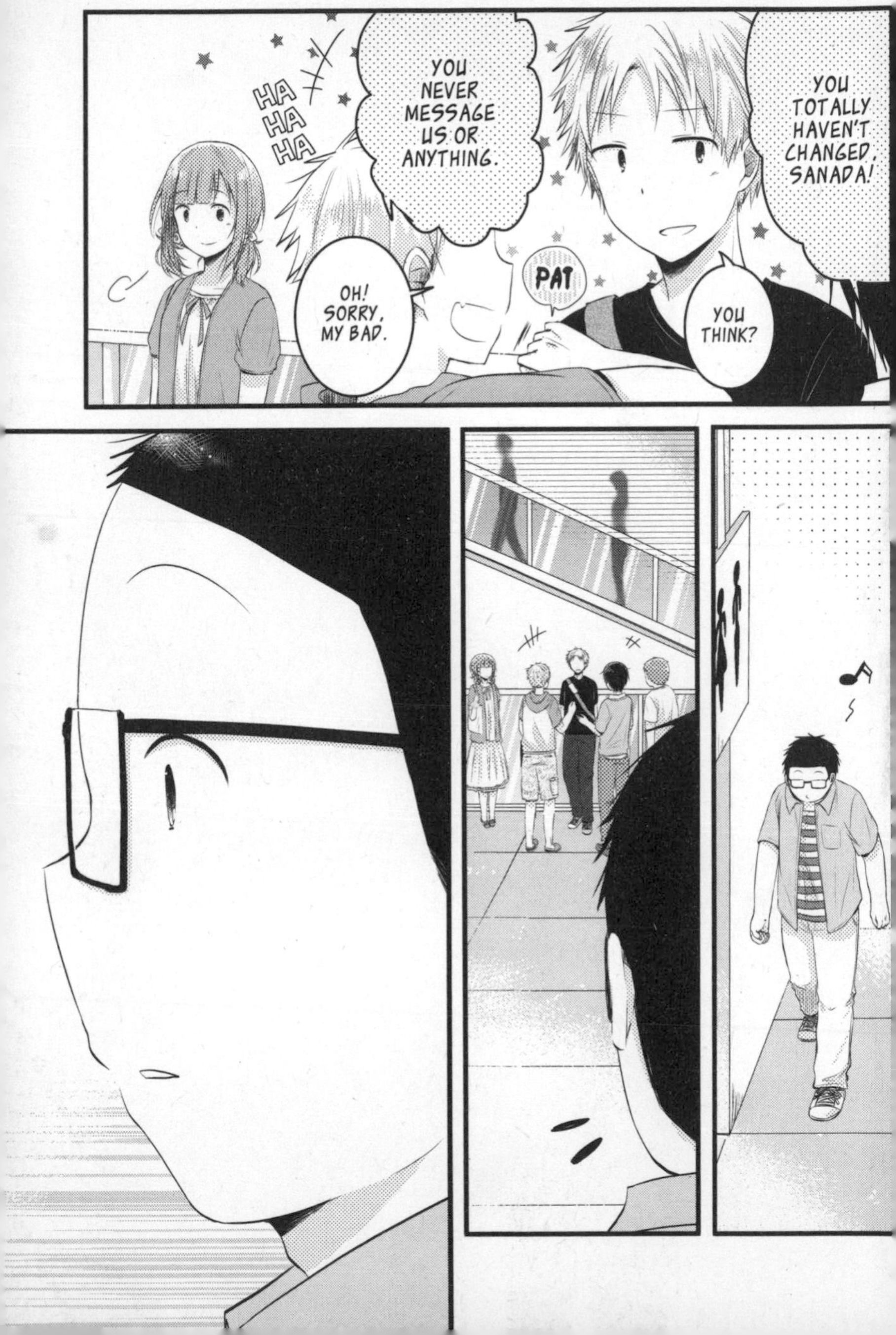
YOU TOTALLY HAVEN'T CHANGED, SANADA!
YOU NEVER MESSAGE US OR ANYTHING.
HA HA HA
YOU THINK?
PAT
OH! SORRY, MY BAD.

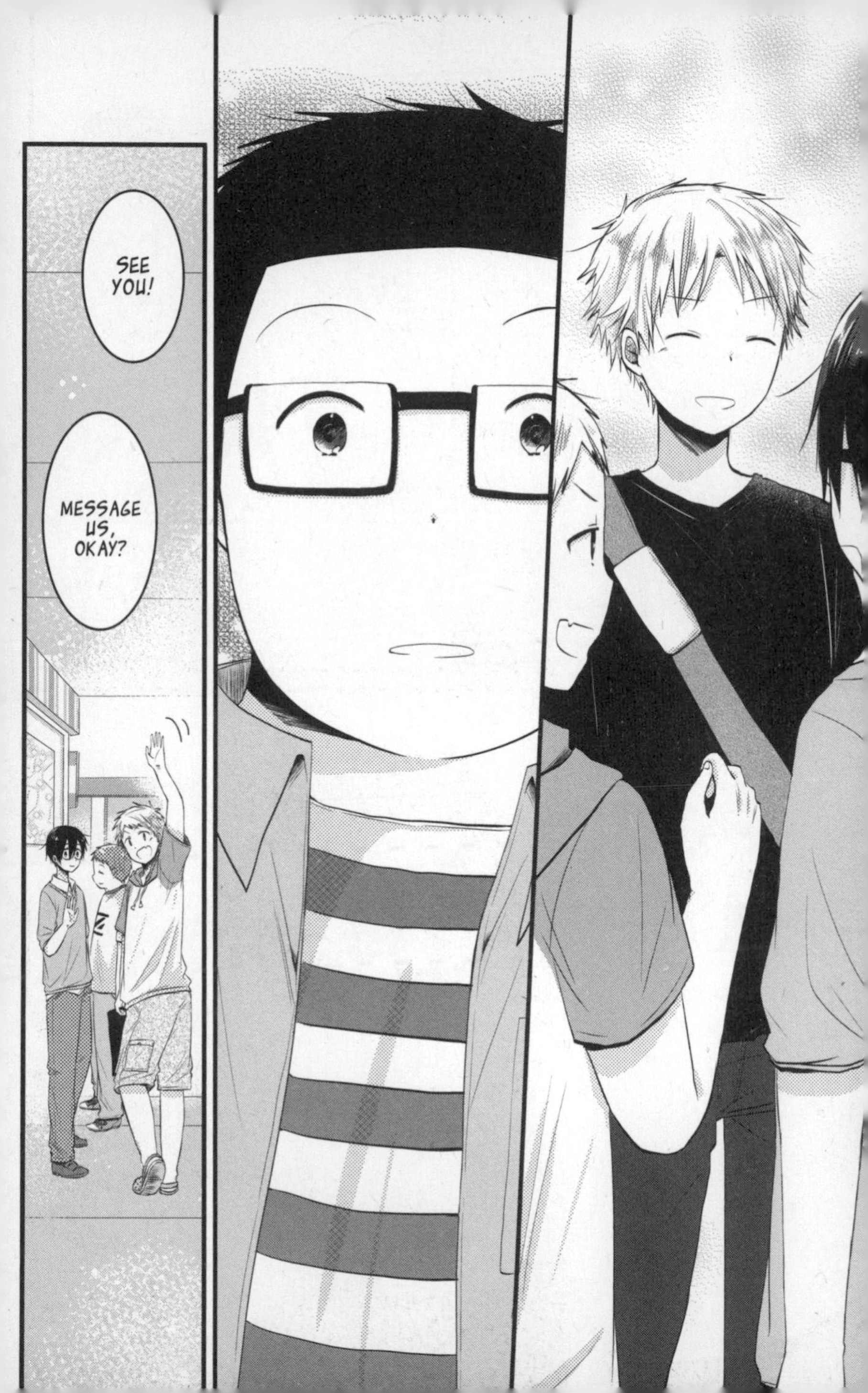
SEE YOU!
MESSAGE US, OKAY?

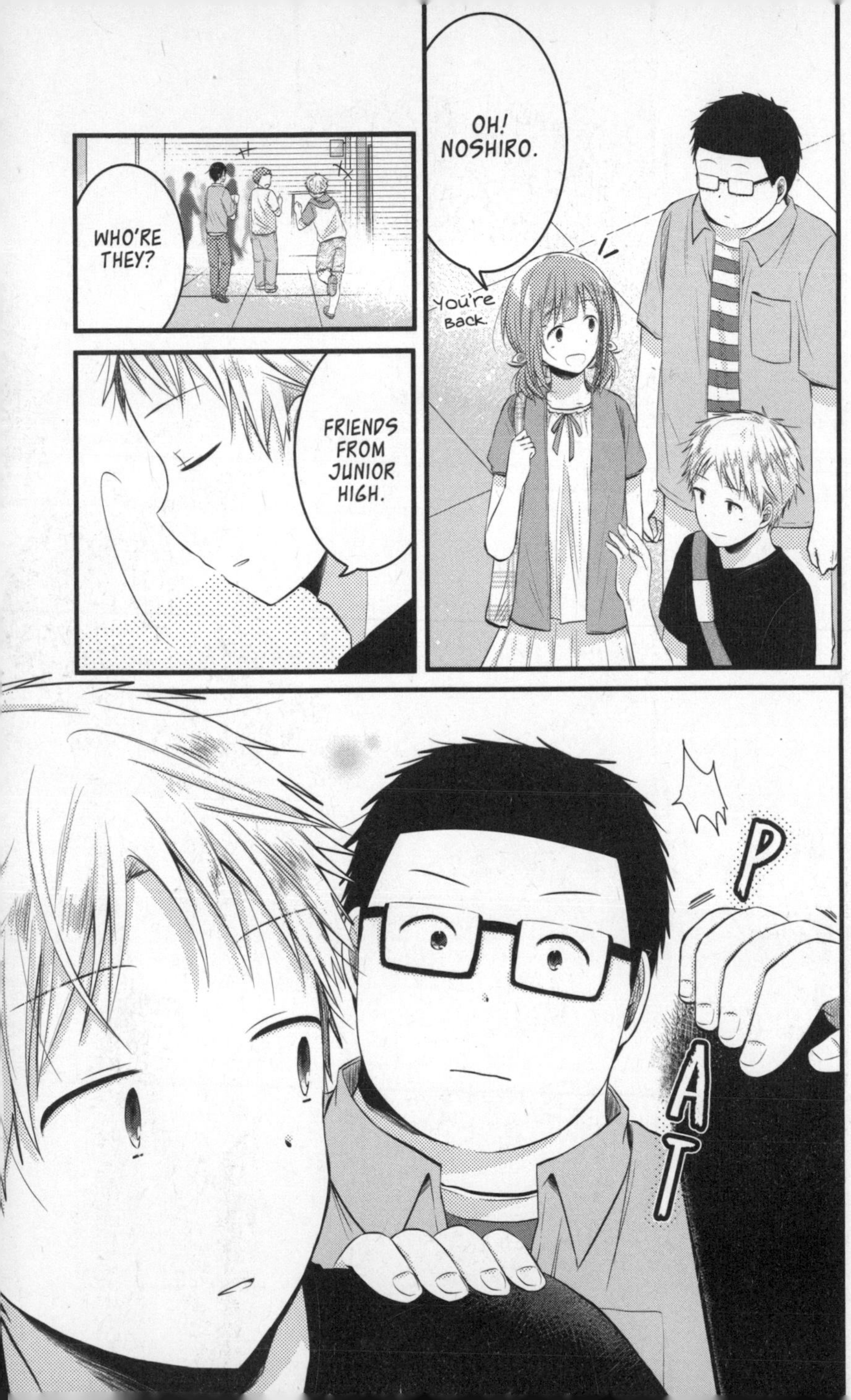
OH! NOSHIRO.
You're Back.
WHO'RE THEY?
FRIENDS FROM JUNIOR HIGH.
PAT

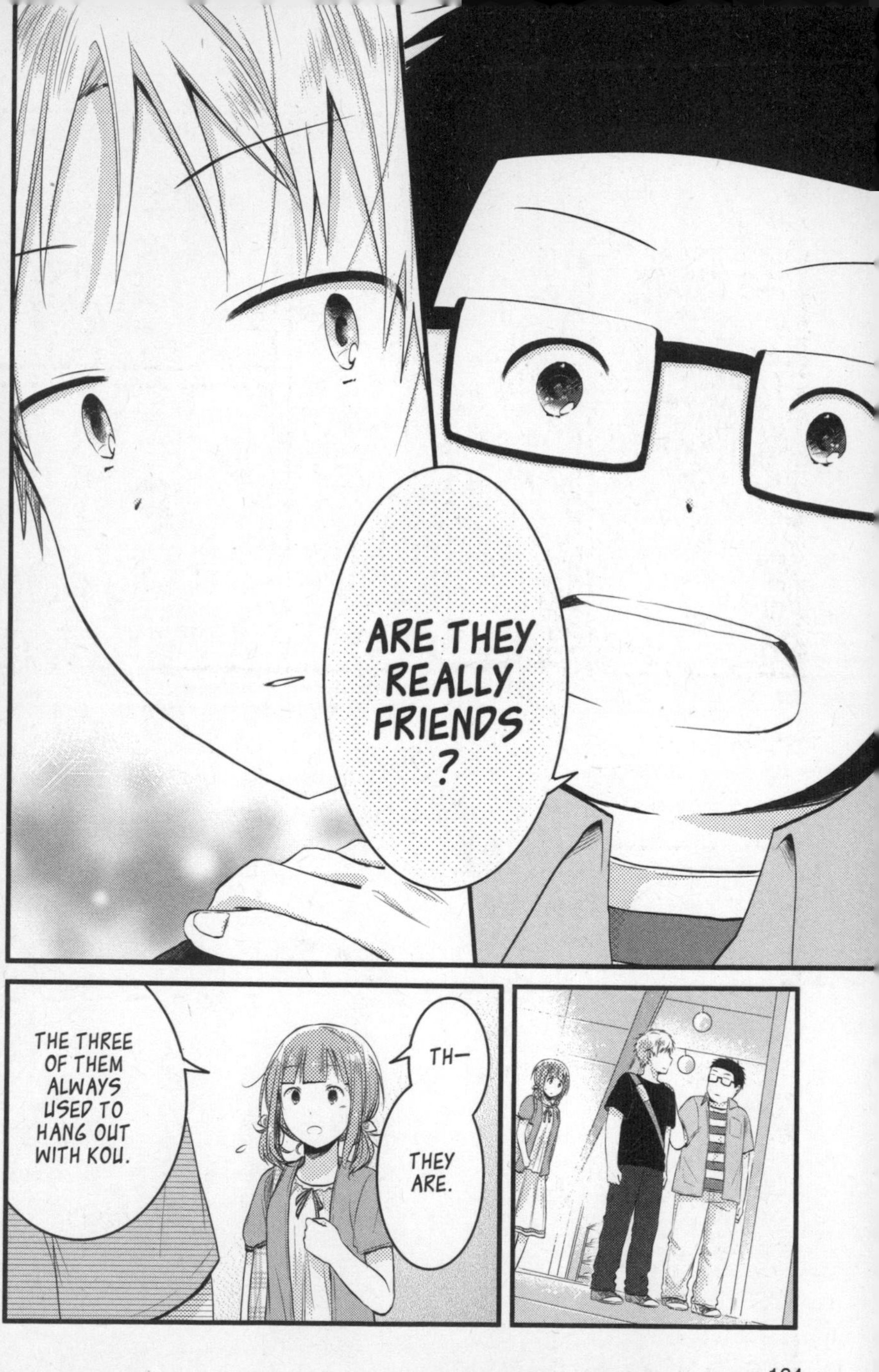
ARE THEY REALLY FRIENDS?
THE THREE OF THEM ALWAYS USED TO HANG OUT WITH KOU.
TH—
THEY ARE.

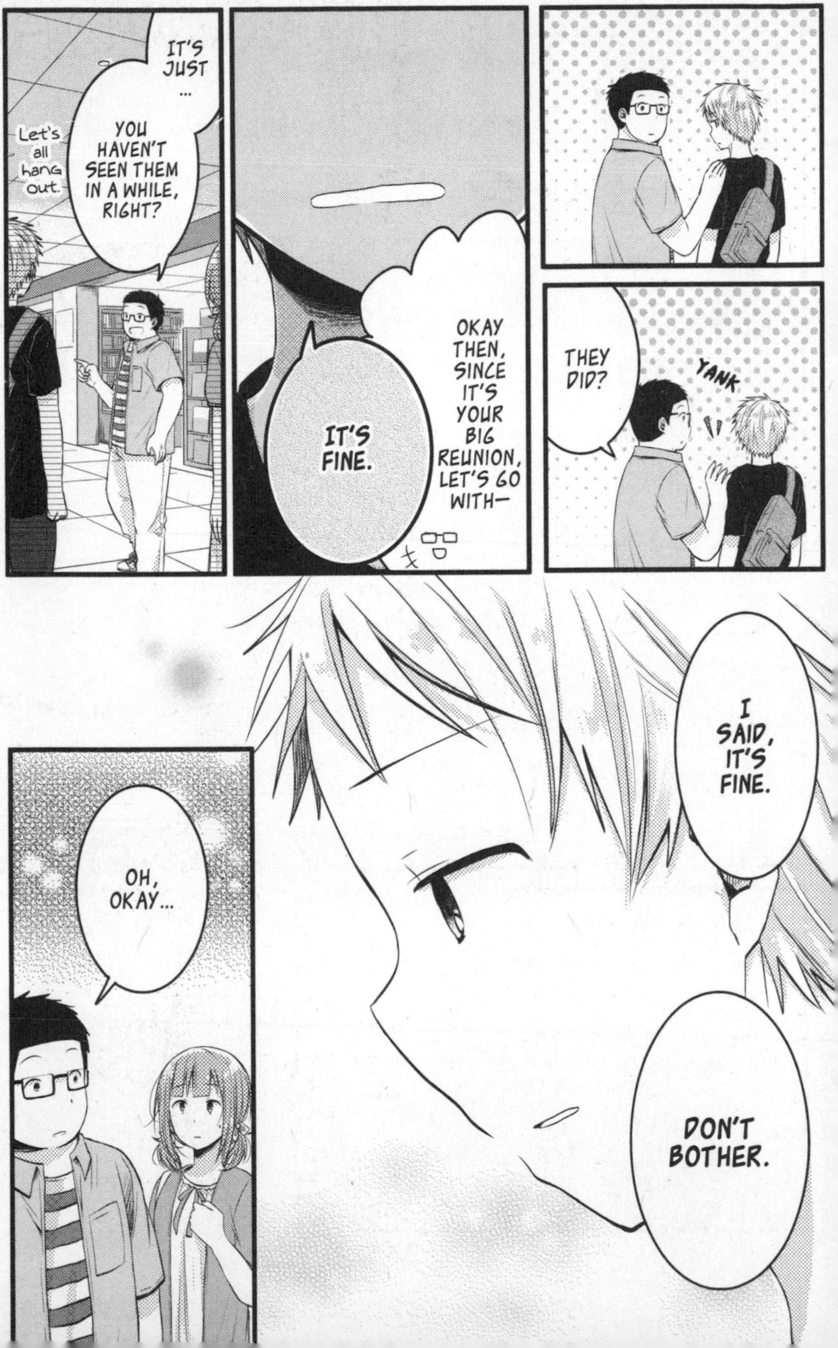
THEY DID?
YANK
OKAY THEN, SINCE IT'S YOUR BIG REUNION, LET'S GO WITH—
IT'S FINE.
IT'S JUST ...
YOU HAVEN'T SEEN THEM IN A WHILE, RIGHT?
Let's all hang out.
I SAID, IT'S FINE.
DON'T BOTHER.
OH, OKAY...

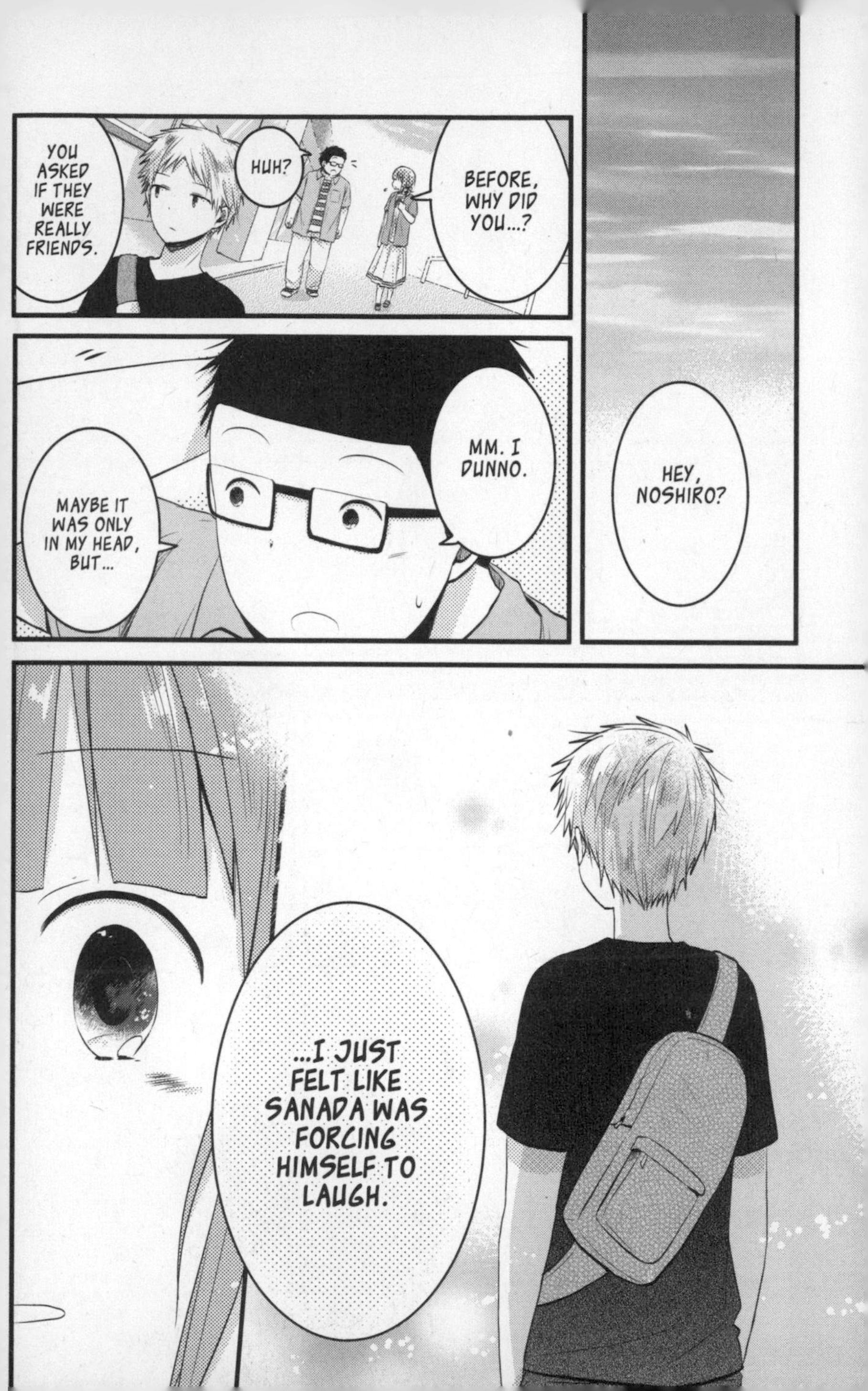
HEY, NOSHIRO?
BEFORE, WHY DID YOU...?
HUH?
YOU ASKED IF THEY WERE REALLY FRIENDS.
MM. I DUNNO.
MAYBE IT WAS ONLY IN MY HEAD, BUT...
...I JUST FELT LIKE SANADA WAS FORCING HIMSELF TO LAUGH.

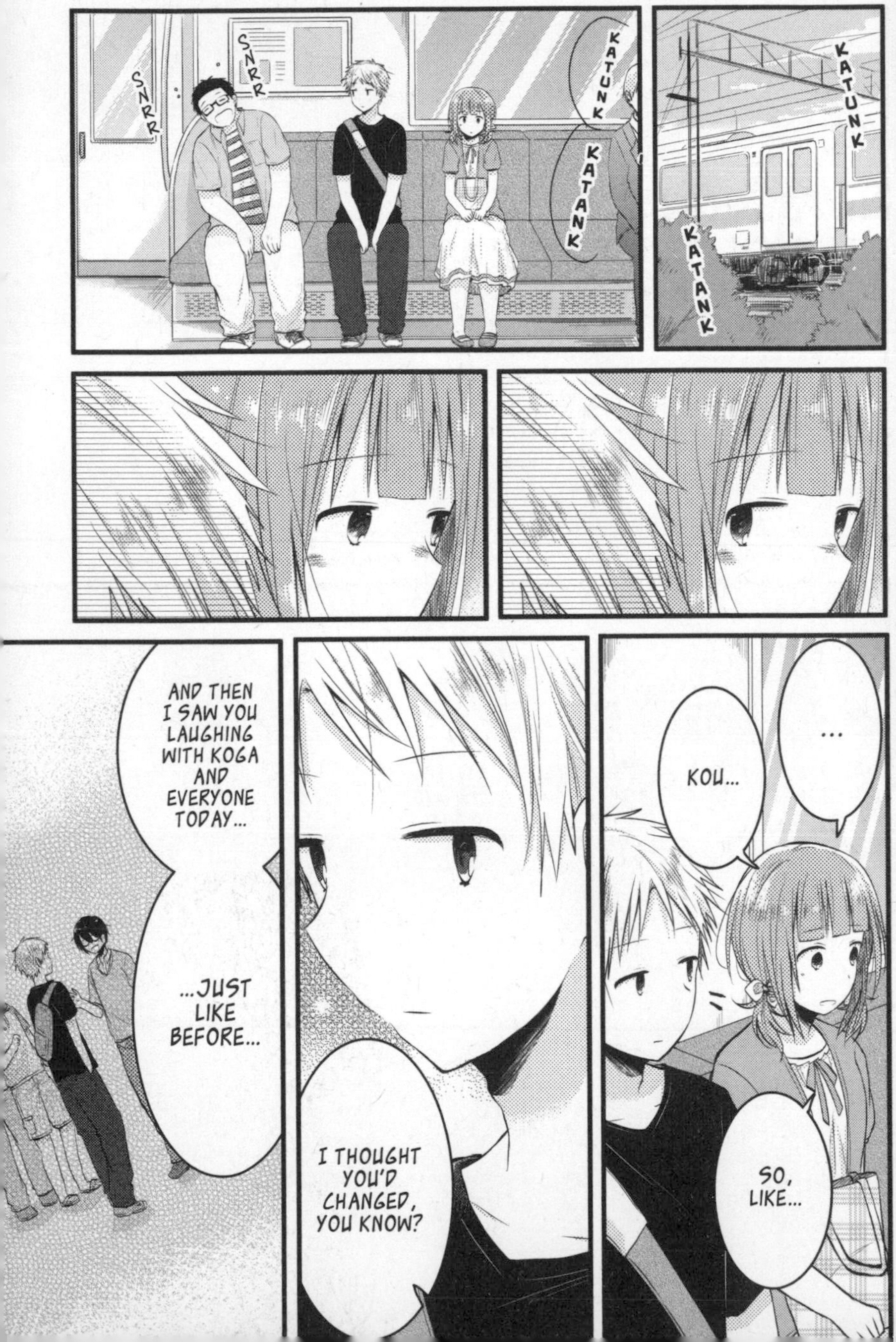
KATUNK
KATANK
KATUNK
KATANK
SNRR
SNRR
...
KOU...
SO, LIKE...
I THOUGHT YOU'D CHANGED, YOU KNOW?
AND THEN I SAW YOU LAUGHING WITH KOGA AND EVERYONE TODAY...
...JUST LIKE BEFORE...

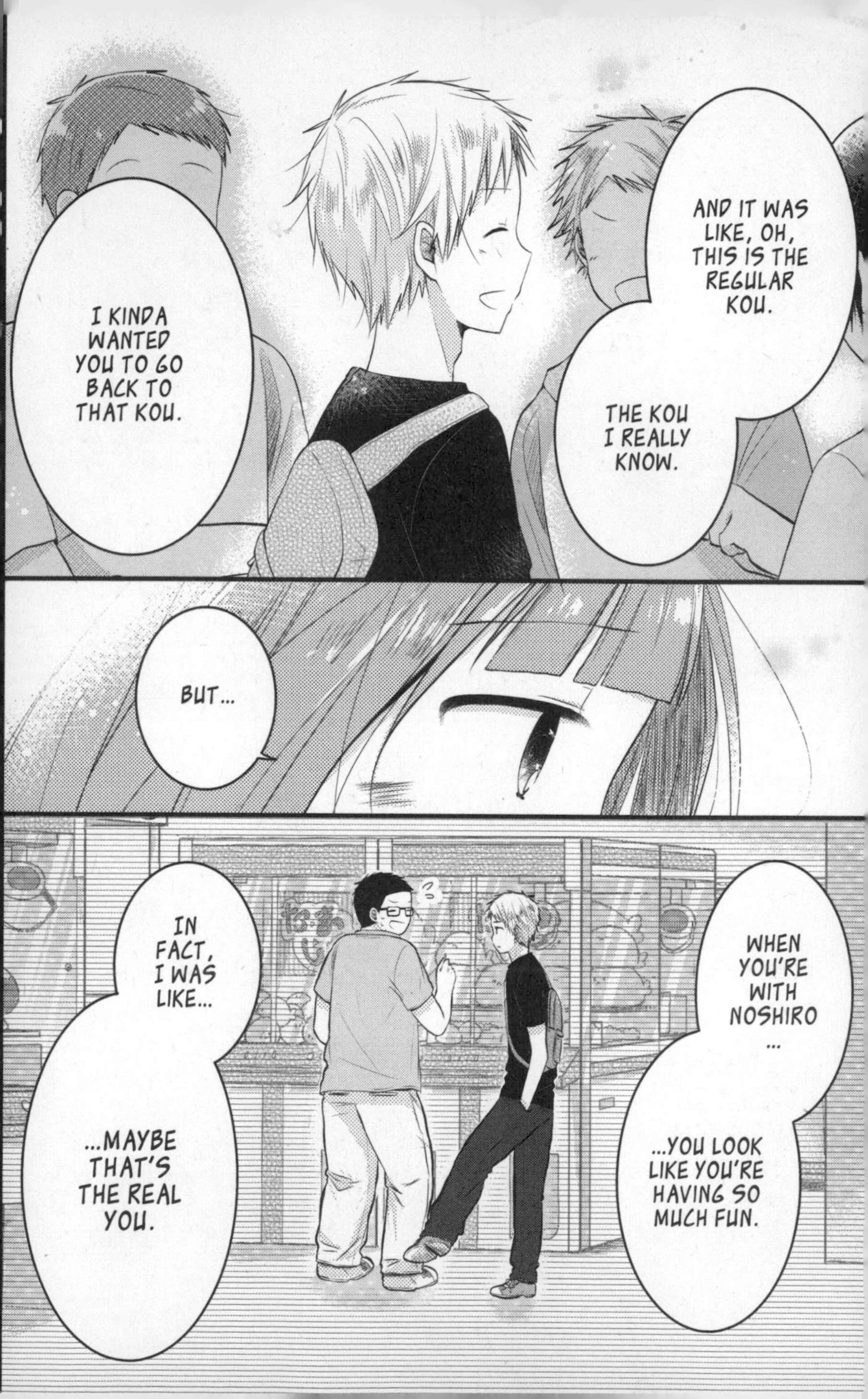
AND IT WAS LIKE, OH, THIS IS THE REGULAR KOU.
THE KOU I REALLY KNOW.
I KINDA WANTED YOU TO GO BACK TO THAT KOU.
BUT...
WHEN YOU'RE WITH NOSHIRO...
...YOU LOOK LIKE YOU'RE HAVING SO MUCH FUN.
IN FACT, I WAS LIKE...
...MAYBE THAT'S THE REAL YOU.

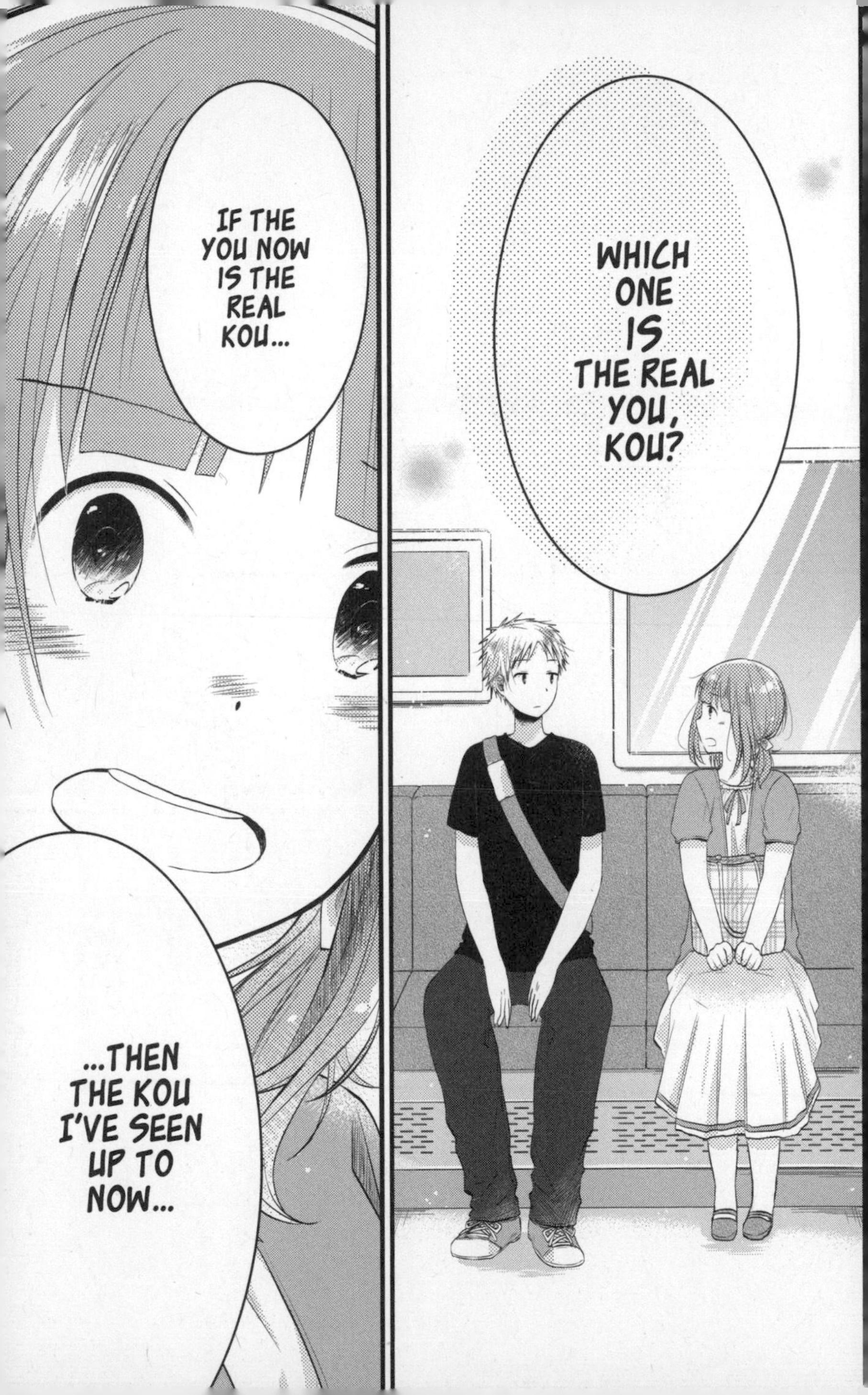
WHICH ONE IS THE REAL YOU, KOU?
IF THE YOU NOW IS THE REAL KOU...
...THEN THE KOU I'VE SEEN UP TO NOW...

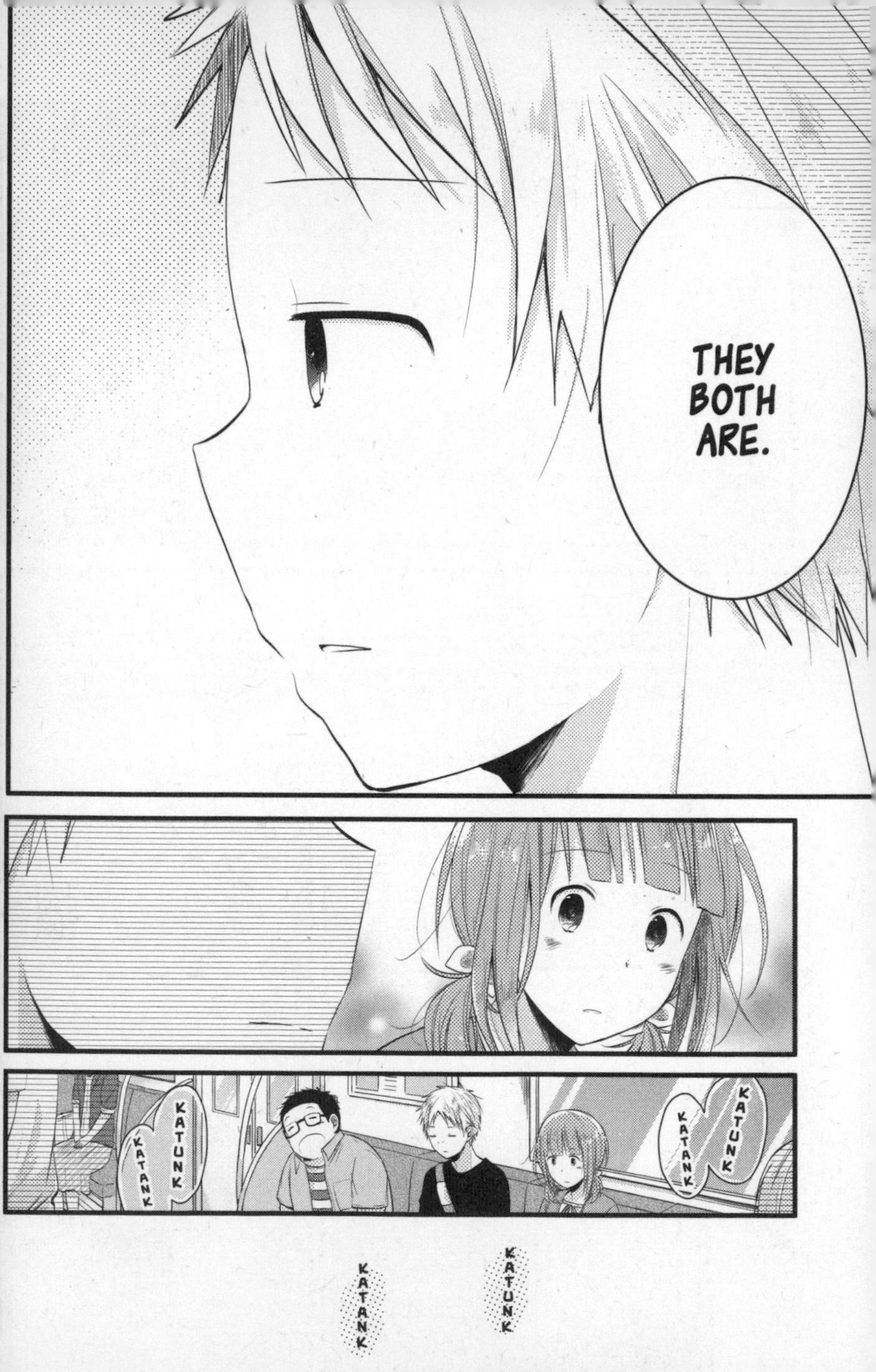
THEY BOTH ARE.
KATUNK
KATANK
KATUNK
KATANK
KATUNK
KATANK

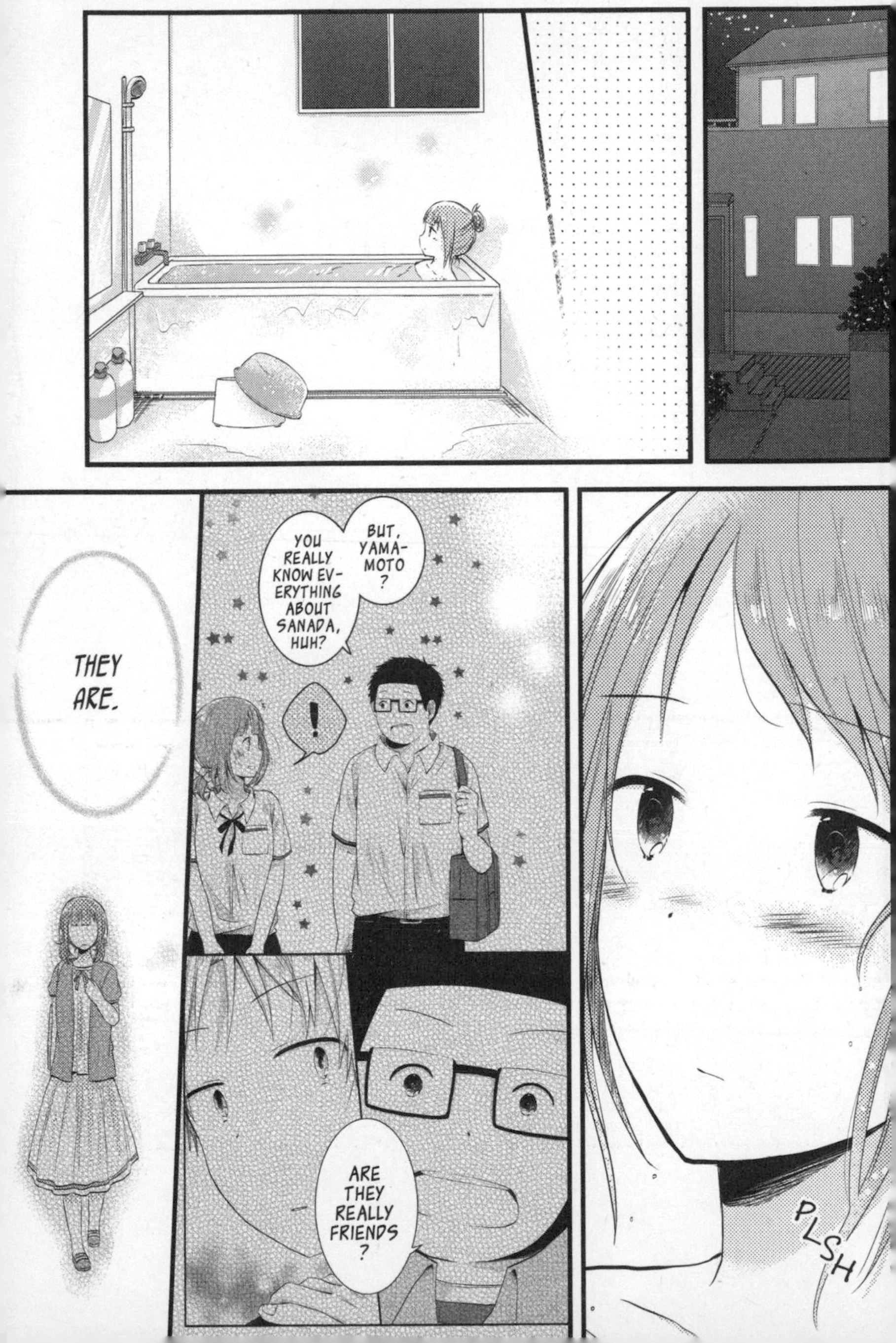
PLSH
BUT, YAMAMOTO?
YOU REALLY KNOW EVERYTHING ABOUT SANADA, HUH?
!
ARE THEY REALLY FRIENDS?
THEY ARE.

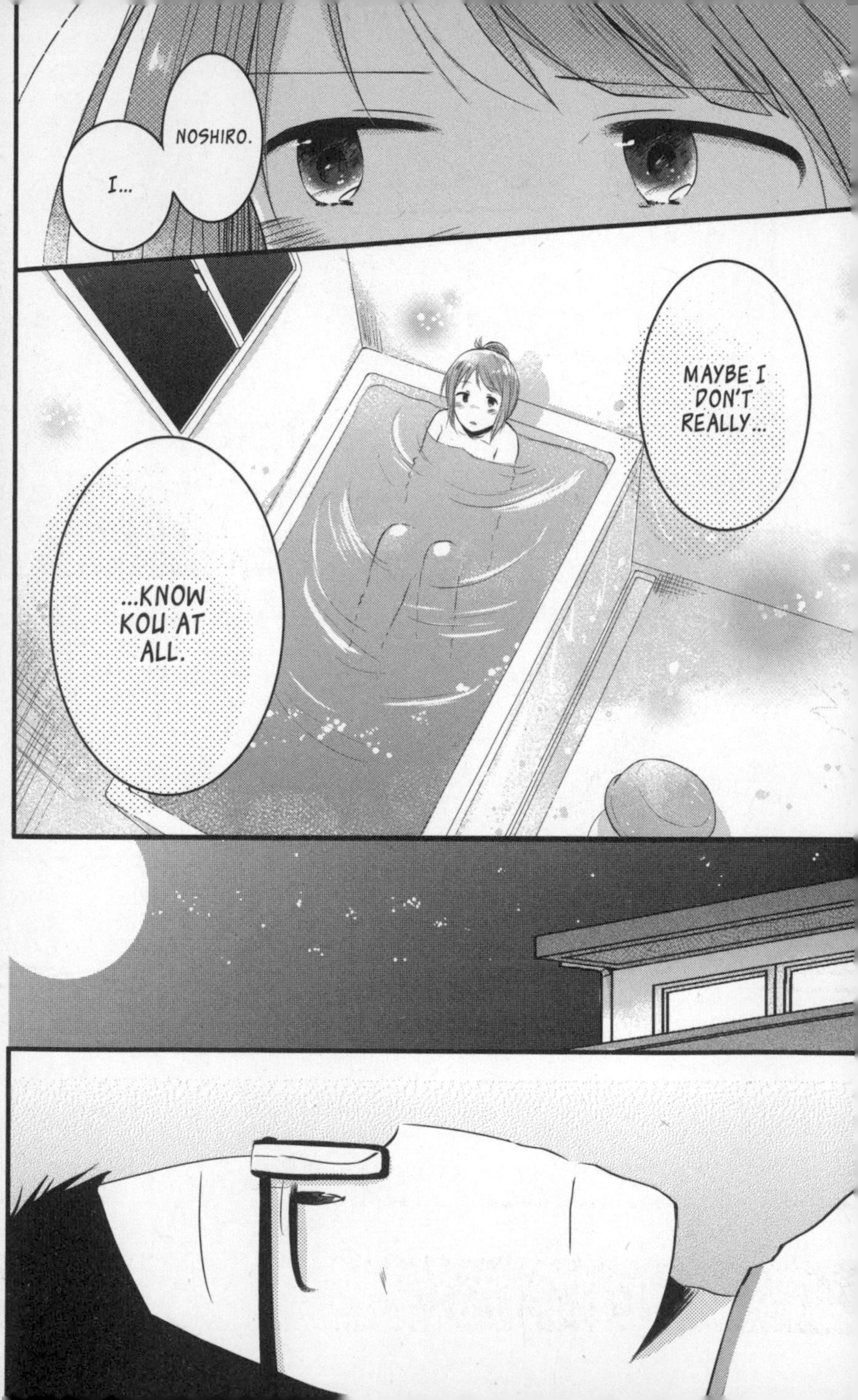
NOSHIRO.
I...
MAYBE I DON'T REALLY...
...KNOW KOU AT ALL.

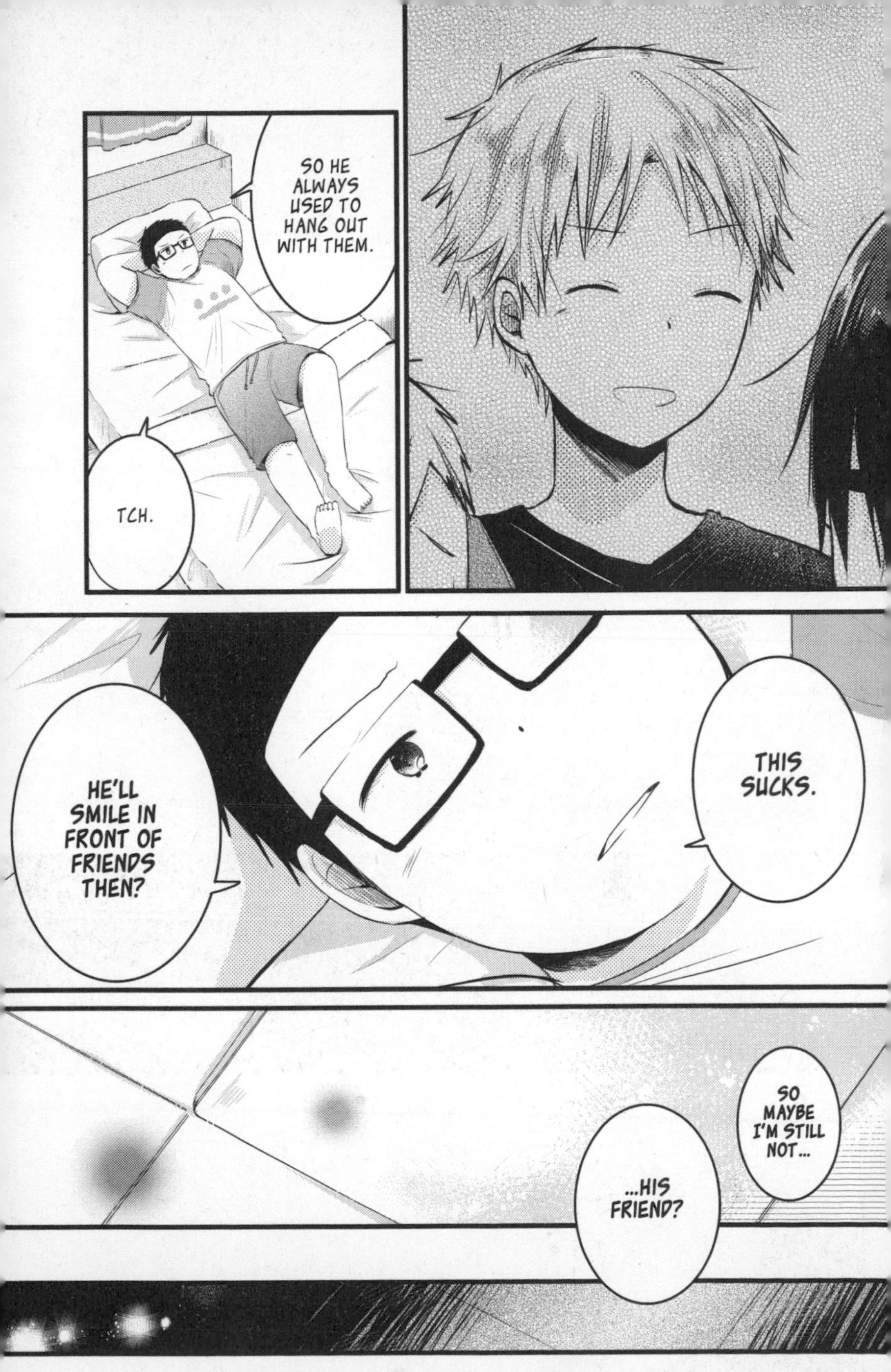
SO HE ALWAYS USED TO HANG OUT WITH THEM.
TCH.
THIS SUCKS.
HE'LL SMILE IN FRONT OF FRIENDS THEN?
SO MAYBE I'M STILL NOT...
...HIS FRIEND?

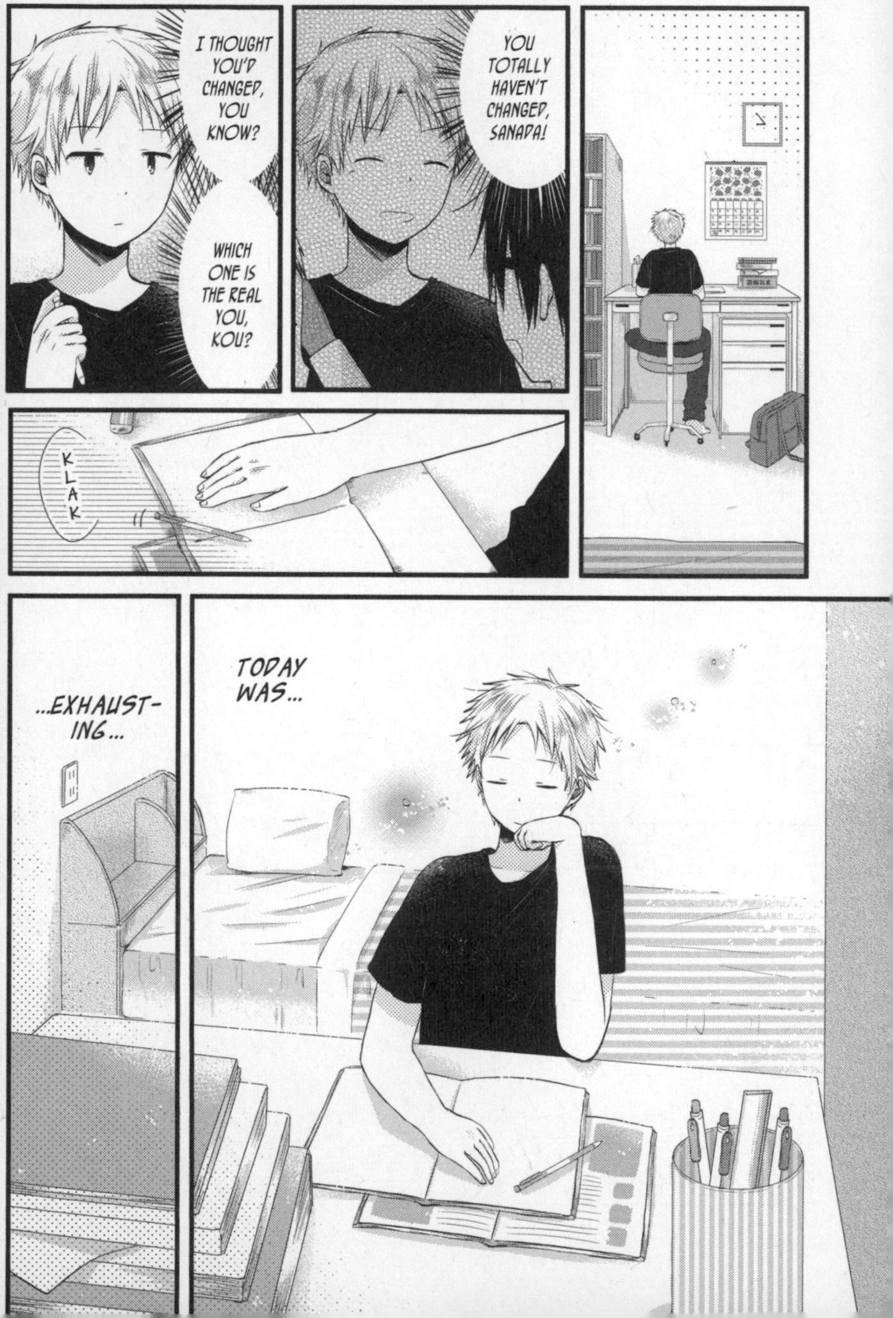
YOU TOTALLY HAVEN'T CHANGED, SANADA!
I THOUGHT YOU'D CHANGED, YOU KNOW?
WHICH ONE IS THE REAL YOU, KOU?
KLAK
TODAY WAS...
...EXHAUST-ING...

That Blue
Sky Feeling

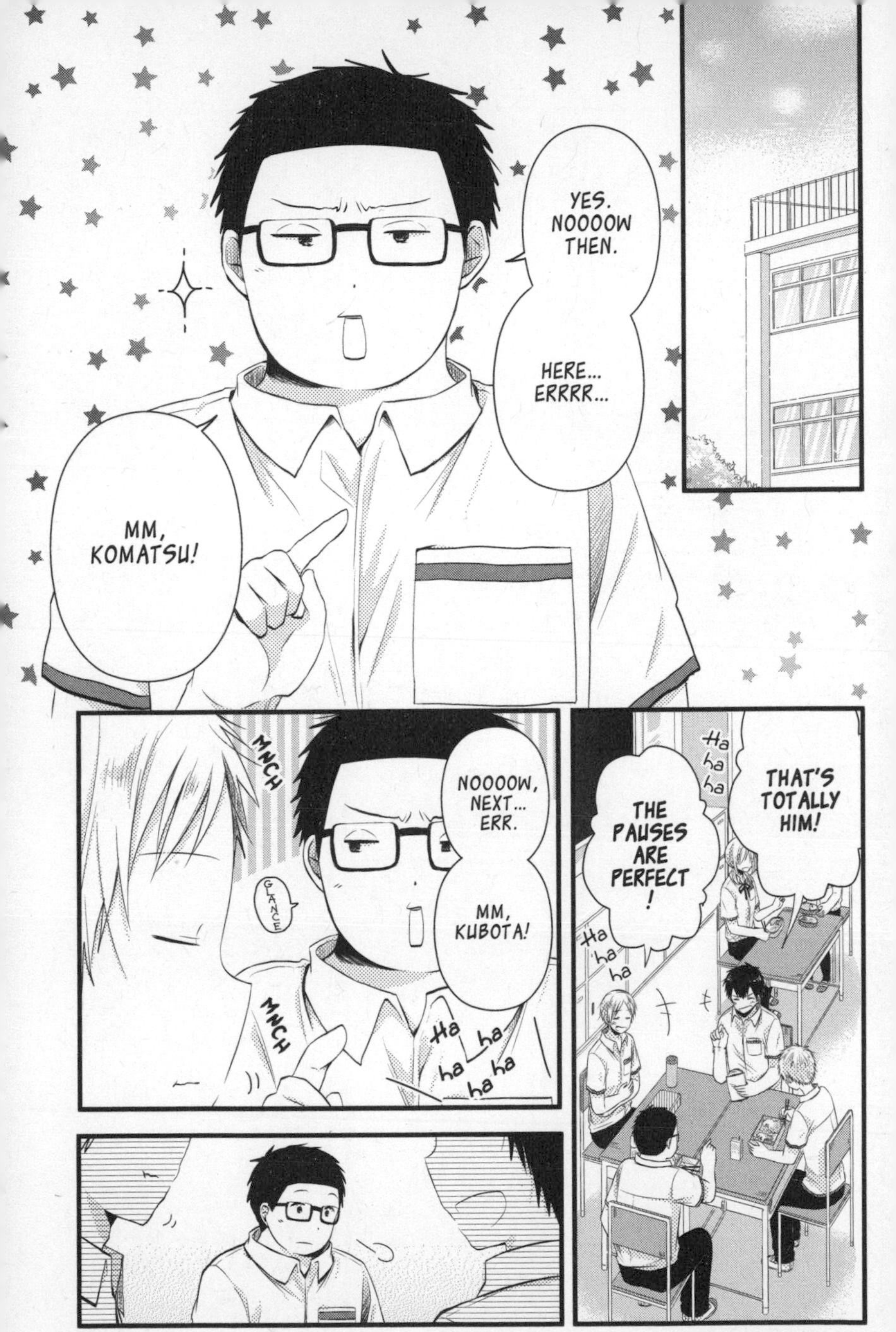
YES. NOOOOW THEN.
HERE... ERRRR...
MM, KOMATSU!
Ha ha ha
THAT'S TOTALLY HIM!
THE PAUSES ARE PERFECT!
Ha ha ha
NOOOOW, NEXT... ERR.
MNCH
MM, KUBOTA!
GLANCE
MNCH
Ha ha ha ha ha

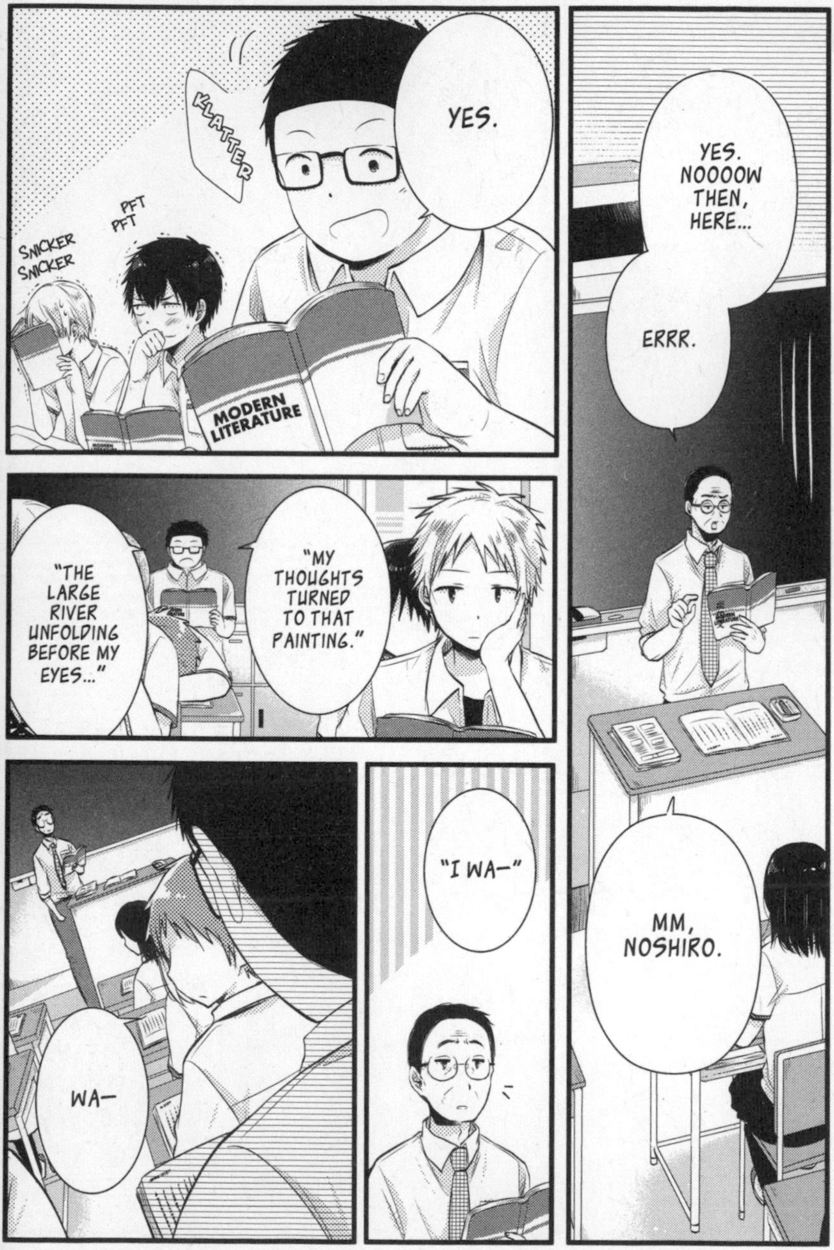
YES. NOOOOW THEN, HERE...
ERRR.
MM, NOSHIRO.
YES.
KLATTER
PFT PFT
SNICKER SNICKER
MODERN LITERATURE
"MY THOUGHTS TURNED TO THAT PAINTING."
"THE LARGE RIVER UNFOLDING BEFORE MY EYES..."
"I WA-"
WA-

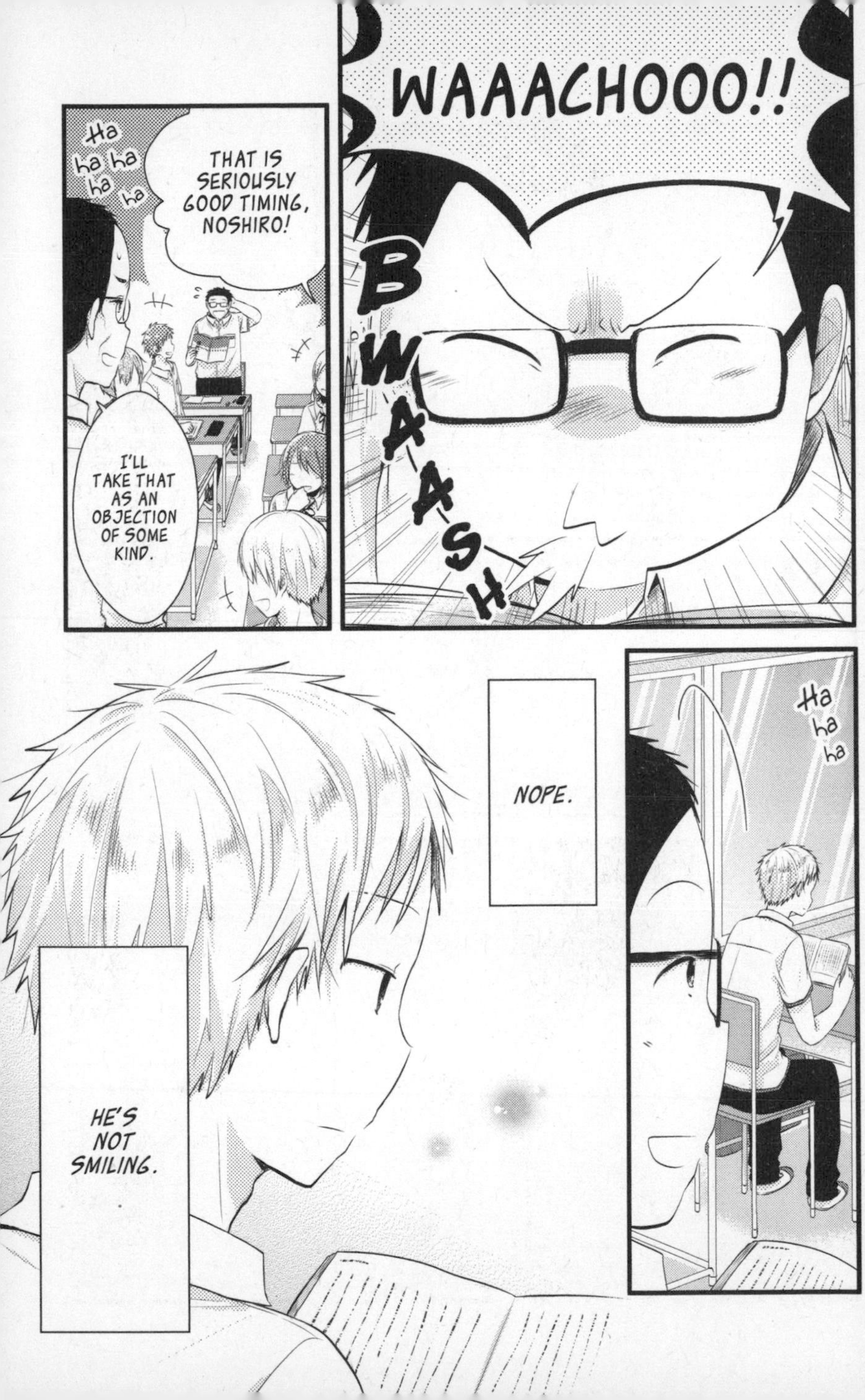
WAAACHOOO!!
BWAASH
Ha ha ha ha ha
THAT IS SERIOUSLY GOOD TIMING, NOSHIRO!
I'LL TAKE THAT AS AN OBJECTION OF SOME KIND.
Ha ha ha
NOPE.
HE'S NOT SMILING.

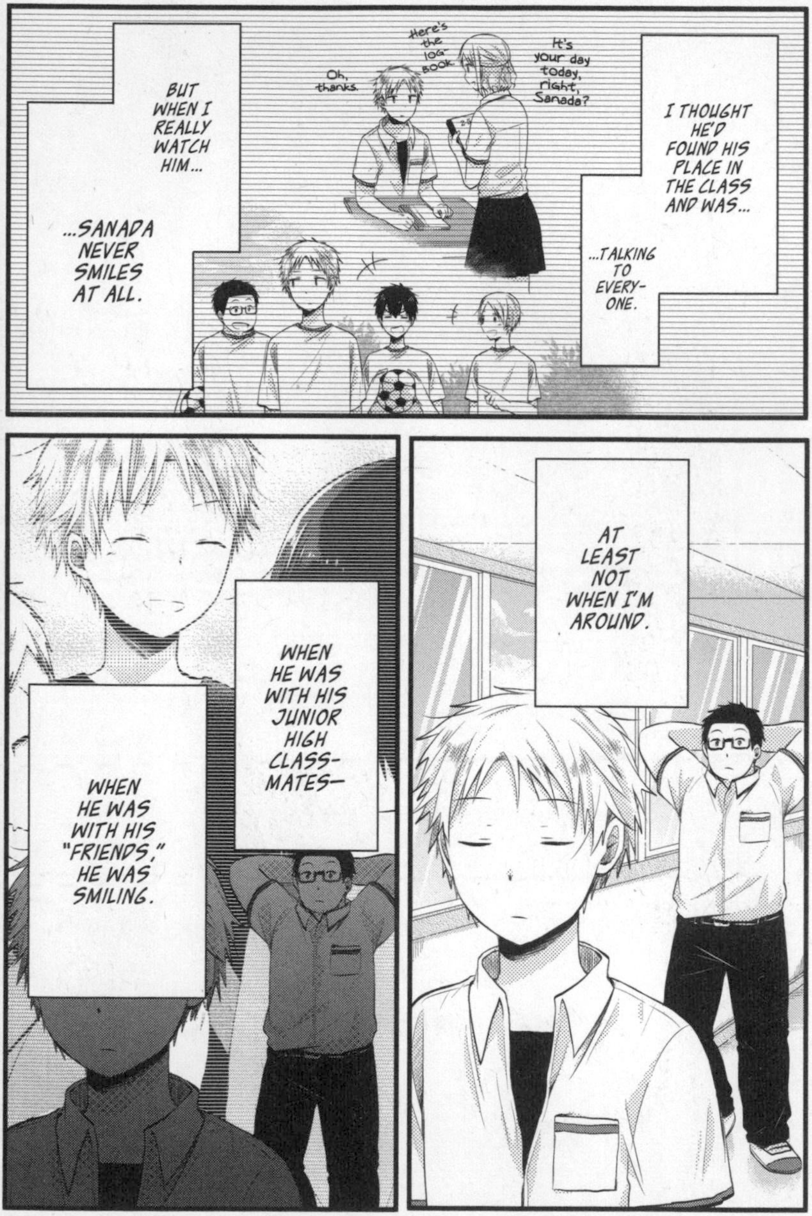
I THOUGHT HE'D FOUND HIS PLACE IN THE CLASS AND WAS...
...TALKING TO EVERYONE.
It's your day today, right, Sanada?
Here's the log book.
Oh, thanks.
BUT WHEN I REALLY WATCH HIM...
...SANADA NEVER SMILES AT ALL.
AT LEAST NOT WHEN I'M AROUND.
WHEN HE WAS WITH HIS JUNIOR HIGH CLASSMATES—
WHEN HE WAS WITH HIS "FRIENDS," HE WAS SMILING.

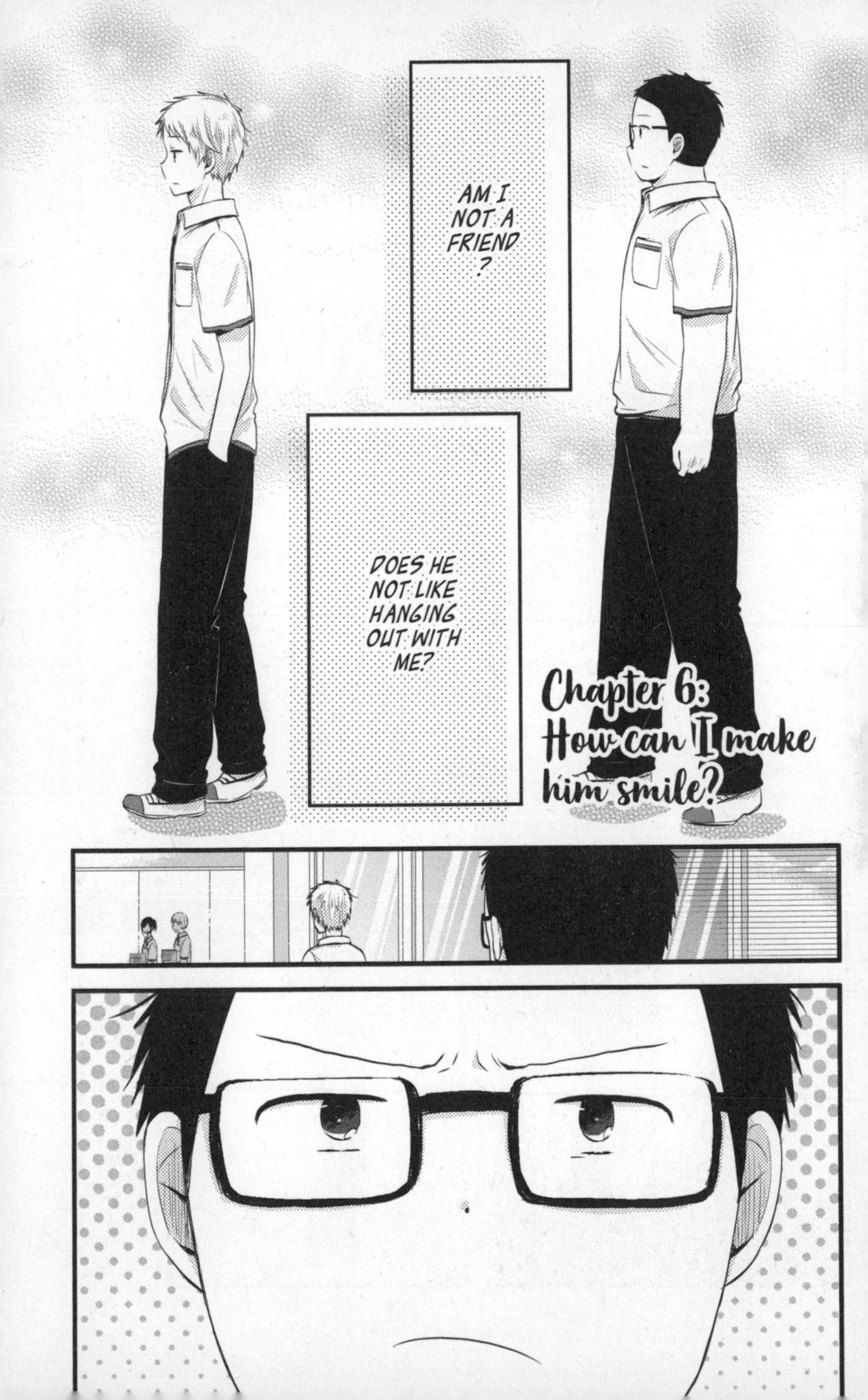
AM I NOT A FRIEND?
DOES HE NOT LIKE HANGING OUT WITH ME?
Chapter 6: How can I make him smile?

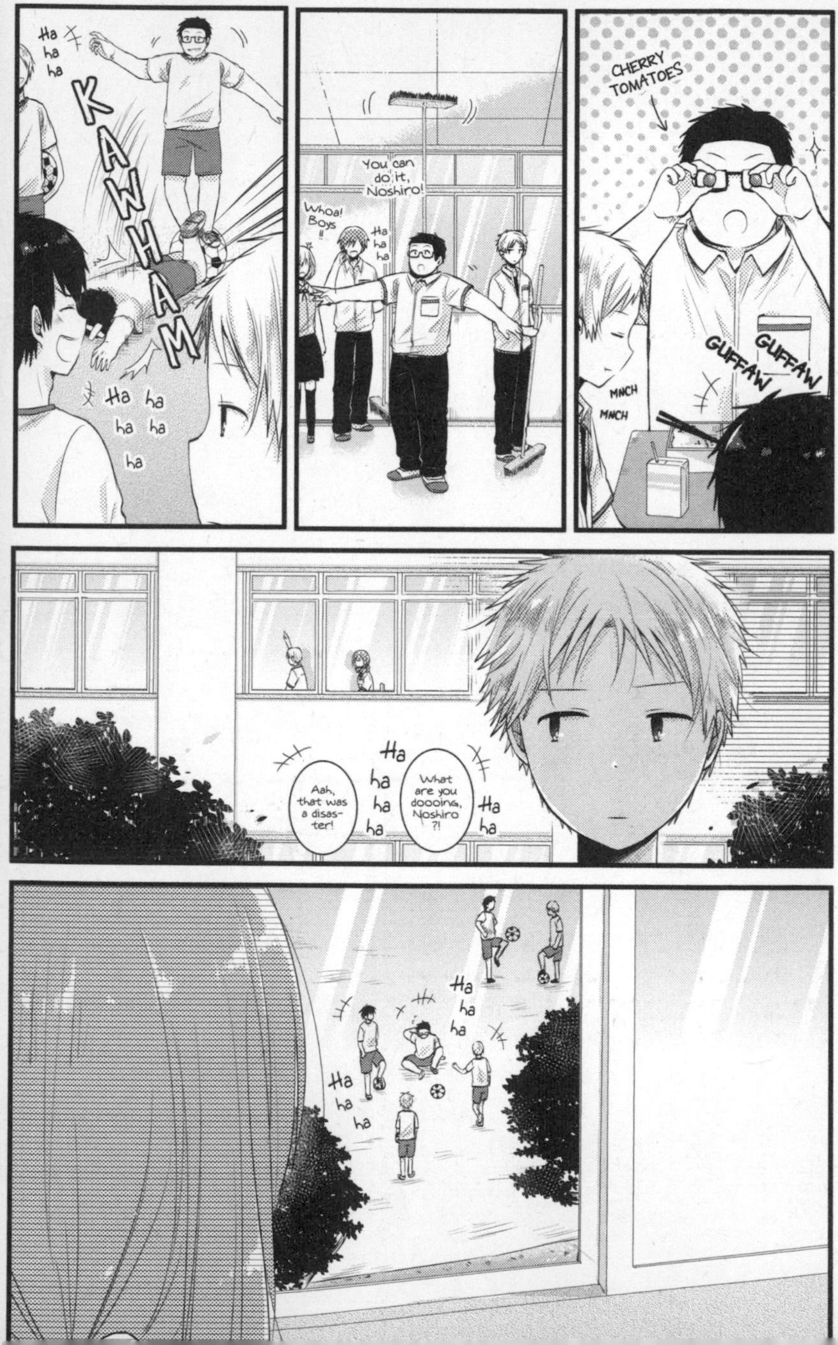
CHERRY TOMATOES
MNCH MNCH
GUFFAW GUFFAW
You can do it, Noshiro!
Ha ha ha
Whoa! Boys !!
Ha ha ha
KAWHAM
Ha ha ha ha ha
Ha ha
What are you doooing, Noshiro?!
Ha ha ha ha
Aah, that was a disaster!
Ha ha ha
Ha ha ha

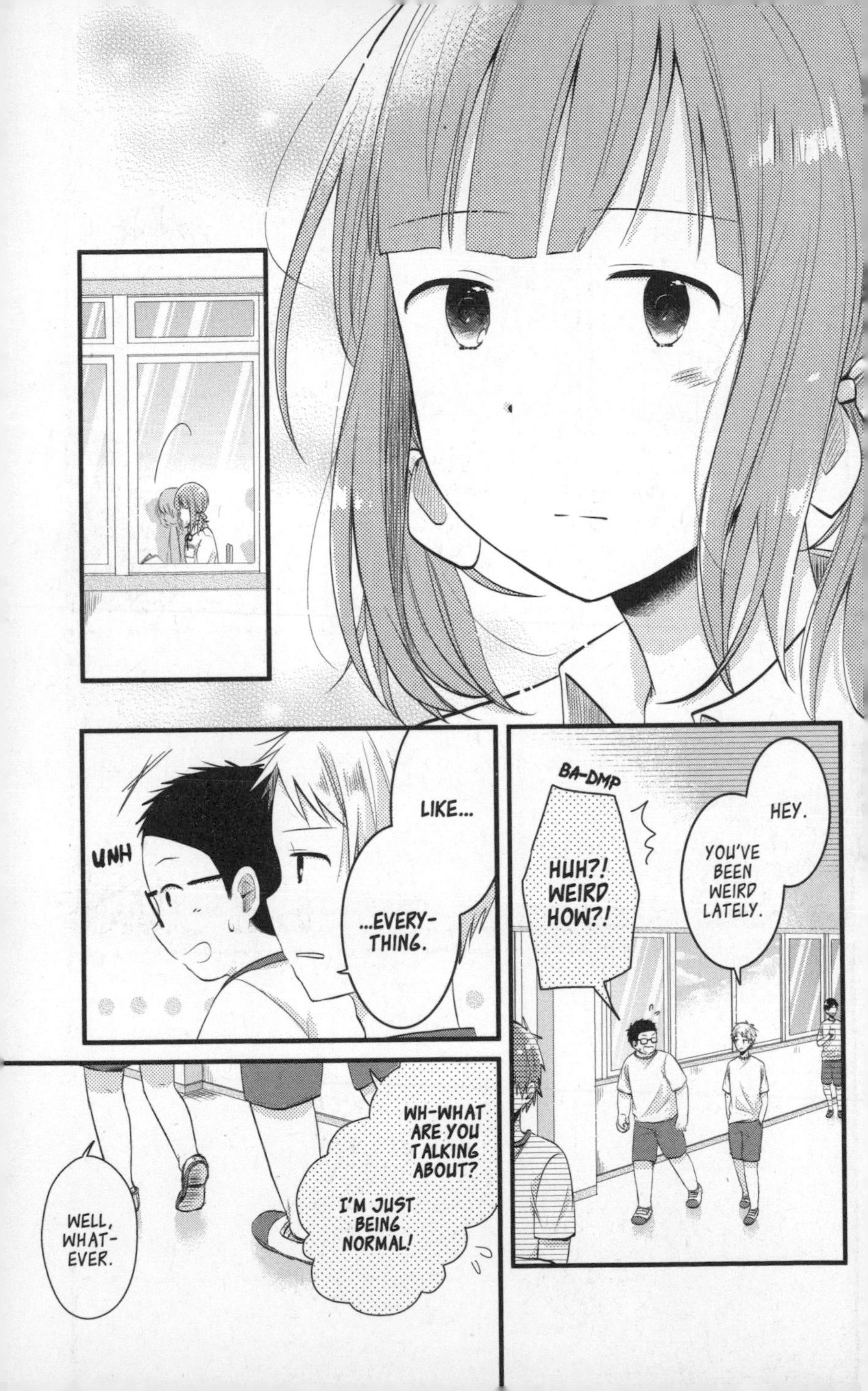
HEY.
YOU'VE BEEN WEIRD LATELY.
BA-DMP
HUH?! WEIRD HOW?!
LIKE...
...EVERYTHING.
UNH
WH-WHAT ARE YOU TALKING ABOUT?
I'M JUST BEING NORMAL!
WELL, WHATEVER.

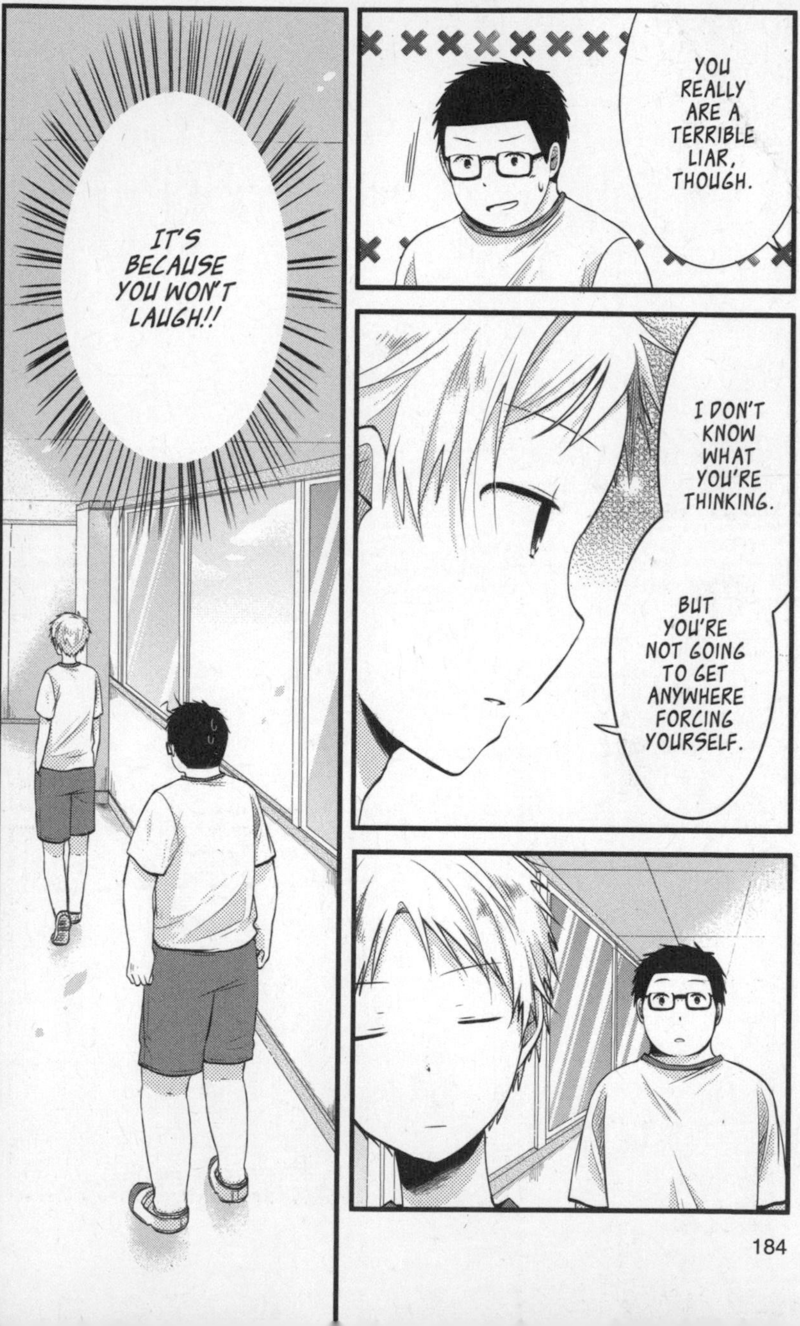
YOU REALLY ARE A TERRIBLE LIAR, THOUGH.
I DON'T KNOW WHAT YOU'RE THINKING.
BUT YOU'RE NOT GOING TO GET ANYWHERE FORCING YOURSELF.
IT'S BECAUSE YOU WON'T LAUGH!!

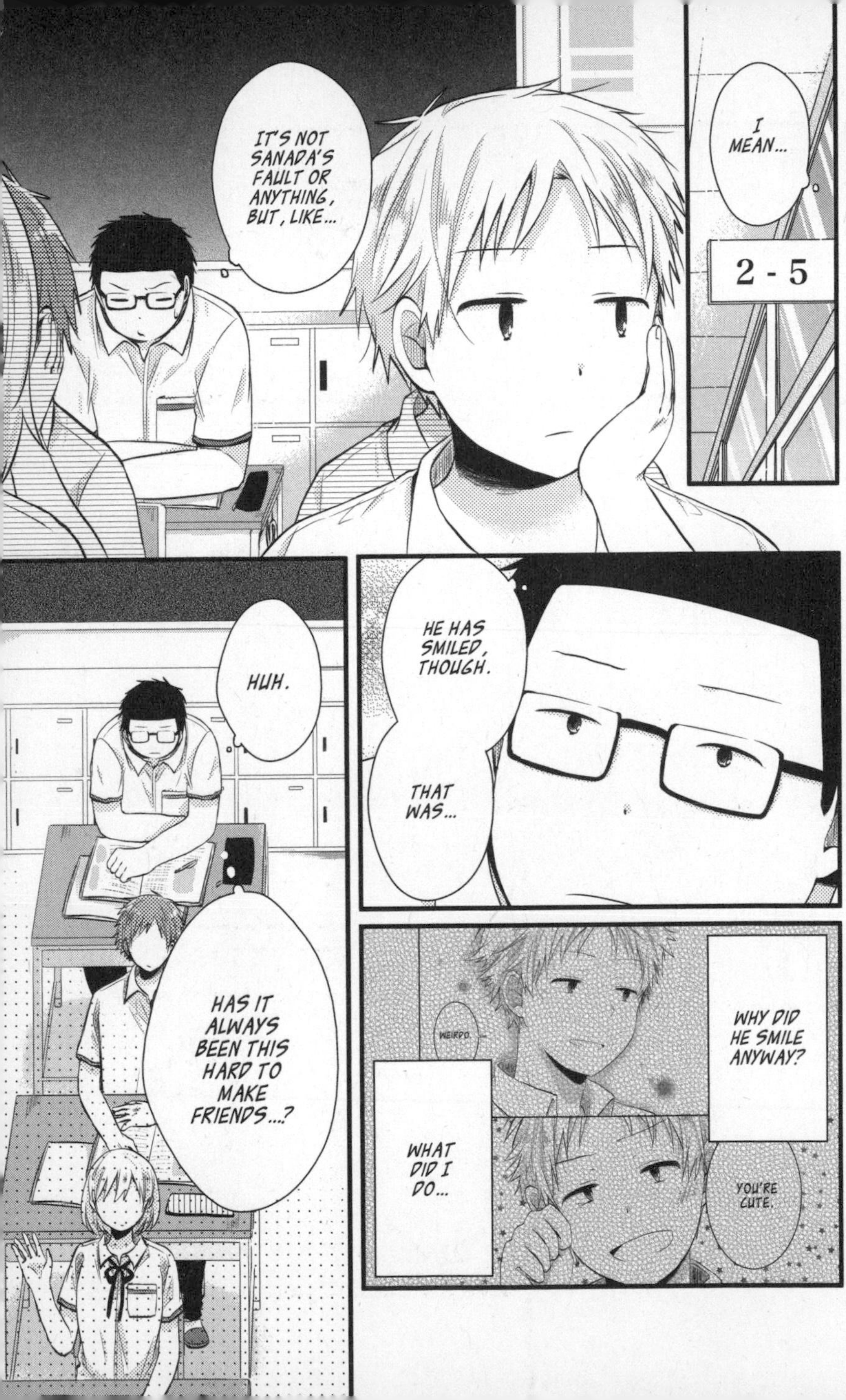
I MEAN...
2 - 5
IT'S NOT SANADA'S FAULT OR ANYTHING, BUT, LIKE...
HE HAS SMILED, THOUGH.
THAT WAS...
WHY DID HE SMILE ANYWAY?
YOU'RE CUTE.
WEIRDO.
WHAT DID I DO...
HUH.
HAS IT ALWAYS BEEN THIS HARD TO MAKE FRIENDS...?

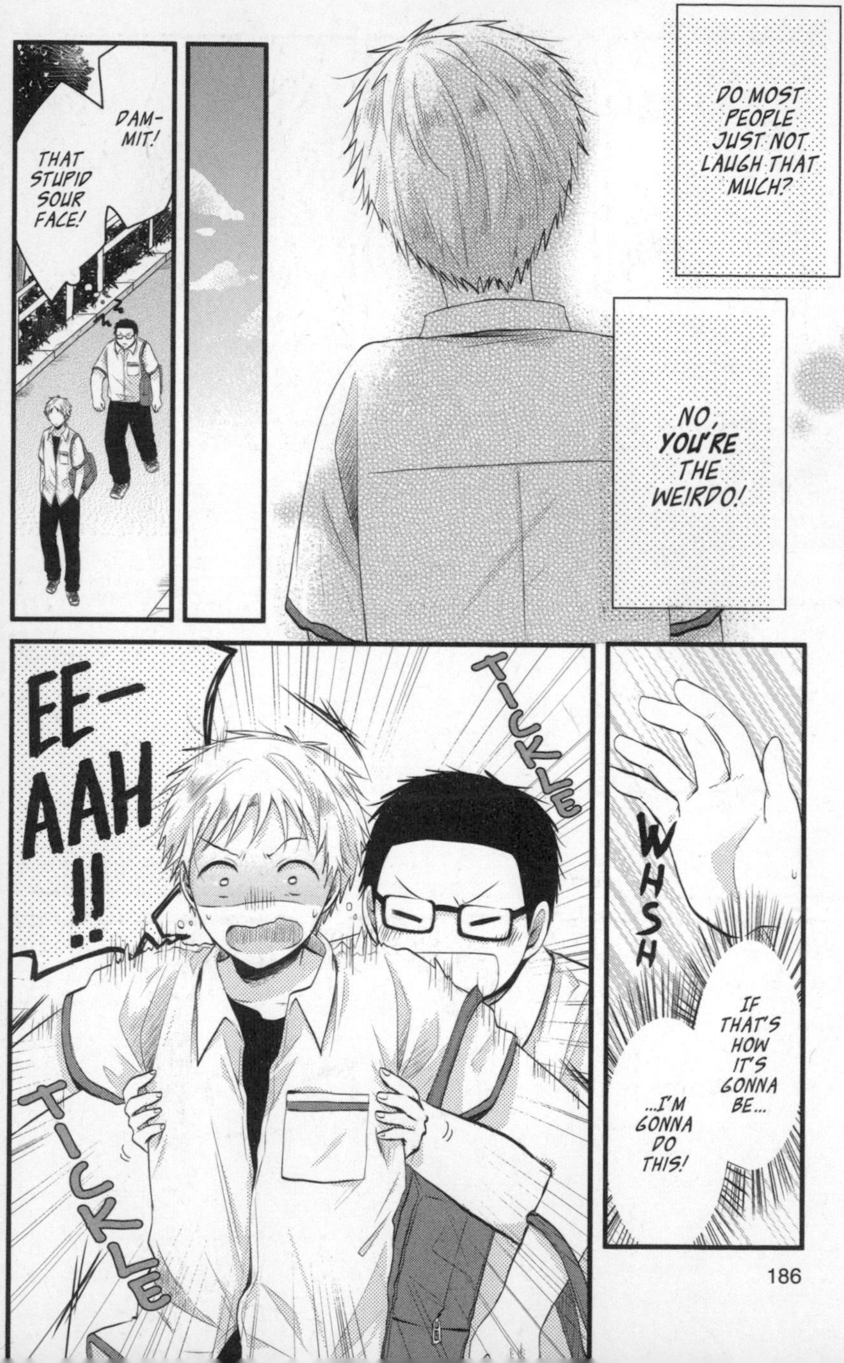
DO MOST PEOPLE JUST NOT LAUGH THAT MUCH?
NO, YOU'RE THE WEIRDO!
DAM-MIT!
THAT STUPID SOUR FACE!
WHSH
IF THAT'S HOW IT'S GONNA BE...
...I'M GONNA DO THIS!
TICKLE
EE-AAH!!
TICKLE

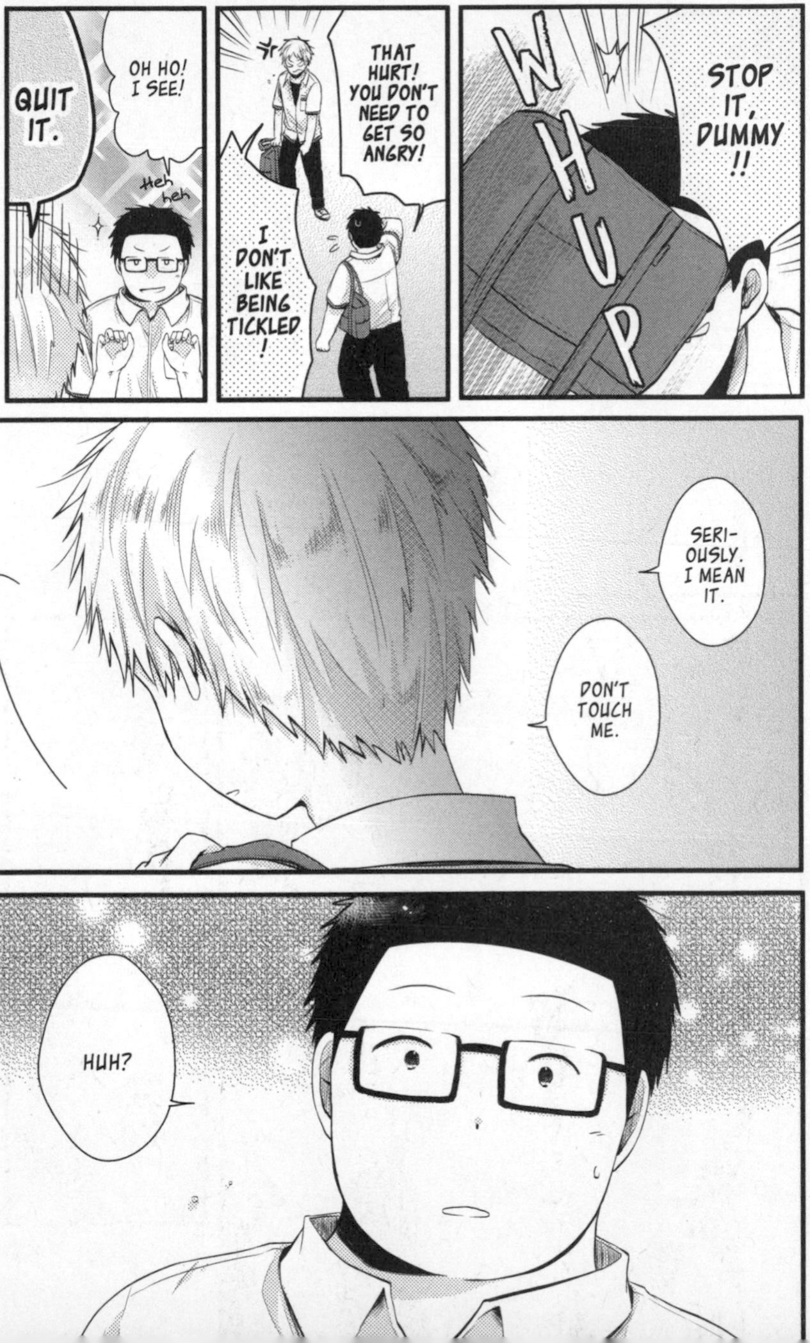
WHUP
STOP IT, DUMMY!!
THAT HURT! YOU DON'T NEED TO GET SO ANGRY!
I DON'T LIKE BEING TICKLED!
OH HO! I SEE!
QUIT IT.
heh heh
SERI-OUSLY. I MEAN IT.
DON'T TOUCH ME.
HUH?

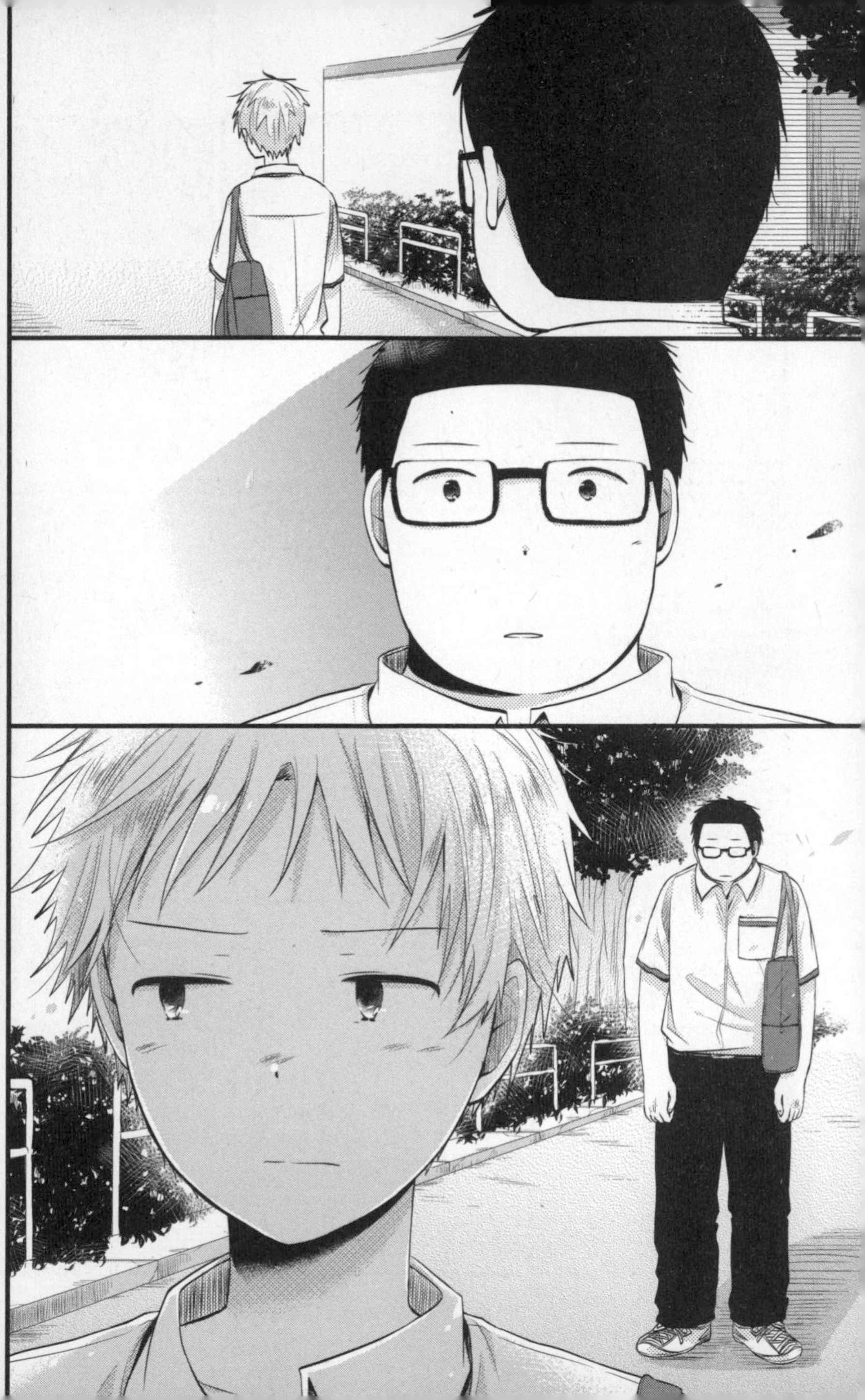

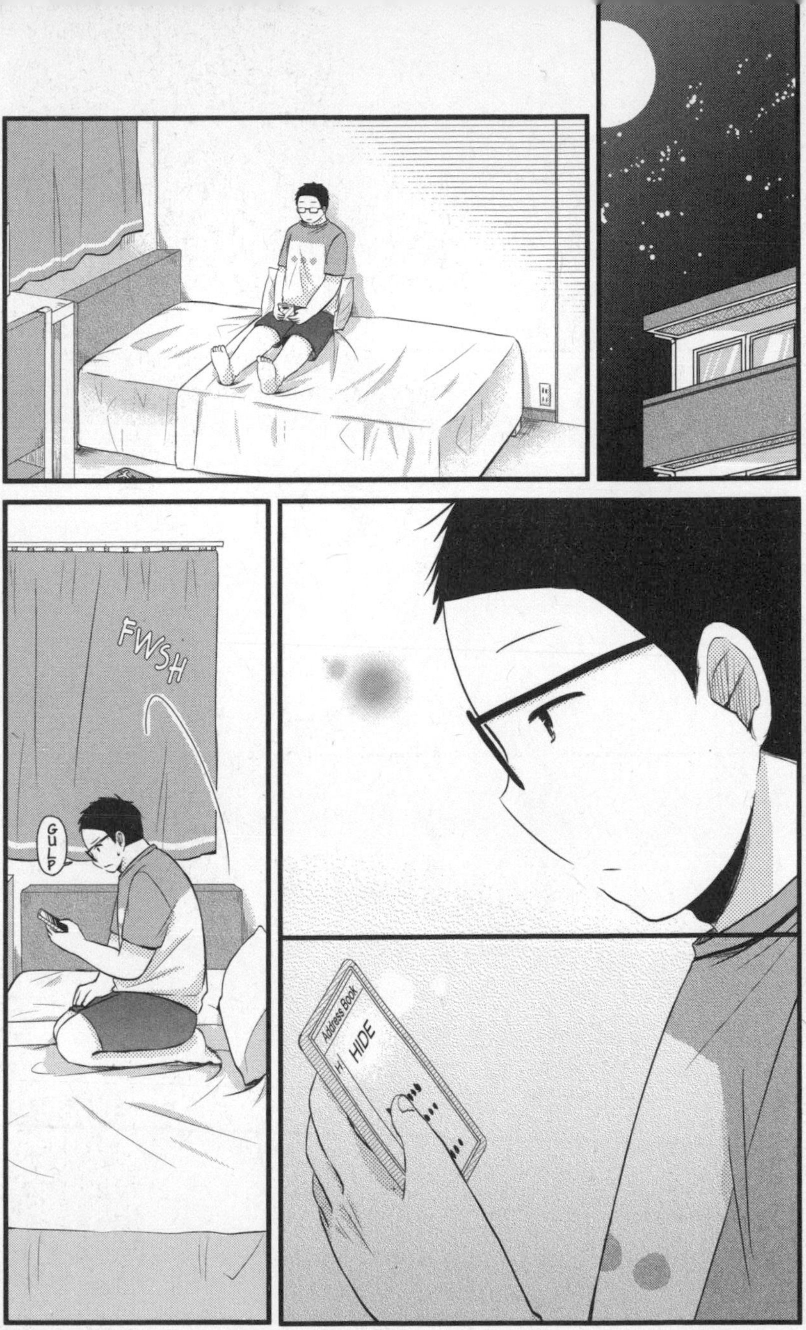
Address Book
H
HIDE
FWSH
GULP

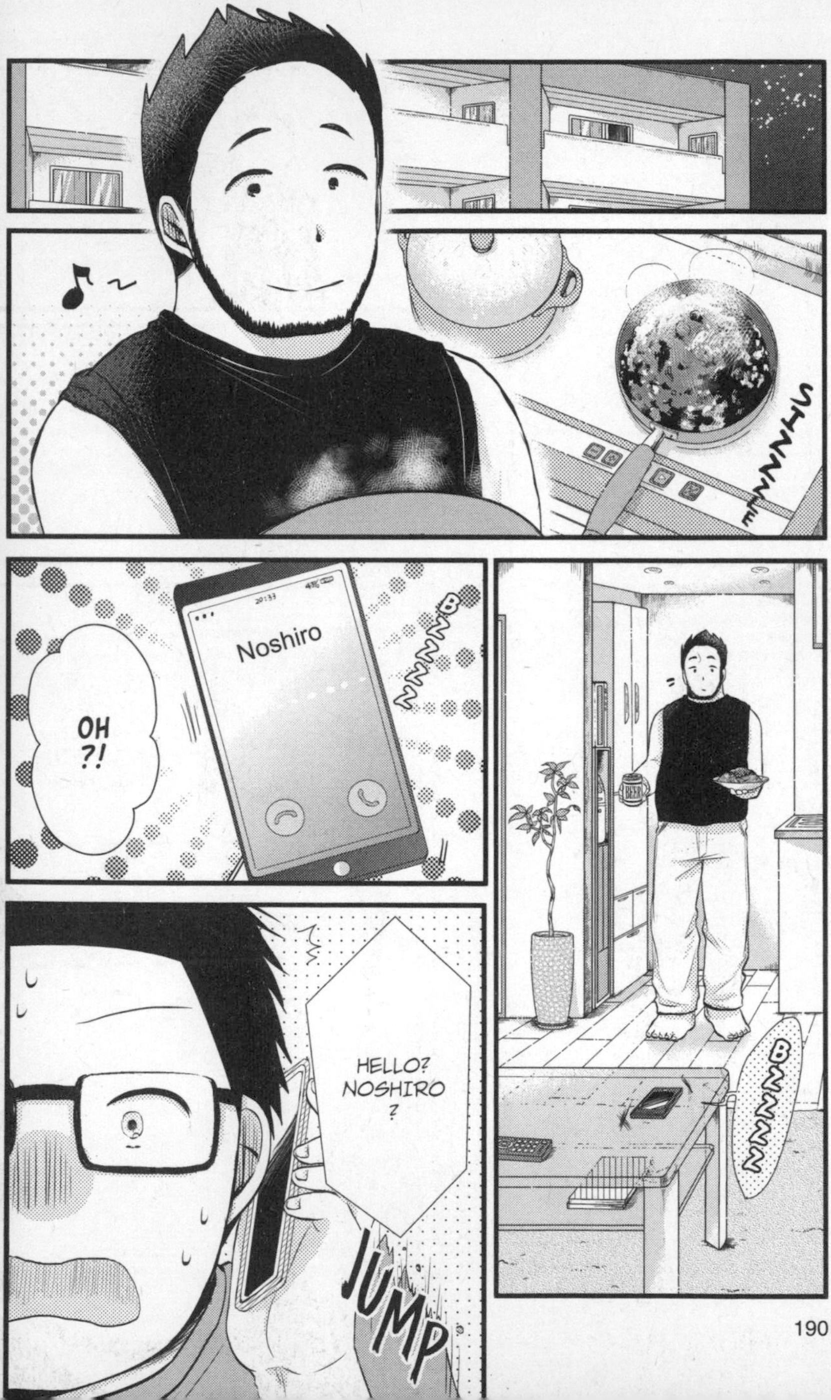

♪~
SHNNNNE
BZZZZZZ
Noshiro
BZZZZZ
OH ?!
HELLO? NOSHIRO ?
JUMP

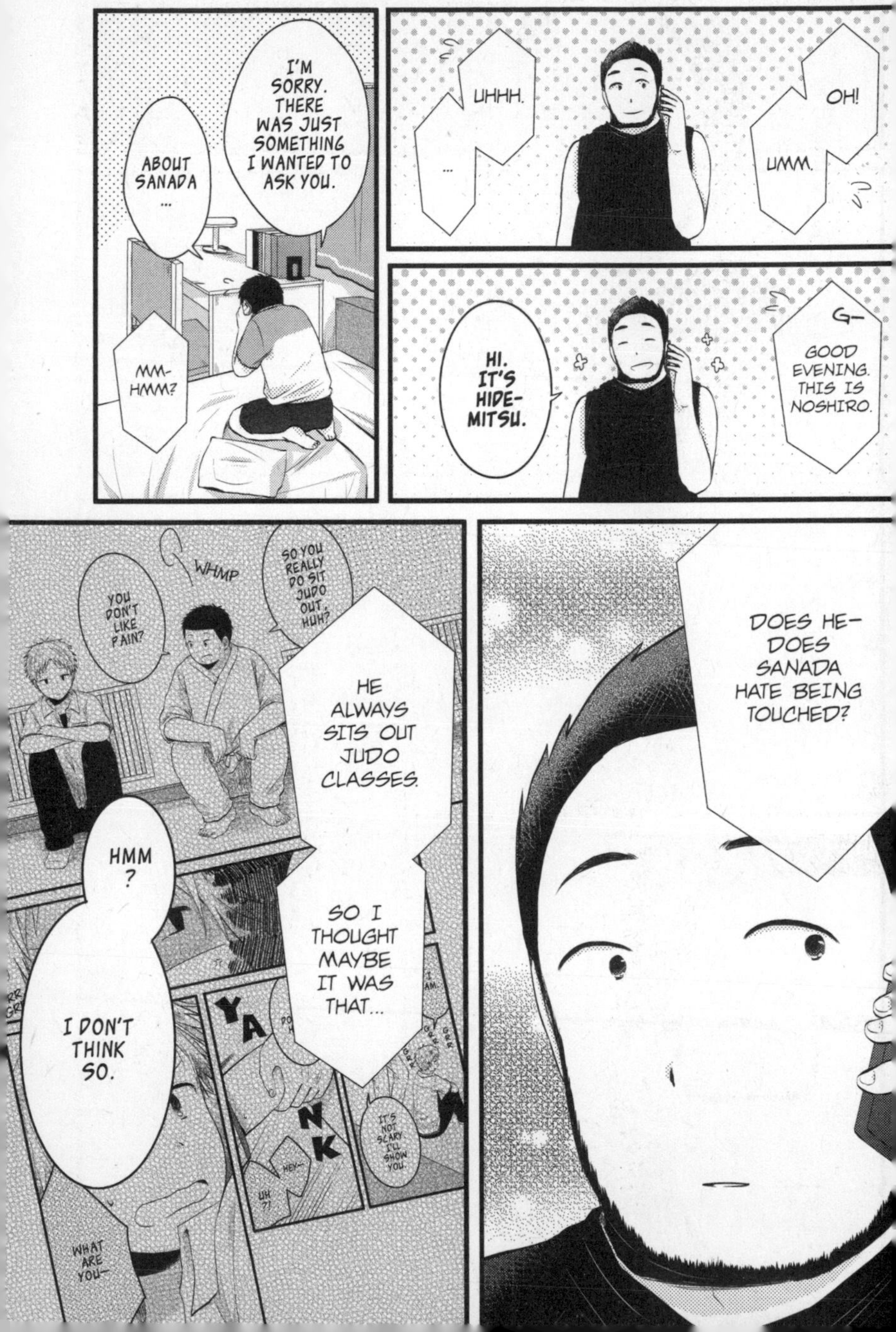
OH!
UMM.
UHHH.
...
G—
GOOD EVENING. THIS IS NOSHIRO.
HI. IT'S HIDE-MITSU.
I'M SORRY. THERE WAS JUST SOMETHING I WANTED TO ASK YOU.
ABOUT SANADA ...
MM-HMM?
DOES HE— DOES SANADA HATE BEING TOUCHED?
SO YOU REALLY DO SIT JUDO OUT, HUH?
WHMP
YOU DON'T LIKE PAIN?
HE ALWAYS SITS OUT JUDO CLASSES.
SO I THOUGHT MAYBE IT WAS THAT...
HMM ?
I AM.
GRR GRR
YANK
IT'S NOT SCARY. I'LL SHOW YOU.
HEY—
UH ?!
GRR GRR
I DON'T THINK SO.
WHAT ARE YOU—

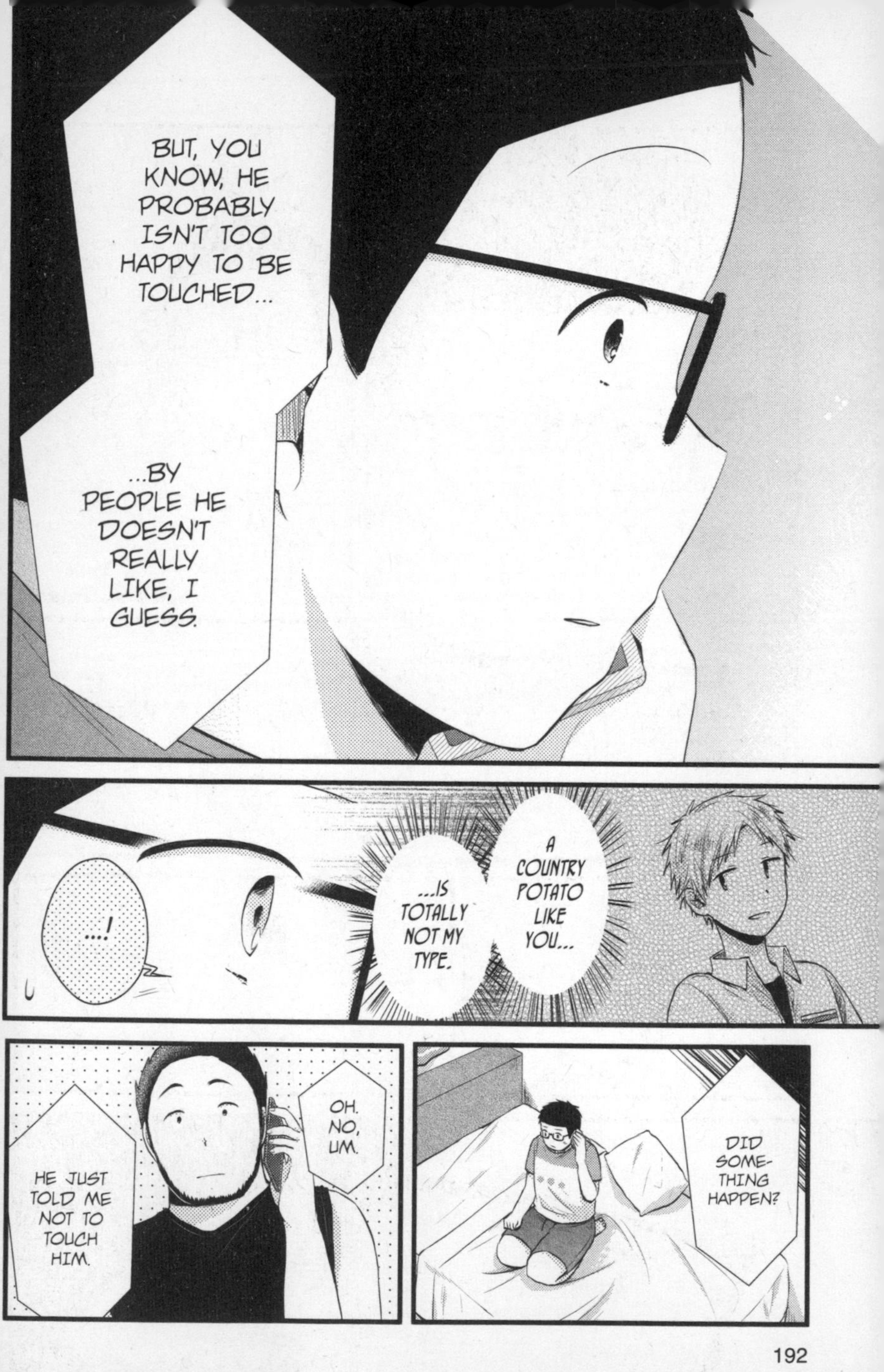
BUT, YOU KNOW, HE PROBABLY ISN'T TOO HAPPY TO BE TOUCHED...
...BY PEOPLE HE DOESN'T REALLY LIKE, I GUESS.
A COUNTRY POTATO LIKE YOU...
...IS TOTALLY NOT MY TYPE.
...!
DID SOME-THING HAPPEN?
OH. NO, UM.
HE JUST TOLD ME NOT TO TOUCH HIM.

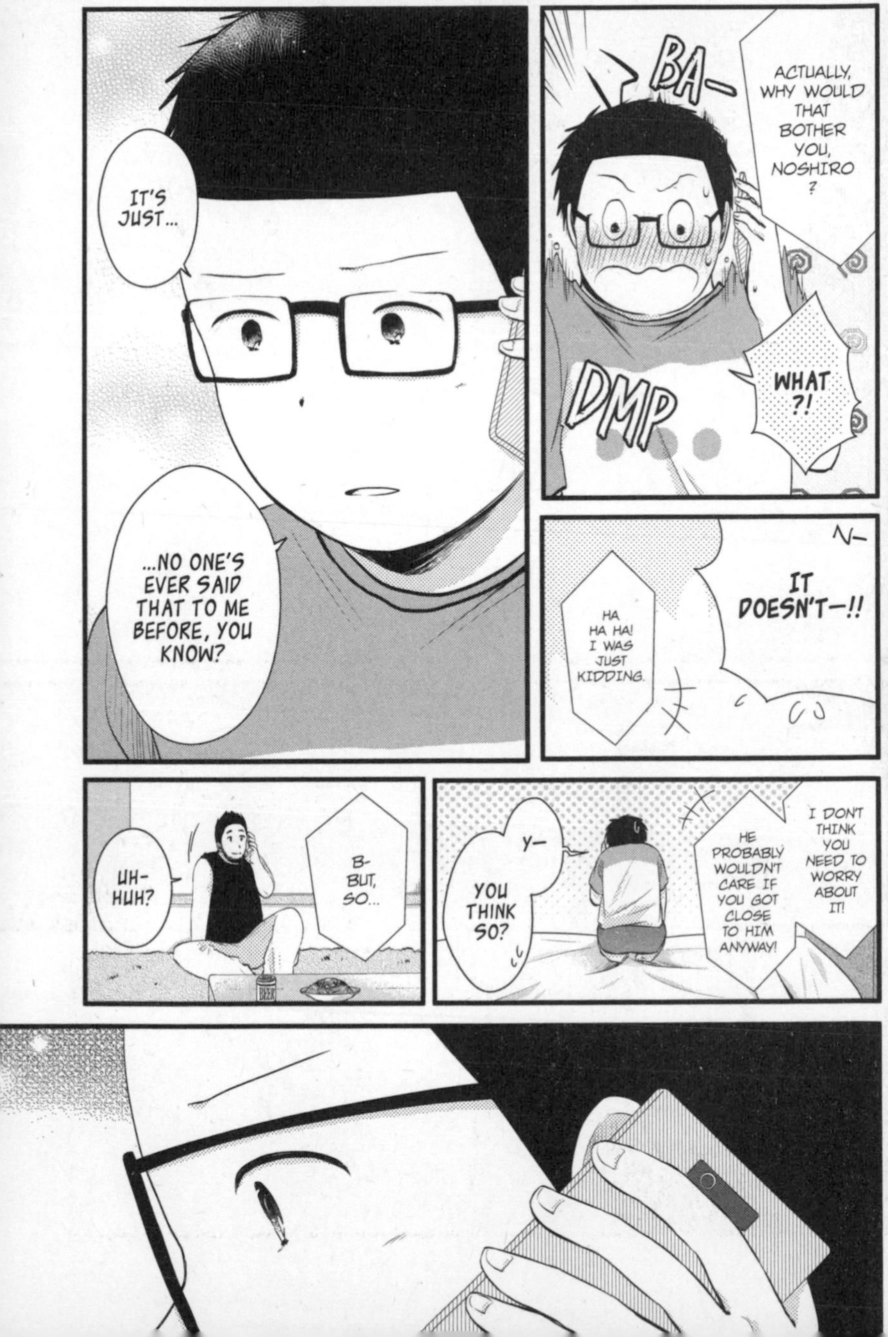
ACTUALLY, WHY WOULD THAT BOTHER YOU, NOSHIRO?
BA—
WHAT?!
DMP
N—
IT DOESN'T—!!
HA HA HA! I WAS JUST KIDDING.
IT'S JUST...
...NO ONE'S EVER SAID THAT TO ME BEFORE, YOU KNOW?
I DON'T THINK YOU NEED TO WORRY ABOUT IT!
HE PROBABLY WOULDN'T CARE IF YOU GOT CLOSE TO HIM ANYWAY!
Y— YOU THINK SO?
B-BUT, SO...
UH-HUH?

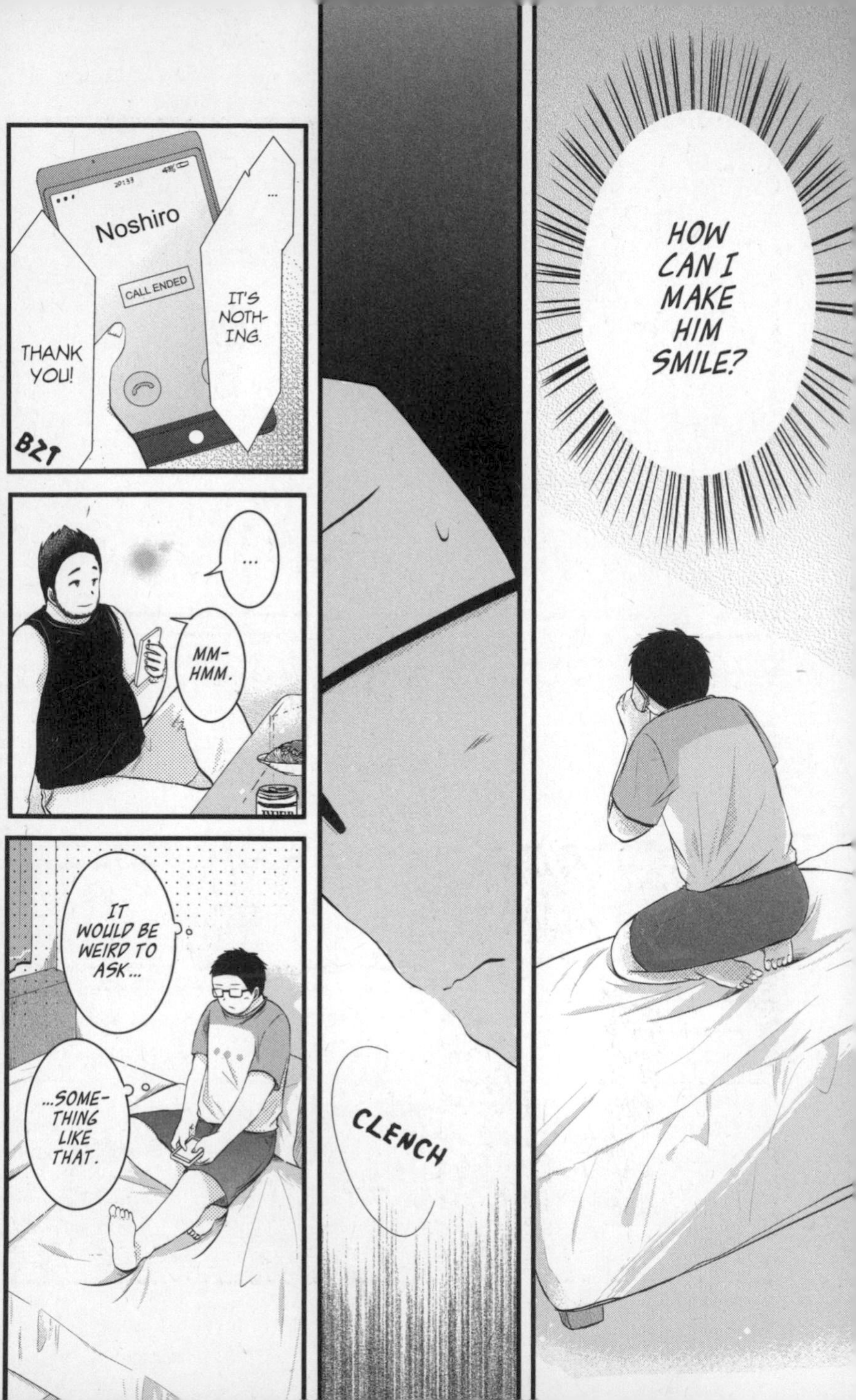
HOW CAN I MAKE HIM SMILE?
CLENCH
...
IT'S NOTHING.
Noshiro
CALL ENDED
THANK YOU!
BZT
...
MM-HMM.
IT WOULD BE WEIRD TO ASK...
...SOMETHING LIKE THAT.

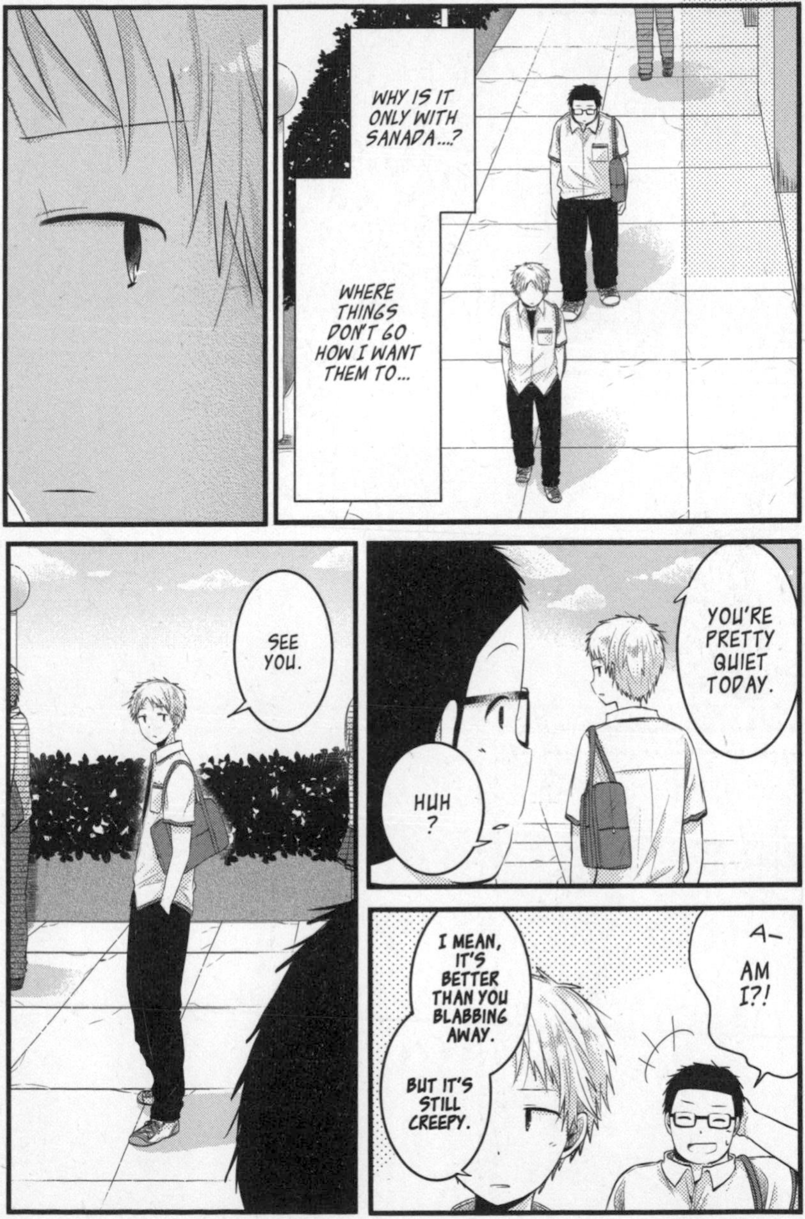
WHY IS IT ONLY WITH SANADA...?
WHERE THINGS DON'T GO HOW I WANT THEM TO...
YOU'RE PRETTY QUIET TODAY.
HUH?
A- AM I?!
I MEAN, IT'S BETTER THAN YOU BLABBING AWAY.
BUT IT'S STILL CREEPY.
SEE YOU.

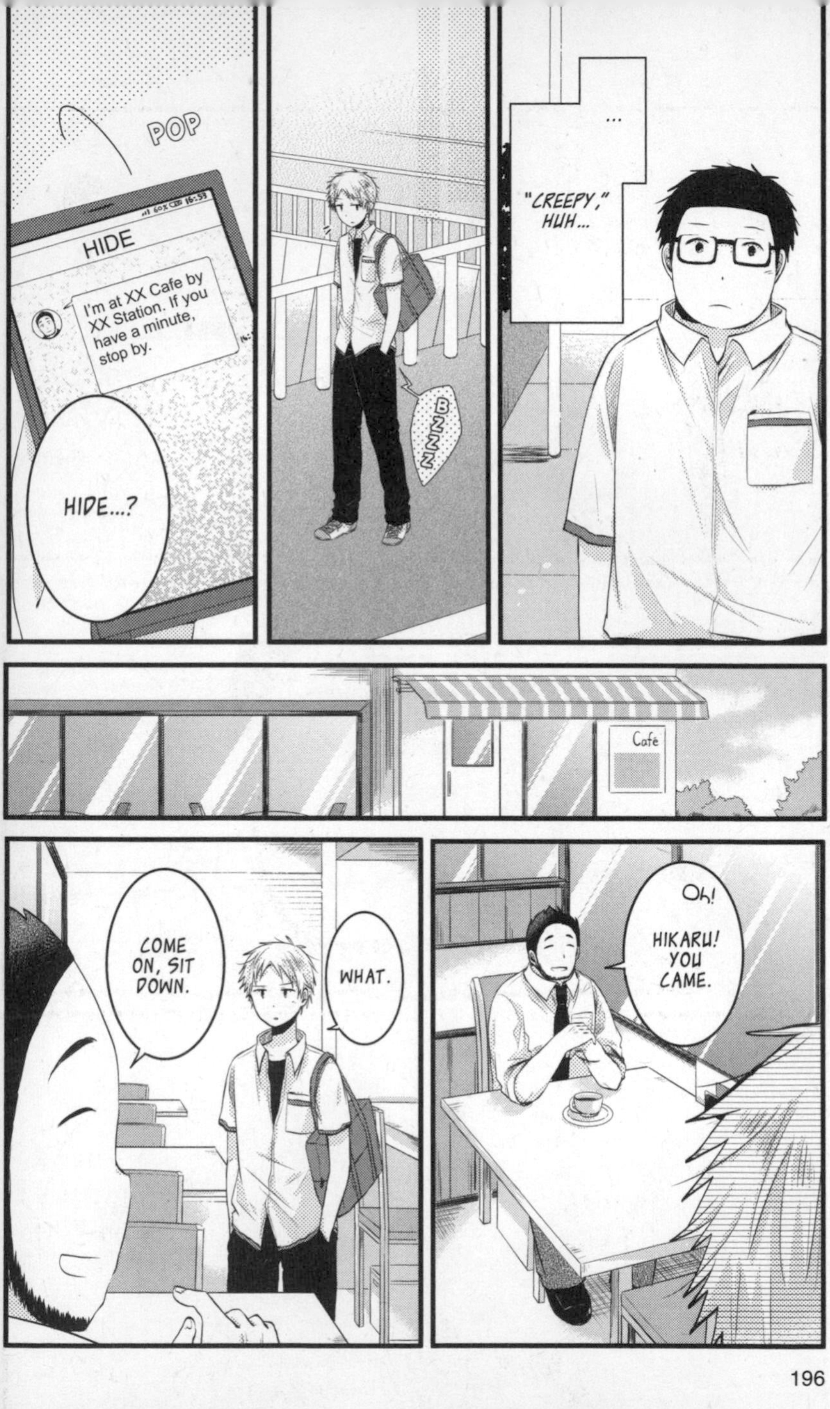
...
"CREEPY," HUH...
BZZZ
POP
HIDE
I'm at XX Cafe by XX Station. If you have a minute, stop by.
HIDE...?
Café
Oh!
HIKARU! YOU CAME.
WHAT.
COME ON, SIT DOWN.

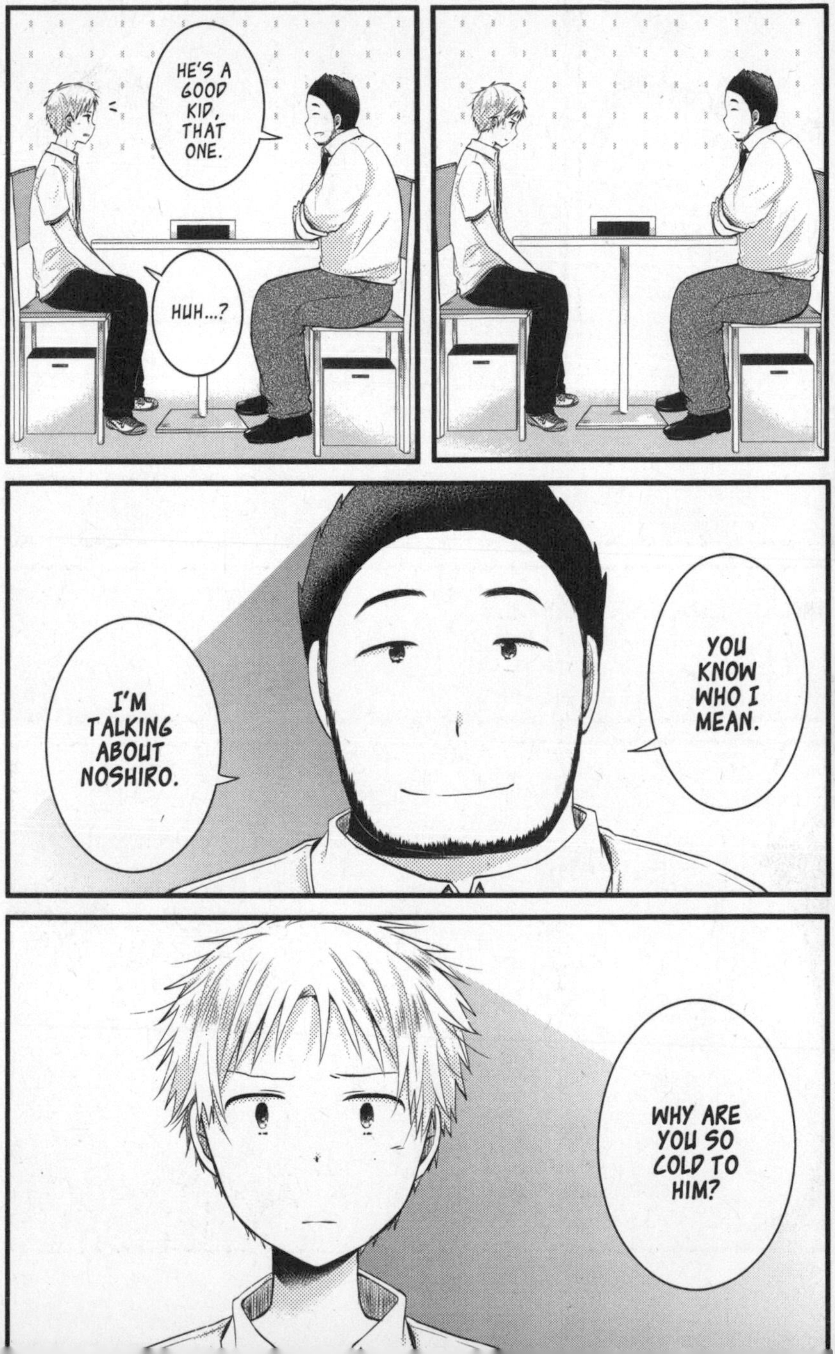
HE'S A GOOD KID, THAT ONE.
HUH...?
YOU KNOW WHO I MEAN.
I'M TALKING ABOUT NOSHIRO.
WHY ARE YOU SO COLD TO HIM?

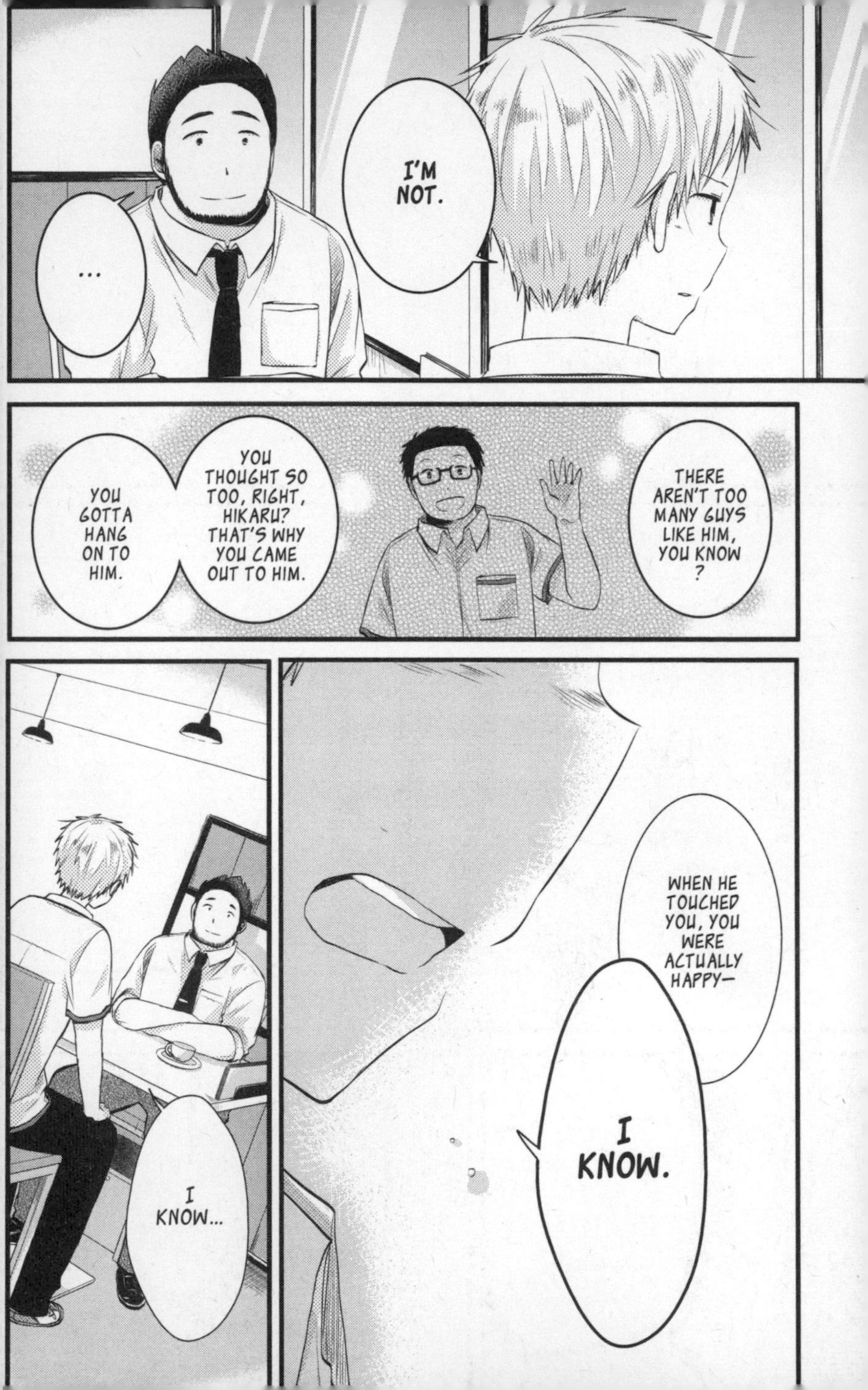
I'M NOT.
...
THERE AREN'T TOO MANY GUYS LIKE HIM, YOU KNOW?
YOU THOUGHT SO TOO, RIGHT, HIKARU? THAT'S WHY YOU CAME OUT TO HIM.
YOU GOTTA HANG ON TO HIM.
WHEN HE TOUCHED YOU, YOU WERE ACTUALLY HAPPY—
I KNOW.
I KNOW...

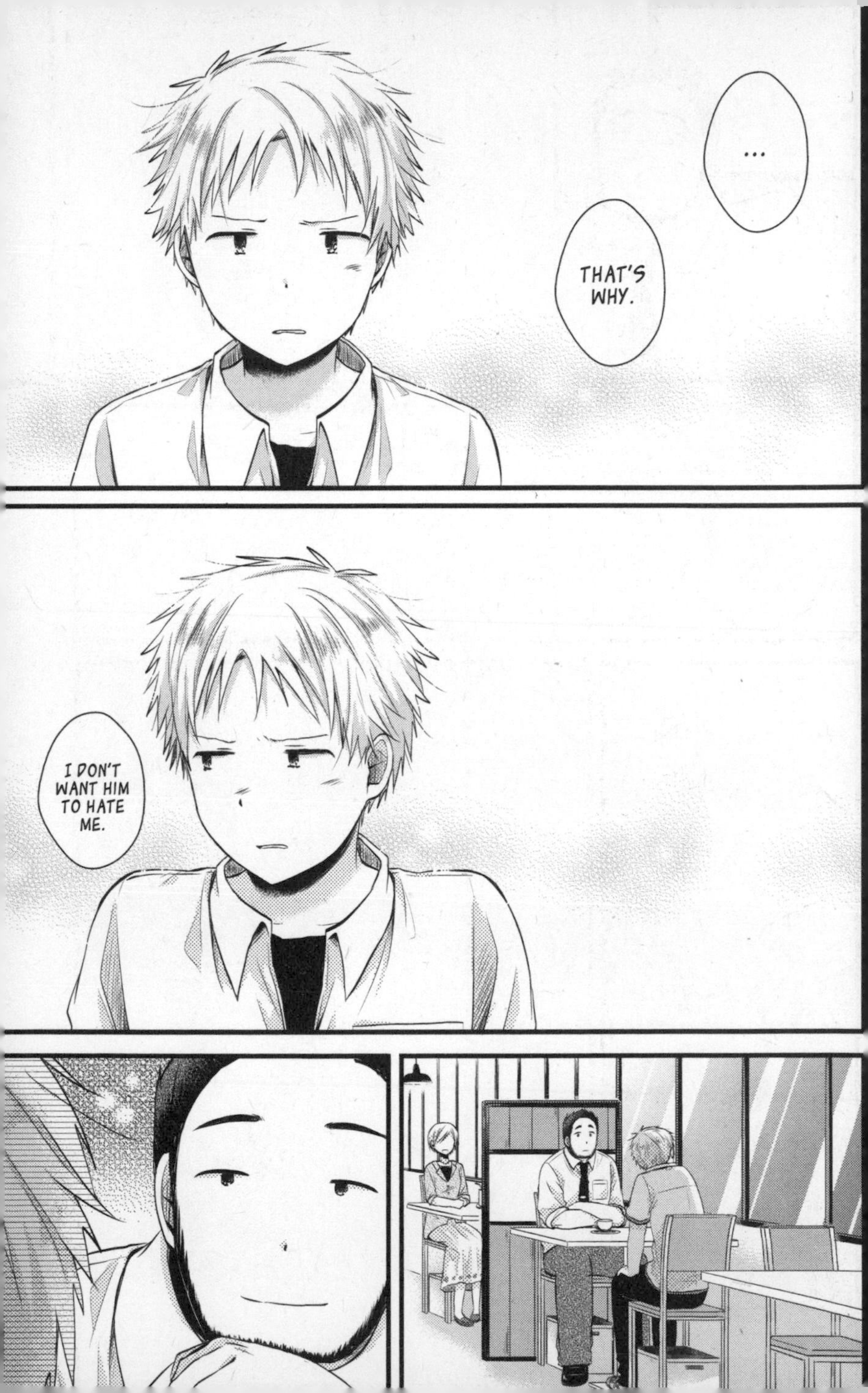
...
THAT'S WHY.
I DON'T WANT HIM TO HATE ME.

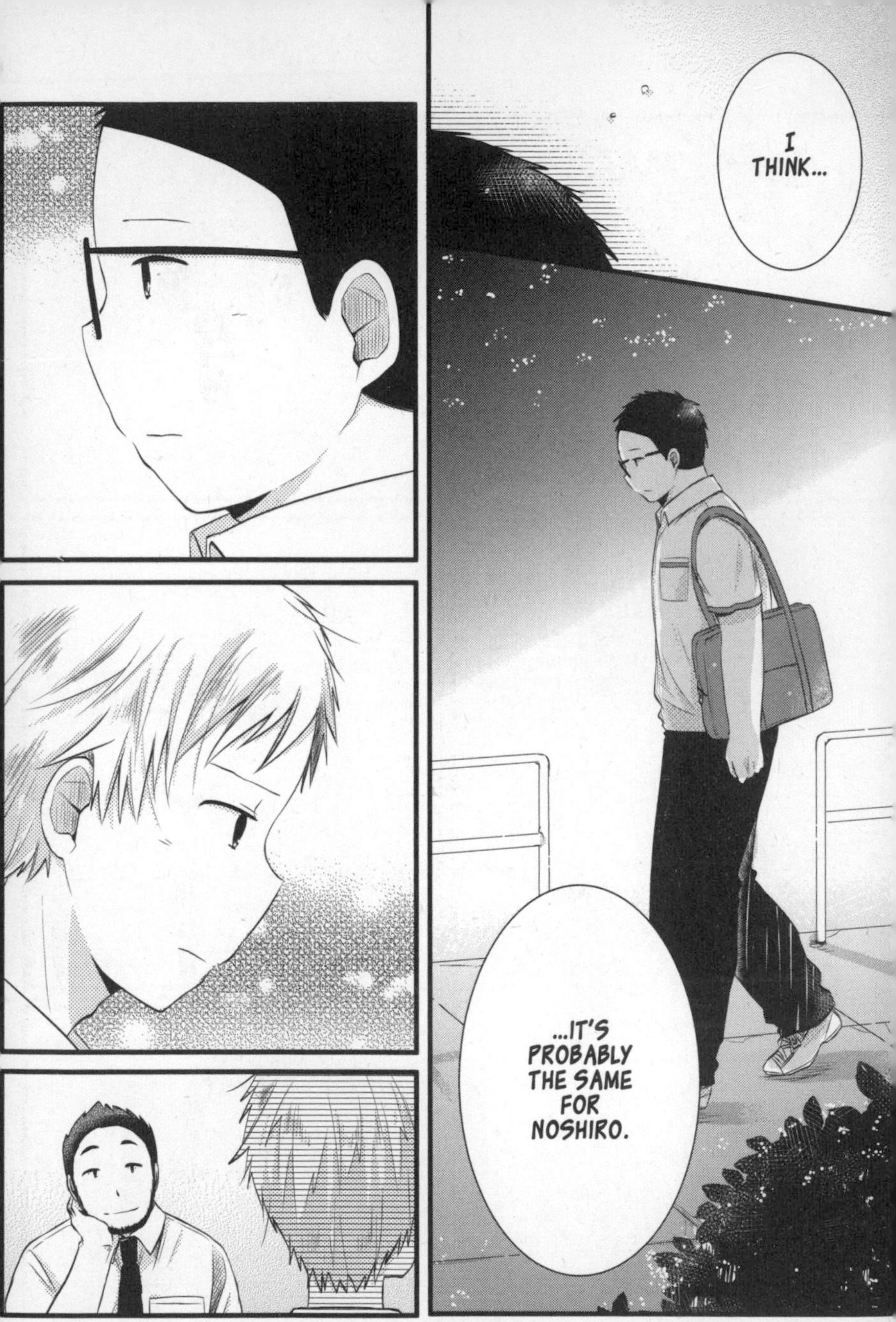
I THINK...
...IT'S PROBABLY THE SAME FOR NOSHIRO.

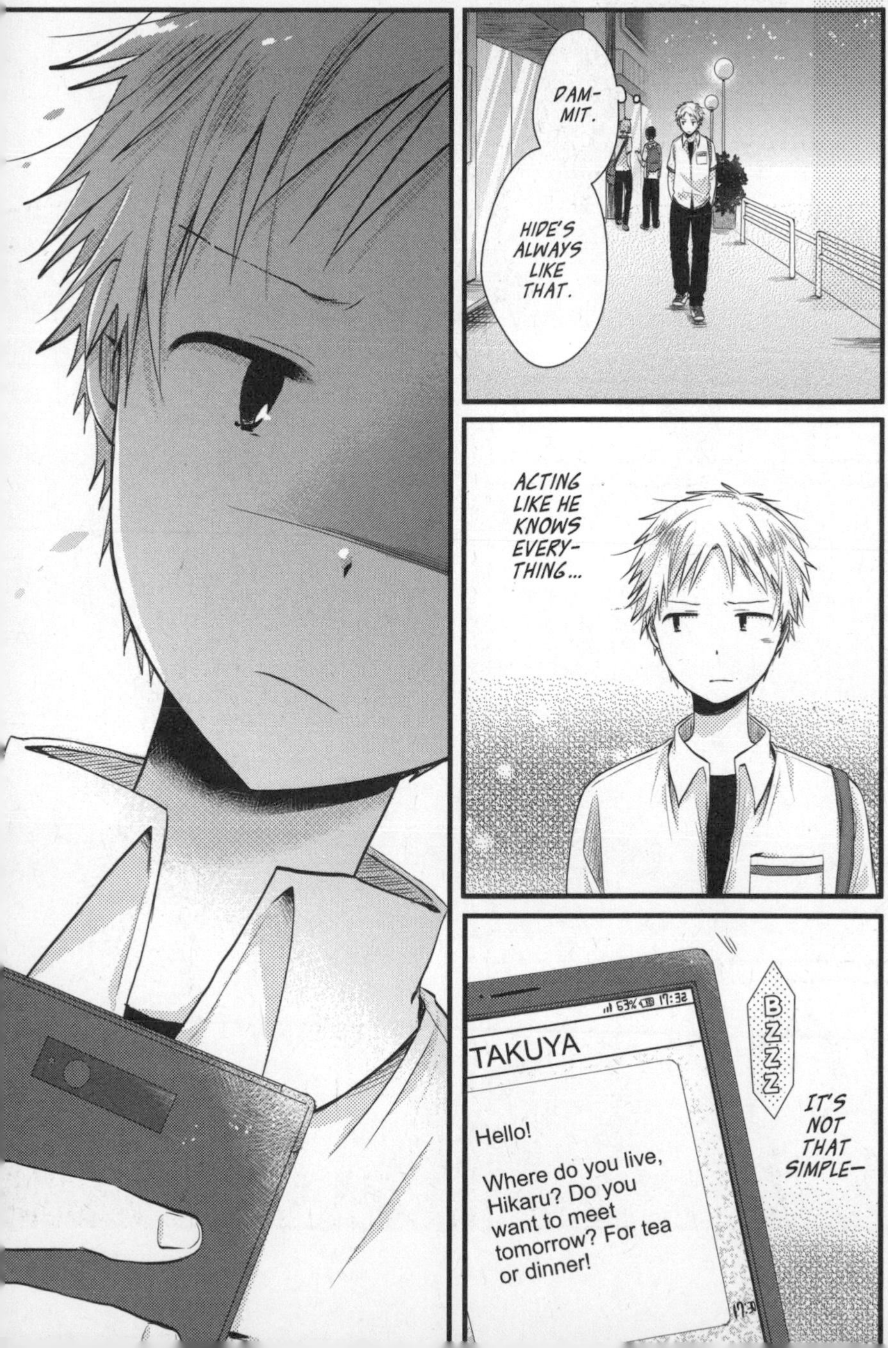
DAM-MIT.
HIDE'S ALWAYS LIKE THAT.
ACTING LIKE HE KNOWS EVERY-THING...
TAKUYA
Hello!
Where do you live, Hikaru? Do you want to meet tomorrow? For tea or dinner!
BZZZ
IT'S NOT THAT SIMPLE—

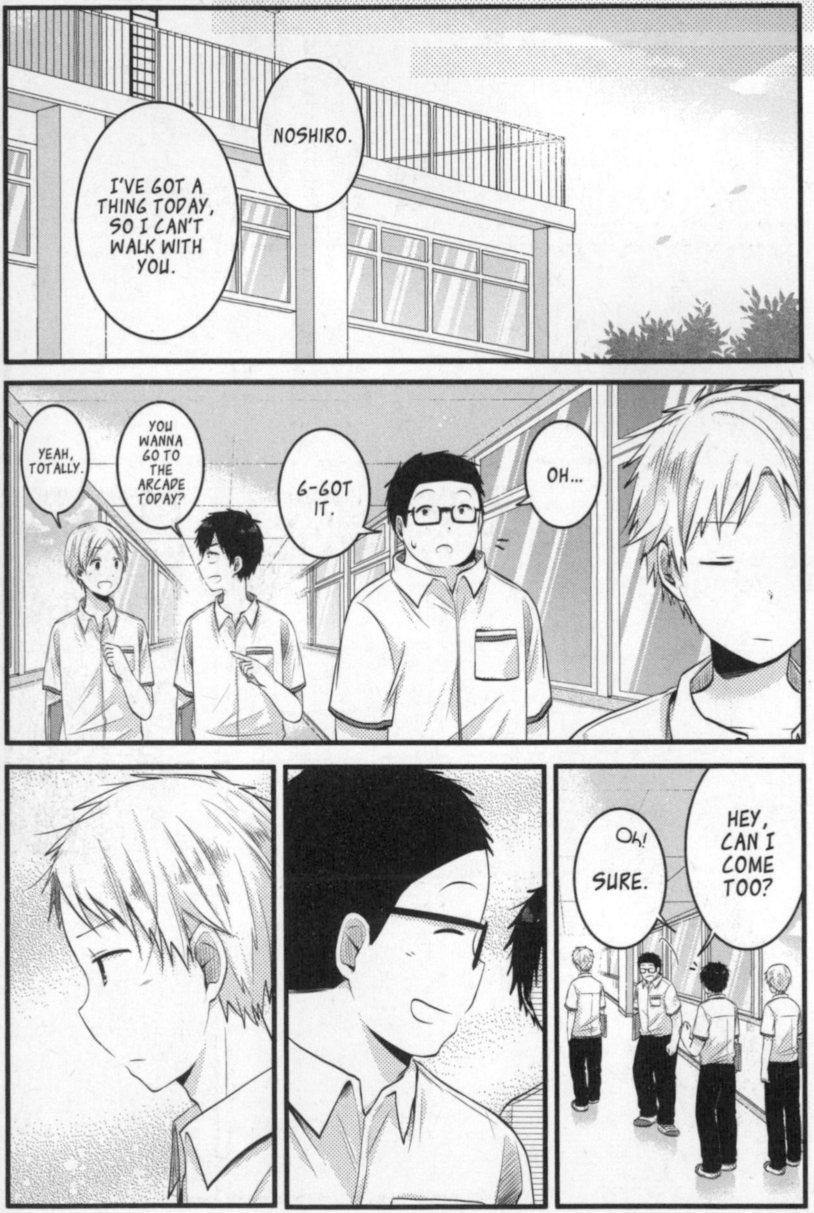
NOSHIRO.
I'VE GOT A THING TODAY, SO I CAN'T WALK WITH YOU.
OH...
G-GOT IT.
YOU WANNA GO TO THE ARCADE TODAY?
YEAH, TOTALLY.
HEY, CAN I COME TOO?
Oh!
SURE.

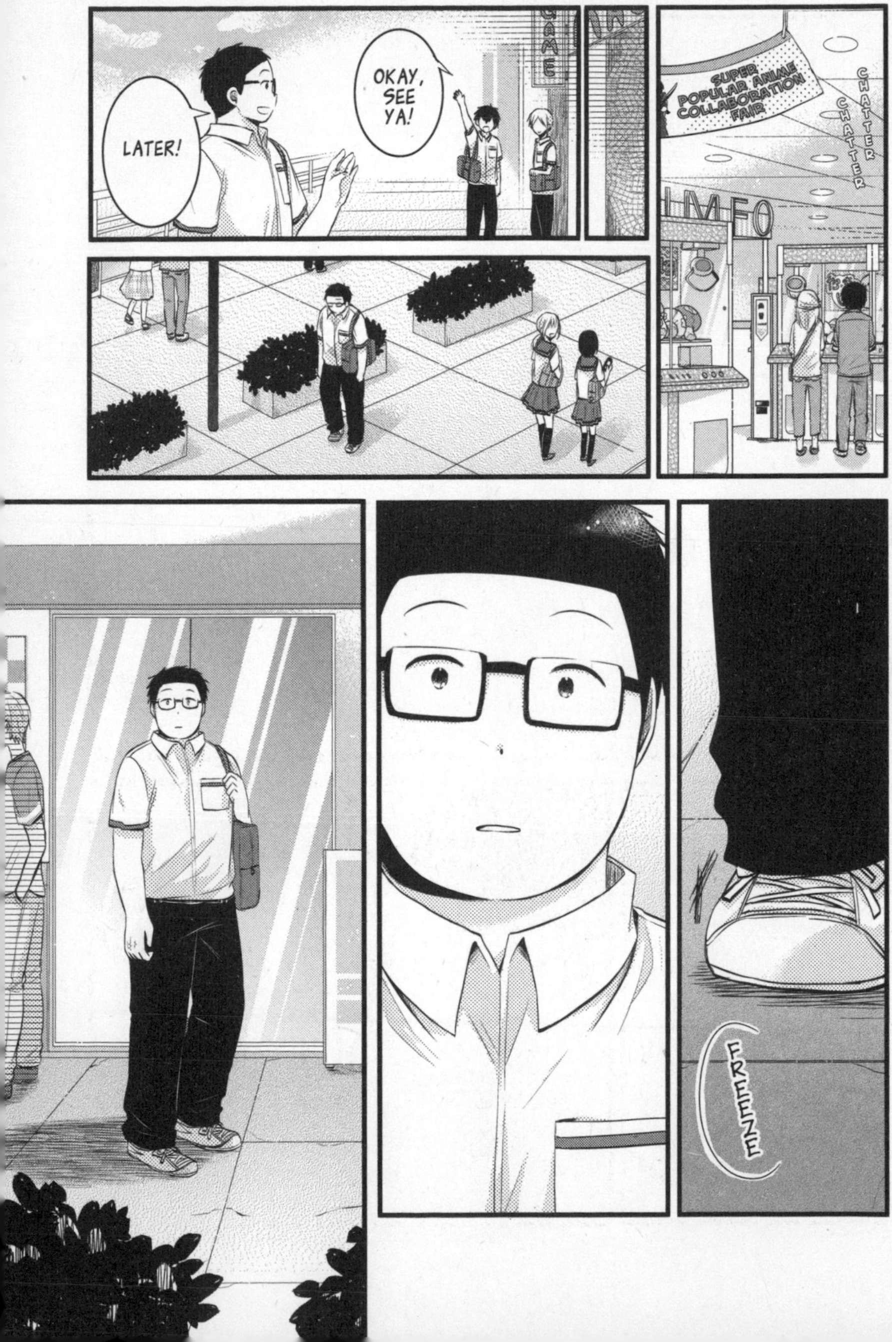
SUPER POPULAR ANIME COLLABORATION FAIR
CHATTER CHATTER
OKAY, SEE YA!
LATER!
FREEZE

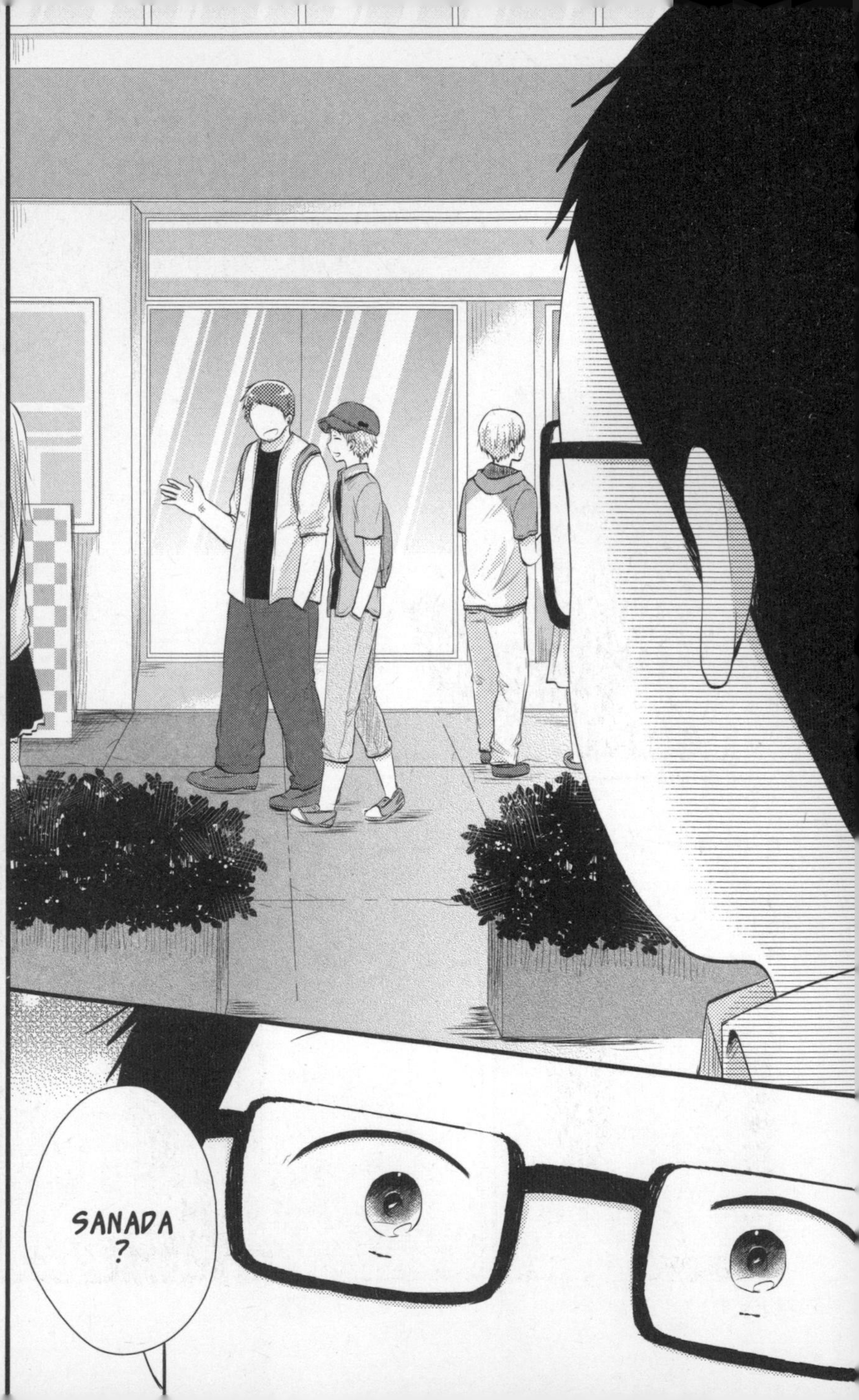
SANADA
?

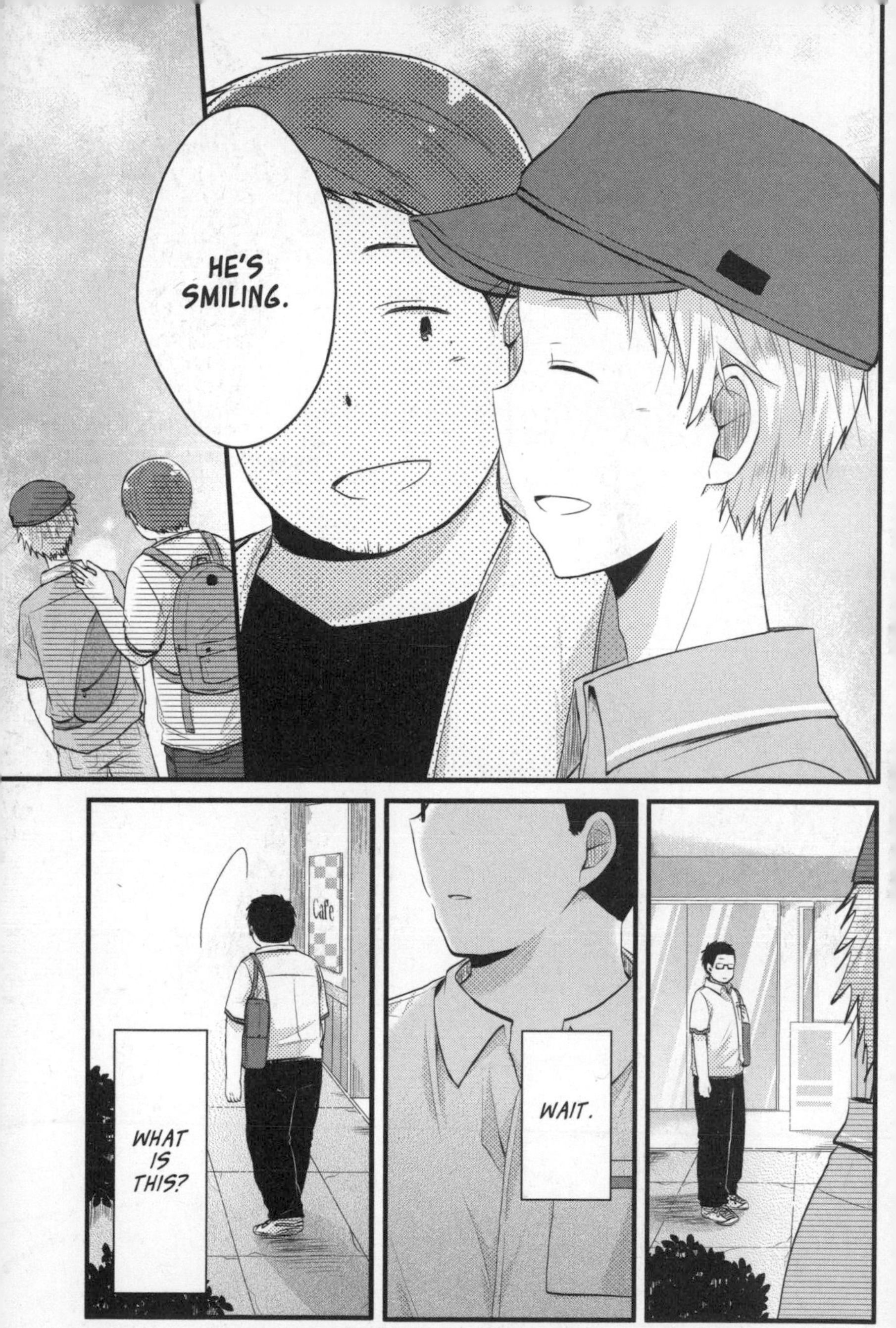

HE'S SMILING.
WAIT.
WHAT IS THIS?

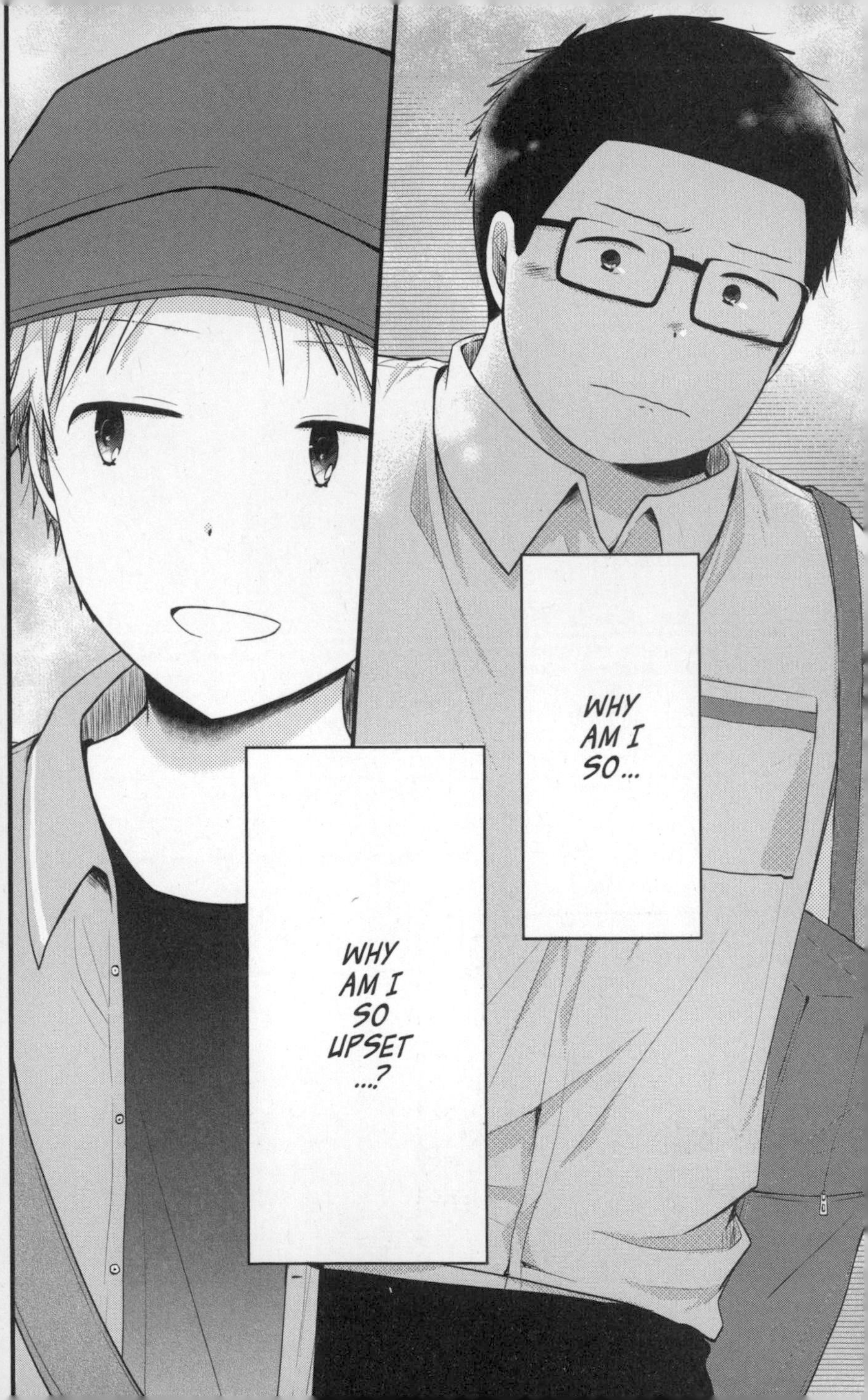
WHY AM I SO...
WHY AM I SO UPSET ...?

That Blue Sky Feeling

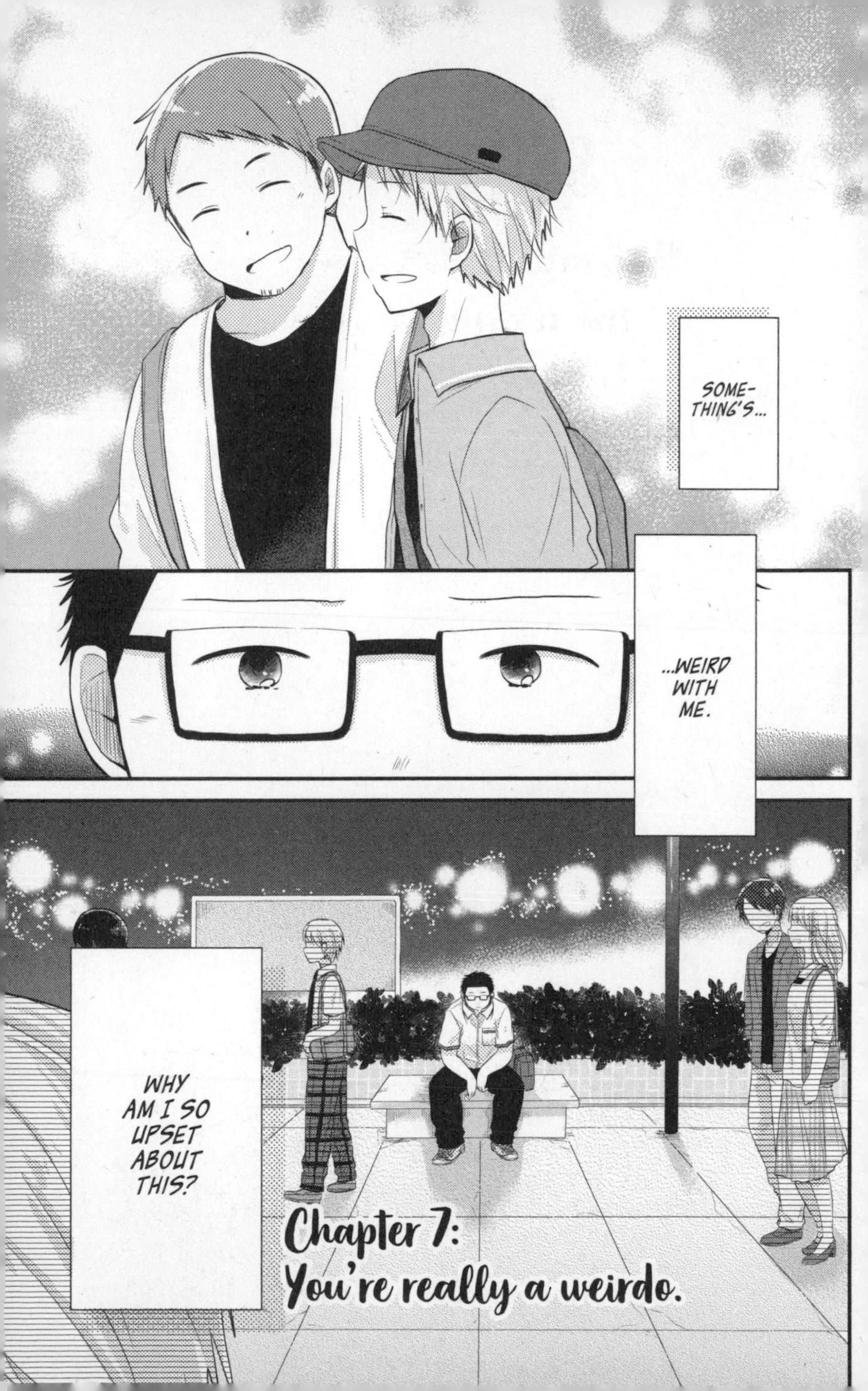
SOME-THING'S...
...WEIRD WITH ME.
WHY AM I SO UPSET ABOUT THIS?
Chapter 7: You're really a weirdo.

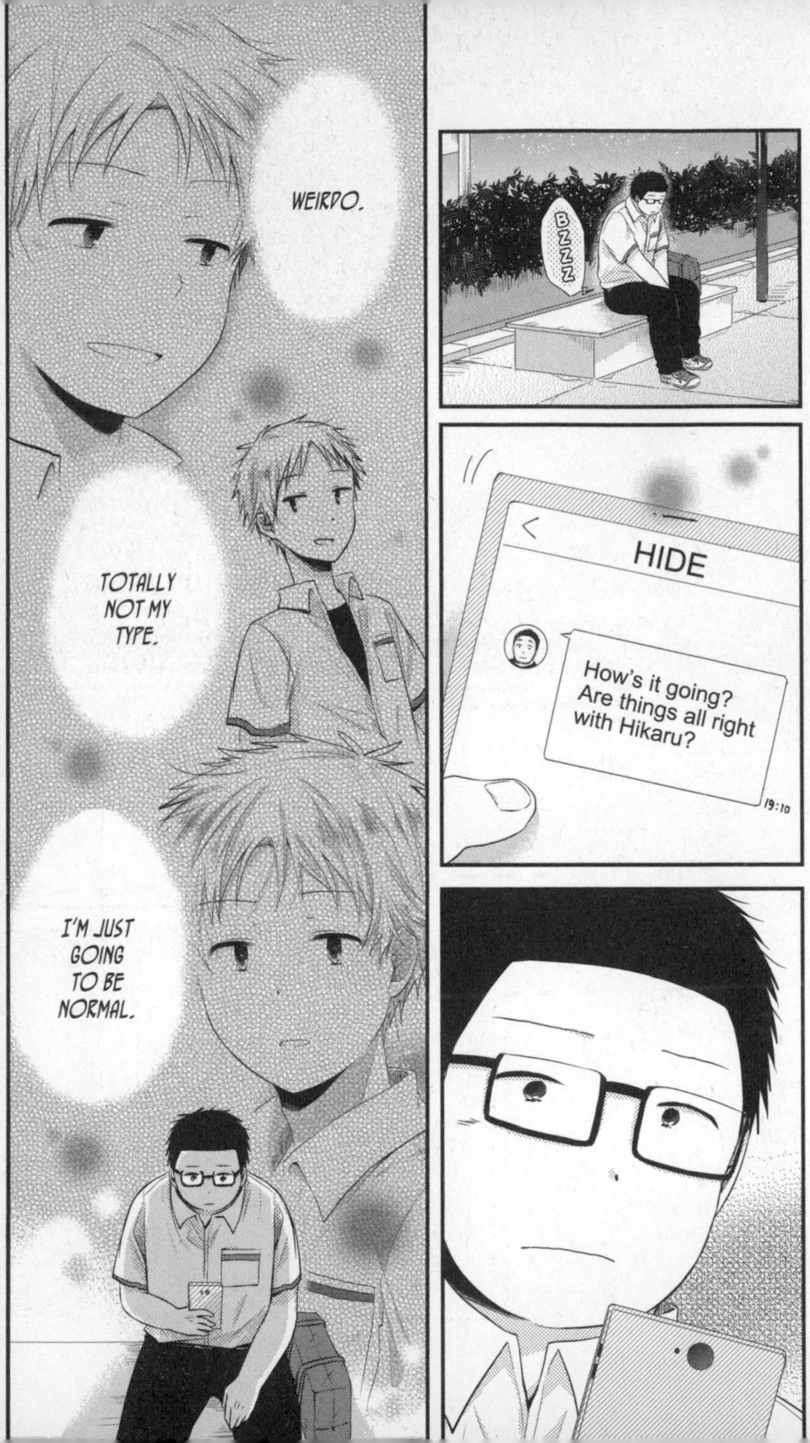
BZZZ
HIDE
How's it going? Are things all right with Hikaru?
19:10
WEIRDO.
TOTALLY NOT MY TYPE.
I'M JUST GOING TO BE NORMAL.

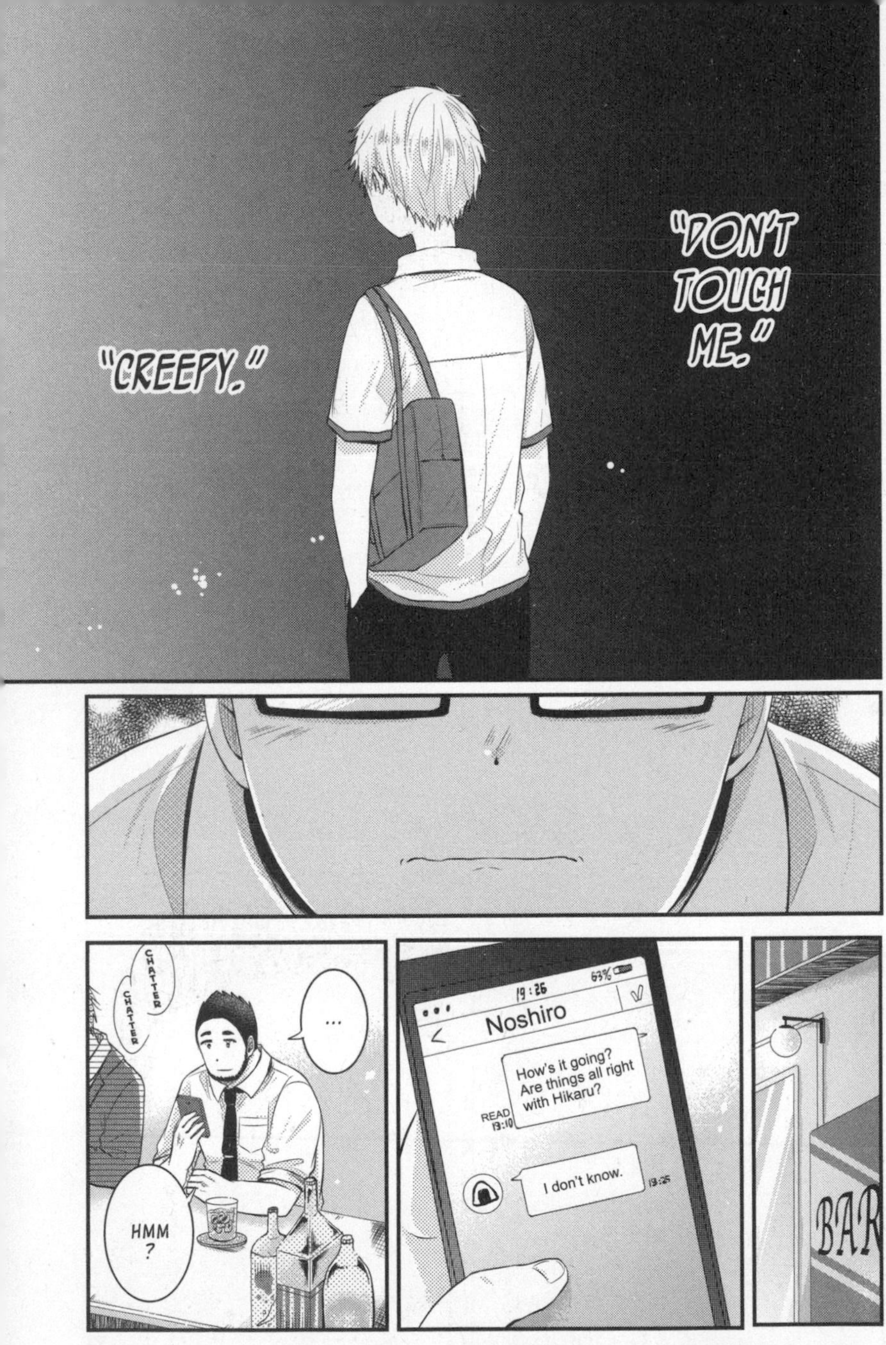
"DON'T TOUCH ME."
"CREEPY."
BAR
19:26
63%
Noshiro
How's it going? Are things all right with Hikaru?
READ 19:10
I don't know.
19:25
...
CHATTER
CHATTER
HMM?

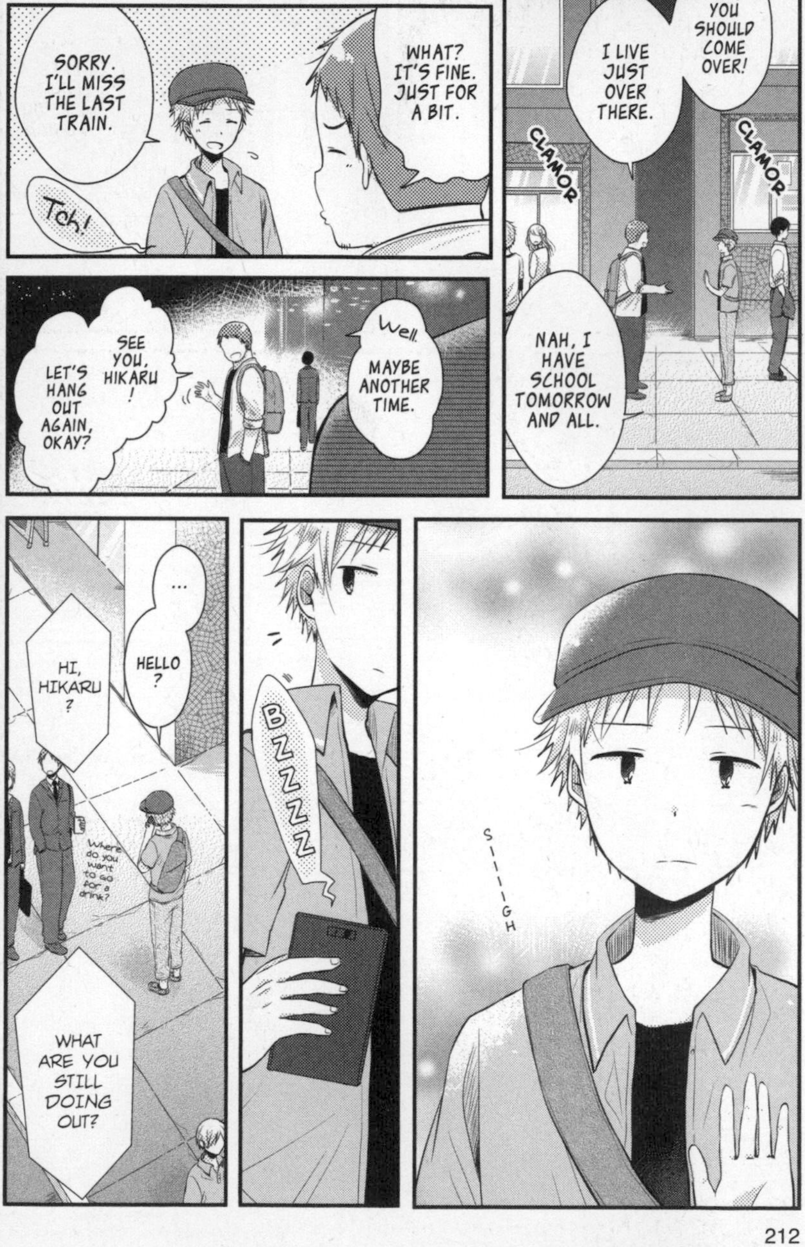
HEY, YOU SHOULD COME OVER!
I LIVE JUST OVER THERE.
CLAMOR
CLAMOR
NAH, I HAVE SCHOOL TOMORROW AND ALL.
WHAT? IT'S FINE. JUST FOR A BIT.
SORRY. I'LL MISS THE LAST TRAIN.
Tch!
Well.
MAYBE ANOTHER TIME.
SEE YOU, HIKARU!
LET'S HANG OUT AGAIN, OKAY?
SIIIIGH
BZZZZ
...
HELLO?
HI, HIKARU?
Where do you want to go for a drink?
WHAT ARE YOU STILL DOING OUT?

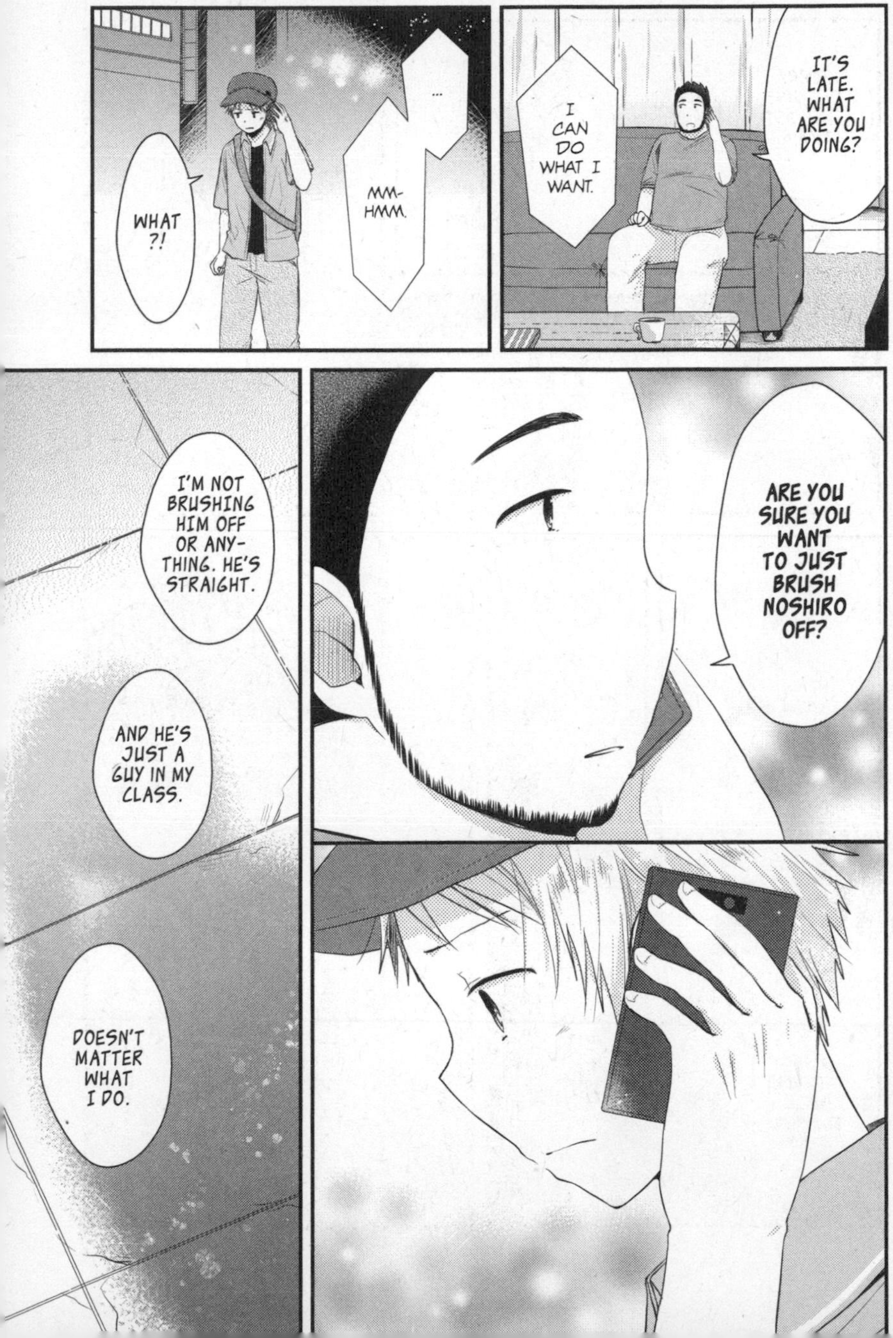
IT'S LATE. WHAT ARE YOU DOING?
I CAN DO WHAT I WANT.
...
MM-HMM.
WHAT?!
ARE YOU SURE YOU WANT TO JUST BRUSH NOSHIRO OFF?
I'M NOT BRUSHING HIM OFF OR ANY-THING. HE'S STRAIGHT.
AND HE'S JUST A GUY IN MY CLASS.
DOESN'T MATTER WHAT I DO.

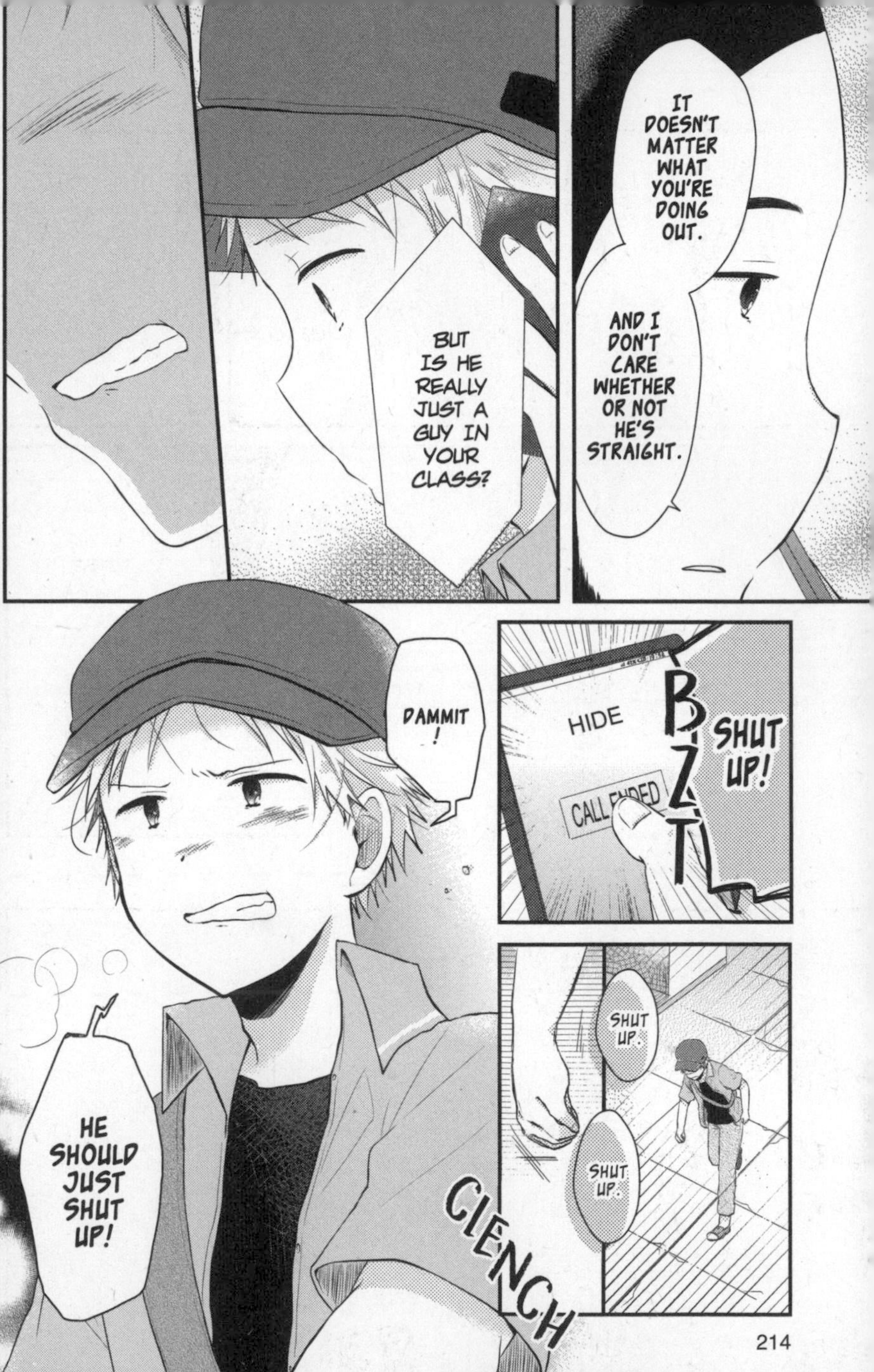
IT DOESN'T MATTER WHAT YOU'RE DOING OUT.
AND I DON'T CARE WHETHER OR NOT HE'S STRAIGHT.
BUT IS HE REALLY JUST A GUY IN YOUR CLASS?
HIDE
CALL ENDED
BZZT
SHUT UP!
SHUT UP.
SHUT UP.
DAMMIT!
HE SHOULD JUST SHUT UP!
CLENCH

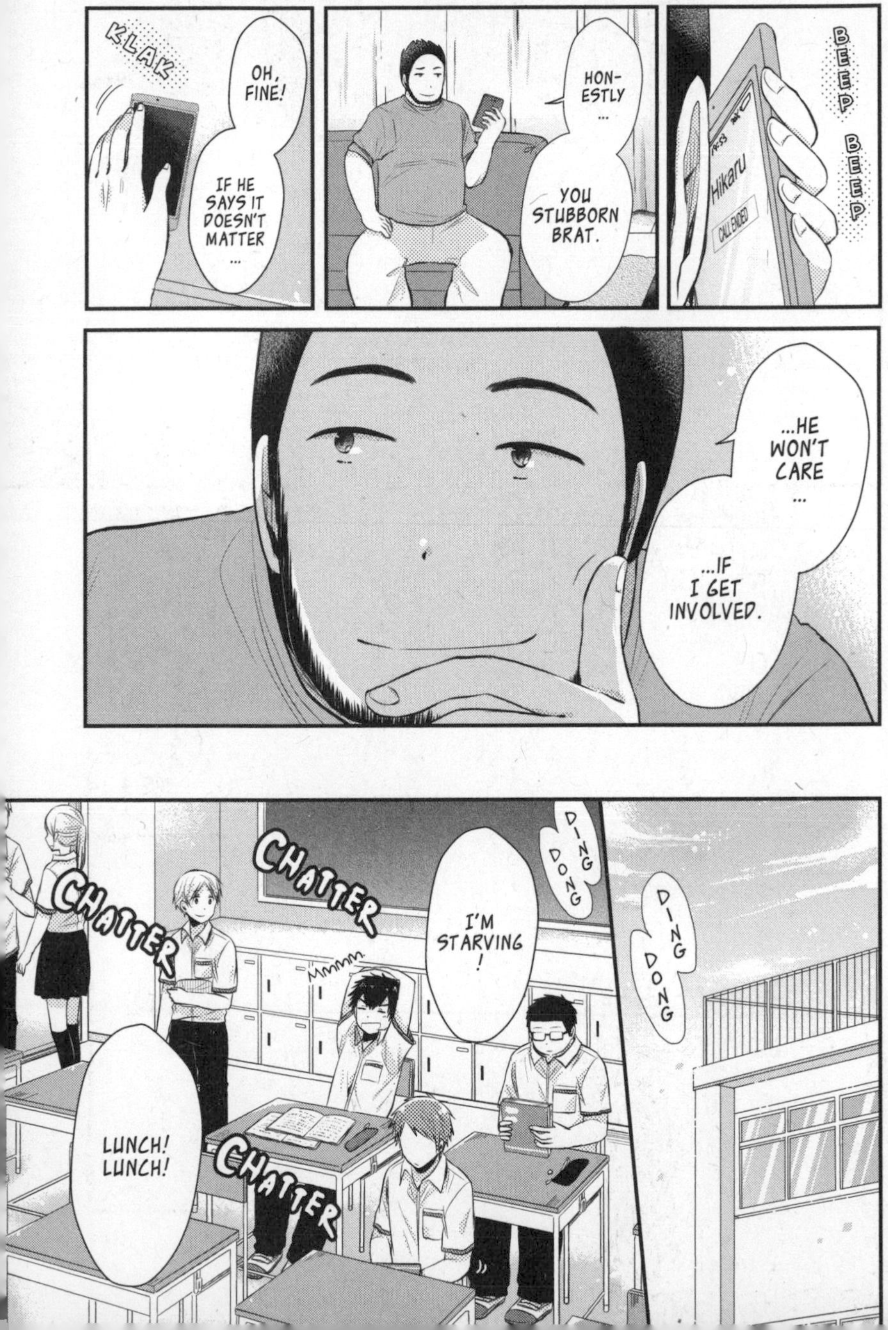
BEEP BEEP
Hikaru
CALL ENDED
HON-ESTLY...
YOU STUBBORN BRAT.
KLAK
OH, FINE!
IF HE SAYS IT DOESN'T MATTER...
...HE WON'T CARE...
...IF I GET INVOLVED.
DING DONG
DING DONG
I'M STARVING!
CHATTER
Mmmm
CHATTER
LUNCH! LUNCH!
CHATTER

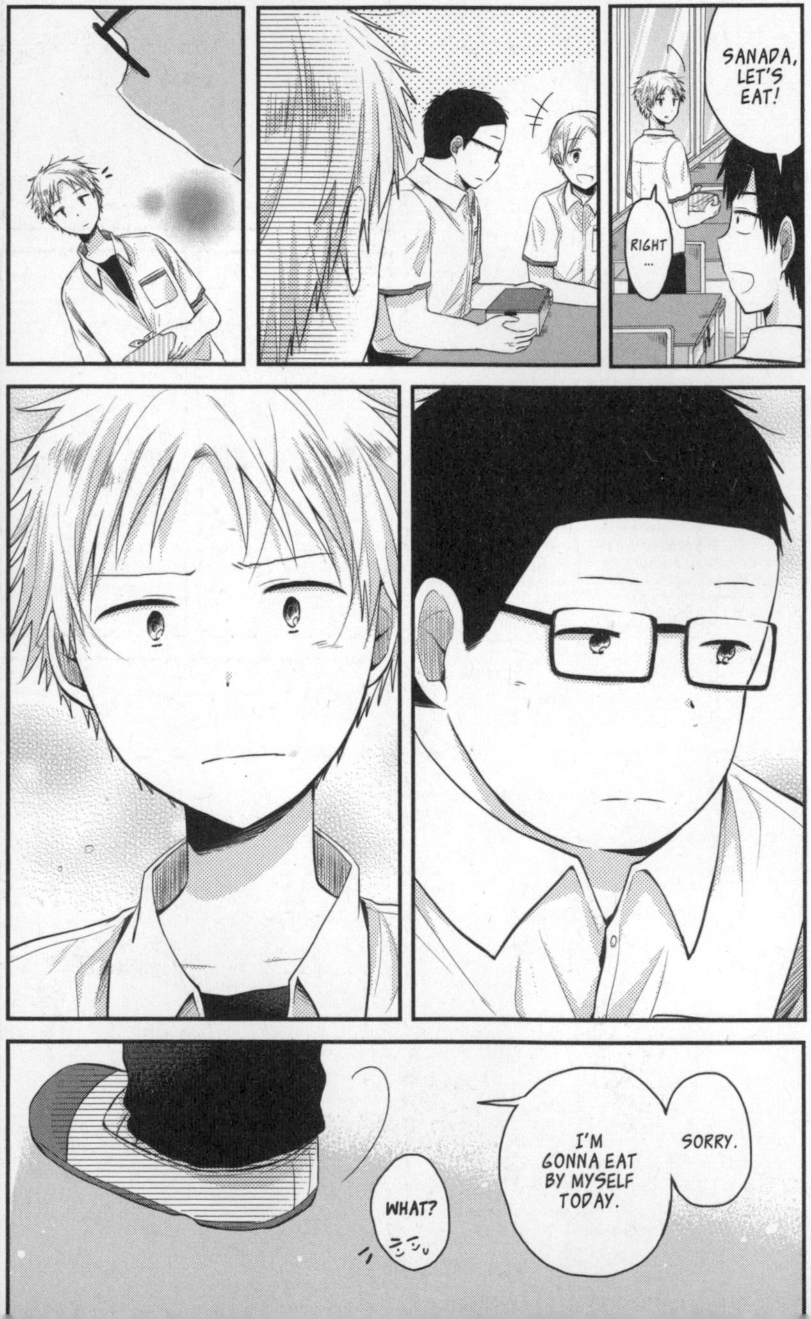
SANADA, LET'S EAT!
RIGHT...
SORRY.
I'M GONNA EAT BY MYSELF TODAY.
WHAT?

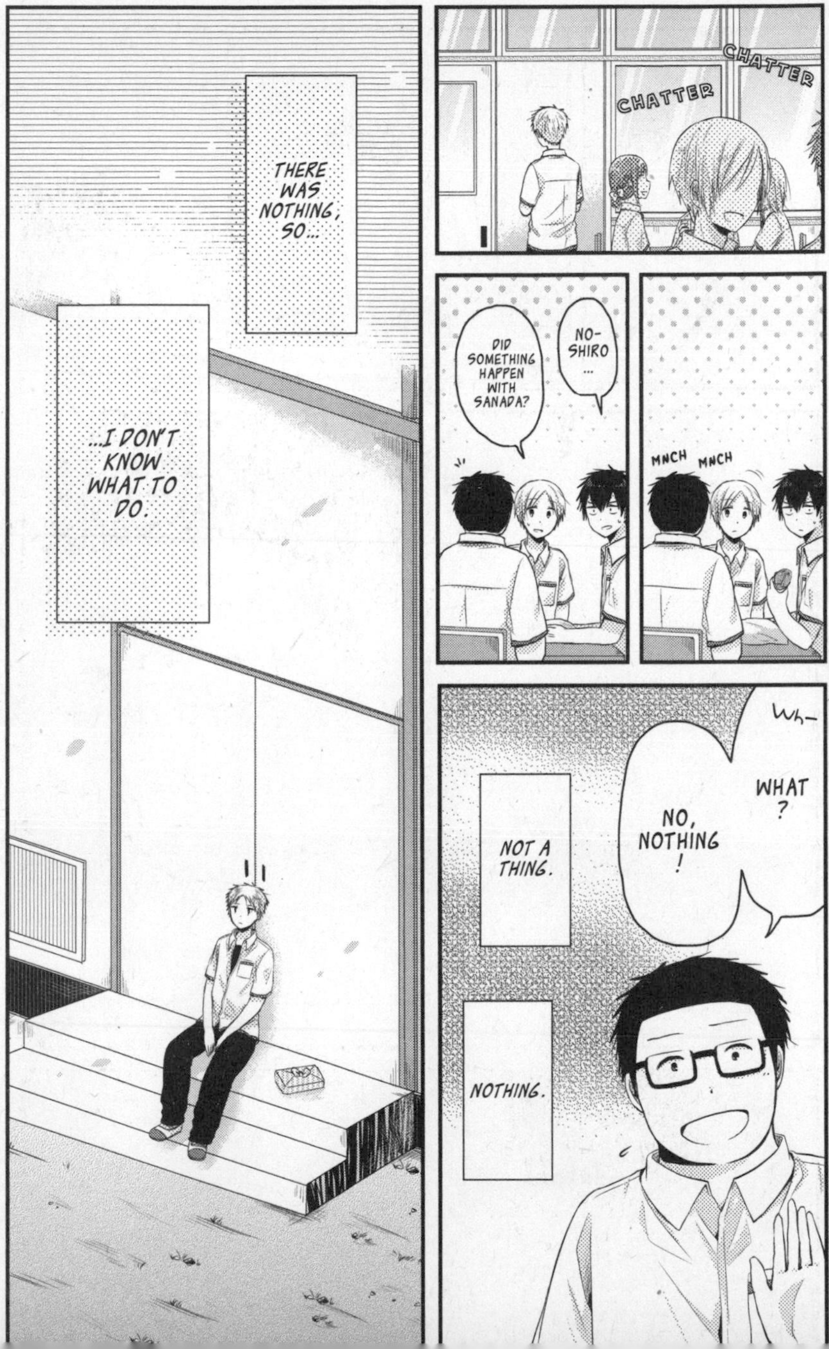
CHATTER
CHATTER
MNCH MNCH
NO-SHIRO...
DID SOMETHING HAPPEN WITH SANADA?
Wh-
WHAT?
NO, NOTHING!
NOT A THING.
NOTHING.
THERE WAS NOTHING, SO...
...I DON'T KNOW WHAT TO DO.

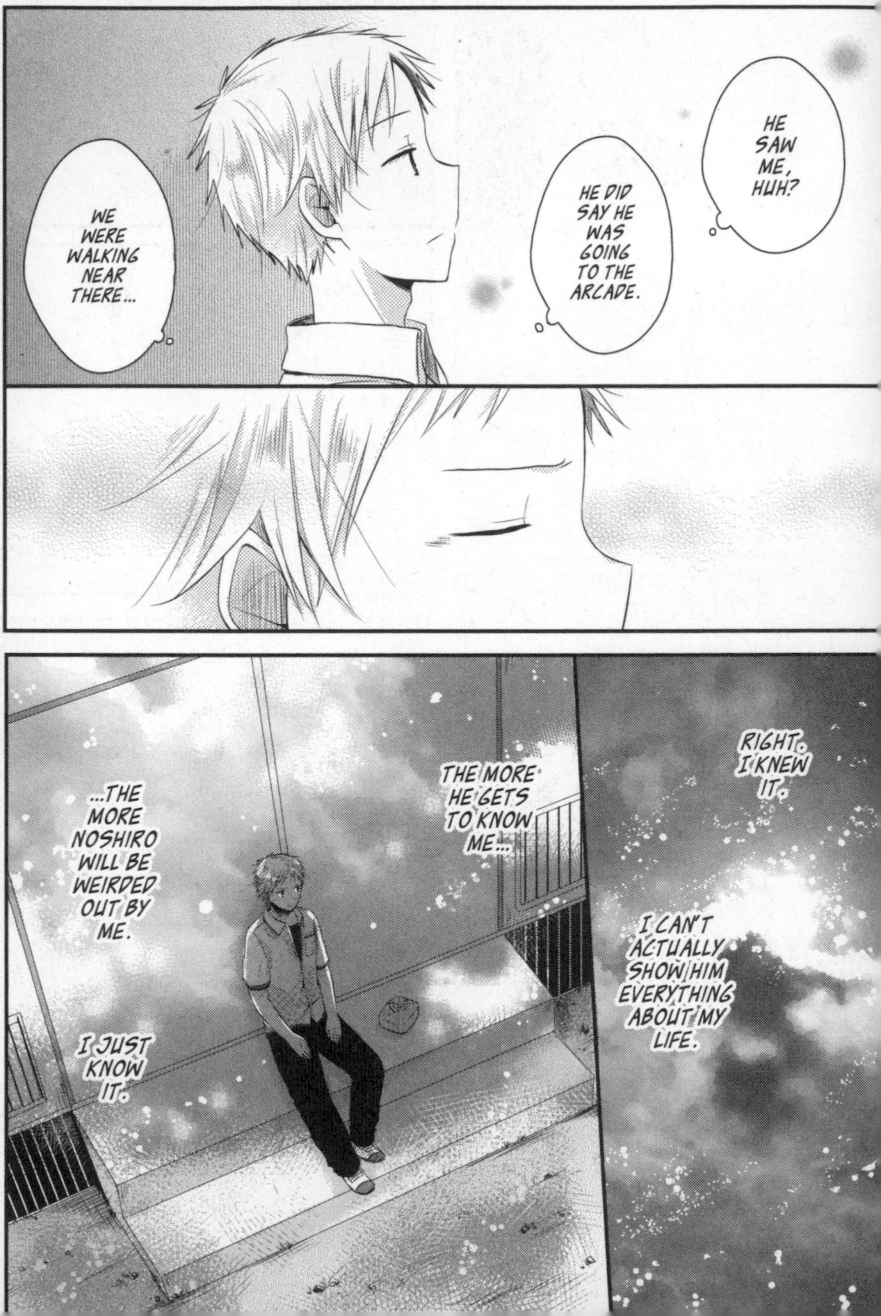
HE SAW ME, HUH?
HE DID SAY HE WAS GOING TO THE ARCADE.
WE WERE WALKING NEAR THERE...
RIGHT. I KNEW IT.
I CAN'T ACTUALLY SHOW HIM EVERYTHING ABOUT MY LIFE.
THE MORE HE GETS TO KNOW ME...
...THE MORE NOSHIRO WILL BE WEIRDED OUT BY ME.
I JUST KNOW IT.

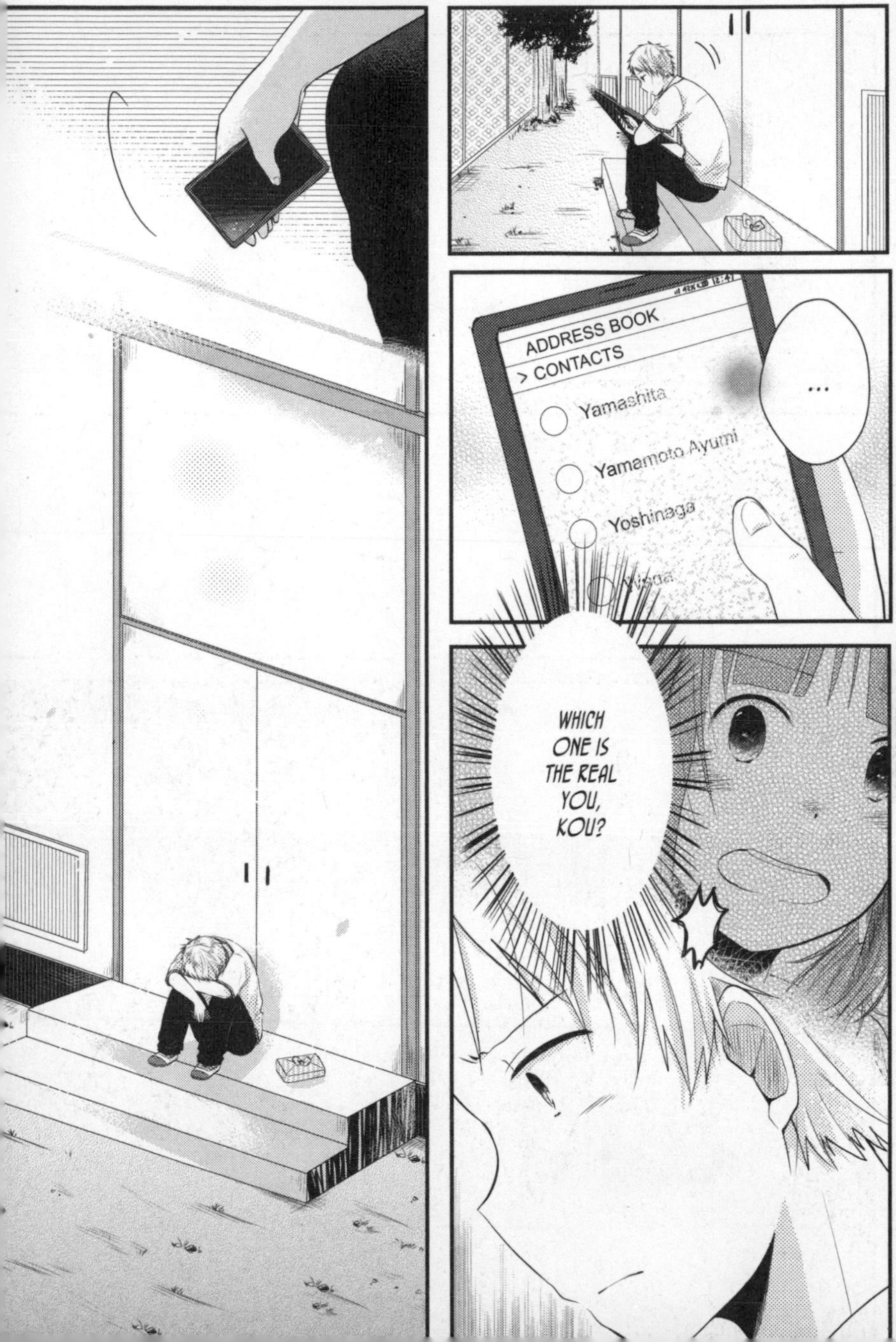
ADDRESS BOOK
> CONTACTS
Yamashita
Yamamoto Ayumi
Yoshinaga
...
WHICH ONE IS THE REAL YOU, KOU?

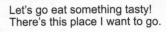

HIDE

Noshiro, meet me when you're done with school today! 😊

Let's go eat something tasty! There's this place I want to go.

How about we meet in front of XX station at five?

13:45

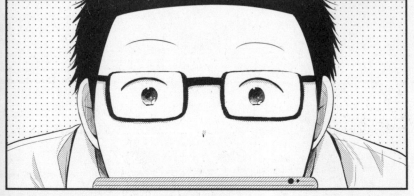

BUT...

WHY ALL OF A SUDDEN ?!

WHAT IS THIS ABOUT, THOUGH ?

... WHAT ?!

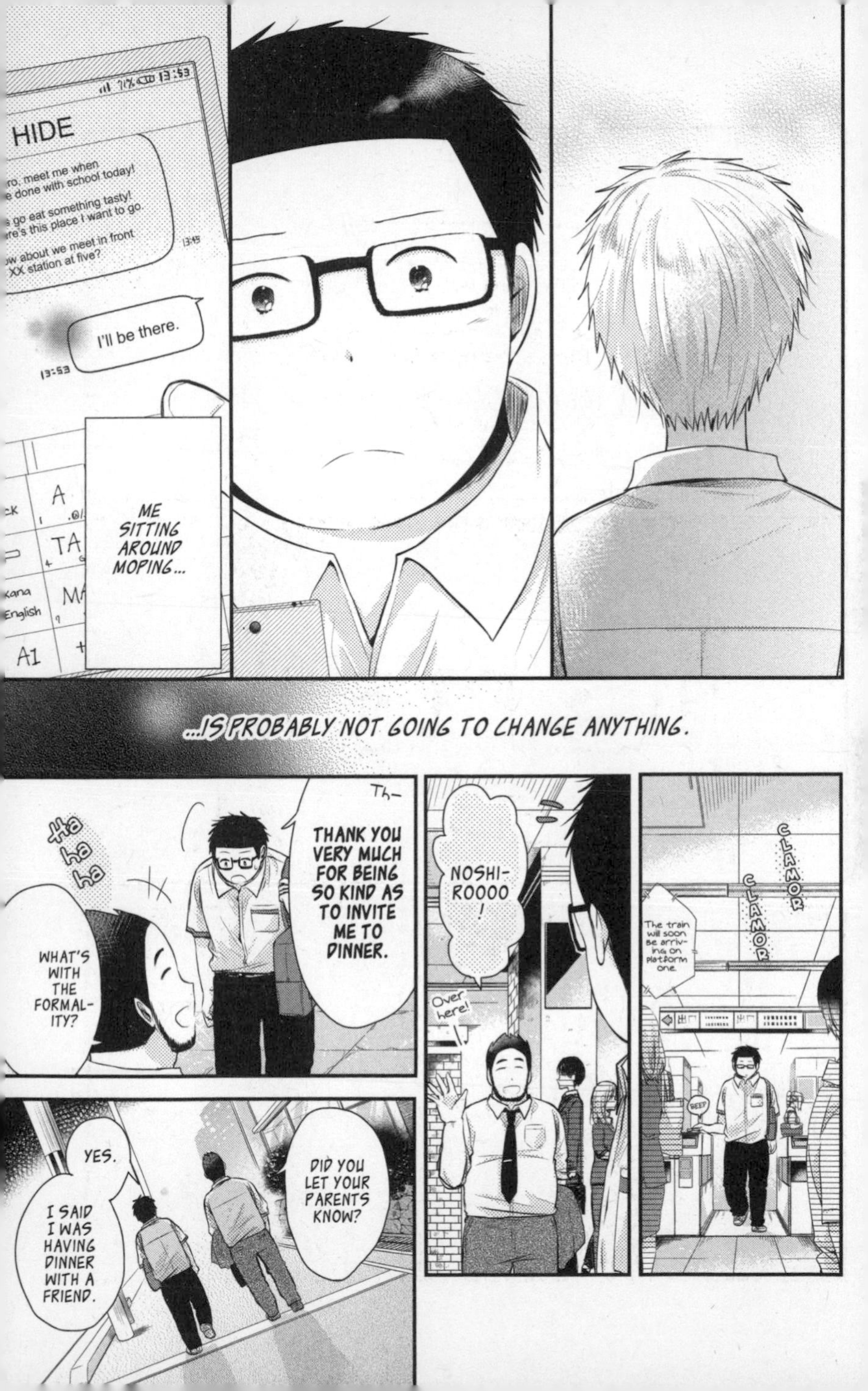
HIDE
ro, meet me when
e done with school today!
s go eat something tasty!
re's this place I want to go.
w about we meet in front
XX station at five?
13:45
I'll be there.
13:53
ME SITTING AROUND MOPING...
...IS PROBABLY NOT GOING TO CHANGE ANYTHING.
CLAMOR
CLAMOR
The train will soon be arriving on platform one.
BEEP
NOSHI-ROOOO!
Over here!
Th-
THANK YOU VERY MUCH FOR BEING SO KIND AS TO INVITE ME TO DINNER.
Ha ha ha
WHAT'S WITH THE FORMALITY?
DID YOU LET YOUR PARENTS KNOW?
YES.
I SAID I WAS HAVING DINNER WITH A FRIEND.

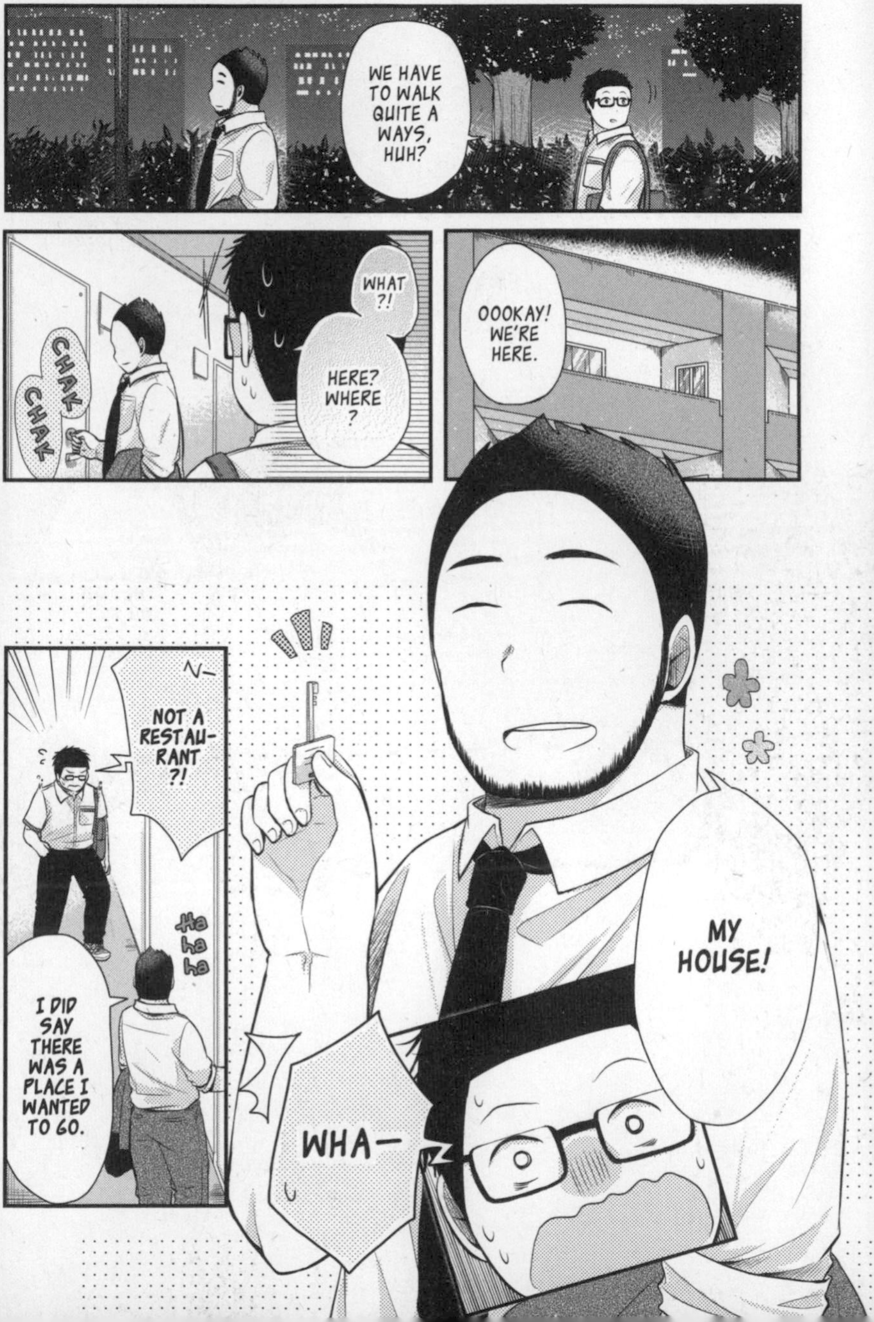
WE HAVE TO WALK QUITE A WAYS, HUH?
OOOKAY! WE'RE HERE.
WHAT?!
HERE? WHERE?
CHAK CHAK
MY HOUSE!
WHA—
N- NOT A RESTAU-RANT?!
Ha ha ha
I DID SAY THERE WAS A PLACE I WANTED TO GO.

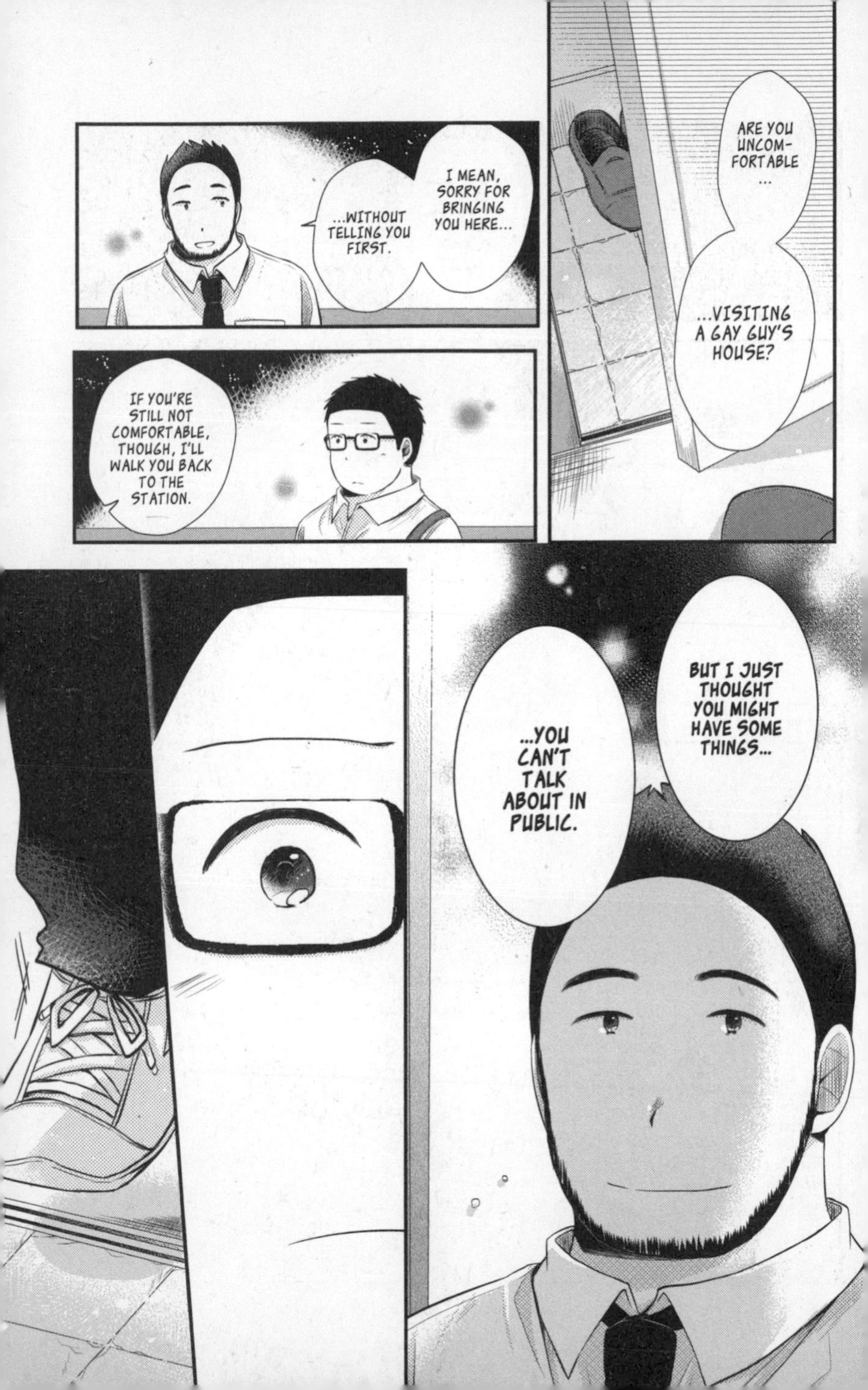
ARE YOU UNCOM-FORTABLE ...
...VISITING A GAY GUY'S HOUSE?
I MEAN, SORRY FOR BRINGING YOU HERE...
...WITHOUT TELLING YOU FIRST.
IF YOU'RE STILL NOT COMFORTABLE, THOUGH, I'LL WALK YOU BACK TO THE STATION.
BUT I JUST THOUGHT YOU MIGHT HAVE SOME THINGS...
...YOU CAN'T TALK ABOUT IN PUBLIC.

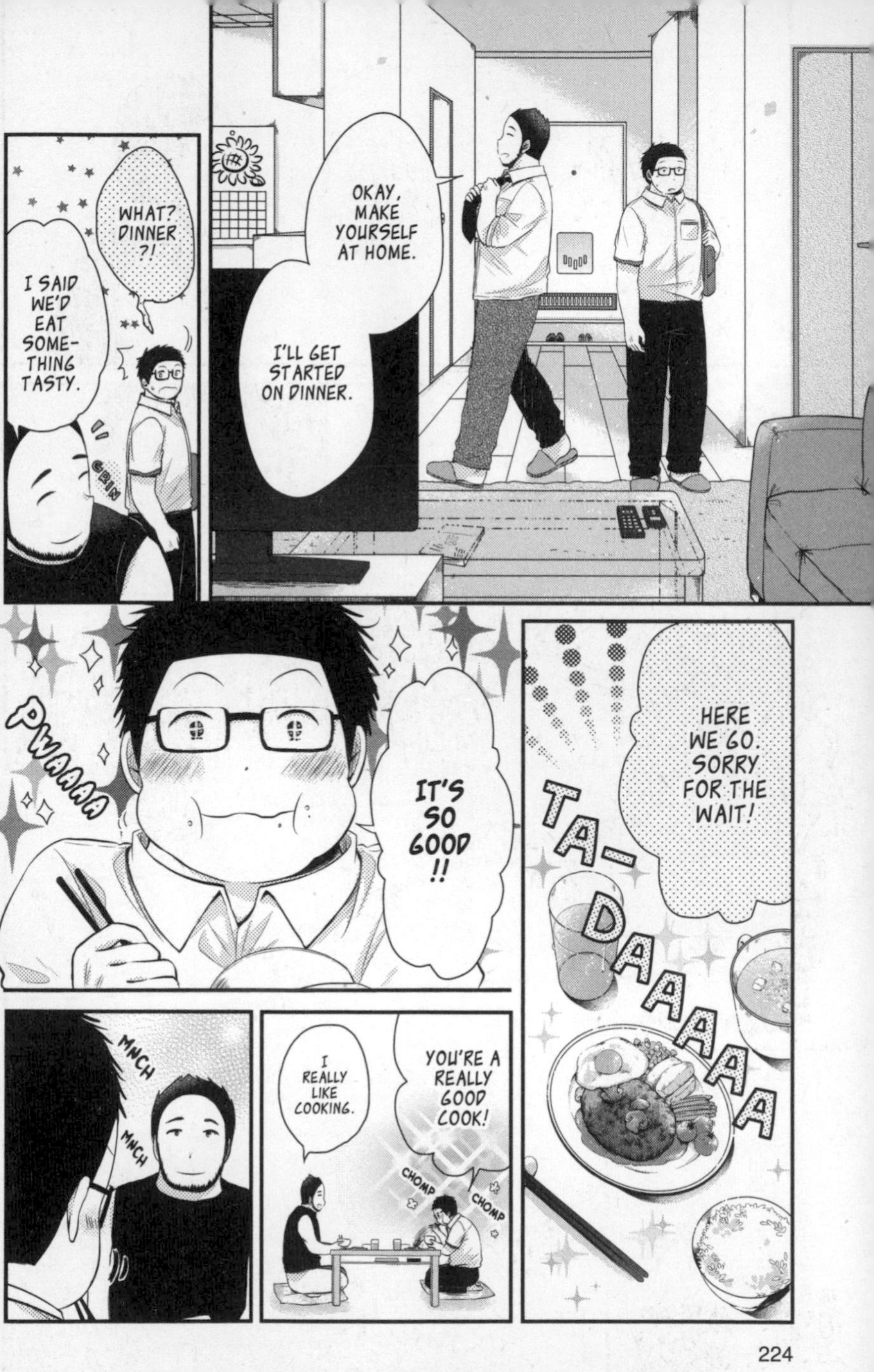
OKAY, MAKE YOURSELF AT HOME.
I'LL GET STARTED ON DINNER.
WHAT? DINNER?!
I SAID WE'D EAT SOME-THING TASTY.
GRIN
HERE WE GO. SORRY FOR THE WAIT!
TA-DAAAAAAA
IT'S SO GOOD!!
PWAAAA
YOU'RE A REALLY GOOD COOK!
I REALLY LIKE COOKING.
CHOMP
CHOMP
MNCH
MNCH

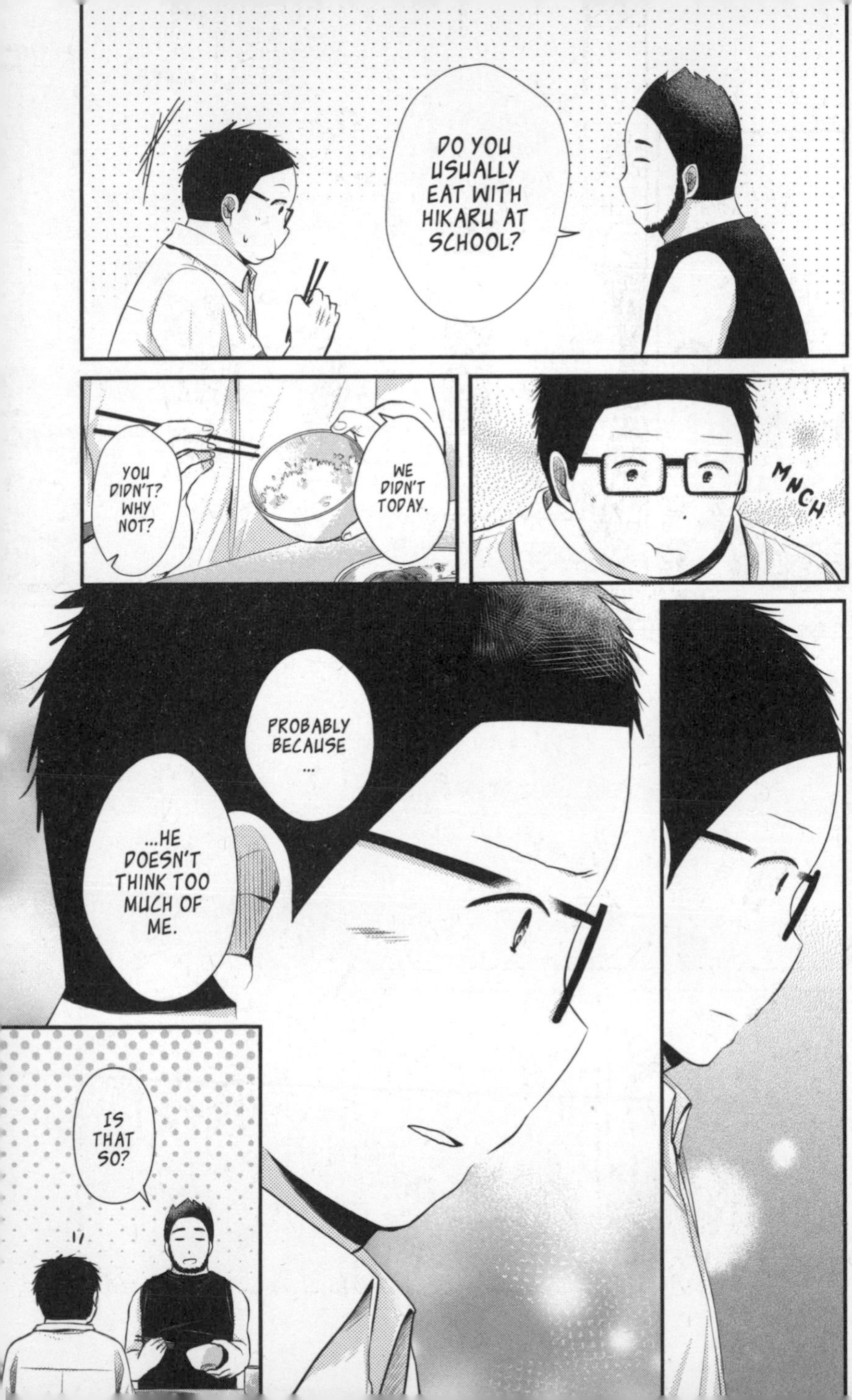
DO YOU USUALLY EAT WITH HIKARU AT SCHOOL?
MNCH
WE DIDN'T TODAY.
YOU DIDN'T? WHY NOT?
PROBABLY BECAUSE ...
...HE DOESN'T THINK TOO MUCH OF ME.
IS THAT SO?

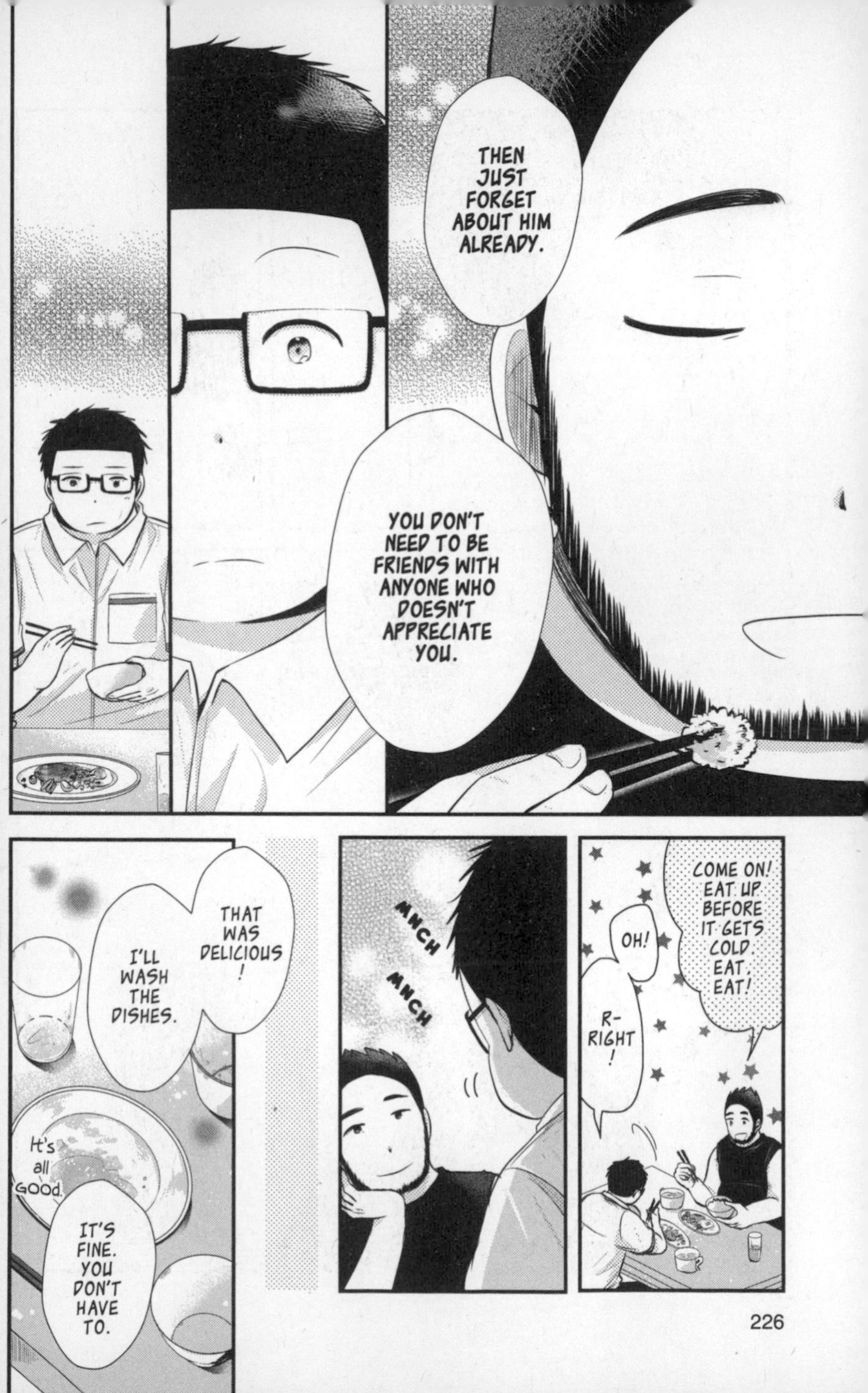
THEN JUST FORGET ABOUT HIM ALREADY.
YOU DON'T NEED TO BE FRIENDS WITH ANYONE WHO DOESN'T APPRECIATE YOU.
COME ON! EAT UP BEFORE IT GETS COLD. EAT, EAT!
OH!
R-RIGHT!
MNCH
MNCH
THAT WAS DELICIOUS!
I'LL WASH THE DISHES.
It's all good.
IT'S FINE. YOU DON'T HAVE TO.

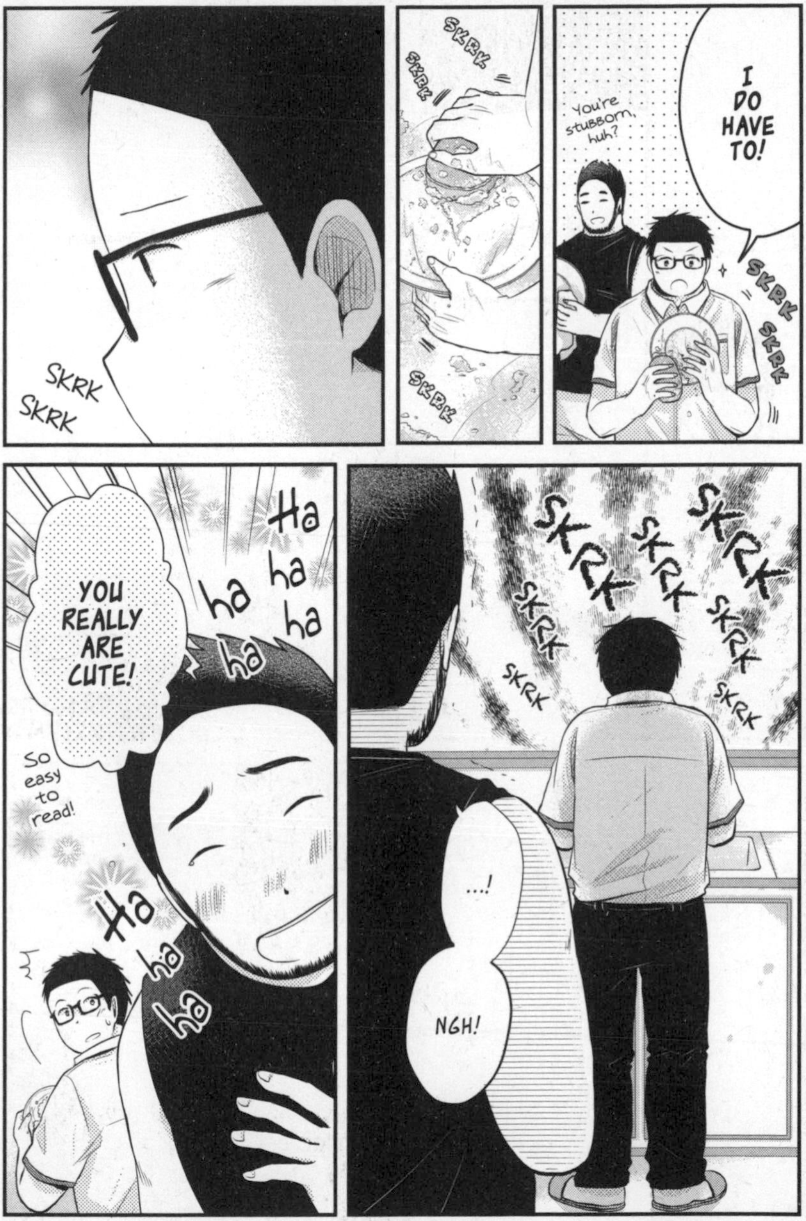

I DO HAVE TO!
You're stubborn, huh?
SKRK SKRK
SKRK
SKRK
SKRK
SKRK SKRK
SKRK SKRK SKRK SKRK SKRK SKRK
...!
NGH!
Ha ha ha ha ha
YOU REALLY ARE CUTE!
So easy to read!
Ha ha ha

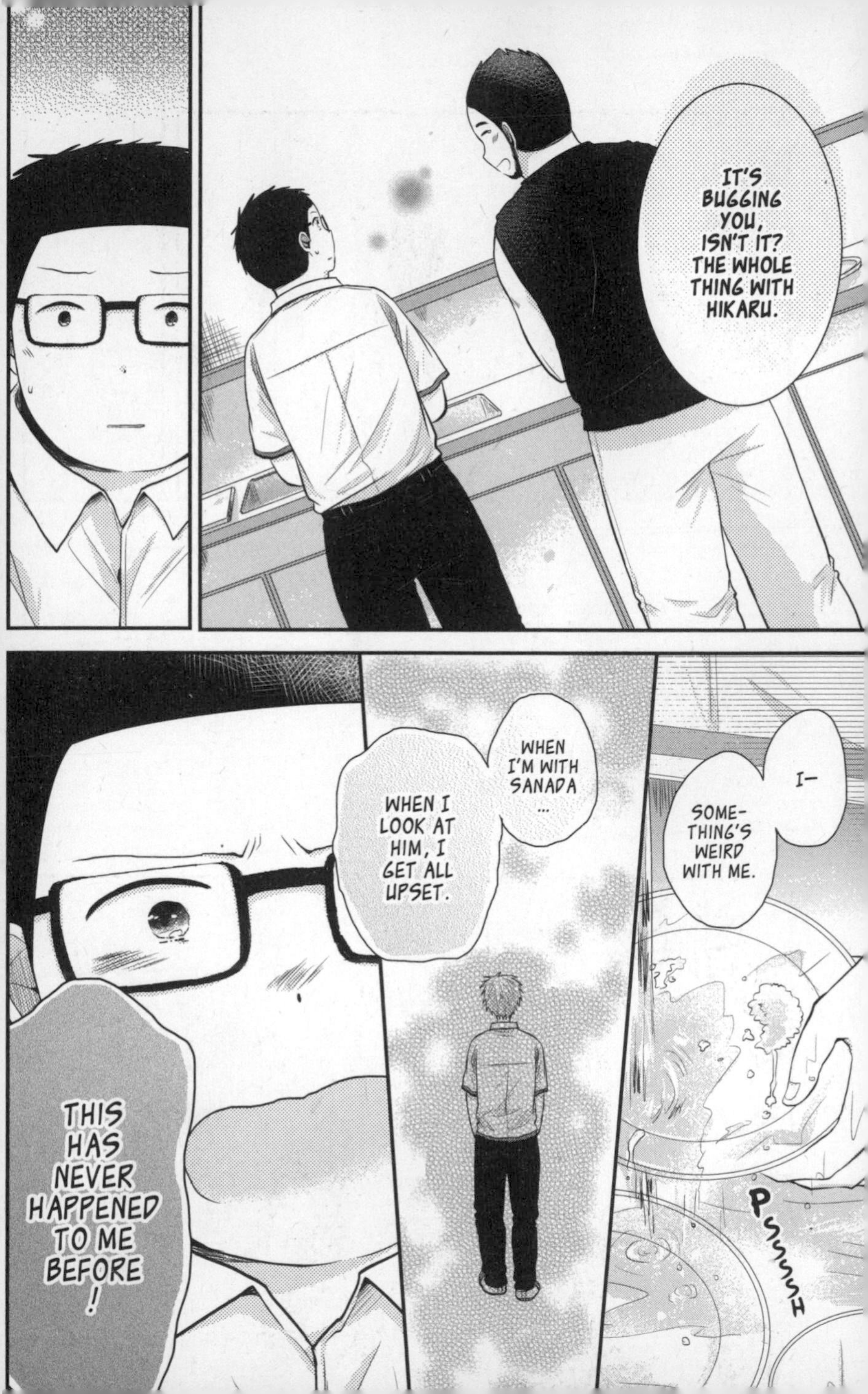
IT'S BUGGING YOU, ISN'T IT? THE WHOLE THING WITH HIKARU.
I—
SOME-THING'S WEIRD WITH ME.
PSSSSH
WHEN I'M WITH SANADA...
WHEN I LOOK AT HIM, I GET ALL UPSET.
THIS HAS NEVER HAPPENED TO ME BEFORE!

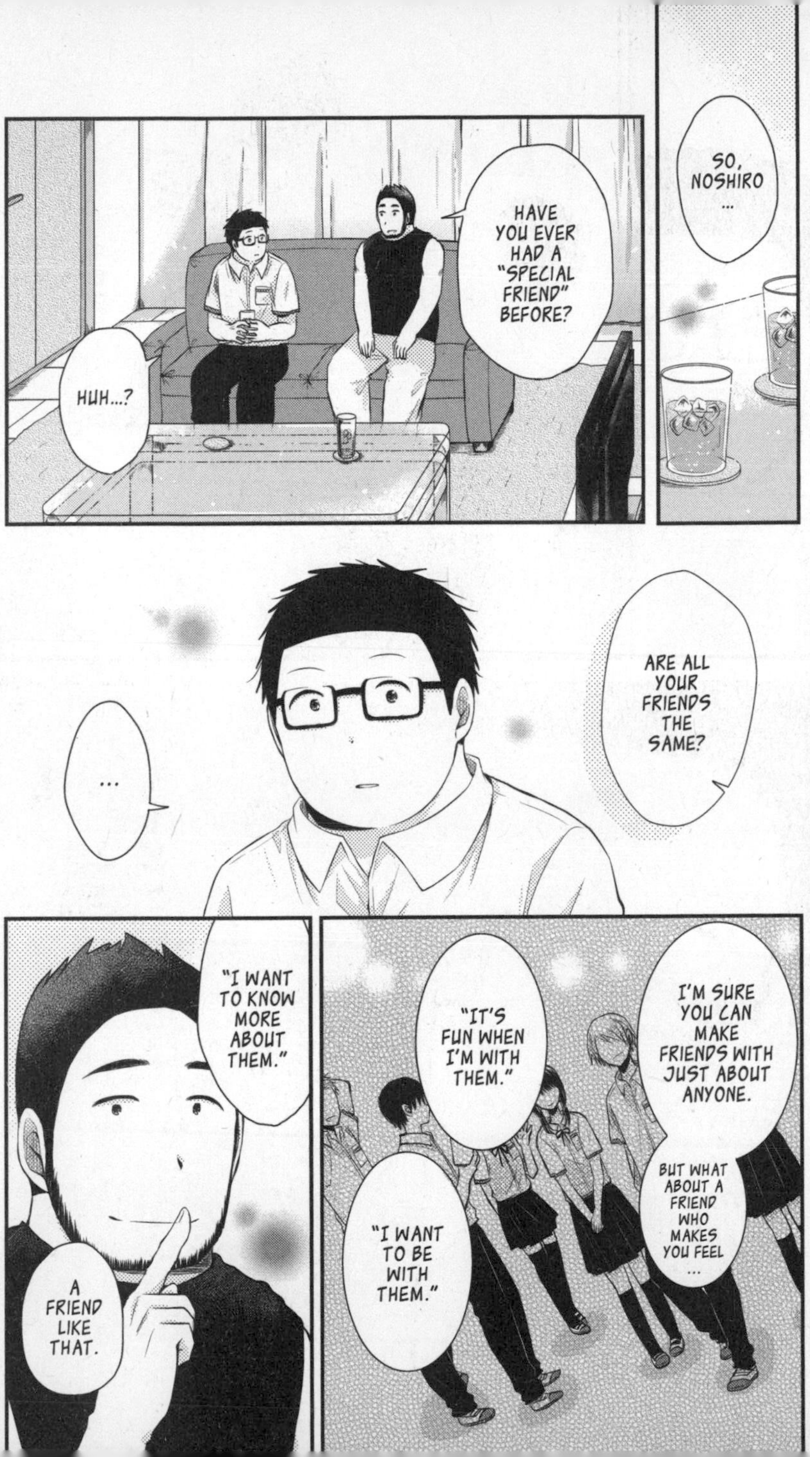
SO, NOSHIRO ...
HAVE YOU EVER HAD A "SPECIAL FRIEND" BEFORE?
HUH...?
ARE ALL YOUR FRIENDS THE SAME?
...
I'M SURE YOU CAN MAKE FRIENDS WITH JUST ABOUT ANYONE.
BUT WHAT ABOUT A FRIEND WHO MAKES YOU FEEL ...
"IT'S FUN WHEN I'M WITH THEM."
"I WANT TO BE WITH THEM."
"I WANT TO KNOW MORE ABOUT THEM."
A FRIEND LIKE THAT.

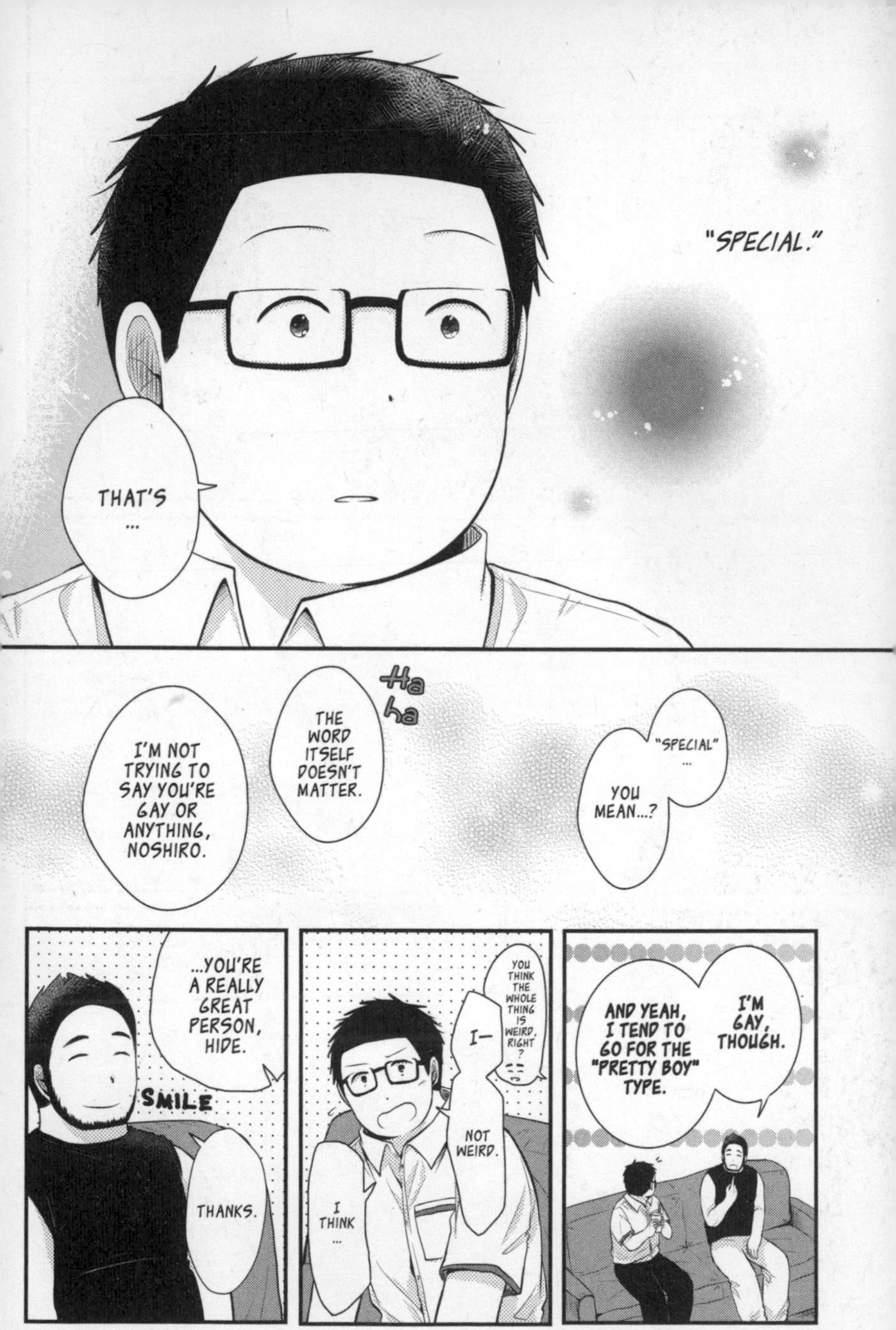
"SPECIAL."
THAT'S ...
"SPECIAL" ... YOU MEAN...?
Ha ha
THE WORD ITSELF DOESN'T MATTER.
I'M NOT TRYING TO SAY YOU'RE GAY OR ANYTHING, NOSHIRO.
I'M GAY, THOUGH.
AND YEAH, I TEND TO GO FOR THE "PRETTY BOY" TYPE.
YOU THINK THE WHOLE THING IS WEIRD, RIGHT?
I—
NOT WEIRD.
I THINK ...
...YOU'RE A REALLY GREAT PERSON, HIDE.
SMILE
THANKS.

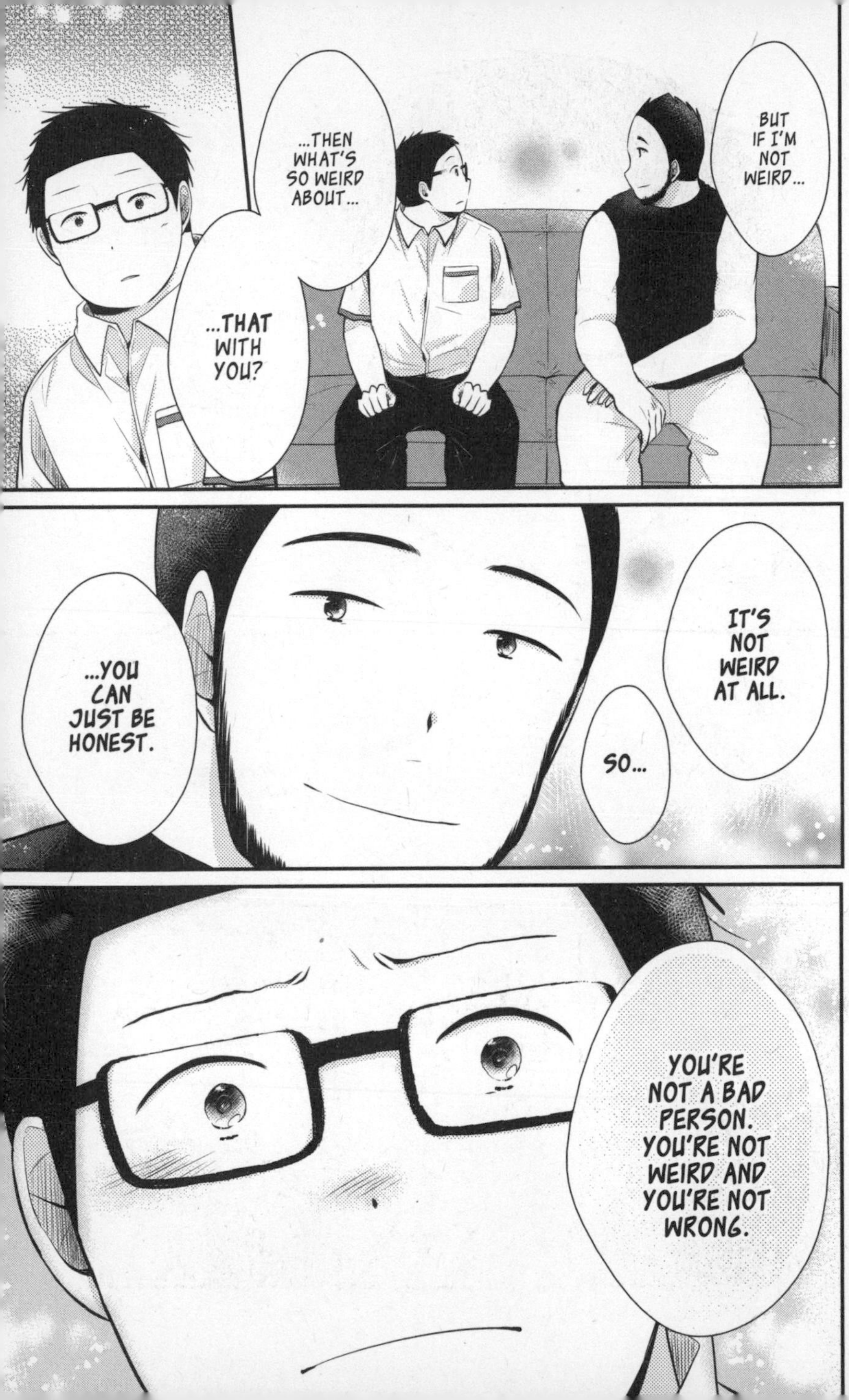
BUT IF I'M NOT WEIRD...
...THEN WHAT'S SO WEIRD ABOUT...
...THAT WITH YOU?
IT'S NOT WEIRD AT ALL.
SO...
...YOU CAN JUST BE HONEST.
YOU'RE NOT A BAD PERSON. YOU'RE NOT WEIRD AND YOU'RE NOT WRONG.

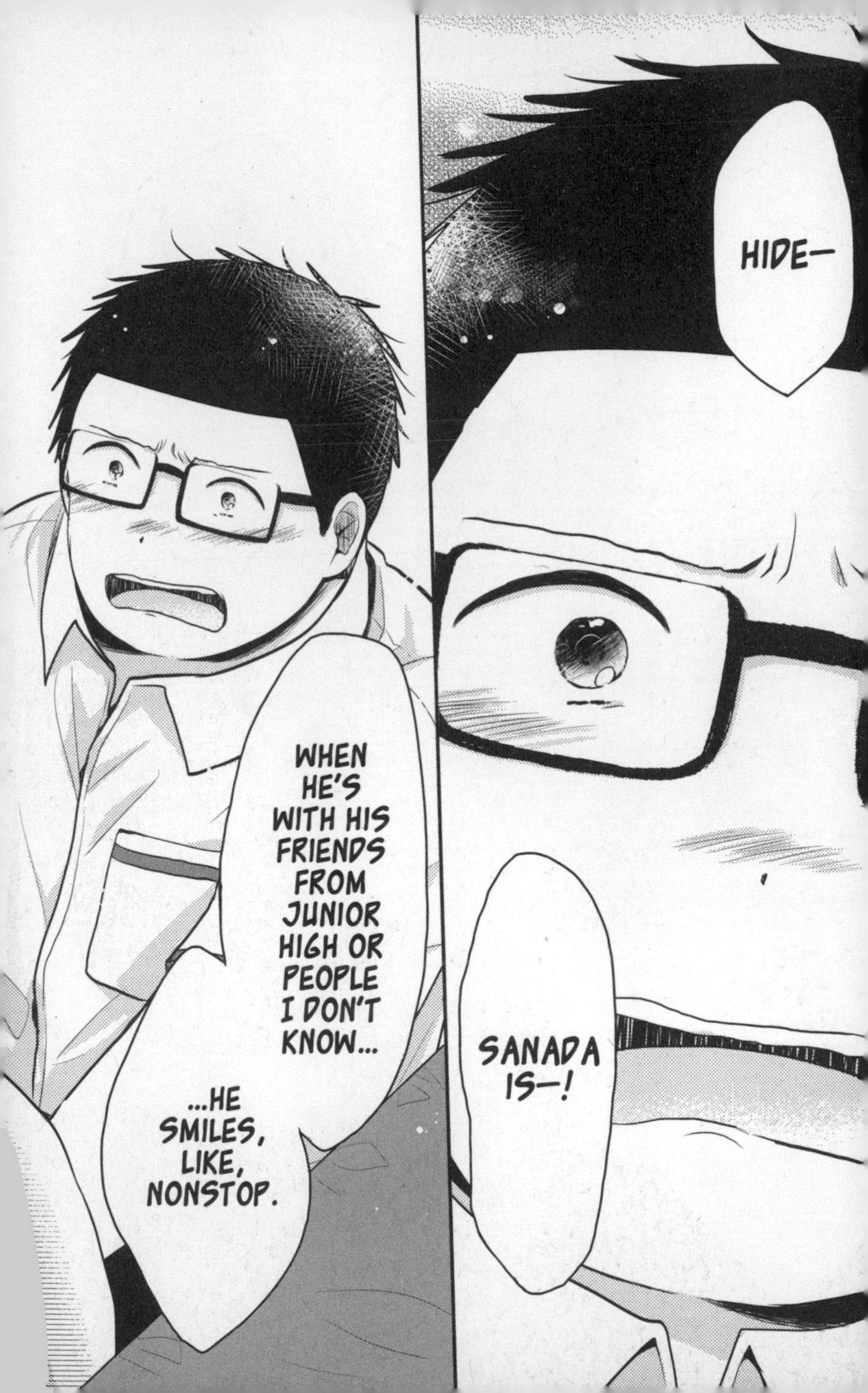
HIDE—
SANADA IS—!
WHEN HE'S WITH HIS FRIENDS FROM JUNIOR HIGH OR PEOPLE I DON'T KNOW...
...HE SMILES, LIKE, NONSTOP.

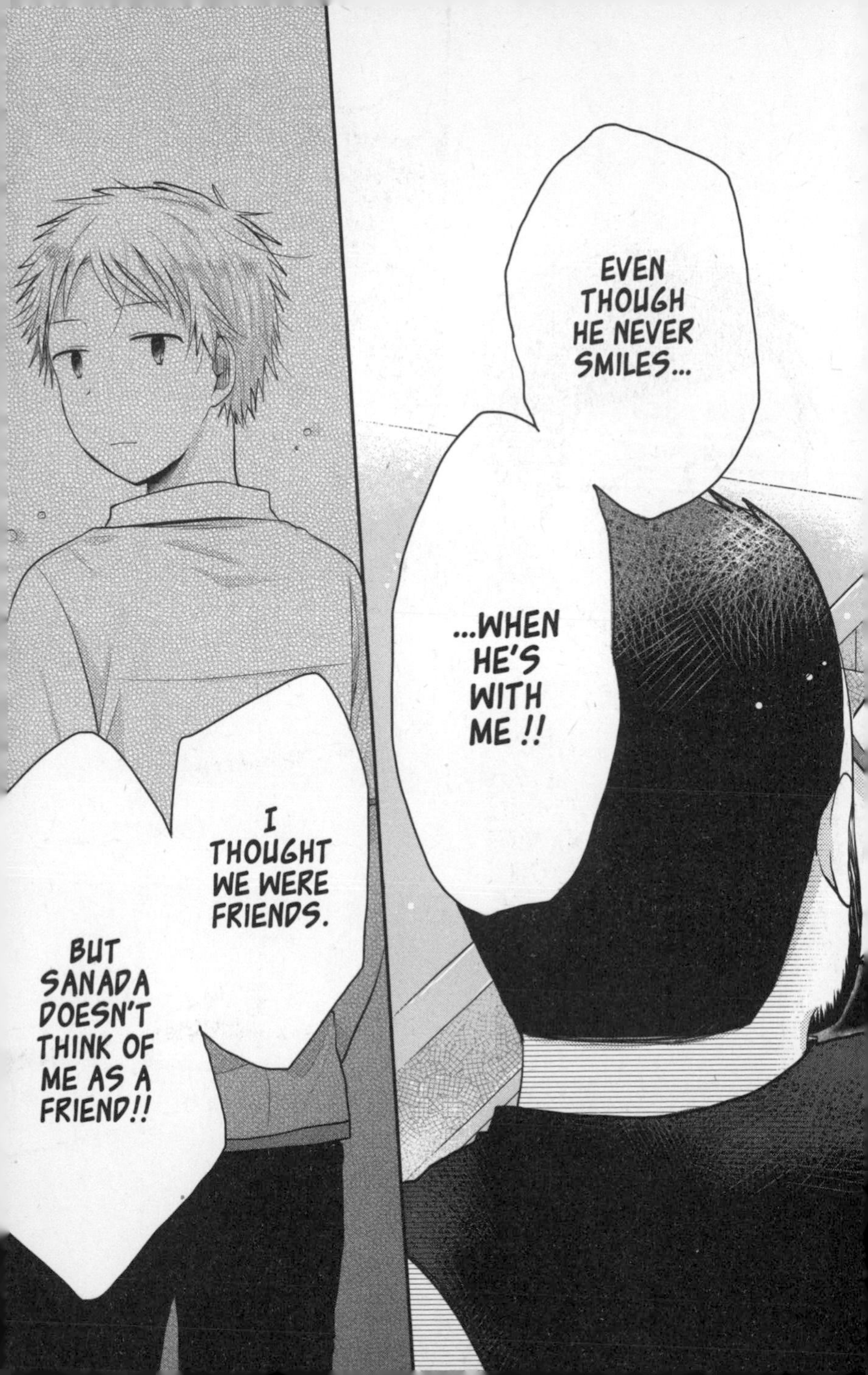
EVEN THOUGH HE NEVER SMILES...
...WHEN HE'S WITH ME!!
I THOUGHT WE WERE FRIENDS.
BUT SANADA DOESN'T THINK OF ME AS A FRIEND!!

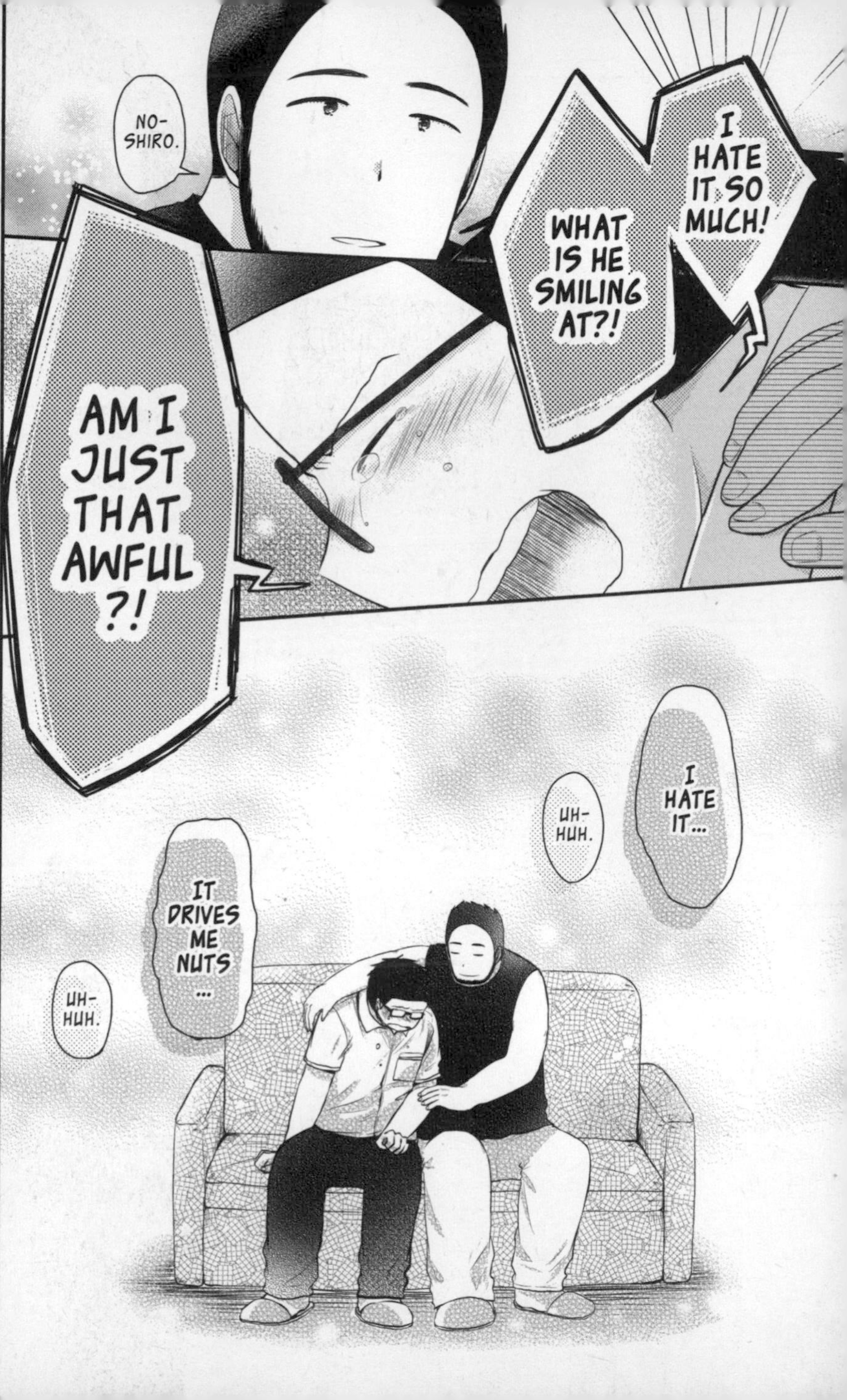
I HATE IT SO MUCH!
WHAT IS HE SMILING AT?!
NO-SHIRO.
AM I JUST THAT AWFUL?!
I HATE IT...
UH-HUH.
IT DRIVES ME NUTS...
UH-HUH.

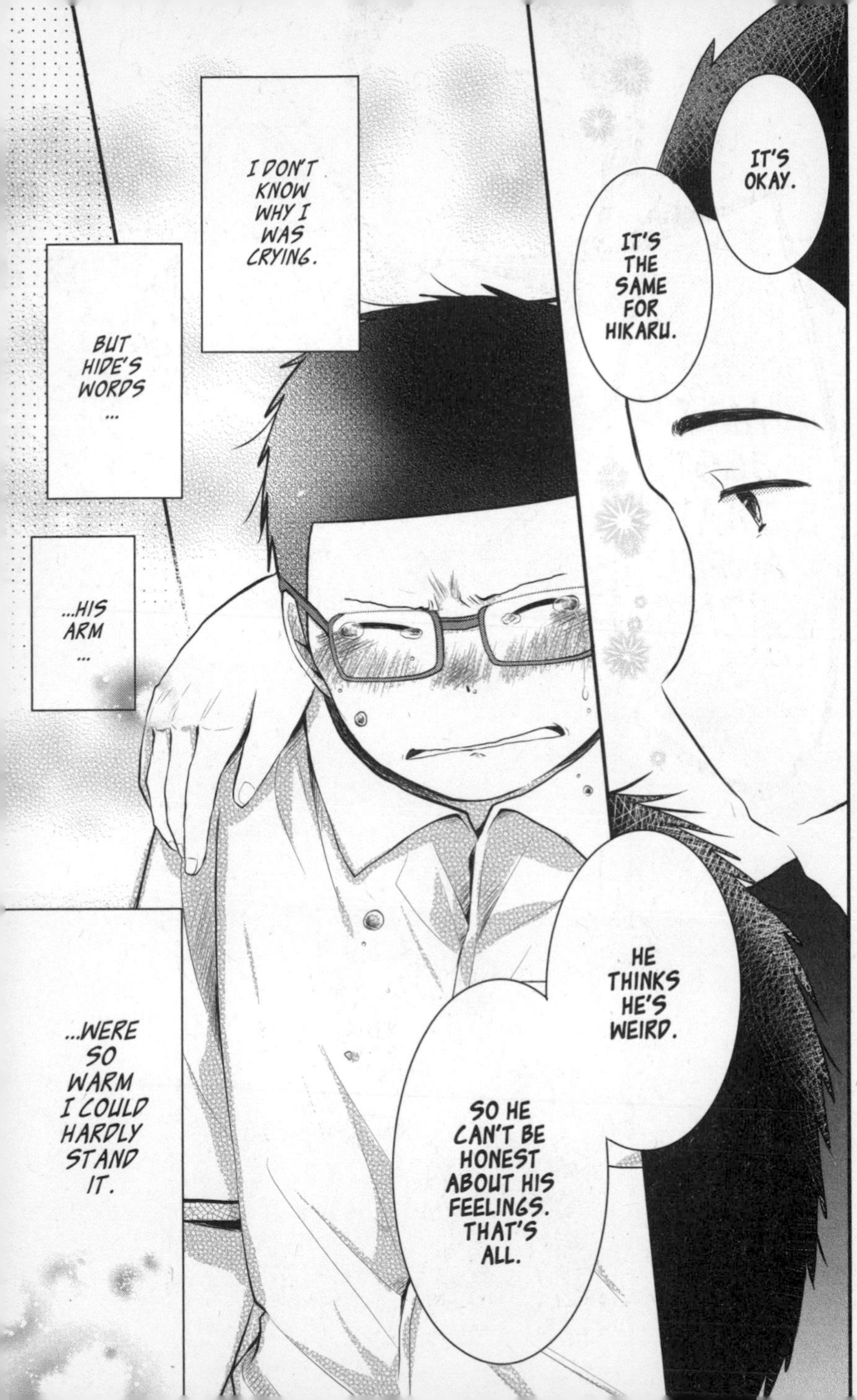
IT'S OKAY.
IT'S THE SAME FOR HIKARU.
HE THINKS HE'S WEIRD.
SO HE CAN'T BE HONEST ABOUT HIS FEELINGS. THAT'S ALL.
I DON'T KNOW WHY I WAS CRYING.
BUT HIDE'S WORDS ...
...HIS ARM ...
...WERE SO WARM I COULD HARDLY STAND IT.

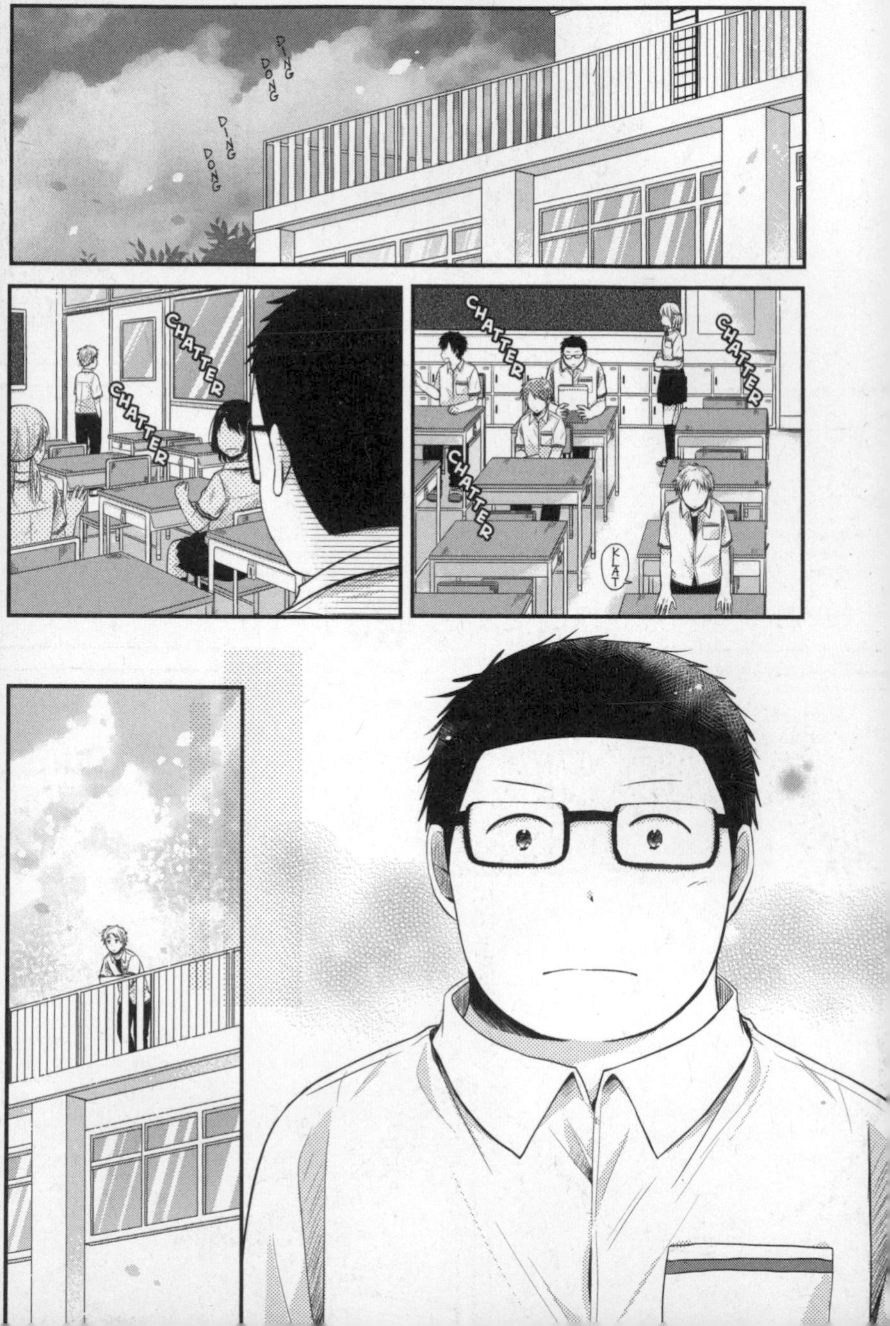
DING DONG
DING DONG
CHATTER
CHATTER
CHATTER
KLAT
CHATTER
CHATTER

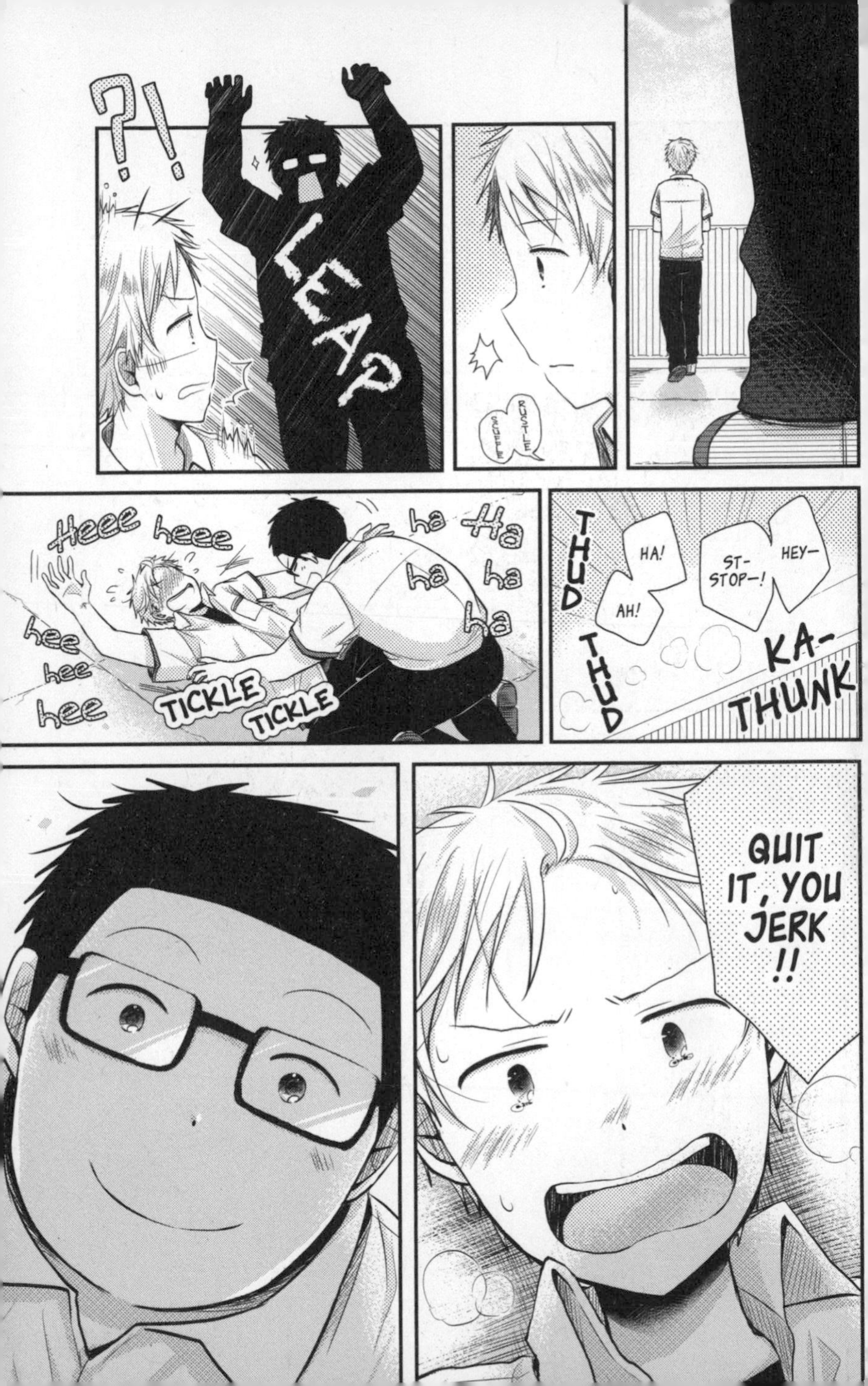
RUSTLE
SCUFFLE
?!
LEAP
HEY—
ST- STOP—!
HA!
AH!
THUD
THUD
KA-THUNK
ha Ha
ha ha
ha
Heee heee
hee hee hee
TICKLE
TICKLE
QUIT IT, YOU JERK!!

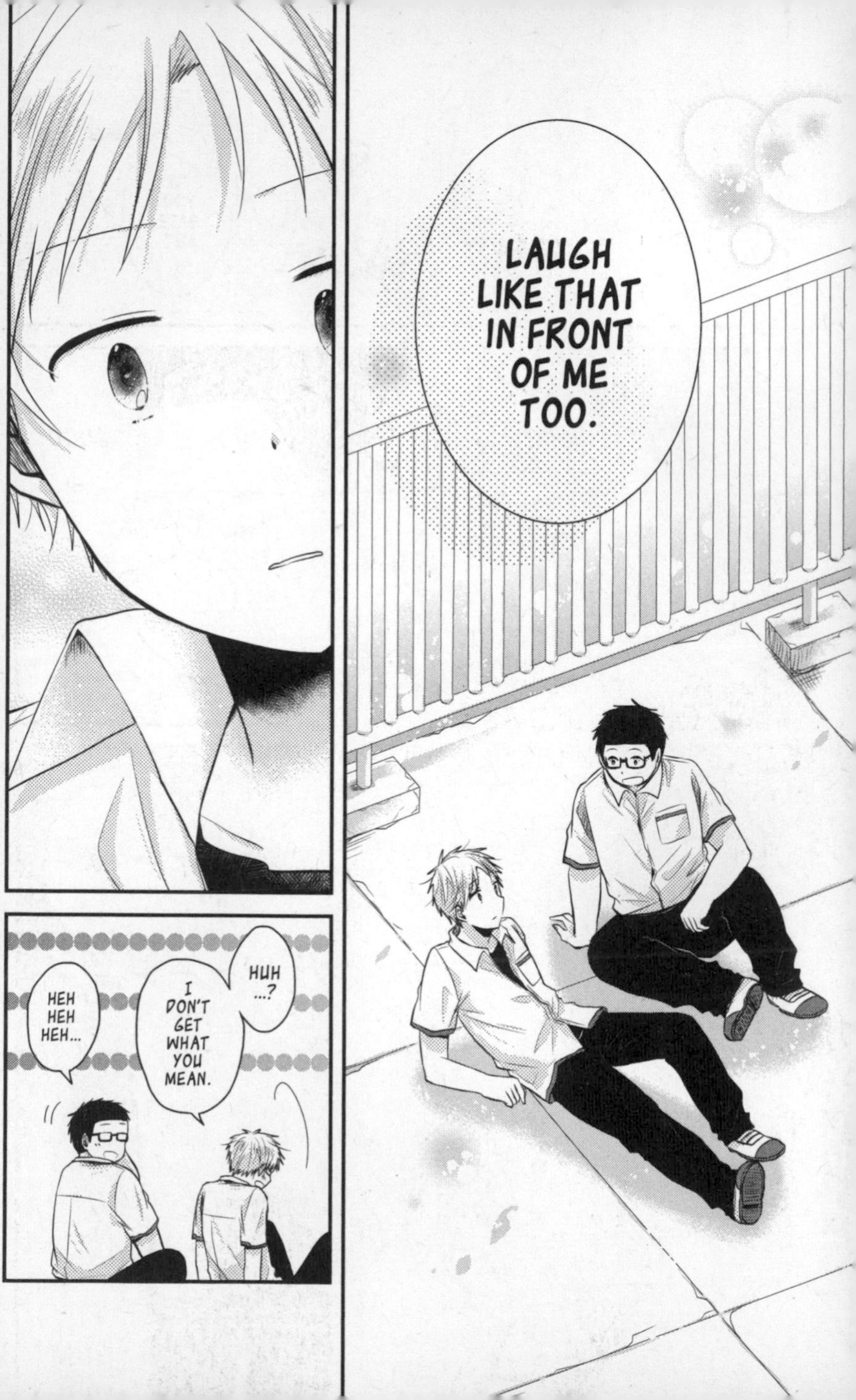
LAUGH LIKE THAT IN FRONT OF ME TOO.
HUH ...?
I DON'T GET WHAT YOU MEAN.
HEH HEH HEH...

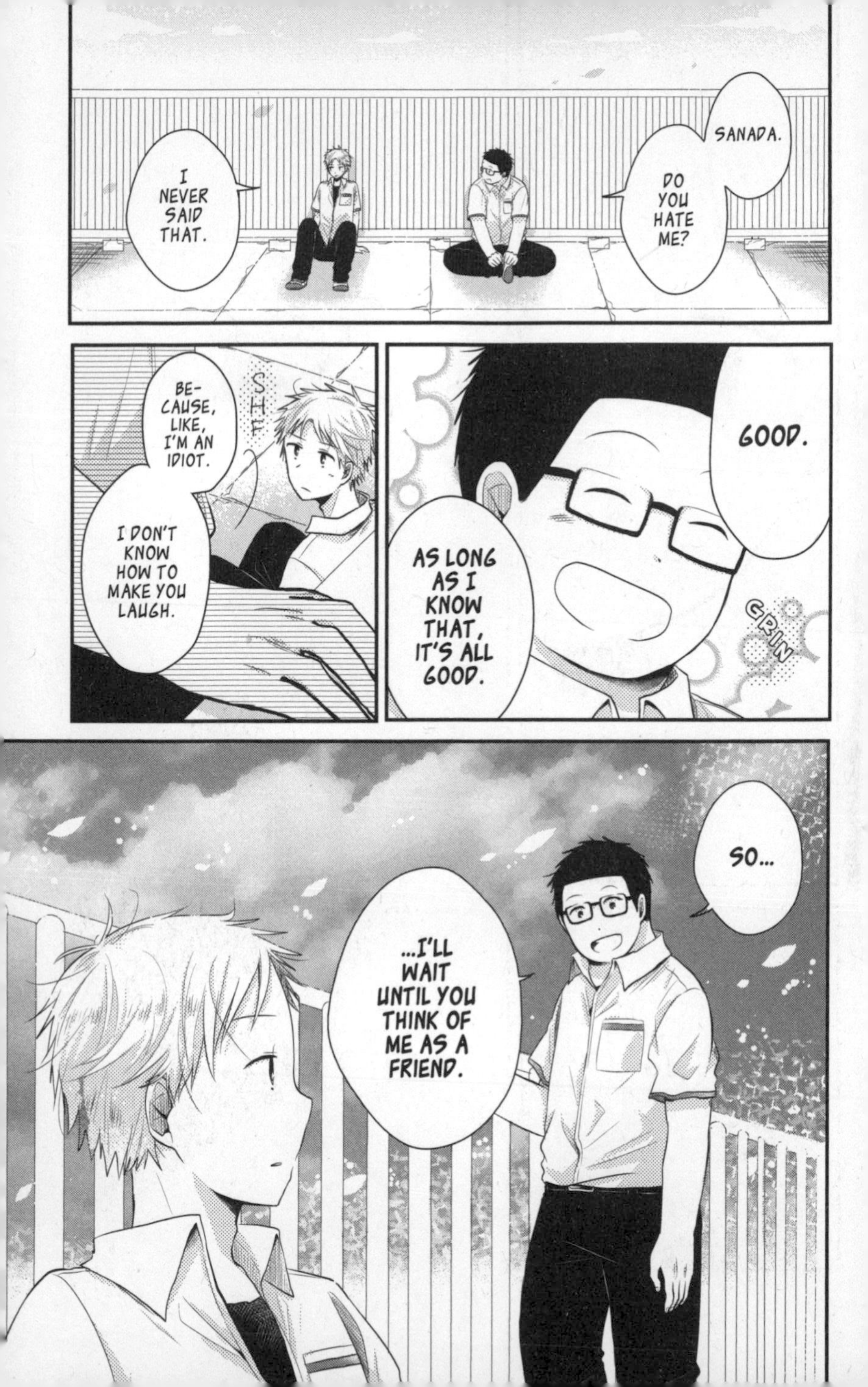
SANADA.
DO YOU HATE ME?
I NEVER SAID THAT.
GOOD.
AS LONG AS I KNOW THAT, IT'S ALL GOOD.
GRIN
BE-CAUSE, LIKE, I'M AN IDIOT.
SHF
I DON'T KNOW HOW TO MAKE YOU LAUGH.
SO...
...I'LL WAIT UNTIL YOU THINK OF ME AS A FRIEND.

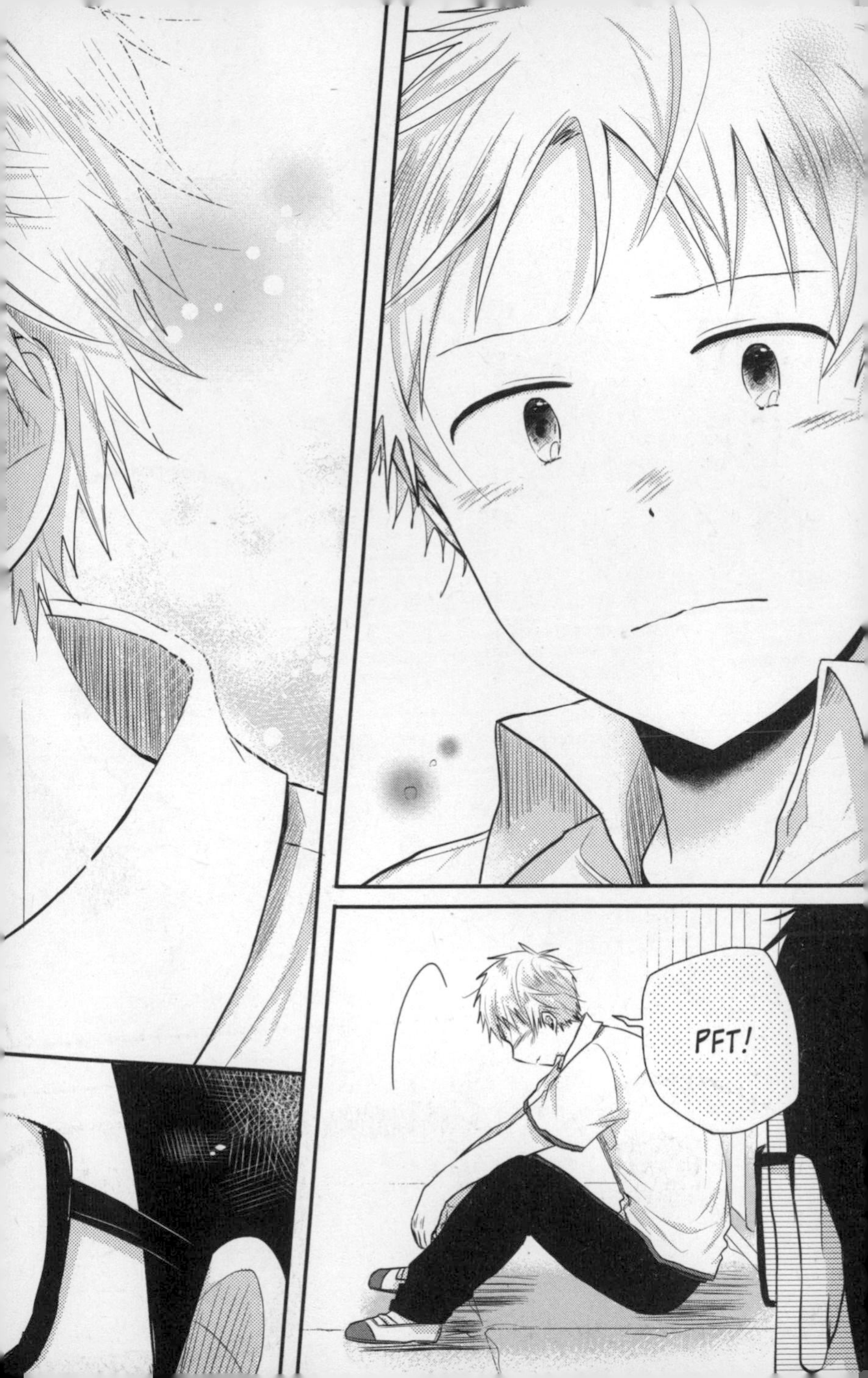
PFT!

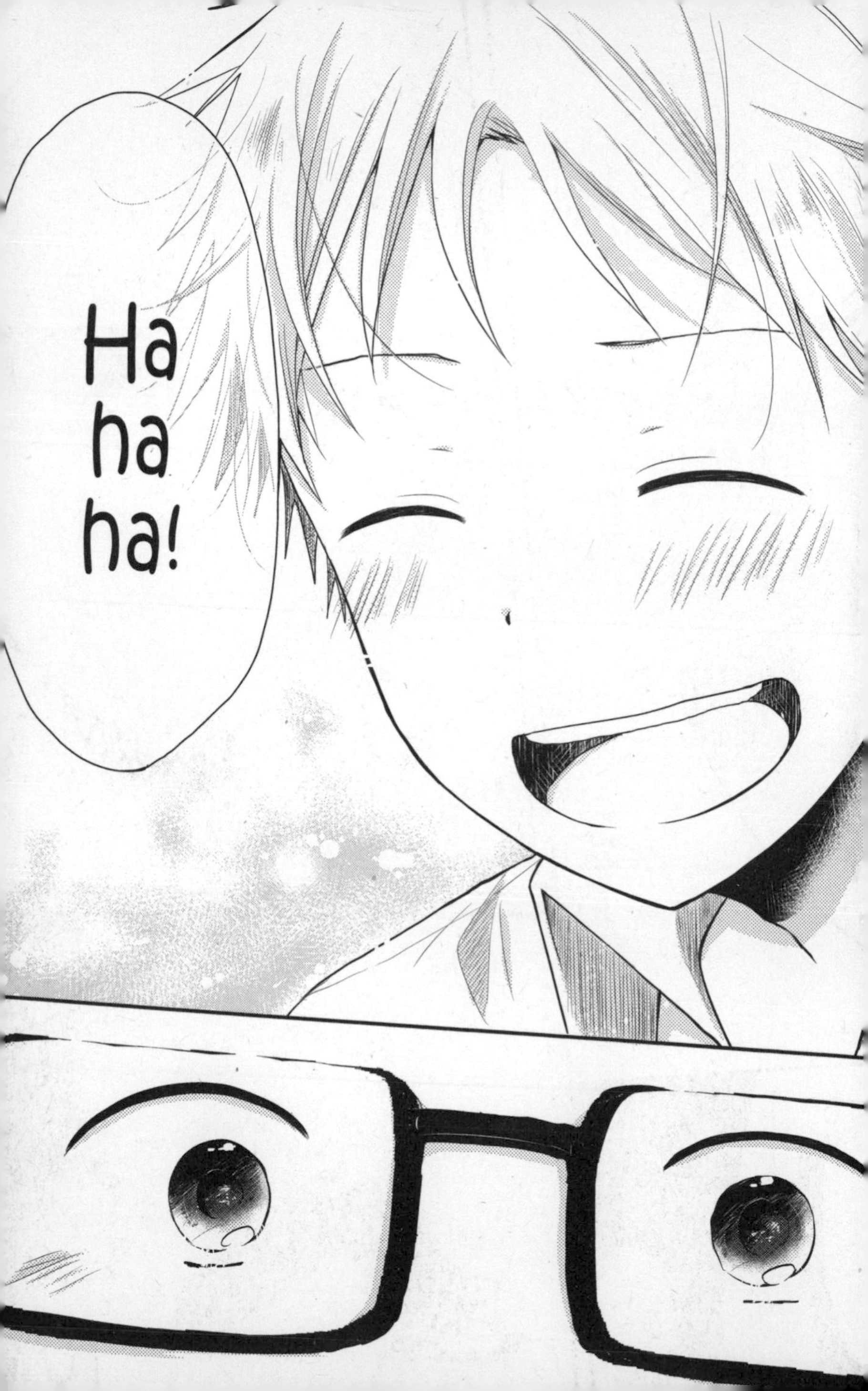
Ha ha ha!

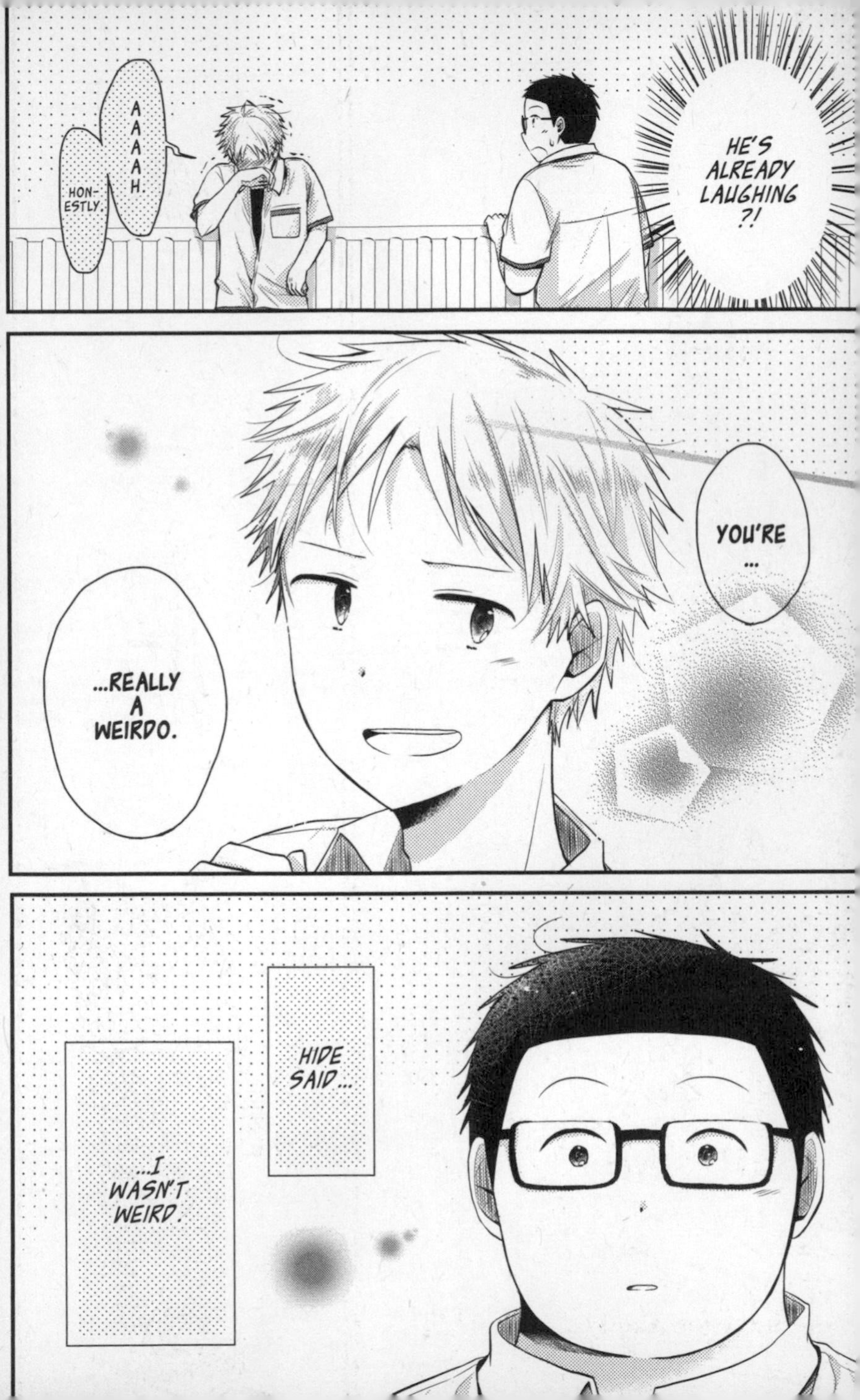
HE'S ALREADY LAUGHING ?!
AAAAH.
HON-ESTLY.
YOU'RE ...
...REALLY A WEIRDO.
HIDE SAID...
...I WASN'T WEIRD.

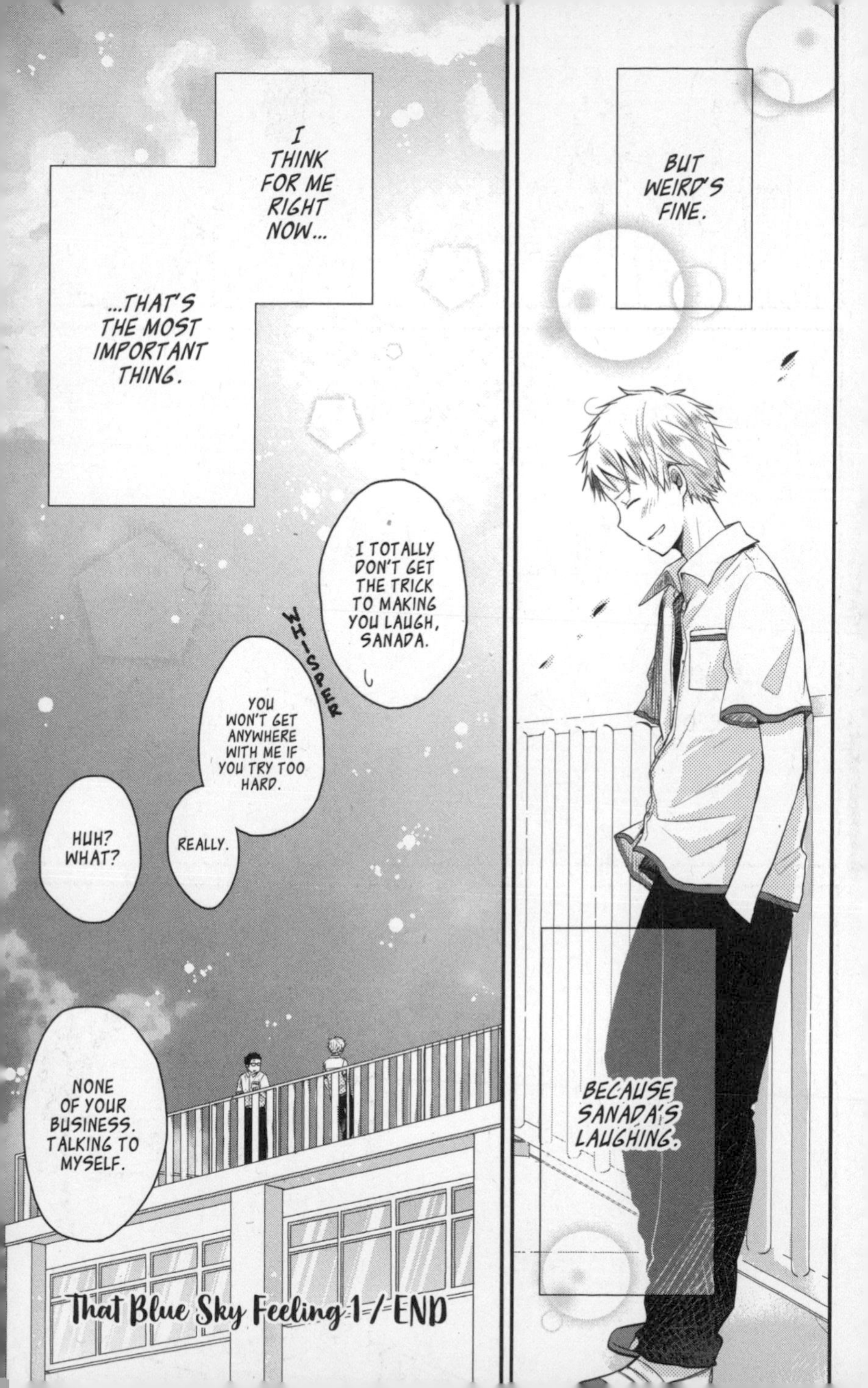
BUT WEIRD'S FINE.
BECAUSE SANADA'S LAUGHING.
I THINK FOR ME RIGHT NOW...
...THAT'S THE MOST IMPORTANT THING.
I TOTALLY DON'T GET THE TRICK TO MAKING YOU LAUGH, SANADA.
WHISPER
YOU WON'T GET ANYWHERE WITH ME IF YOU TRY TOO HARD.
REALLY.
HUH? WHAT?
NONE OF YOUR BUSINESS. TALKING TO MYSELF.
That Blue Sky Feeling 1 / END

Bonus manga by story creator Okura

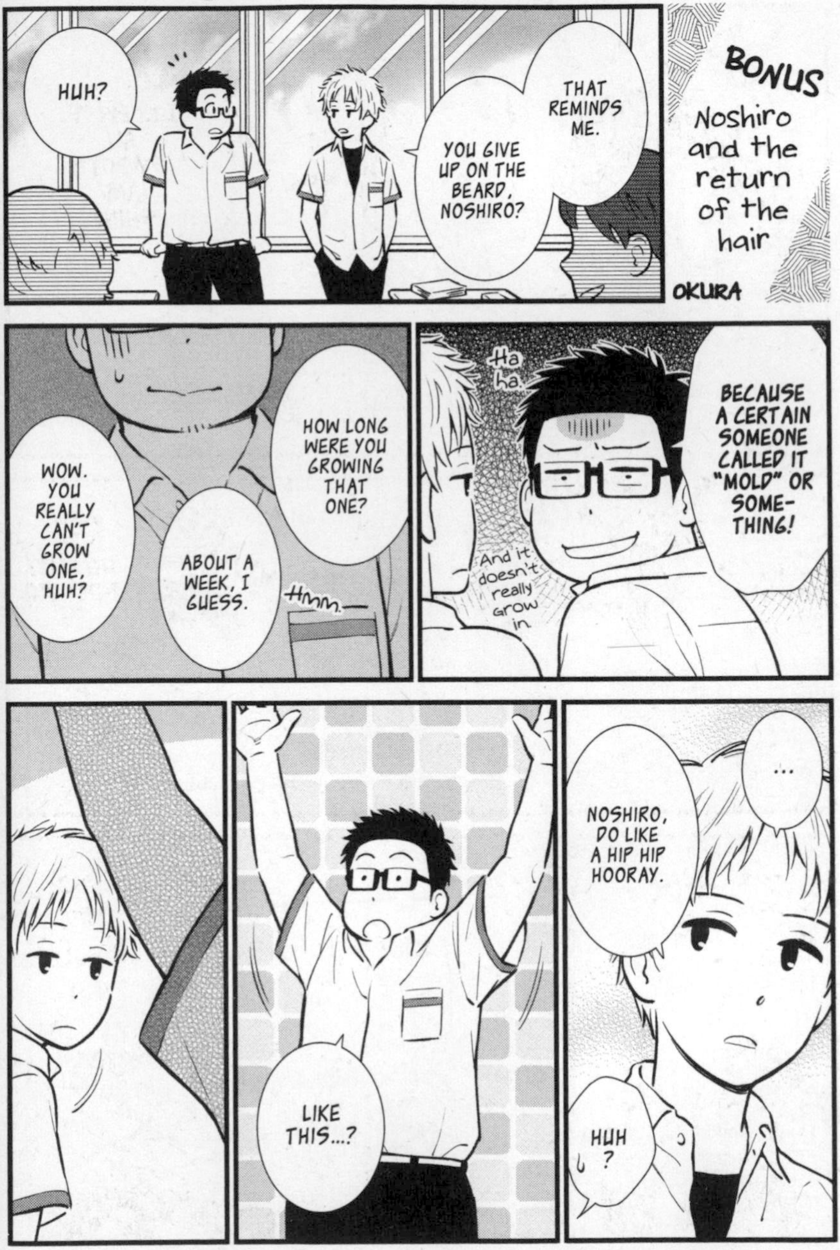
BONUS
Noshiro and the return of the hair
OKURA
THAT REMINDS ME.
YOU GIVE UP ON THE BEARD, NOSHIRO?
HUH?
BECAUSE A CERTAIN SOMEONE CALLED IT "MOLD" OR SOMETHING!
Ha ha.
And it doesn't really grow in.
HOW LONG WERE YOU GROWING THAT ONE?
ABOUT A WEEK, I GUESS.
Hmm.
WOW. YOU REALLY CAN'T GROW ONE, HUH?
...
NOSHIRO, DO LIKE A HIP HIP HOORAY.
HUH?
LIKE THIS...?

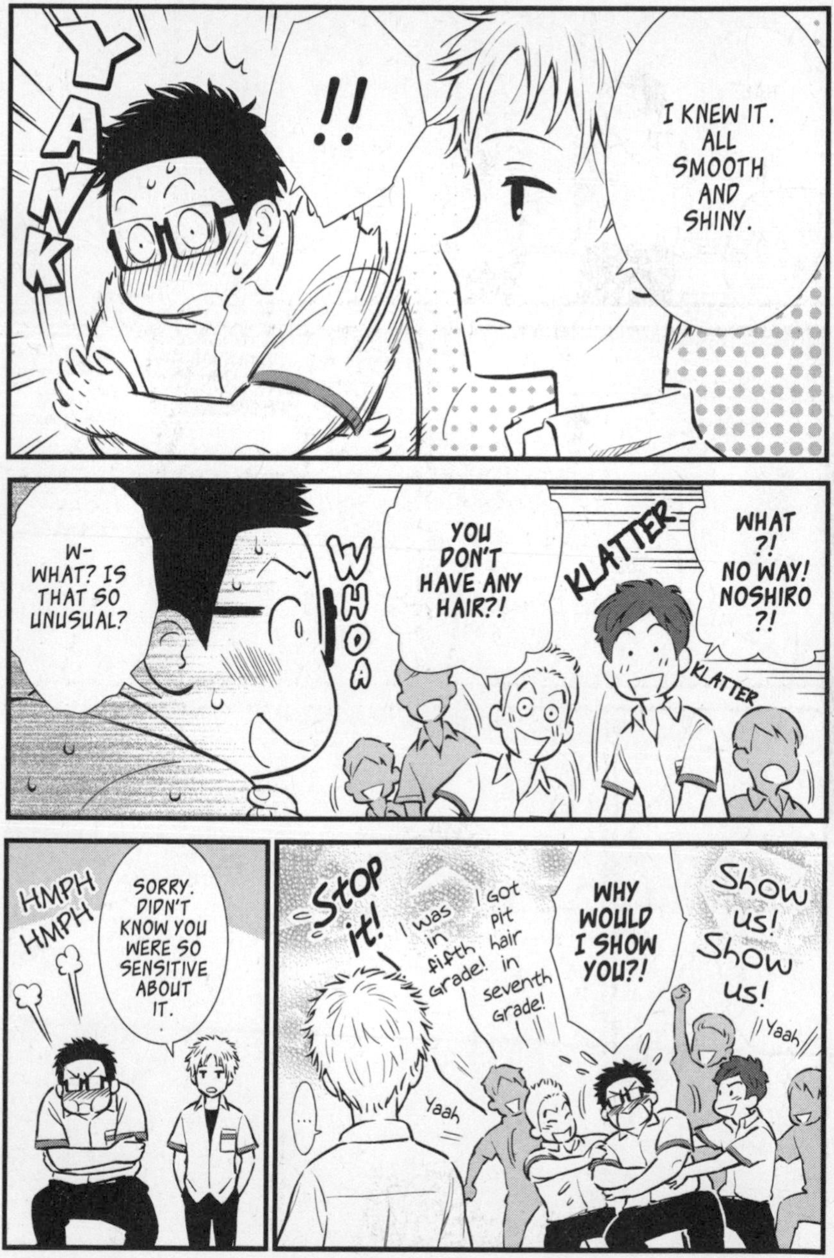
I KNEW IT. ALL SMOOTH AND SHINY.
!!
YANK
WHAT?! NO WAY! NOSHIRO?!
KLATTER
KLATTER
YOU DON'T HAVE ANY HAIR?!
WHOA
W-WHAT? IS THAT SO UNUSUAL?
Show us! Show us!
Yaah
WHY WOULD I SHOW YOU?!
I got pit hair in seventh grade!
I was in fifth grade!
Stop it!
Yaah
...
SORRY. DIDN'T KNOW YOU WERE SO SENSITIVE ABOUT IT.
HMPH HMPH

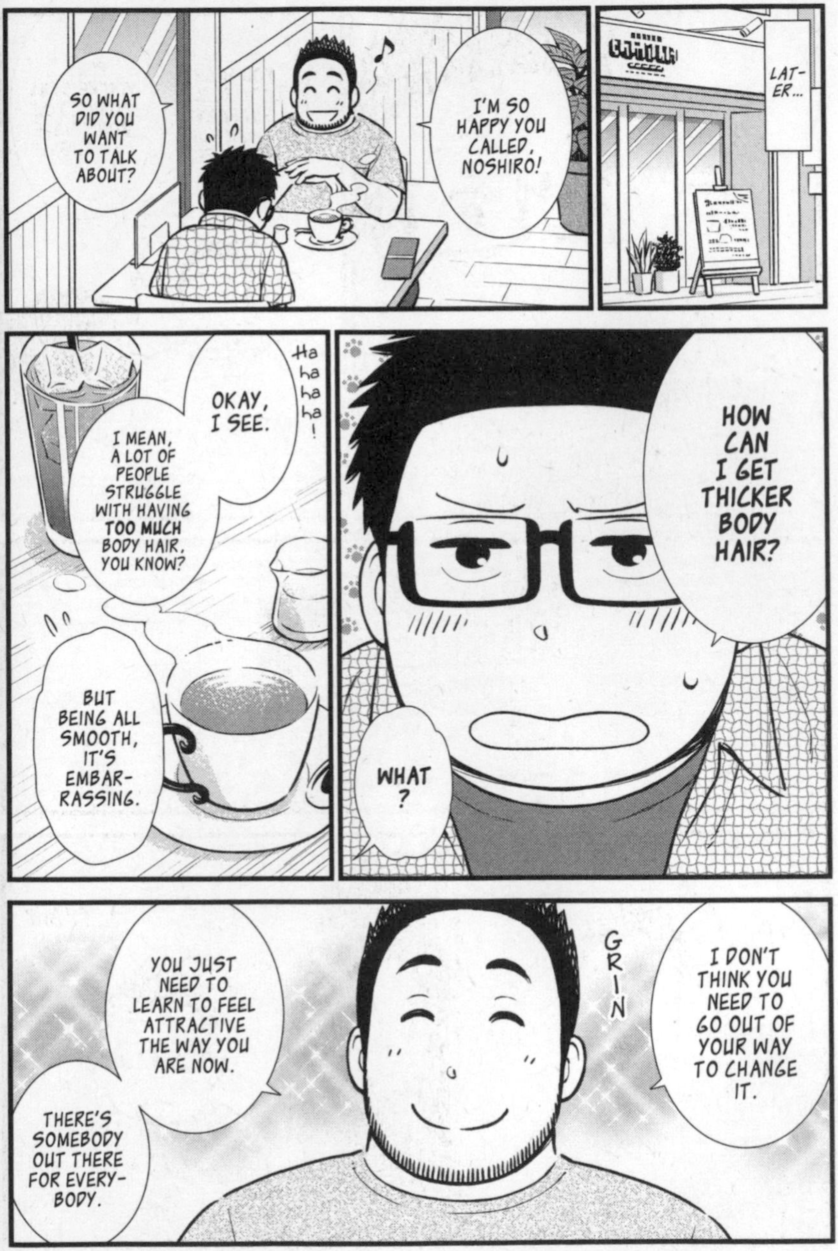
LATER...
I'M SO HAPPY YOU CALLED, NOSHIRO!
SO WHAT DID YOU WANT TO TALK ABOUT?
HOW CAN I GET THICKER BODY HAIR?
WHAT?
Ha ha ha ha!
OKAY, I SEE.
I MEAN, A LOT OF PEOPLE STRUGGLE WITH HAVING TOO MUCH BODY HAIR, YOU KNOW?
BUT BEING ALL SMOOTH, IT'S EMBARRASSING.
I DON'T THINK YOU NEED TO GO OUT OF YOUR WAY TO CHANGE IT.
GRIN
YOU JUST NEED TO LEARN TO FEEL ATTRACTIVE THE WAY YOU ARE NOW.
THERE'S SOMEBODY OUT THERE FOR EVERY-BODY.

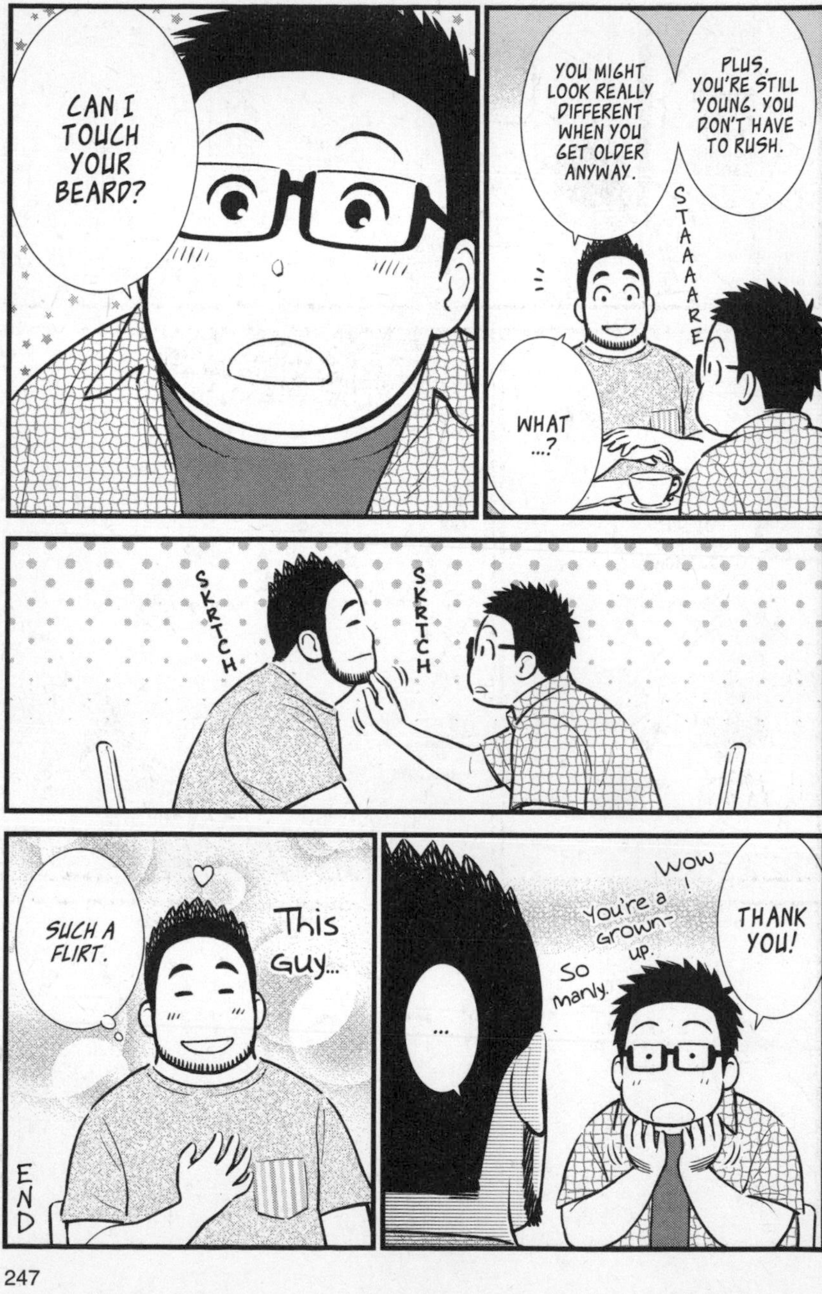
PLUS, YOU'RE STILL YOUNG. YOU DON'T HAVE TO RUSH.
YOU MIGHT LOOK REALLY DIFFERENT WHEN YOU GET OLDER ANYWAY.
STAAAARE
WHAT ...?
CAN I TOUCH YOUR BEARD?
SKRTCH
SKRTCH
THANK YOU!
Wow!
You're a grown-up.
So manly.
...
This guy...
SUCH A FLIRT.
END

CHANGES IN THE REMAKE VERSION

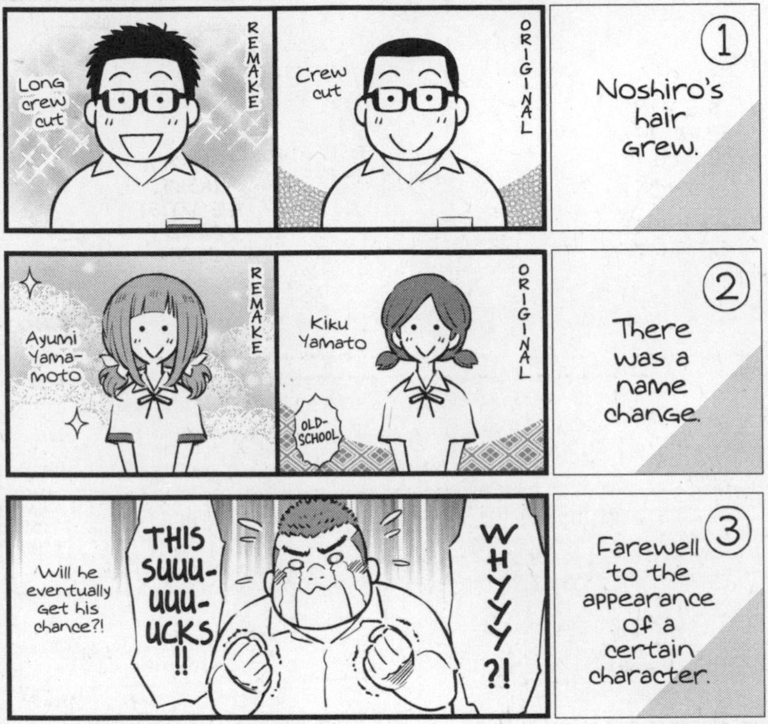
①
Noshiro's hair grew.
ORIGINAL
Crew cut
REMAKE
Long crew cut
②
There was a name change.
ORIGINAL
Kiku Yamato
OLD-SCHOOL
REMAKE
Ayumi Yamamoto
③
Farewell to the appearance of a certain character.
WHYYYY ?!
THIS SUUUUUU-UCKS !!
Will he eventually get his chance?!

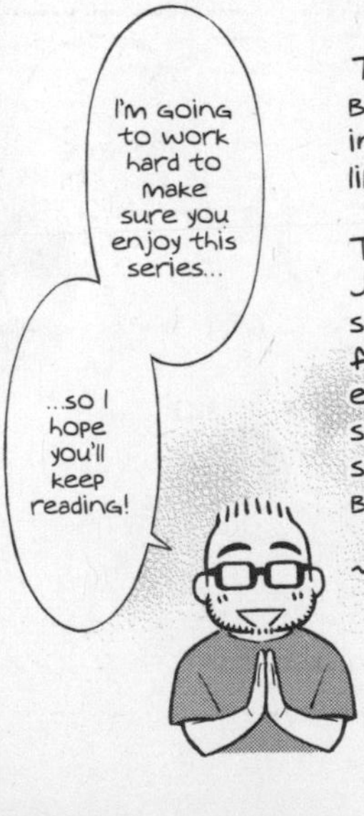
I'm going to work hard to make sure you enjoy this series...
...so I hope you'll keep reading!

That *Blue Sky Feeling* is a webcomic that began in 2009 on a private site and ended in 2012. That it would be turned into a book like this feels like a dream.

To the editorial department at GanGan Joker for giving me the opportunity to serialize the remake, to Coma Hashii for doing the art, and—more than anyone else—to the readers who have been supporting *Blue Sky* since it was being serialized online, thank you from the very bottom of my heart.

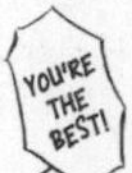
YOU'RE THE BEST!

~Okura

Afterword

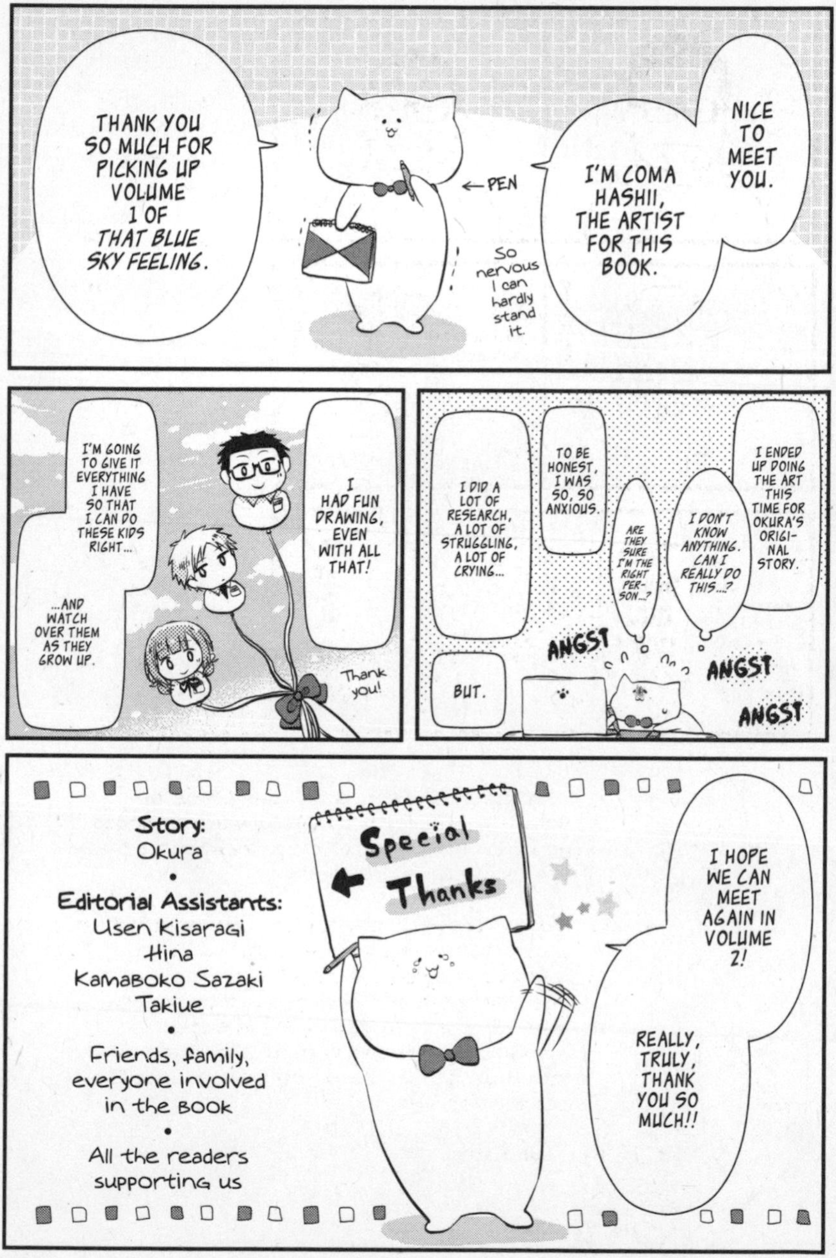

NICE TO MEET YOU.
I'M COMA HASHII, THE ARTIST FOR THIS BOOK.
← PEN
So nervous I can hardly stand it.
THANK YOU SO MUCH FOR PICKING UP VOLUME 1 OF *THAT BLUE SKY FEELING*.
I ENDED UP DOING THE ART THIS TIME FOR OKURA'S ORIGINAL STORY.
I DON'T KNOW ANYTHING. CAN I REALLY DO THIS...?
ARE THEY SURE I'M THE RIGHT PERSON...?
TO BE HONEST, I WAS SO, SO ANXIOUS.
I DID A LOT OF RESEARCH, A LOT OF STRUGGLING, A LOT OF CRYING...
ANGST
ANGST
ANGST
BUT.
I HAD FUN DRAWING, EVEN WITH ALL THAT!
Thank you!
I'M GOING TO GIVE IT EVERYTHING I HAVE SO THAT I CAN DO THESE KIDS RIGHT...
...AND WATCH OVER THEM AS THEY GROW UP.
I HOPE WE CAN MEET AGAIN IN VOLUME 2!
REALLY, TRULY, THANK YOU SO MUCH!!
Special Thanks
Story:
Okura
•
Editorial Assistants:
Usen Kisaragi
Hina
Kamaboko Sazaki
Takiue
•
Friends, family, everyone involved in the book
•
All the readers supporting us

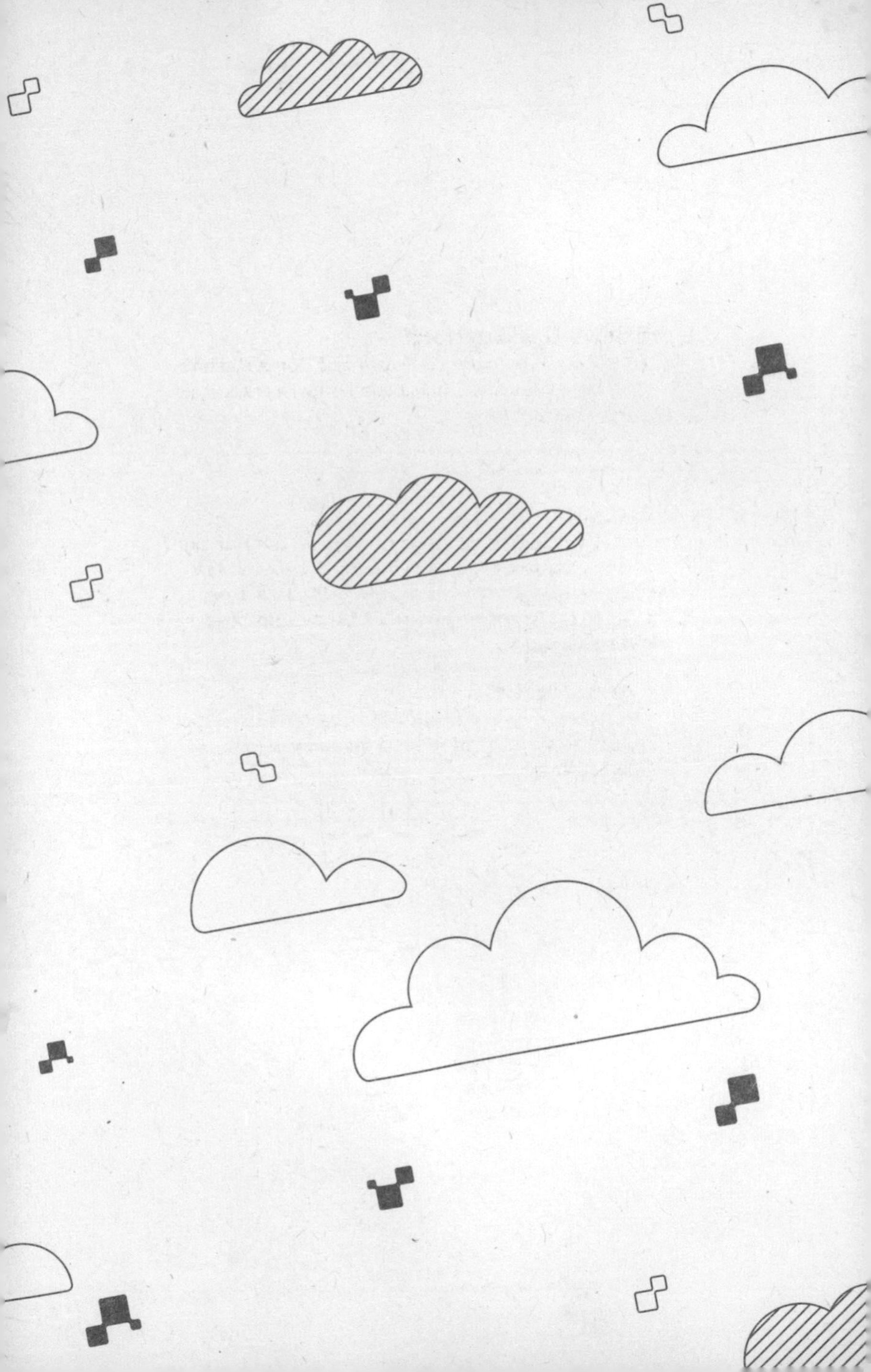

About the Authors
That Blue Sky Feeling is Okura and Coma Hashii's first manga series and is based on writer Okura's original webcomic.

Okura
This is the book I've been waiting for, the remake of the webcomic from my personal website. I'm truly delighted that I'm able to bring this story to even more people and to all those who have cheered me on.

Coma Hashii
I think this is a work that welcomes all kinds of "likes." I'd be so happy if you found even just one "like" in here.

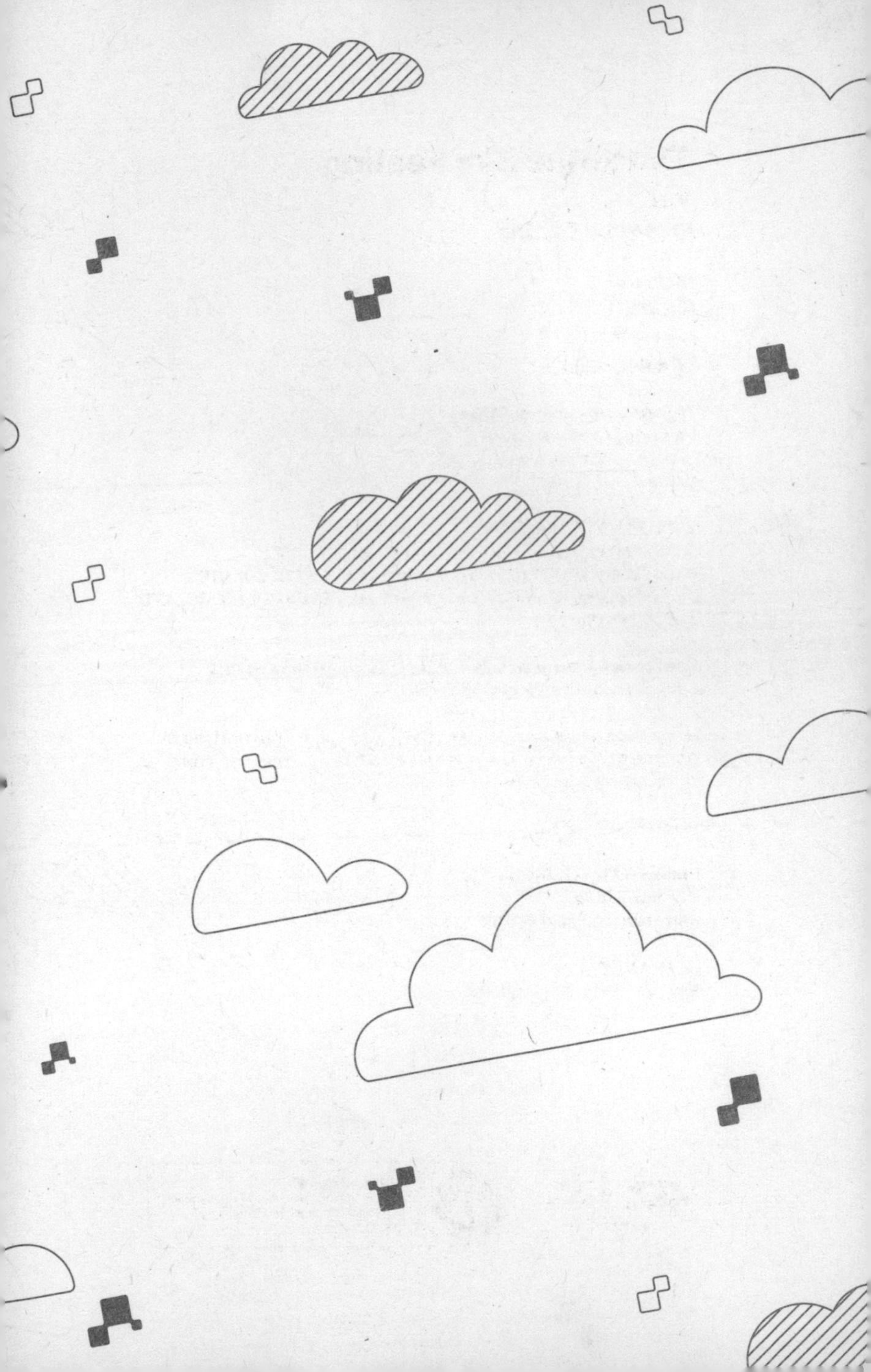

That Blue Sky Feeling
Vol. 1
VIZ Media Edition

STORY BY
Okura

ART BY
Coma Hashii

Translation/Jocelyne Allen
Lettering/Joanna Estep
Design/Yukiko Whitley
Editor/Joel Enos

SORAIRO FLUTTER vol. 1
© 2017 Okura, Coma Hashii/SQUARE ENIX CO., LTD.
First published in Japan in 2017 by SQUARE ENIX CO., LTD.
English translation rights arranged with SQUARE ENIX CO., LTD.
and VIZ Media, LLC

Printed in Canada

Published by VIZ Media, LLC
P.O. Box 77010
San Francisco, CA 94107

10 9 8 7 6 5 4 3 2 1
First printing, August 2018

VIZ MEDIA
viz.com

PARENTAL ADVISORY
THAT BLUE SKY FEELING is rated T for Teen and
is recommended for ages 13 and up. Contains
suggestive themes.

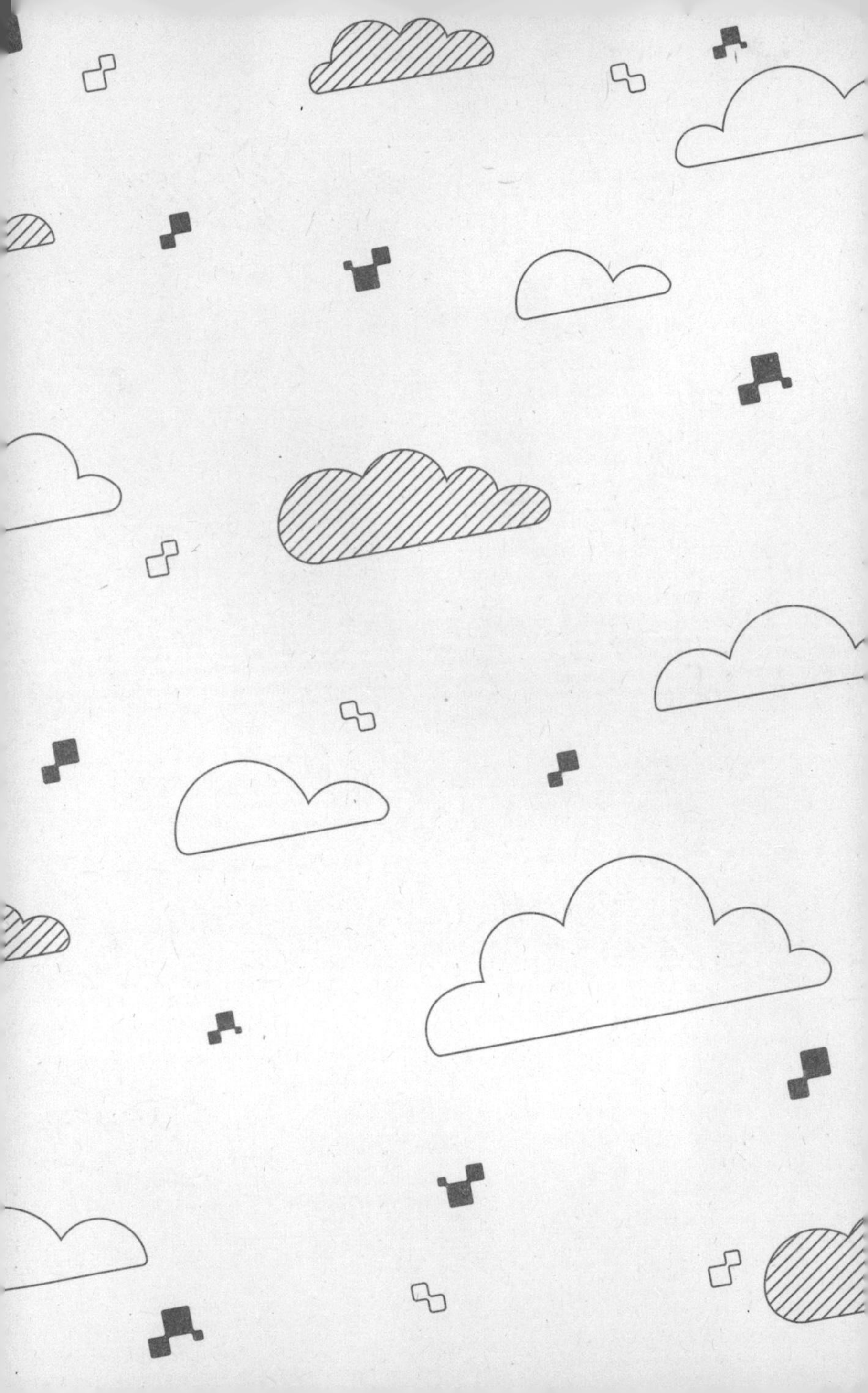

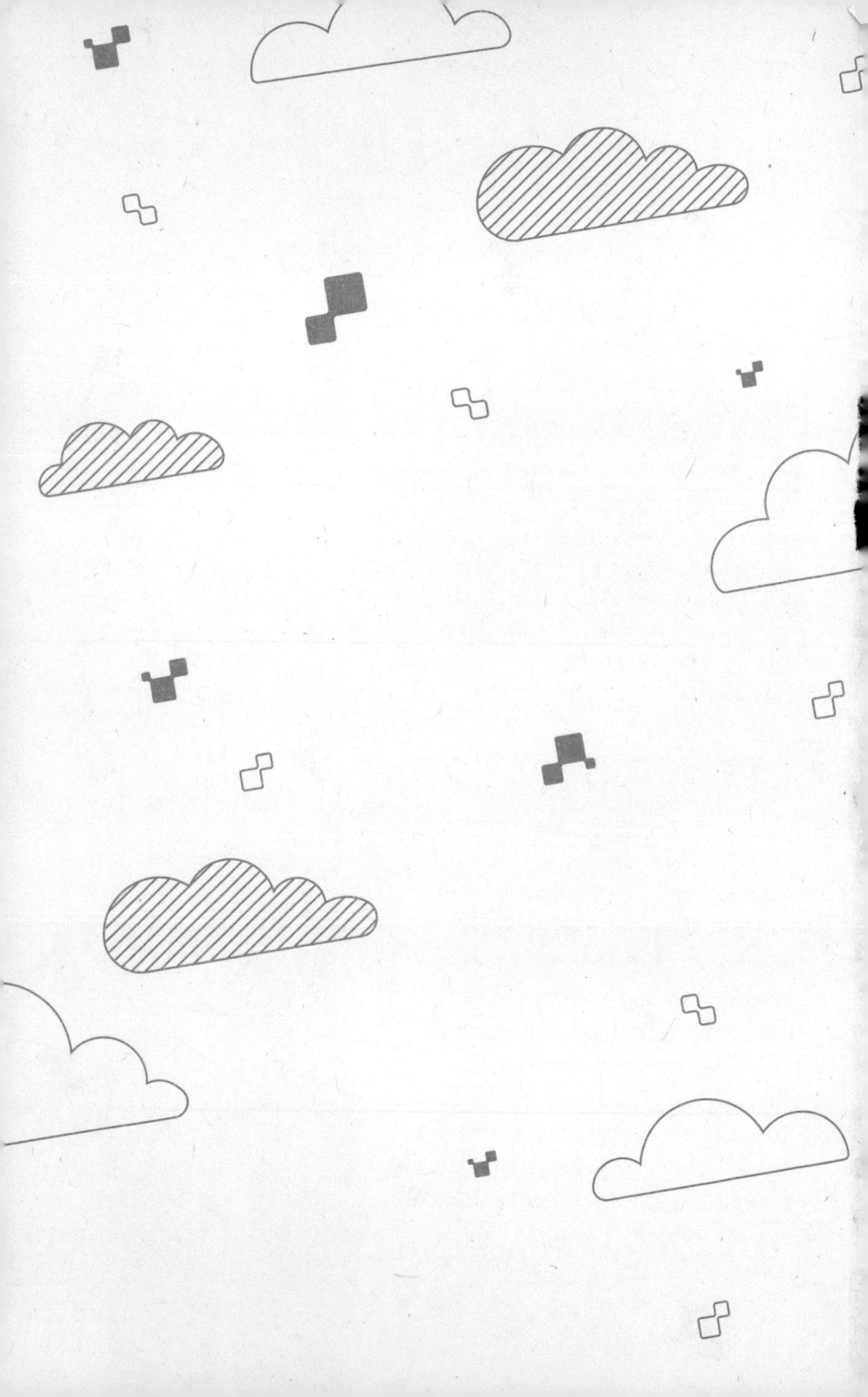

Surprise!

You may be reading the wrong way!

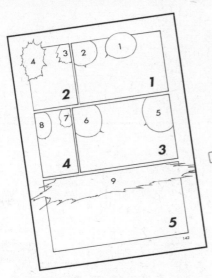

It's true: In keeping with the original Japanese comic format, this book reads from right to left—so action, sound effects and word balloons are completely reversed. This preserves the orientation of the original artwork—plus, it's fun! Check out the diagram shown here to get the hang of things, and then turn to the other side of the book to get started!